Windows Kernel Programming

Pavel Yosifovich

Windows Kernel Programming

Pavel Yosifovich

ISBN 9781977593375

Leanpub

Contents

Introduction

Windows kernel programming is considered by many a dark art, available to select few that managed to somehow unlock the mysteries of the Windows kernel. Kernel development, however, is no different than user-mode development, at least in general terms. In both cases, a good understanding of the platform is essential for high quality code to be produced.

The book is a guide to programming within the Windows kernel, using the well-known Visual Studio integrated development environment (IDE). This environment is familiar to many developers in the Microsoft space, so that the learning curve is restricted to kernel understanding, coding and debugging, with less friction from the development tools.

The book targets software device drivers, a term I use to refer to drivers that do not deal with hardware. Software kernel drivers have full access to the kernel, allowing these to perform any operation allowed by the kernel. Some software drivers are more specific, such as file system mini filters, also described in the book.

Who Should Read This Book

The book is intended for software developers that target the Windows kernel, and need to write kernel drivers to achieve their goals. Common scenarios where kernel drivers are employed is in the Cyber Security space, where kernel drivers are the chief mechanism to get notified of important events, withe the power to intercept certain operations. The book uses C and C++ for code examples, as the kernel API is all C. C++ is used where it makes sense, where its advantages are obvious in terms of maintenance, clarity, resource management, or any combination of the above. The book does not use non-trivial C++ constructs, such as template metaprogramming. The book is not about C++, it's about the Windows kernel.

What You Should Know to Use This Book

Readers should be very comfortable with the C programming language, especially with pointers, structures, and its standard library, as these occur very frequently when working with kernel APIs. Basic C++ knowledge is highly recommended, although it is possible to traverse the book with C proficiency only.

Sample Code

All the sample code from the book is freely available in the book's Github repository at https://github. com/zodiacon/windowskernelprogrammingbook. Updates to the code samples will be pushed to this repository. It's recommended the reader clone the repository to the local machine, so it's easy to experiment with the code directly.

All code samples have been compiled with Visual Studio 2019. It's possible to compile most code samples with earlier versions of Visual Studio if desired. There might be few features of the latest C++ standards that may not be supported in earlier versions, but these should be easy to fix.

Happy reading!

Pavel Yosifovich

June 2019

Chapter 1: Windows Internals Overview

This chapters describes the most important concepts in the internal workings of Windows. Some of the topics will be described in greater detail later in the book, where it's closely related to the topic at hand. Make sure you understand the concepts in this chapter, as these make the foundations upon any driver and even user mode low-level code, is built.

In this chapter:

- **Processes**
- **Virtual Memory**
- **Threads**
- **System Services**
- **System Architecture**
- **Handles and Objects**

Processes

A process is a containment and management object that represents a running instance of a program. The term "process runs" which is used fairly often, is inaccurate. Processes don't run – processes manage. Threads are the ones that execute code and technically run. From a high-level perspective, a process owns the following:

- An executable program, which contains the initial code and data used to execute code within the process.
- A private virtual address space, used for allocating memory for whatever purposes the code within the process needs it.
- A primary token, which is an object that stores the default security context of the process, used by threads executing code within the process (unless a thread assumes a different token by using impersonation).

- A private handle table to executive objects, such as events, processes, threads, semaphores, and files.
- One or more threads of execution. A normal user-mode process is created with one thread (executing the classic main/WinMain function). A user-mode process without threads is mostly useless and under normal circumstances will be destroyed by the kernel.

These elements of a process are depicted in figure 1-1.

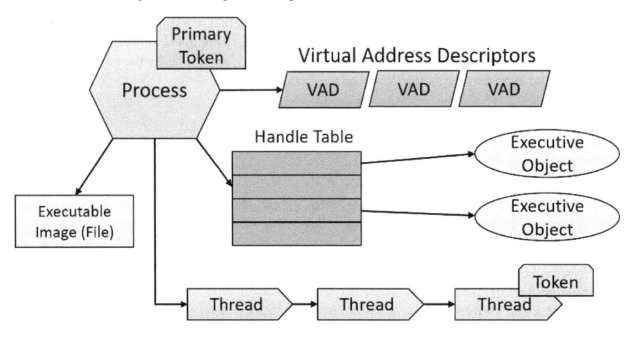

Figure 1-1: Important ingredients of a process

A process is uniquely identified by its Process ID, which remains unique as long as the kernel process object exists. Once it's destroyed, the same ID may be reused for new processes. It's important to realize that the executable file itself is not a unique identifier of a process. For example, there may be five instances of notepad.exe running at the same time. Each process has its own address space, its own threads, its own handle table, its own unique process ID, etc. All those five processes are using the same image file (notepad.exe) as their initial code and data. Figure 1-2 shows a screen shot of Task Manager's Details tab showing five instances of Notepad.exe, each with its own attributes.

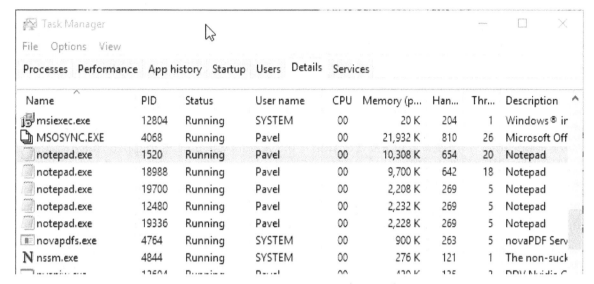

Figure 1-2: Five instances of notepad

Virtual Memory

Every process has its own virtual, private, linear address space. This address space starts out empty (or close to empty, since the executable image and NtDll.Dll are the first to be mapped, followed by more subsystem DLLs). Once execution of the main (first) thread begins, memory is likely to be allocated, more DLLs loaded, etc. This address space is private, which means other processes cannot access it directly. The address space range starts at zero (although technically the first 64KB of address cannot be allocated or used in any way), and goes all the way to a maximum which depends on the process "bitness" (32 or 64 bit) and the operating system "bitness" as follows:

- For 32-bit processes on 32-bit Windows systems, the process address space size is 2 GB by default.
- For 32-bit processes on 32-bit Windows systems that use the increase user address space setting (LARGEADDRESSAWARE flag in the Portable Executable header), that process address space size can be as large as 3 GB (depending on the exact setting). To get the extended address space range, the executable from which the process was created must have been marked with the LARGEADDRESSAWARE linker flag in its header. If it was not, it would still be limited to 2 GB.
- For 64-bit processes (on a 64-bit Windows system, naturally), the address space size is 8 TB (Windows 8 and earlier) or 128 TB (Windows 8.1 and later).
- For 32-bit processes on a 64-bit Windows system, the address space size is 4 GB if the executable image is linked with the LARGEADDRESSAWARE flag. Otherwise, the size remains at 2 GB.

 The requirement of the LARGEADDRESSAWARE flag stems from the fact that a 2 GB address range requires 31 bits only, leaving the most significant bit (MSB) free for application use. Specifying this flag indicates that the program is not using bit 31 for anything and so setting that bit to 1 (which would happen for addresses larger than 2 GB) is not an issue.

Each process has its own address space, which makes any process address relative, rather than absolute. For example, when trying to determine what lies in address 0x20000, the address itself is not enough; the process to which this address relates to must be specified.

The memory itself is called *virtual*, which means there is an indirect relationship between an address range and the exact location where it's found in physical memory (RAM). A buffer within a process may be mapped to physical memory, or it may temporarily reside in a file (such as a page file). The term virtual refers to the fact that from an execution perspective, there is no need to know if the memory about to be accessed is in RAM or not; if the memory is indeed mapped to RAM, the CPU will access the data directly. If not, the CPU will raise a page fault exception that will cause the memory manager's page fault handler to fetch the data from the appropriate file, copy it to RAM, make the required changes in the page table entries that map the buffer, and instruct the CPU to try again. Figure 1-3 shows this mapping from virtual to physical memory for two processes.

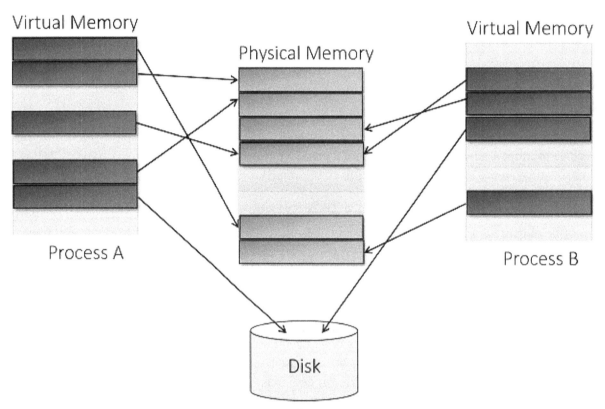

Figure 1-3: virtual memory mapping

The unit of memory management is called a *page*. Every attribute related to memory is always at a page's granularity, such as its protection. The size of a page is determined by CPU type (and on some processors, may be configurable), and in any case the memory manager must follow suit. Normal (sometimes called small) page size is 4 KB on all Windows supported architectures.

Apart from the normal (small) page size, Windows also supports large pages. The size of a large page is 2 MB (x86/x64/ARM64) and 4 MB (ARM). This is based using the Page Directory Entry (PDE) to map the large page without using a page table. This results in quicker translation, but most importantly better use the Translation Lookaside Buffer (TLB) – a cache of recently translated pages maintained by the CPU. In the case of a large page, a single TLB entry is able to map significantly more memory than a small page.

 The downside of large pages is the need to have the memory contiguous in RAM, which can fail if memory is tight or very fragmented. Also, large pages are always non-pageable and must be protected with read/write access only. Huge pages of 1 GB in size are supported on Windows 10 and Server 2016 and later. These are used automatically with large pages if an allocation is at least 1 GB in size and that page can be located as contiguous in RAM.

Page States

Each page in virtual memory can be in one of three states:

- Free – the page is not allocated in any way; there is nothing there. Any attempt to access that page would cause an access violation exception. Most pages in a newly created process are free.
- Committed – the reverse of free; an allocated page that can be accessed successfully (assuming non-conflicting protection attributes; for example, writing to a read-only page causes an access violation). Committed pages are usually mapped to RAM or to a file (such as a page file).
- Reserved – the page is not committed, but the address range is reserved for possible future commitment. From the CPU's perspective, it's the same as Free – any access attempt raises an access violation exception. However, new allocation attempts using the VirtualAlloc function (or NtAllocateVirtualMemory, the related native API) that does not specify a specific address would not allocate in the reserved region. A classic example of using reserved memory to maintain contiguous virtual address space while conserving memory is described later in this chapter in the section "Thread Stacks".

System Memory

The lower part of the address space is for processes' use. While a certain thread is executing, its associated process address space is visible from address zero to the upper limit as described in the previous section. The operating system, however, must also reside somewhere – and that somewhere is the upper address range that's supported on the system, as follows:

- On 32-bit systems running without the *increase user virtual address space* setting, the operating system resides in the upper 2 GB of virtual address space, from address 0x80000000 to 0xFFFFFFFF.
- On 32-bit systems configured with the *increase user virtual address space* setting, the operating system resides in the address space left. For example, if the system is configured with 3 GB user address space per process (the maximum), the OS takes the upper 1 GB (from address 0xC0000000 to 0xFFFFFFFF). The entity that suffers mostly from this address space reduction is the file system cache.

- On 64-bit systems on Windows 8, Server 2012 and earlier, the OS takes the upper 8 TB of virtual address space.
- On 64-bit systems on Windows 8.1, Server 2012 R2 and later, the OS takes the upper 128 TB of virtual address space.

System space is not process-relative – after all, it's the same "system", the same kernel, the same drivers that service every process on the system (the exception is some system memory that is on a per-session basis but is not important for this discussion). It follows that any address in system space is absolute rather than relative, since it "looks" the same from every process context. Of course, actual access from user mode into system space results in an access violation exception.

System space is where the kernel itself, the Hardware Abstraction Layer (HAL) and kernel drivers reside once loaded. Thus, kernel drivers are automatically protected from direct user mode access. It also means they have a potentially system-wide impact. For example, if a kernel driver leaks memory, that memory will not be freed even after the driver unloads. User-mode processes, on the other hand, can never leak anything beyond their life time. The kernel is responsible for closing and freeing everything private to a dead process (all handles are closed and all private memory is freed).

Threads

The actual entities that execute code are threads. A Thread is contained within a process, using the resources exposed by the process to do work (such as virtual memory and handles to kernel objects). The most important information a thread owns is the following:

- Current access mode, either user or kernel.
- Execution context, including processor registers and execution state.
- One or two stacks, used for local variable allocations and call management.
- Thread Local Storage (TLS) array, which provides a way to store thread-private data with uniform access semantics.
- Base priority and a current (dynamic) priority.
- Processor affinity, indicating on which processors the thread is allowed to run on.

The most common states a thread can be in are:

- Running – currently executing code on a (logical) processor.
- Ready – waiting to be scheduled for execution because all relevant processors are busy or unavailable.
- Waiting – waiting for some event to occur before proceeding. Once the event occurs, the thread goes to the Ready state.

Figure 1-4 shows the state diagram for these states. The numbers in parenthesis indicate the state numbers, as can be viewed by tools such as Performance Monitor. Note that the Ready state has a sibling state called Deferred Ready, which is similar, and really exists to minimize some internal locking.

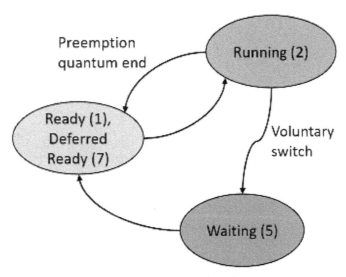

Figure 1-4: Common thread states

Thread Stacks

Each thread has a stack it uses while executing, used for local variables, parameter passing to functions (in some cases) and where return addresses are stored prior to function calls. A thread has at least one stack residing in system (kernel) space, and it's pretty small (default is 12 KB on 32-bit systems and 24 KB on 64-bit systems). A user mode thread has a second stack in its process user space address range and is considerably larger (by default can grow to 1 MB). An example with three user-mode threads and their stacks is shown in figure 1-5. In the figure, threads 1 and 2 are in process A and thread 3 is in process B.

The kernel stack always resides in RAM while the thread is in the Running or Ready states. The reason for this is subtle and will be discussed later in this chapter. The user mode stack, on the other hand, may be paged out, just like any user-mode memory.

The user-mode stack is handled differently than the kernel mode stack, in terms of its size. It starts out with a small amount of memory committed (could be as small as a single page), with the rest of the stack address space as reserved memory, meaning it's not allocated in any way. The idea is to be able to grow the stack in case the thread's code needs to use more stack space. To make this work, the next page (sometimes more than one) right after the committed part is marked with a special protection called PAGE_GUARD – this is a guard page. If the thread needs more stack space it would write to the guard page which would throw an exception that is handled by the memory manager. The memory manager then removes the guard protection and commits the page and marks the next page as a guard page. This way, the stack grows as needed and the entire stack memory is not committed upfront. Figure 1-6 shows the way a user mode's thread stack looks like.

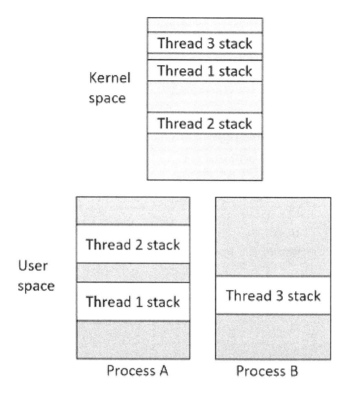

Figure 1-5: User-mode threads and their stacks

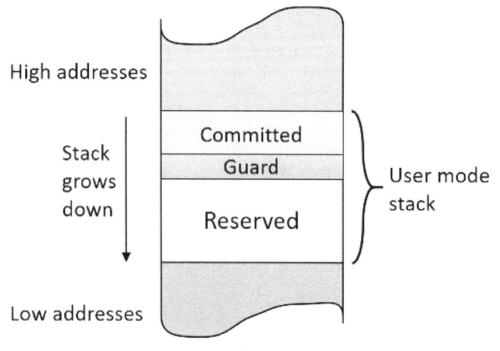

Figure 1-6: Thread's stack in user space

The sizes of a thread's user-mode stack are determined as follows:

- The executable image has a stack commit and reserved values in its Portable Executable (PE) header. These are taken as defaults if a thread does not specify alternative values.
- When a thread is created with CreateThread (and similar functions), the caller can specify its required stack size, either the upfront committed size or the reserved size (but not both), depending on a flag provided to the function; specifying zero goes with the default according the above bullet.

 Curiously enough, the functions CreateThread and CreateRemoteThread(Ex) only allow specifying a single value for the stack size and can be the committed or the reserved size, but not both. The native (undocumented) function, NtCreateThreadEx allows specifying both values.

System Services (a.k.a. System Calls)

Applications need to perform various operations that are not purely computational, such as allocating memory, opening files, creating threads, etc. These operations can only be ultimately performed by code running in kernel mode. So how would user-mode code be able to perform such operations? Let's take a classic example: a user running a Notepad process uses the File menu to request opening a file. Notepad's code responds by calling the CreateFile documented Windows API function. CreateFile is documented as implemented in kernel32.Dll, one of the Windows subsystem DLLs. This function still runs in user mode, so there is no way it can directly open a file. After some error checking, it calls NtCreateFile, a function implemented in NTDLL.dll, a foundational DLL that implements the API known as the "Native API", and is in fact the lowest layer of code which is still in user mode. This (officially undocumented) API is the one that makes the transition to kernel mode. Before the actual transition, it puts a number, called system service number, into a CPU register (EAX on Intel/AMD architectures). Then it issues a special CPU instruction (syscall on x64 or sysenter on x86) that makes the actual transition to kernel mode while jumping to a predefined routine called the system service dispatcher.

The system service dispatcher, in turn, uses the value in that EAX register as an index into a System Service Dispatch Table (SSDT). Using this table, the code jumps to the system service (system call) itself. For our Notepad example, the SSDT entry would point to the I/O manager's NtCreateFile function. Notice the function has the same name as the one in NTDLL.dll and in fact has the same arguments as well. Once the system service is complete, the thread returns to user mode to execute the instruction following sysenter/syscall. This sequence of events is depicted in figure 1-7.

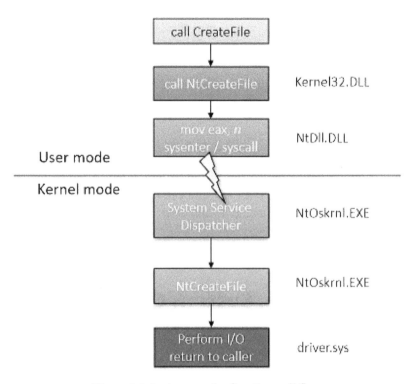

Figure 1-7: System service function call flow

General System Architecture

Figure 1-8 shows the general architecture of Windows, comprising of user mode and kernel mode components.

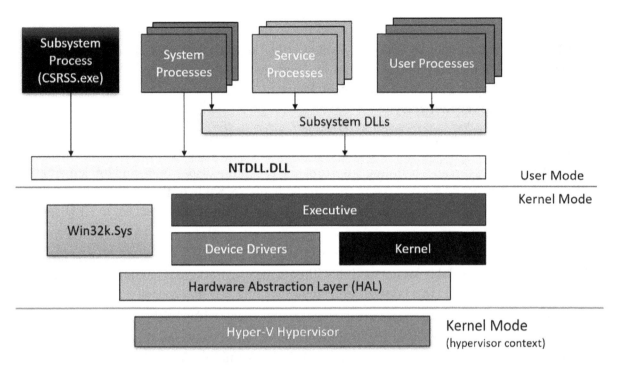

Figure 1-8: Windows system architecture

Here's a quick rundown of the named boxes appearing in figure 1-8:

- **User processes**

  These are normal processes based on image files, executing on the system, such as instances of Notepad.exe, cmd.exe, explorer.exe and so on.

- **Subsystem DLLs**

  Subsystem DLLs are dynamic link libraries (DLLs) that implement the API of a subsystem. A subsystem is a certain view of the capabilities exposed by the kernel. Technically, starting from Windows 8.1, there is only a single subsystem – the Windows Subsystem. The subsystem DLLs include well-known files, such as kernel32.dll, user32.dll, gdi32.dll, advapi32.dll, combase.dll and many others. These include mostly the officially documented API of Windows.

- **NTDLL.DLL**

  A system-wide DLL, implementing the Windows native API. This is the lowest layer of code which is still in user mode. Its most important role is to make the transition to kernel mode for system call invocation. NTDLL also implements the Heap Manager, the Image Loader, and some parts of the user-mode thread pool.

- **Service Processes**

  Service processes are normal Windows processes that communicate with the Service Control Manager (SCM, implemented in services.exe) and allow some control over their lifetime. The SCM can start, stop, pause, resume and send other messages to services. Services typically execute under one of the special Windows accounts – local system, network service or local service.

- **Executive**

  The Executive is the upper layer of NtOskrnl.exe (the "kernel"). It hosts most of the code that is in kernel mode. It includes mostly the various "managers": Object Manager, Memory Manager, I/O Manager, Plug & Play Manager, Power Manager, Configuration Manager, etc. It's by far larger than the lower Kernel layer.

- **Kernel**

  The Kernel layer implements the most fundamental and time-sensitive parts of kernel-mode OS code. This includes thread scheduling, interrupt and exception dispatching, and implementation of various kernel primitives such as mutex and semaphore. Some of the kernel code is written in CPU-specific machine language for efficiency and for getting direct access to CPU-specific details.

- **Device Drivers**

  Device drivers are loadable kernel modules. Their code executes in kernel mode and so has the full power of the kernel. This book is dedicated to writing certain types of kernel drivers.

- **Win32k.sys**

  The "kernel mode component of the Windows subsystem". Essentially this is a kernel module (driver) that handles the user interface part of Windows and the classic Graphics Device Interface (GDI) APIs. This means that all windowing operations (`CreateWindowEx`, `GetMessage`, `PostMessage`, etc.) are handled by this component. The rest of the system has little-to-none knowledge of UI.

- **Hardware Abstraction Layer (HAL)**

  The HAL is an abstraction layer over the hardware closest to the CPU. It allows device drivers to use APIs that do not require detailed and specific knowledge of things like Interrupt Controller or DMA controller. Naturally, this layer is mostly useful for device drivers written to handle hardware devices.

- **System Processes**

  System processes is an umbrella term used to describe processes that are typically "just there", doing their thing where normally these processes are not communicated with directly. They are important nonetheless, and some in fact, critical to the system's well-being. Terminating some of them is fatal and causes a system crash. Some of the system processes are native processes, meaning they use the native API only (the API implemented by NTDLL). Example system processes include `Smss.exe`, `Lsass.exe`, `Winlogon.exe`, `Services.exe` and others.

- **Subsystem Process**

  The Windows subsystem process, running the image `Csrss.exe`, can be viewed as a helper to the kernel for managing processes running under the Windows system. It is a critical process, meaning if killed, the system would crash. There is normally one `Csrss.exe` instance per session, so on a standard system two instances would exist – one for session 0 and one for the logged-on user session (typically 1). Although `Csrss.exe` is the "manager" of the Windows subsystem (the only one left these days), its importance goes beyond just this role.

- **Hyper-V Hypervisor**

The Hyper-V hypervisor exists on Windows 10 and server 2016 (and later) systems if they support Virtualization Based Security (VBS). VBS provides an extra layer of security, where the actual machine is in fact a virtual machine controlled by Hyper-V. VBS is beyond the scope of this book. For more information, check out the *Windows Internals* book.

> Windows 10 version 1607 introduced the Windows Subsystem for Linux (WSL). Although this may look like yet another subsystem, like the old POSIX and OS/2 subsystems supported by Windows, it is not quite like that at all. The old subsystems were able to execute POSIX and OS/2 apps if theses were compiled on a Windows compiler. WSL, on the other hand, has no such requirement. Existing executables from Linux (stored in ELF format) can be run as-is on Windows, without any recompilation.
>
> To make something like this work, a new process type was created – the Pico process together with a Pico provider. Briefly, a Pico process is an empty address space (minimal process) that is used for WSL processes, where every system call (Linux system call) must be intercepted and translated to the Windows system call(s) equivalent using that Pico provider (a device driver). There is a true Linux (the user-mode part) installed on the Windows machine.

Handles and Objects

The Windows kernel exposes various types of objects for use by user-mode processes, the kernel itself and kernel-mode drivers. Instances of these types are data structures in system space, created by the Object Manager (part of the executive) when requested to do so by user or kernel-mode code. Objects are reference counted – only when the last reference to the object is released will the object be destroyed and freed from memory.

Since these object instances reside in system space, they cannot be accessed directly by user mode. User mode must use an indirect access mechanism, known as handles. A handle is an index to an entry in a table maintained on a process by process basis that points logically to a kernel object residing in system space. There are various `Create*` and `Open*` functions to create/open objects and retrieve back handles to these objects. For example, the `CreateMutex` user mode function allows creating or opening a mutex (depending on whether the object is named and exists). If successful, the function returns a handle to the object. A return value of zero means an invalid handle (and a function call failure). The `OpenMutex` function, on the other hand, tries to open a handle to a named mutex. If the mutex with that name does not exist, the function fails and returns null (0).

Kernel (and driver) code can use either a handle or a direct pointer to an object. The choice is usually based on the API the code wants to call. In some cases, a handle given by user mode to the driver must be turned into a pointer with the `ObReferenceObjectByHandle` function. We'll discuss these details in a later chapter.

> Most functions return null (zero) on failure, but some do not. Most notably, the `CreateFile` function returns `INVALID_HANDLE_VALUE` (-1) if it fails.

Handle values are multiples of 4, where the first valid handle is 4; Zero is never a valid handle value.

Kernel mode code can use handles when creating/opening objects, but they can also use direct pointers to kernel objects. This is typically done when a certain API demands it. Kernel code can get a pointer to an object given a valid handle using the `ObReferenceObjectByHandle` function. If successful, the reference count on the object is incremented, so there is no danger that if the user mode client holding the handle decided to close it while kernel code holds a pointer to the object would now hold a dangling pointer. The object is safe to access regardless of the handle-holder until the kernel code calls `ObDereferenceObject`, which decrements the reference count; if the kernel code missed this call, that's a resource leak which will only be resolved in the next system boot.

All objects are reference counted. The object manager maintains a handle count and total reference count for objects. Once an object is no longer needed, its client should close the handle (if a handle was used to access the object) or dereference the object (if kernel client using a pointer). From that point on, the code should consider its handle/pointer to be invalid. The Object Manager will destroy the object if its reference count reaches zero.

Each object points to an object type, which holds information on the type itself, meaning there is a single type object for each type of object. These are also exposed as exported global kernel variables, some of which are defined in the kernel headers and are actually useful in certain cases, as we'll see in later chapters.

Object Names

Some types of objects can have names. These names can be used to open objects by name with a suitable *Open* function. Note that not all objects have names; for example, processes and threads don't have names – they have IDs. That's why the `OpenProcess` and `OpenThread` functions require a process/thread identifier (a number) rather than a string-base name. Another somewhat weird case of an object that does not have a name is a file. The file name is not the object's name – these are different concepts.

From user mode code, calling a *Create* function with a name creates the object with that name if an object with that name does not exist, but if it exists it just opens the existing object. In the latter case, calling `GetLastError` returns `ERROR_ALREADY_EXISTS`, indicating this is not a new object, and the returned handle is yet another handle to an existing object.

The name provided to a *Create* function is not actually the final name of the object. It's prepended with *\Sessions\x\BaseNamedObjects* where x is the session ID of the caller. If the session is zero, the name is prepended with *\BaseNamedObjects*. If the caller happens to be running in an AppContainer (typically a Universal Windows Platform process), then the prepended string is more complex and consists of the unique AppContainer SID: *\Sessions\x\AppContainerNamedObjects\{AppContainerSID}*.

All the above means is that object names are session-relative (and in the case of AppContainer – package relative). If an object must be shared across sessions it can be created in session 0 by prepending the object name with *Global*; for example, creating a mutex with the `CreateMutex` function named *Global\MyMutex* will create it under *\BaseNamedObjects*. Note that AppContainers do not have the power to use session 0 object namespace. This hierarchy can be viewed with the Sysinternals *WinObj* tool (run elevated) as shown in figure 1-9.

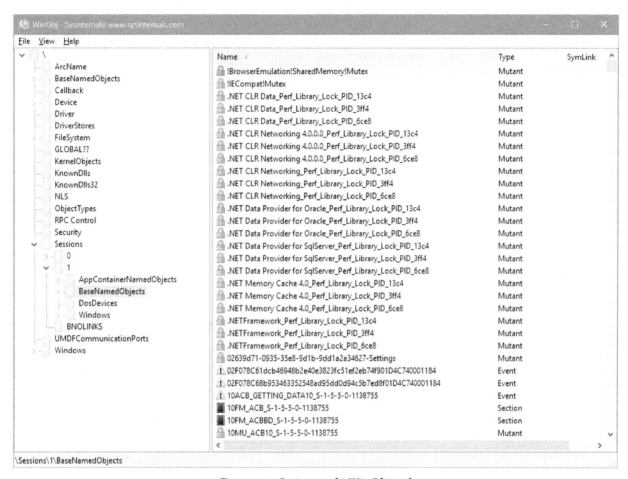

Figure 1-9: Sysinternals *WinObj* tool

The view shown in figure 1-9 is the object manager namespace, comprising of a hierarchy of named objects. This entire structure is held in memory and manipulated by the Object Manager (part of the Executive) as required. Note that unnamed objects are not part of this structure, meaning the objects seen in *WinObj* do not comprise all the existing objects, but rather all the objects that were created with a name.

Every process has a private handle table to kernel objects (whether named or not), which can be viewed with the *Process Explorer* and/or *Handles* Sysinternals tools. A screen shot of Process Explorer showing handles in some process is shown in figure 1-10. The default columns shown in the handles view are the object type and name only. However, there are other columns available, as shown in figure 1-10.

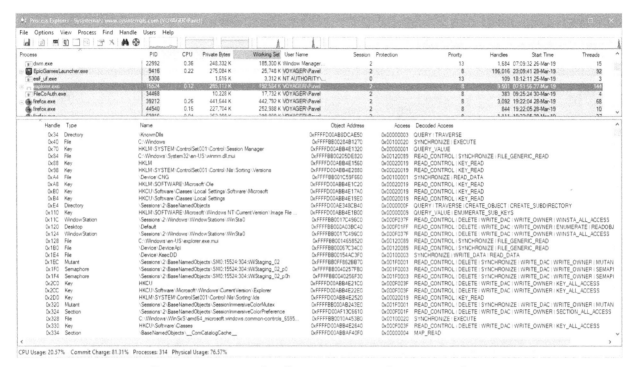

Figure 1-10: Viewing handles in processes with Process Explorer

By default, Process Explorer shows only handles for objects which have names (according to Process Explorer's definition of a name, discussed shortly). To view all handles in a process, select *Show Unnamed Handles and Mappings* from Process Explorer's *View* menu.

The various columns in the handle view provide more information for each handle. The handle value and the object type are self explanatory. The name column is tricky. It shows true object names for Mutexes (Mutants), Semaphores, Events, Sections, ALPC Ports, Jobs, Timers, and other, less used object types. Yet others are shown with a name that has a different meaning than a true named object:

- Process and Thread objects, the name is shown as their unique ID.
- For File objects it shows the file name (or device name) pointed to by the file object. It's not the same as an object's name, as there is no way to get a handle to a file object given the file name - only a new file object may be created that accesses the same underlying file or device (assuming sharing settings for the original file object allow it).
- (Registry) Key objects names are shown with the path to the registry key. This is not a name, for the same reasoning as for file objects.
- Directory objects show the path, rather than a true object name. A Directory is not a file system object, but rather it's an object manager directory - these can be easily viewed with the Sysinternals *WinObj* tool.
- Token object names are shown with the user name stored in the token.

Accessing Existing Objects

The *Access* column in Process Explorer's handles view shows the access mask which was used to open or create the handle. This access mask is key to what operations are allowed to be performed with a specific handle. For example, if client code wants to terminate a process, it must call the OpenProcess function first, to obtain a handle to the required process with an access mask of (at least) PROCESS_TERMINATE, otherwise there is no way to terminate the process with that handle. If the call succeeds, then the call to TerminateProcess is bound to succeed. Here's a user mode example for terminating a process given a process ID:

```
bool KillProcess(DWORD pid) {
    // open a powerful-enough handle to the process

    HANDLE hProcess = OpenProcess(PROCESS_TERMINATE, FALSE, pid);
    if (!hProcess)
        return false;

    // now kill it with some arbitrary exit code
    BOOL success = TerminateProcess(hProcess, 1);

    // close the handle
    CloseHandle(hProcess);

    return success != FALSE;
}
```

The *Decoded Access* column provides a textual description of the access mask (for some object types), making it easier to recognize the exact access allowed for a particular handle.

Double clicking a handle entry shows some of the object's properties. Figure 1-11 shows a screen shot of an example event object's properties.

Figure 1-11: Object properties in Process Explorer

The properties in figure 1-11 include the object's name (if any), its type, a description, its address in kernel memory, the number of open handles, and some specific object information, such as the state and type of the event object shown. Note that the *References* shown do not indicate the actual number of outstanding references to the object. A proper way to see the actual reference count for the object is to use the kernel debugger's `!trueref` command, as shown here:

```
lkd> !object 0xFFFFA08F948AC0B0
Object: ffffa08f948ac0b0  Type: (ffffa08f684df140) Event
    ObjectHeader: ffffa08f948ac080 (new version)
    HandleCount: 2  PointerCount: 65535
    Directory Object: ffff90839b63a700  Name: ShellDesktopSwitchEvent
lkd> !trueref ffffa08f948ac0b0
ffffa08f948ac0b0: HandleCount: 2 PointerCount: 65535 RealPointerCount: 3
```

We'll look more closely at the attributes of objects and the kernel debugger in later chapters.

Now let's start writing a very simple driver to show and use many of the tools we'll need later in this book.

Chapter 2: Getting Started with Kernel Development

This chapter deals with the fundamentals needed to get up and running with kernel driver development. During the course of this chapter, you'll install the necessary tools and write a very basic driver that can be loaded and unloaded.

In this chapter:

- **Installing the Tools**
- **Creating a Driver Project**
- **The `DriverEntry` and Unload routines**
- **Deploying the Driver**
- **Simple Tracing**

Installing the Tools

In the old days (pre-2012), the process of developing and building drivers included using a dedicated build tool from the Device Driver Kit (DDK), without having an integrated development experience developers were used to when developing user mode applications. There were some workarounds, but none of them was perfect nor officially supported. Fortunately, starting with Visual Studio 2012 and Windows Driver Kit 8, Microsoft started officially supporting building drivers with Visual Studio (and msbuild), without the need to use a separate compiler and build tools.

To get started with driver development, the following tools must be installed (in this order):

- Visual Studio 2017 or 2019 with latest updates. Make sure the C++ workload is selected during installation. At the time of this writing Visual Studio 2019 has just been released and can be used for driver development. Note that any SKU will do, including the free Community edition.
- Windows 10 SDK (generally the latest is best). Make sure at least the *Debugging Tools for Windows* item is selected during installation.
- Windows 10 Driver Kit (WDK). The latest should be fine, but make sure you also installs the project templates for Visual Studio at the end of the standard installation.

- The *Sysinternals* tools, which are invaluable in any "internals" work, can be downloaded for free from http://www.sysinternals.com. Click on *Sysinternals Suite* on the left of that web page and download the Sysinternals Suite zip file. Unzip to any folder and the tools are ready to go.

A quick way to make sure the WDK templates are installed correctly is to open Visual Studio and select New Project and look for driver projects, such as "Empty WDM Driver".

Creating a Driver Project

With the above installations in place, a new driver project can be created. The template you'll use in this section is "WDM Empty Driver". Figure 2-1 shows what the New Project dialog looks like for this type of driver in Visual Studio 2017. Figure 2-2 shows the same initial wizard with Visual Studio 2019. The project in both figures is named "Sample".

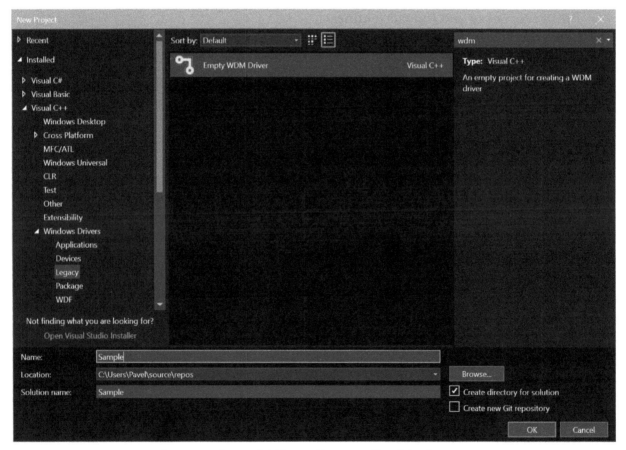

Figure 2-1: New WDM Driver Project in Visual Studio 2017

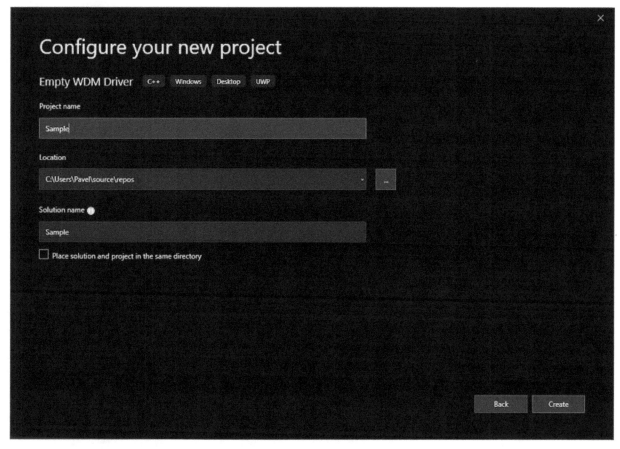

Figure 2-2: New WDM Driver Project in Visual Studio 2019

Once the project is created, the Solution Explorer shows a single file - `Sample.inf`. You won't need this file in this example, so just delete it.

Now it's time to add a source file. Right-click the *Source Files* node in Solution Explorer and select *Add / New Item...* from the File menu. Select a C++ source file and name it `Sample.cpp`. Click OK to create it.

The DriverEntry and Unload Routines

Every driver has an entry point called `DriverEntry` by default. This can be considered the "main" of the driver, comparable to the classic main of a user mode application. This function is called by a system thread at IRQL PASSIVE_LEVEL (0). (IRQLs will be discussed in detail in chapter 8.)

`DriverEntry` has a predefined prototype, shown here:

```
NTSTATUS
DriverEntry(_In_ PDRIVER_OBJECT DriverObject, _In_ PUNICODE_STRING RegistryPath);
```

The _In_ annotations are part of the *Source (Code) Annotation Language (SAL)*. These annotations are transparent to the compiler, but provide metadata useful for human readers and static analysis tools. We'll try to use these as much as possible to improve code clarity.

A minimal DriverEntry routine could just return a successful status, like so:

```
NTSTATUS
DriverEntry(_In_ PDRIVER_OBJECT DriverObject, _In_ PUNICODE_STRING RegistryPath) {
    return STATUS_SUCCESS;
}
```

This code would not yet compile. First, you'll need to include a header that has the required definitions for the types present in DriverEntry. Here's one possibility:

```
#include <ntddk.h>
```

Now the code has better chance of compiling, but would still fail. One reason is that by default, the compiler is set to treat warnings as errors, and the function does not make use of its given arguments. Removing *treat warnings as errors* is not recommended, as some warnings may be errors in disguise. These warnings can be solved by removing the argument names entirely (or commenting them out), which is fine for C++ files. There is another, classic way to solve this, which is to use the UNREFERENCED_PARAMETER macro:

```
NTSTATUS
DriverEntry(_In_ PDRIVER_OBJECT DriverObject, _In_ PUNICODE_STRING RegistryPath) {
    UNREFERENCED_PARAMETER(DriverObject);
    UNREFERENCED_PARAMETER(RegistryPath);

    return STATUS_SUCCESS;
}
```

As it turns out, this macro actually references the argument given just by writing its value as is, and this shuts the compiler up, making the argument "referenced".

Building the project now compiles fine, but causes a linker error. The DriverEntry function must have C-linkage, which is not the default in C++ compilation. Here's the final version of a successful build of the driver consisting of a DriverEntry function only:

```
extern "C"
NTSTATUS
DriverEntry(_In_ PDRIVER_OBJECT DriverObject, _In_ PUNICODE_STRING RegistryPath) {
    UNREFERENCED_PARAMETER(DriverObject);
    UNREFERENCED_PARAMETER(RegistryPath);

    return STATUS_SUCCESS;
}
```

At some point the driver may be unloaded. At that time, anything done in the DriverEntry function must be undone. Failure to do so creates a leak, which the kernel will not clean until the next reboot. Drivers can have an Unload routine that is automatically called before the driver is unloaded from memory. Its pointer must be set using the DriverUnload member of the driver object:

```
DriverObject->DriverUnload = SampleUnload;
```

The unload routine accepts the driver object (the same one passed in to DriverEntry) and returns void. As our sample driver has done nothing in terms of resource allocation in DriverEntry, there is nothing to do in the Unload routine, so we can leave it empty for now:

```
void SampleUnload(_In_ PDRIVER_OBJECT DriverObject) {
    UNREFERENCED_PARAMETER(DriverObject);
}
```

Here is the complete driver source at this point:

```
#include <ntddk.h>

void SampleUnload(_In_ PDRIVER_OBJECT DriverObject) {
    UNREFERENCED_PARAMETER(DriverObject);
}

extern "C"
NTSTATUS
DriverEntry(_In_ PDRIVER_OBJECT DriverObject, _In_ PUNICODE_STRING RegistryPath) {
    UNREFERENCED_PARAMETER(RegistryPath);

    DriverObject->DriverUnload = SampleUnload;

    return STATUS_SUCCESS;
}
```

Deploying the Driver

Now the we have a successfully compiled *Sample.sys* driver file, let's install it on a system and then load it. Normally, you would install and load a driver on a virtual machine, to remove the risk of crashing your primary machine. Feel free to do so, or take the slight risk with this minimalist driver.

Installing a software driver, just like installing a user-mode service, requires calling the `Create-Service` API with proper arguments or using existing tools. One of the well-known tools for this purpose is *Sc.exe*, a built-in Windows tool for manipulating services. We'll use this tool to install and then load the driver. Note that installation and loading of drivers is a privileged operation, normally only allowed for administrators.

Open an elevated command window and type the following (the last part should be the path on your system where the SYS file resides):

```
sc create sample type= kernel binPath= c:\dev\sample\x64\debug\sample.sys
```

Note there is no space between *type* and the equal sign, and there is a space between the equal sign and *kernel*; same goes for the second part.

If all goes well, the output should indicate success. To test the installation, you can open the registry editor (*regedit.exe*) and look for the driver in *HKLM\System\CurrentControlSet\Services\Sample*. Figure 2-3 shows a screen shot of the registry editor after the previous command.

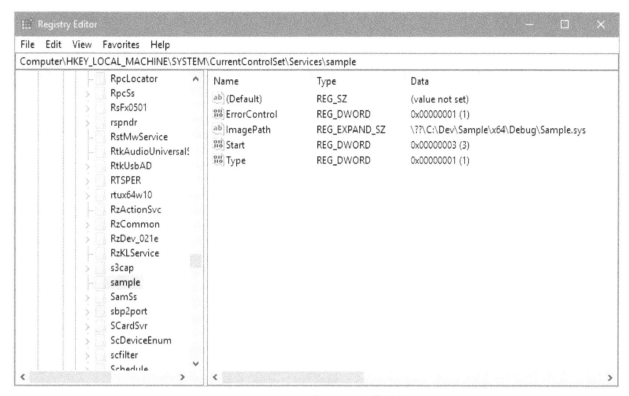

Figure 2-3: **Registry for an installed driver**

To load the driver, we can use the *Sc.exe* tool again, this time with the *start* option, which uses the `StartService` API to load the driver (the same API used to load services). However, on 64 bit systems drivers must be signed, and so normally the following command would fail:

```
sc start sample
```

Since it's inconvenient to sign a driver during development (maybe even not possible if you don't have a proper certificate), a better option is to put the system into test signing mode. In this mode, unsigned drivers can be loaded without a hitch.

With an elevated command window, test signing can be turned on like so:

```
bcdedit /set testsigning on
```

Unfortunately, this command requires a reboot to take effect. Once rebooted, the previous start command should succeed.

 If you are testing on Windows 10 with Secure Boot enabled, changing the test signing mode would fail. This is one of the settings protected by Secure Boot (also protected is local kernel debugging). If you can't disable Secure Boot through BIOS setting, because of IT policy or some other reason, your best option is to test on a virtual machine.

There is yet another setting that you may need to specify if you intend to test the driver on pre-Windows 10 machine. In this case, you have to set the target OS version in the project properties dialog, as shown in figure 2-4. Notice that I have selected all configurations and all platforms, so that when switching configurations (Debug/Release) or platforms (x86/x64/ARM/ARM64), the setting is maintained.

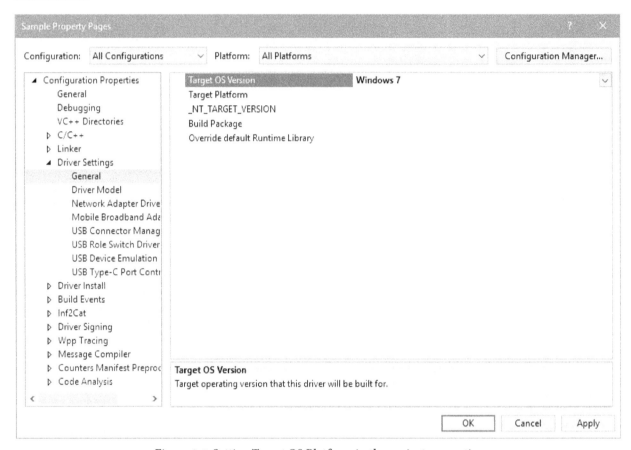

Figure 2-4: Setting Target OS Platform in the project properties

Once test signing mode is on and the driver is loaded, this is the output you should see:

```
SERVICE_NAME: sample
        TYPE                : 1   KERNEL_DRIVER
        STATE               : 4   RUNNING
                                  (STOPPABLE, NOT_PAUSABLE, IGNORES_SHUTDOWN)
        WIN32_EXIT_CODE     : 0   (0x0)
        SERVICE_EXIT_CODE   : 0   (0x0)
        CHECKPOINT          : 0x0
        WAIT_HINT           : 0x0
        PID                 : 0
        FLAGS               :
```

This means everything is well and the driver is loaded. To confirm, we can open *Process Explorer* and find the *Sample.Sys* driver image file. Figure 2-5 shows the details of the sample driver image loaded into system space.

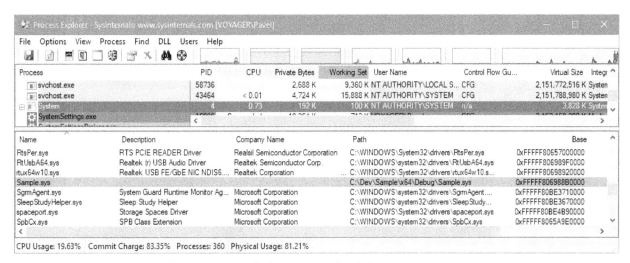

Figure 2-5: sample driver image loaded into system space

At this point we can unload the driver using the following command:

```
sc stop sample
```

Behind the scenes, *sc.exe* calls the `ControlService` API with the `SERVICE_CONTROL_STOP` value. Unloading the driver causes the Unload routine to be called, which at this time does nothing. You can verify the driver is indeed unloaded by looking at Process Explorer again; the driver image should not be there.

Simple Tracing

How can we know for sure that the `DriverEntry` and Unload routines actually executed? Let's add basic tracing to these functions. Drivers can use the `KdPrint` macro to output printf-style text that can be viewed using the kernel debugger and other tools. `KdPrint` is a macro that is only compiled in Debug builds and calls the underlying `DbgPrint` kernel API.

Here is updated versions for `DriverEntry` and the Unload routine that use `KdPrint` to trace the fact their code executed:

```
void SampleUnload(_In_ PDRIVER_OBJECT DriverObject) {
    UNREFERENCED_PARAMETER(DriverObject);

    KdPrint(("Sample driver Unload called\n"));
}

extern "C"
NTSTATUS
DriverEntry(_In_ PDRIVER_OBJECT DriverObject, _In_ PUNICODE_STRING RegistryPath) {
    UNREFERENCED_PARAMETER(RegistryPath);

    DriverObject->DriverUnload = SampleUnload;

    KdPrint(("Sample driver initialized successfully\n"));

    return STATUS_SUCCESS;
}
```

Notice the double parenthesis when using KdPrint. This is required because KdPrint is a macro, but apparently accepts any number of arguments, a-la printf. Since macros cannot receive a variable number of arguments, a compiler trick is used to call the real DbgPrint function.

With these statements in place, we would like to load the driver again and see these messages. We'll use a kernel debugger in chapter 4, but for now we'll use a useful *Sysinternals* tool named *DebugView*. Before running *DebugView*, you'll need to make some preparations. First, starting with Windows Vista, DbgPrint output is not actually generated unless a certain value is in the registry. You'll have to add a key named *Debug Print Filter* under *HKLM\SYSTEM\CurrentControlSet\Control\Session Manager* (the key typically does not exist). Within this new key, add a DWORD value named *DEFAULT* (not the default value that exists in any key) and set its value to 8 (technically, any value with bit 3 set will do). Figure 2-6 shows the setting in *RegEdit*. Unfortunately, you'll have to restart the system for this setting to take effect.

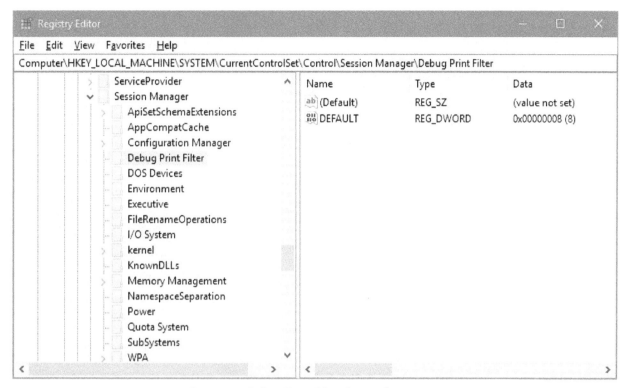

Figure 2-6: Debug Print Filter key in the registry

Once this setting has been applied, run *DebugView* (*DbgView.exe*) elevated. In the *Options* menu, make sure *Capture Kernel* is selected (or press *Ctrl+K*). You can safely deselect *Capture Win32* and *Capture Global Win32* so output from various processes does not clutter the display.

Build the driver, if you haven't already. Now you can load the driver again from an elevated command window (`sc start sample`). You should see output in *DebugView* as shown in figure 2-7. If you unload the driver, you'll see another message appearing because the Unload routine was called. (The third output line is from another driver and has nothing to do with our sample driver)

Figure 2-7: Sysinternals *DebugView* Output

Exercises

1. Add code to the sample `DriverEntry` to output the Windows OS version: major, minor and build number. Use the `RtlGetVersion` function to retrieve the information. Check the results with *DebugView*.

Summary

We've seen the tools you need to have for kernel development and wrote a very minimalistic driver to prove the basic tools work. In the next chapter, we'll look at the fundamental building blocks of kernel APIs, concepts and structures.

Chapter 3: Kernel Programming Basics

In this chapter we'll dig deeper into kernel APIs, structures and definitions. We'll also examine some of the mechanisms that invoke code in a driver. Finally, we'll put all that knowledge together to create our first functional driver.

In this chapter:

- **General Kernel Programming Guidelines**
- **Debug vs. Release Builds**
- **The Kernel API**
- **Functions and Error Codes**
- **Strings**
- **Dynamic Memory Allocation**
- **Lists**
- **The Driver Object**
- **Device Objects**

General Kernel Programming Guidelines

Developing kernel drivers requires the Windows Driver Kit (WDK), where the appropriate headers and libraries needed are located. The kernel APIs consists of C functions, very similar in essence to user mode development. There are several differences, however. Table 3-1 summarizes the important differences between user mode programming and kernel mode programming.

Table 3-1: Differences between user mode and kernel mode development

	User Mode	Kernel Mode
Unhandled Exception	Unhandled exception crashes the process	Unhandled exception crashes the system
Termination	When a process terminates, all private memory and resources are freed automatically	If a driver unloads without freeing everything it was using, there is a leak, only resolved in the next boot
Return values	API errors are sometimes ignored	Should (almost) never ignore errors
IRQL	Always PASSIVE_LEVEL (0)	May be DISPATCH_LEVEL (2) or higher
Bad coding	Typically localized to the process	Can have system-wide effect
Testing and Debugging	Typical testing and debugging done on the developer's machine	Debugging must be done with another machine
Libraries	Can use almost and C/C++ library (e.g. STL, boost)	Most standard libraries cannot be used
Exception Handling	Can use C++ exceptions or Structured Exception Handling (SEH)	Only SEH can be used
C++ Usage	Full C++ runtime available	No C++ runtime

Unhandled Exceptions

Exceptions occurring in user mode that are not caught by the program cause the process to terminate prematurely. Kernel mode code, on the other hand, being implicitly trusted, cannot recover from an unhandled exception. Such an exception causes the system to crash with the infamous *Blue screen of death* (BSOD) (newer versions of Windows have more diverse colors for the crash screen). The BSOD may first appear to be a punishment, but it's essentially a protective mechanism. The rational being that allowing the code to continue execution could cause irreversible damage to Windows (such as deleting important files or corrupting the registry) that may cause the system to fail boot. It's better, then, to stop everything immediately to prevent potential damage. We'll discuss the BSOD in more detail in chapter 6.

All this leads to at least one simple conclusion: kernel code must be carefully coded, meticulous, and not skipping any details or error checks.

Termination

When a process terminates, for whatever reason - either normally, because of an unhandled exception or terminated by external code - it never leaks anything: all private memory is freed, all handles are closed, etc. Of course premature handle closing may cause some loss of data, such as a file handle being closed before flushing some data to disk - but there is no resource leaks; this is guaranteed by the kernel.

Kernel drivers, on the other hand, don't provide such a guarantee. If a driver unloads while still holding onto allocated memory or open kernel handles - these resources will not be freed automatically, only released at the next system boot.

Why is that? Can't the kernel keep track of a driver's allocations and resource usage so these can be freed automatically when the driver unloads?

Theoretically, this would have been possible to achieve (although currently the kernel does not track such resource usage). The real issue is that it would be too dangerous for the kernel to attempt such cleanup. The kernel has no way of knowing whether the driver leaked those resources for a reason; for example, the driver could allocate some buffer and then pass it to another driver, with which it cooperates. That second driver may use the memory buffer and free it eventually. if the kernel attempted to free the buffer when the first driver unloads, the second driver would cause an access violation when accessing that now-freed buffer, causing a system crash.

This again emphasizes the responsibility of a kernel driver to properly clean up after itself; no one else will do it.

Function Return Values

In typical user mode code, return values from API functions are sometimes ignored, the developer being somewhat optimistic that the called function is unlikely to fail. This may or may not be appropriate for one function or another. In the worst case, an unhandled exception would later crash the process; the system, however, remains intact.

Ignoring return values from kernel APIs is much more dangerous (see the previous Termination section), and generally should be avoided. Even seemingly "innocent" looking functions can fail for unexpected reasons, so the golden rule here is - always check return status values from kernel APIs.

IRQL

Interrupt Request Level (IRQL) is an important kernel concept that will be further discussed in chapter 6. Suffice it to say at this point that normally a processor's IRQL is zero, and more specifically, it's always zero when user mode code is executing. In kernel mode, it's still zero most of the time - but not all the time. The effects of higher than zero IRQL will be discussed in chapter 6.

C++ Usage

In user mode programming, C++ has been used for many years and it works well when combined with user mode API calls. With kernel code, Microsoft started officially supporting C++ with Visual Studio 2012 and WDK 8. C++ is not mandatory, of course, but it has some important benefits related to resource cleanup, using an C++ idiom called *Resource Acquisition Is Initialization* (RAII). We'll use this RAII idiom quite a bit to make sure we don't leak resources.

C++ as a language is almost fully supported for kernel code. But there is no C++ runtime in the kernel, and so some C++ features just cannot be used:

- The `new` and `delete` operators are not supported and will fail to compile. This is because their normal operation is to allocate from a user-mode heap, which of course is irrelevant within the kernel. The kernel API has "replacement" functions that are more closely modeled after the C functions `malloc` and `free`. We'll discuss these functions later in this chapter. It is possible, however, to overload these operators similarly as it's done in user mode C++ and invoke the kernel allocation and free functions. We'll see how to do that later in this chapter as well.
- Global variables that have non-default constructors will not be called - there is no-one to call these constructors. These situations can be avoided in several ways:
  - Avoid any code in the constructor and instead create some `Init` function to be called explicitly from driver code (e.g. from `DriverEntry`).
  - Allocate a pointer only as a global variable, and create the actual instance dynamically. The compiler will generate the correct code to invoke the constructor. This works assuming the `new` and `delete` operators have been overloaded as described later in this chapter.
- The C++ exception handling keywords (`try`, `catch`, `throw`) do not compile. This is because the C++ exception handling mechanism requires its own runtime, which is not present in the kernel. Exception handling can only be done using *Structured Exception Handling* (SEH) - a kernel mechanism to handle exceptions. We'll take a detailed look at SEH in chapter 6.
- The standard C++ libraries are not available in the kernel. Although most are template-based, these do not compile, because they depend on user mode libraries and semantics. That said, C++ templates as a language feature works just fine and can be used, for example, to create alternative types for user mode library types such as `std::vector<>`, `std::wstring`, etc.

The code examples in this book make some use of C++. The features mostly used in the code examples are:

- The `nullptr` keyword, representing a true `NULL` pointer.
- The `auto` keyword that allows type inference when declaring and initializing variables. This is useful to reduce clutter, save some typing, and focus on the important pieces.
- Templates will be used when they make sense.
- Overloading of the `new` and `delete` operators.
- Constructors and destructors, especially for building RAII types.

Strictly speaking, drivers can be written in pure C without any issues. If you prefer to go that route, use files with a C extension rather than CPP. This will automatically invoke the C compiler.

Testing and Debugging

With user mode code, testing is generally done on the developer's machine (if all required dependencies can be satisfied). Debugging is typically done by attaching the debugger (Visual Studio in most cases) to the running process (or processes).

With kernel code, testing is typically done on another machine, usually a virtual machine hosted on the developer's machine. This ensures that if a BSOD occurs, the developer's machine is unaffected.

Debugging kernel code must be done with another machine, where the actual driver is executing. This is because in kernel mode, hitting a breakpoint freezes the entire machine, not just a particular process. This means the developer's machine hosts the debugger itself, while the second machine (again, usually a virtual machine) executes the driver code. These two machines must be connected through some mechanism so data can flow between the host (where the debugger is running) and the target. We'll look at kernel debugging in more detail in chapter 5.

Debug vs. Release Builds

Just like with user mode projects, building kernel drivers can be done in Debug or Release mode. The differences are similar to their user mode counterparts - Debug build uses no optimizations by default, but easier to debug. Release builds utilize compiler optimizations to produce the fastest code possible. There are a few differences, however.

The actual terms in kernel terminology are Checked (Debug) and Free (Release). Although Visual Studio kernel projects continue to use the Debug/Release terms, older documentation uses the Checked/Free terms. From a compilation perspective, kernel Debug builds define the symbol DBG and set its value to 1 (compared to the _DEBUG symbol defined in user mode). This means you can use the DBG symbol to distinguish between Debug and Release builds with conditional compilation. This is in fact what the KdPrint macro does: in Debug builds it compiles to calling DbgPrint, while in Release build it compiles to nothing, resulting in KdPrint calls having no effect in Release builds. This is usually what you want because these calls are relatively expensive. We'll discuss other ways of logging information in chapter 10.

The Kernel API

Kernel drivers use exported functions from kernel components. These functions will be referred to as the *Kernel API*. Most functions are implemented within the kernel module itself (*NtOskrnl.exe*), but some may be implemented by other kernel modules, such the HAL (*hal.dll*).

The Kernel API is a large set of C functions. Most of these start with a prefix suggesting the component implementing that function. Table 3-2 shows some of the common prefixes and their meaning:

Table 3-2: Common kernel API prefixes

Prefix	Meaning	Example
Ex	general executive functions	`ExAllocatePool`
Ke	general kernel functions	`KeAcquireSpinLock`
Mm	memory manager	`MmProbeAndLockPages`
Rtl	general runtime library	`RtlInitUnicodeString`
FsRtl	file system runtime library	`FsRtlGetFileSize`
Flt	file system mini-filter library	`FltCreateFile`
Ob	object manager	`ObReferenceObject`
Io	I/O manager	`IoCompleteRequest`
Se	security	`SeAccessCheck`
Ps	process structure	`PsLookupProcessByProcessId`
Po	power manager	`PoSetSystemState`
Wmi	Windows management instrumentation	`WmiTraceMessage`
Zw	native API wrappers	`ZwCreateFile`
Hal	hardware abstraction layer	`HalExamineMBR`
Cm	configuration manager (registry)	`CmRegisterCallbackEx`

If you take a look at the exported functions list from *NtOsKrnl.exe*, you'll find many functions that are not documented in the Windows Driver Kit; this is just a fact of a kernel developer's life - not everything is documented.

One set of functions bears discussion at this point - the *Zw* prefixed functions. These functions mirror native APIs available as gateways from *NtDll.Dll* with the actual implementation within the Executive. When an *Nt* function is called from user mode, such as `NtCreateFile`, it reaches the Executive at the actual `NtCreateFile` implementation. At this point, `NtCreateFile` might do various checks based on the fact that the original caller is from user mode. This caller information is stored on a thread-by-thread basis, in the undocumented `PreviousMode` member in the `KTHREAD` structure for each thread.

On the other hand, if a kernel driver needs to call a system service, it should not be subjected to the same checks and constraints imposed on user-mode callers. This is where the *Zw* functions come into play. Calling a *Zw* function sets the previous caller mode to `KernelMode` (0) and then invokes the native function. For example, calling `ZwCreateFile` sets the previous caller to `KernelMode` and then calls `NtCreateFile`, causing `NtCreateFile` to bypass some security and buffer checks that would otherwise be performed. The bottom line is, that kernel drivers should call the *Zw* functions unless there is a compelling reason to do otherwise.

Functions and Error Codes

Most kernel API functions return a status indicating success or failure of an operation. This is typed as `NTSTATUS`, a signed 32-bit integer. The value `STATUS_SUCCESS` (0) indicates success. A negative value indicates some kind of error. You can find all the defined `NTSTATUS` values in the file *ntstatus.h*.

Most code paths don't care about the exact nature of the error, and so testing the most significant bit is enough. This can be done with the NT_SUCCESS macro. Here is an example that tests for failure and logs an error if that is the case:

```
NTSTATUS DoWork() {
    NTSTATUS status = CallSomeKernelFunction();
    if(!NT_SUCCESS(Statue)) {
        KdPrint((L"Error occurred: 0x%08X\n", status));
        return status;
    }

    // continue with more operations

    return STATUS_SUCCESS;
}
```

In some cases, NTSTATUS values are returned from functions that eventually bubble up to user mode. In these cases, the *STATUS_xxx* value is translated to some *ERROR_yyy* value that is available to user mode through the GetLastError function. Note that these are not the same numbers; for one, the error code in user mode have positive values. Second, the mapping is not one-to-one. In any case, this is not generally a concern for a kernel driver.

Internal kernel driver functions also typically return NTSTATUS to indicate their success/failure status. This is usually convenient, as these functions make calls to kernel APIs and so can propagate any error by simply returning the same status they got back from the particular API. This also implies that the "real" return values from driver functions is typically returned through pointers and references provided as arguments to the function.

Strings

The kernel API uses strings in many cases where needed. In some cases these strings are simple Unicode pointers (wchar_t* or one of their typedefs such as WCHAR), but most functions dealing with strings expect a structure of type UNICODE_STRING.

> The term *Unicode* as used in this book is roughly equivalent to UTF-16, which means 2 bytes per character. This is how strings are stored internally within kernel components.

The UNICODE_STRING structure represents a string with its length and maximum length known. Here is a simplified definition of the structure:

```
typedef struct _UNICODE_STRING {
    USHORT Length;
    USHORT MaximumLength;
    PWCH   Buffer;
} UNICODE_STRING;
typedef UNICODE_STRING *PUNICODE_STRING;
typedef const UNICODE_STRING *PCUNICODE_STRING;
```

THe Length member is in bytes (not characters) and does not include a Unicode-NULL terminator, if one exists (a NULL terminator is not mandatory). The MaximumLength member is the number of bytes the string can grow to without requiring a memory reallocation.

Manipulating UNICODE_STRING structures is typically done with a set of *Rtl* functions that deal specifically with strings. Table 3-3 lists some of the common functions for string manipulation provided by the *Rtl* functions.

Table 3-3: Common UNICODE_STRING functions

Function	Description
RtlInitUnicodeString	Initializes a UNICODE_STRING based on an existing C-string pointer. It sets Buffer, then calculates the Length and sets MaximumLength to the same value. Note that this function does not allocate any memory - it just initializes the internal members.
RtlCopyUnicodeString	Copies one UNICODE_STRING to another. The destination string pointer (Buffer) must be allocated before the copy and MaximumLength set appropriately.
RtlCompareUnicodeString	Compares two UNICODE_STRINGs (equal, less, greater), specifying whether to do a case sensitive or insensitive comparison.
RtlEqualUnicodeString	Compares two UNICODE_STRINGs for equality, with case sensitivity specification.
RtlAppendUnicodeStringToString	Appends one UNICODE_STRING to another.
RtlAppendUnicodeToString	Appends UNICODE_STRING to a C-style string.

In addition to the above functions, there are functions that work on C-string pointers. Moreover, some of the well-known string functions from the C Runtime Library are implemented within the kernel as well for convenience: wcscpy, wcscat, wcslen, wcscpy_s, wcschr, strcpy, strcpy_s and others.

 The *wcs* prefix works with C Unicode strings, while the *str* prefix works with C Ansi strings. The suffix _s in some functions indicates a *safe* function, where an additional argument indicating the maximum length of the string must be provided so the function would not transfer more data than that size.

Dynamic Memory Allocation

Drivers often need to allocate memory dynamically. As discussed in chapter 1, kernel stack size is rather small, so any large chunk of memory should be allocated dynamically.

The kernel provides two general memory pools for drivers to use (the kernel itself uses them as well).

- Paged pool - memory pool that can be paged out if required.
- Non Paged Pool - memory pool that is never paged out and is guaranteed to remain in RAM.

Clearly, the non-paged pool is a "better" memory pool as it can never incur a page fault. We'll see later in this book that some cases require allocating from non-paged pool. Drivers should use this pool sparingly, only when required. In all other cases drivers should use the paged pool. The POOL_TYPE enumeration represents the pool types. This enumeration includes many "types" of pools, but only three should be used by drivers: PagedPool, NonPagedPool, NonPagedPoolNx (non-page pool without execute permissions).

Table 3-4 summarizes the most useful functions used for working with the kernel memory pools.

Table 3-4: Functions for kernel memory pool allocation

Function	Description
ExAllocatePool	Allocate memory from one of the pools with a default tag. This function is considered obsolete. The next function in this table should be used instead.
ExAllocatePoolWithTag	Allocate memory from one of the pools with the specified tag.
ExAllocatePoolWithQuotaTag	Allocate memory from one of the pools with the specified tag and charges the current process' quota for the allocation.
ExFreePool	Free an allocation. The function knows from which pool the allocation was made.

The tag argument in some of the functions allows tagging an allocation with a 4 byte value. Typically this value is comprised of up to 4 ASCII characters logically identifying the driver, or some part of the driver. These tags can be used to indicate memory leaks - if any allocations tagged with the driver's tag remain after the driver is unloaded. These pool allocations (with their tags) can be viewed with the *Poolmon* WDK tool, or my own *PoolMonX* tool (downloadable from http://www.github.com/zodiacon/AllTools). Figure 3-1 shows a screen shot of *PoolMonX (v2)*.

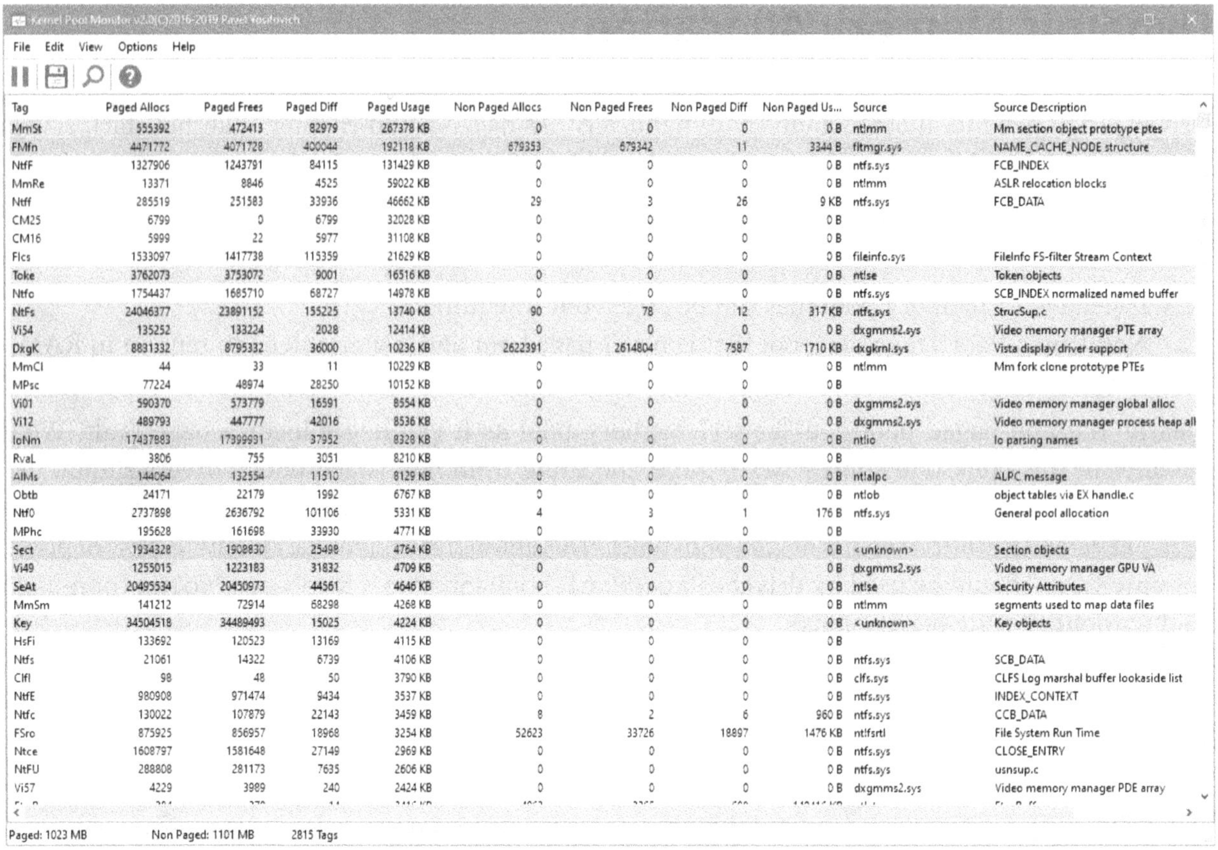

Tag	Paged Allocs	Paged Frees	Paged Diff	Paged Usage	Non Paged Allocs	Non Paged Frees	Non Paged Diff	Non Paged Us...	Source	Source Description
MmSt	555392	472413	82979	267378 KB	0	0	0	0 B	ntlmm	Mm section object prototype ptes
FMfn	4471772	4071728	400044	192118 KB	679353	679342	11	3344 B	fltmgr.sys	NAME_CACHE_NODE structure
NtfF	1327906	1243791	84115	131429 KB	0	0	0	0 B	ntfs.sys	FCB_INDEX
MmRe	13371	9846	4525	59022 KB	0	0	0	0 B	ntlmm	ASLR relocation blocks
Ntff	285519	251583	33936	46662 KB	29	3	26	9 KB	ntfs.sys	FCB_DATA
CM25	6799	0	6799	32028 KB	0	0	0	0 B		
CM16	5999	22	5977	31108 KB	0	0	0	0 B		
Flcs	1533097	1417738	115359	21629 KB	0	0	0	0 B	fileinfo.sys	FileInfo FS-filter Stream Context
Toke	3762073	3753072	9001	16516 KB	0	0	0	0 B	ntlse	Token objects
Ntfo	1754437	1685710	68727	14978 KB	0	0	0	0 B	ntfs.sys	SCB_INDEX normalized named buffer
NtFs	24046377	23891152	155225	13740 KB	90	78	12	317 KB	ntfs.sys	StrucSup.c
Vi54	135252	133224	2028	12414 KB	0	0	0	0 B	dxgmms2.sys	Video memory manager PTE array
DxgK	8831332	8795332	36000	10236 KB	2622391	2614804	7587	1710 KB	dxgkrnl.sys	Vista display driver support
MmCl	44	33	11	10229 KB	0	0	0	0 B	ntlmm	Mm fork clone prototype PTEs
MPsc	77224	48974	28250	10152 KB	0	0	0	0 B		
Vi01	590370	573779	16591	8554 KB	0	0	0	0 B	dxgmms2.sys	Video memory manager global alloc
Vi12	489793	447777	42016	8536 KB	0	0	0	0 B	dxgmms2.sys	Video memory manager process heap all
IoNm	17437883	17399931	37952	8328 KB	0	0	0	0 B	ntlio	Io parsing names
RvaL	3806	755	3051	8210 KB	0	0	0	0 B		
AlMs	144064	132554	11510	8129 KB	0	0	0	0 B	ntlalpc	ALPC message
Obtb	24171	22179	1992	6767 KB	0	0	0	0 B	ntlob	object tables via EX handle.c
Ntf0	2737898	2636792	101106	5331 KB	4	3	1	176 KB	ntfs.sys	General pool allocation
MPhc	195628	161698	33930	4771 KB	0	0	0	0 B		
Sect	1934328	1908830	25498	4764 KB	0	0	0	0 B	<unknown>	Section objects
Vi49	1255015	1223183	31832	4709 KB	0	0	0	0 B	dxgmms2.sys	Video memory manager GPU VA
SeAt	20495534	20450973	44561	4646 KB	0	0	0	0 B	ntlse	Security Attributes
MmSm	141212	72914	68298	4268 KB	0	0	0	0 B	ntlmm	segments used to map data files
Key	34504518	34489493	15025	4224 KB	0	0	0	0 B	<unknown>	Key objects
HsFi	133692	120523	13169	4115 KB	0	0	0	0 B		
Ntfs	21061	14322	6739	4106 KB	0	0	0	0 B	ntfs.sys	SCB_DATA
Clfl	98	48	50	3790 KB	0	0	0	0 B	clfs.sys	CLFS Log marshal buffer lookaside list
NtfE	980908	971474	9434	3537 KB	0	0	0	0 B	ntfs.sys	INDEX_CONTEXT
Ntfc	130022	107879	22143	3459 KB	8	2	6	960 B	ntfs.sys	CCB_DATA
FSro	875925	856957	18968	3254 KB	52623	33726	18897	1476 KB	ntlfsrtl	File System Run Time
Ntce	1608797	1581648	27149	2969 KB	0	0	0	0 B	ntfs.sys	CLOSE_ENTRY
NtFU	288808	281173	7635	2606 KB	0	0	0	0 B	ntfs.sys	usnsup.c
Vi57	4229	3989	240	2424 KB	0	0	0	0 B	dxgmms2.sys	Video memory manager PDE array

Paged: 1023 MB   Non Paged: 1101 MB   2815 Tags

Figure 3-1: *PoolMonX (v2)*

The following code example shows memory allocation and string copying to save the registry path passed to `DriverEntry`, and freeing that string in the Unload routine:

```cpp
// define a tag (because of little endianess, viewed in PoolMon as 'abcd')

#define DRIVER_TAG 'dcba'

UNICODE_STRING g_RegistryPath;

extern "C" NTSTATUS
DriverEntry(_In_ PDRIVER_OBJECT DriverObject, _In_ PUNICODE_STRING RegistryPath) {
    DriverObject->DriverUnload = SampleUnload;

    g_RegistryPath.Buffer = (WCHAR*)ExAllocatePoolWithTag(PagedPool,
        RegistryPath->Length, DRIVER_TAG);
    if (g_RegistryPath.Buffer == nullptr) {
        KdPrint(("Failed to allocate memory\n"));
        return STATUS_INSUFFICIENT_RESOURCES;
    }
```

```
    g_RegistryPath.MaximumLength = RegistryPath->Length;
    RtlCopyUnicodeString(&g_RegistryPath, (PCUNICODE_STRING)RegistryPath);

    // %wZ is for UNICODE_STRING objects
    KdPrint(("Copied registry path: %wZ\n", &g_RegistryPath));
    //...
    return STATUS_SUCCESS;
}

void SampleUnload(_In_ PDRIVER_OBJECT DriverObject) {
    UNREFERENCED_PARAMETER(DriverObject);

    ExFreePool(g_RegistryPath.Buffer);
    KdPrint(("Sample driver Unload called\n"));
}
```

Lists

The kernel uses circular doubly linked lists in many of its internal data structures. For example, all processes on the system are managed by EPROCESS structures, connected in a circular doubly linked list, where its head is stored the kernel variable PsActiveProcessHead.

All these lists are built in a similar fashion, around the LIST_ENTRY structure defined like so:

```
typedef struct _LIST_ENTRY {
    struct _LIST_ENTRY *Flink;
    struct _LIST_ENTRY *Blink;
} LIST_ENTRY, *PLIST_ENTRY;
```

Figure 3-2 depicts an example of such a list containing a head and three instances.

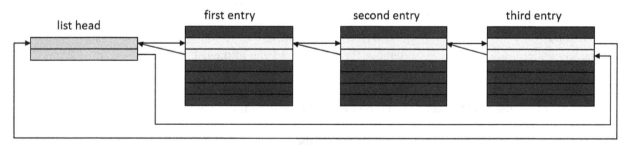

Figure 3-2: Circular linked list

One such structure is embedded inside the real structure of interest. For example, in the EPROCESS structure, the member ActiveProcessLinks is of type LIST_ENTRY, pointing to the next and previous LIST_ENTRY objects of other EPROCESS structures. The head of a list is stored separately; in the case of the process, that's PsActiveProcessHead. To get the pointer to the actual structure of interest given the address of a LIST_ENTRY can be obtained with the CONTAINING_RECORD macro.

For example, suppose you want to manage a list of structures of type *MyDataItem* defined like so:

```
struct MyDataItem {
    // some data members
    LIST_ENTRY Link;
    // more data members
};
```

When working with these linked lists, we have a head for the list, stored in a variable. This means that natural traversal is done by using the Flink member of the list to point to the next LIST_ENTRY in the list. Given a pointer to the LIST_ENTRY, what we're really after is the MyDataItem that contains this list entry member. This is where the CONTAINING_RECORD comes in:

```
MyDataItem* GetItem(LIST_ENTRY* pEntry) {
    return CONTAINING_RECORD(pEntry, MyDataItem, Link);
}
```

The macro does the proper offset calculation and does the casting to the actual data type (*My-DataItem* in the example).

Table 3-5 shows the common functions for working with these linked lists. All operations use constant time.

Table 3-5: Functions for working with circular linked lists

Function	Description
InitializeListHead	Initializes a list head to make an empty list. The forward and back pointers point to the forward pointer.
InsertHeadList	Insert an item to the head of the list.
InsertTailList	Insert an item to the tail of the list.
IsListEmpty	Check if the list is empty.
RemoveHeadList	Remove the item at the head of the list.
RemoveTailList	Remove the item at the tail of the list.
RemoveEntryList	Remove a specific item from the list.
ExInterlockedInsertHeadList	Insert an item at the head of the list atomically by using the specified spinlock.
ExInterlockedInsertTailList	Insert an item at the tail of the list atomically by using the specified spinlock.
ExInterlockedRemoveHeadList	Remove an item from the head of the list atomically by using the specified spinlock.

The last three functions in table 3-4 perform the operation atomically using a synchronization primitive called a spinlock. Spinlocks will be discussed in chapter 6.

The Driver Object

We've already seen that the `DriverEntry` function accepts two arguments, the first is a driver object of some kind. This is a semi-documented structure called `DRIVER_OBJECT` defined in the WDK headers. "Semi-documented" means that some of its members are documented for driver's use and some are not. This structure is allocated by the kernel and partially initialized. Then it's provided to `DriverEntry` (and before the driver unloads to the Unload routine as well). The role of the driver at this point is to further initialize the structure to indicate what operations are supported by the driver.

We've seen One such "operation" in chapter 2 - the Unload routine. The other important set of operations to initialize is called *Dispatch Routines*. This is an array of function pointers, in the `MajorFunction` member of `DRIVER_OBJECT`. This set specifies which particular operations the driver supports, such as Create, Read, Write and so on. These indices are defined with the *IRP_MJ_* prefix. Table 3-6 shows some common major function codes and their meaning.

Table 3-6: Common major function codes

Major function	Description
IRP_MJ_CREATE (0)	Create operation. Typically invoked for `CreateFile` or `ZwCreateFile` calls.
IRP_MJ_CLOSE (2)	Close operation. Normally invoked for `CloseHandle` or `ZwClose` calls.
IRP_MJ_READ (3)	Read operation. Typically invoked for `ReadFile`, `ZwReadFile` and similar read APIs.
IRP_MJ_WRITE (4)	Write operation. Typically invoked for `WriteFile`, `ZwWriteFile` and similar write APIs.
IRP_MJ_DEVICE_CONTROL (14)	Generic call to a driver, invoked because of `DeviceIoControl` or `ZwDeviceIoControlFile` calls.
IRP_MJ_INTERNAL_DEVICE_CONTROL (15)	Similar to the previous one, but only available for kernel-mode callers.
IRP_MJ_PNP (31)	Plug and play callback invoked by the Plug and Play Manager. Generally interesting for hardware-based drivers or filters to such drivers.
IRP_MJ_POWER (22)	Power callback invoked by the Power Manager. Generally interesting for hardware-based drivers or filters to such drivers.

Initially the `MajorFunction` array is initialized by the kernel to point to a kernel internal routine, `IopInvalidDeviceRequest`, which returns a failure status to the caller, indicating the operation is not supported. This means the driver, in its `DriverEntry` routine only needs to initialize the actual operations it supports, leaving all the other entries in their default values.

For example, our Sample driver at this point does not support any dispatch routines, which means there is no way to communicate with the driver. A driver must at least support the IRP_MJ_CREATE and IRP_MJ_CLOSE operations, to allow opening a handle to one the device objects for the driver. We'll put these ideas into practice in the next chapter.

Device Objects

Although a driver object may look like a good candidate for clients to talk to, this is not the case. The actual communication endpoints for clients to talk to drivers are device objects. Device objects are instances of the semi-documented DEVICE_OBJECT structure. Without device objects, there is no one to talk to. This means at least one device object should be created by the driver and given a name, so that it may be contacted by clients.

The CreateFile function (and its variants) accepts a first argument which is called "file name", but really this should point to a device object's name, where an actual file is just once particular case. The name CreateFile is somewhat misleading - the word "file" here actually means file object. Opening a handle to a file or device creates a instance of the kernel structure FILE_OBJECT, another semi-documented structure.

More precisely, CreateFile accepts a *symbolic link*, a kernel object that knows how to point to another kernel object. (You can think of a symbolic link as similar in concept to a file system shortcut.) All the symbolic links that can be used from user mode CreateFile or CreateFile2 call are located in the Object Manager directory named *??*. This can be viewed with the Sysinternals tool *WinObj*. Figure 3-3 shows this directory (named *Global??* in *WinObj*).

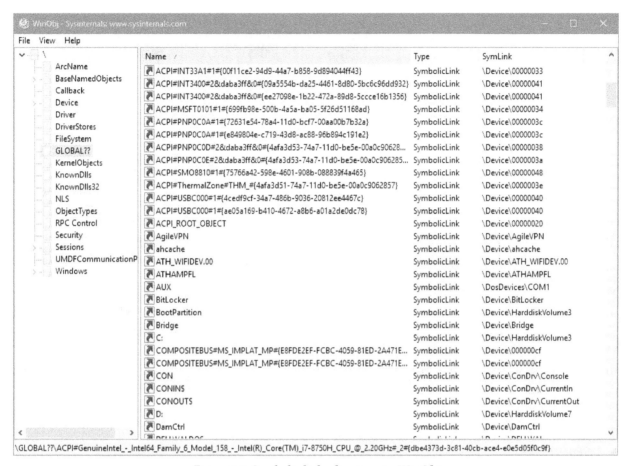

Figure 3-3: Symbolic links directory in *WinObj*

Some of the names seem familiar, such as *C:*, *Aux*, *Con*, and others. Indeed, these are valid "file names" for `CreateFile` calls. Other entries look like long cryptic strings, and these in fact are generated by the I/O system for hardware-based drivers that call the `IoRegisterDeviceInterface` API. These types of symbolic links are not useful for the purpose of this book.

Most of the symbolic links in the *\??* directory point to an internal device name under the *\Device* directory. The names in this directory are not directly accessible by user-mode callers. But they can be accessed by kernel callers using the `IoGetDeviceObjectPointer` API.

A canonical example is the device driver for *Process Explorer*. When *Process Explorer* is launched with administrator rights, it installs a driver. This driver give *Process Explorer* powers beyond those that can be obtained by user-mode callers, even if running elevated. For example, *Process Explorer* in its *Threads* dialog for a process can show the complete call stack of a thread, including functions in kernel mode. This type of information is not possible to obtain from user mode; its driver provides the missing information.

The driver installed by *Process Explorer* creates a single device object so that *Process Explorer* can open a handle to that device and make requests. This means that device objects must be named and must have a symbolic link in the *??* directory; and it's there, named *PROCEXP152*, probably indicating driver version 15.2 (at the time of this writing). Figure 3-4 shows this symbolic link in

WinObj.

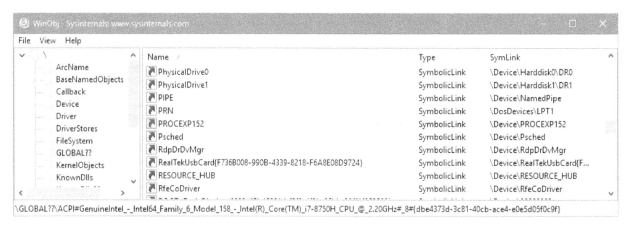

Figure 3-4: Process Explorer's symbolic link in WinObj

Notice the symbolic link for *Process Explorer*'s device points to \Device\PROCEXP152, which is the internal name only accessible to kernel (and native user-mode) callers. The actual CreateFile call made by *Process Explorer* (or any other client) based on the symbolic link must be prepended with \\.\. This is necessary so that the object manager's parser will not assume the string "PROCEXP152" indicates a file in the current directory. Here is how *Process Explorer* would open a handle to its device (note the double backslash because of the backslash escape character):

```
HANDLE hDevice = CreateFile(L"\\\\.\\PROCEXP152",
    GENERIC_WRITE | GENERIC_READ, 0, nullptr, OPEN_EXISTING, 0, nullptr);
```

It is possible to open a handle to the device with the internal name with the native NtOpenFile or NtCreateFile APIs. An alternative is to create the symbolic link from user-mode using DefineDosDevice. Such a symbolic link would work for the current user only, however.

A driver creates a device object using the IoCreateDevice function. This function allocates and initializes a device object structure and returns its pointer to the caller. The device object instance is stored in the DeviceObject member of the DRIVER_OBJECT structure. If more than one device object is created, they form a singly linked list, where the member NextDevice of the DEVICE_-OBJECT points to the next device object. Note that the device objects are inserted at the head of the list, so the first device object created is stored last; its NextDevice points to NULL. These relationships are depicted in figure 3-3.

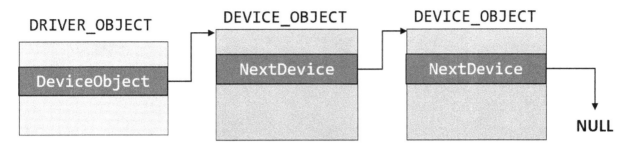

Figure 3-5: Driver and Device objects

Summary

We've looked at some of the fundamental kernel data structures and APIs. In the next chapter, we'll build a complete driver and client and expand on the information presented thus far.

Chapter 4: Driver from Start to Finish

In this chapter, we'll use many of the concepts we learned in previous chapters and build a simple, yet complete driver and client application, while filling in some of the missing details. We'll deploy the driver and use its capabilities - perform some operation in kernel mode that is not available to user mode.

In this chapter:

- **Introduction**
- **Driver Initialization**
- **Client Code**
- **The Create and Close Dispatch Routines**
- **The DeviceIoControl Dispatch Routine**
- **Installing and Testing**

Introduction

The problem we'll solve with a simple kernel driver is the inflexibility of setting thread priorities using the Windows API. In user mode, a thread's priority is determined by a combination of its process *Priority Class* with an offset on a per thread basis that has a limited number of levels. Changing a process priority class can be achieved with the SetPriorityClass function that accepts a process handle and one of the six supported priority classes. Each priority class corresponds to a priority level, which is the default priority of threads created in that process. A particular thread's priority can be changed with the SetThreadPriority function, accepting a thread handle and one of several constants corresponding to offsets around the base priority class. Table 4-1 shows the available thread priorities based on the process priority class and the thread's priority offset.

Table 4-1: Legal values for thread priorities with the Windows APIs

Priority Class	- Sat	-2	-1	0 (default)	+1	+2	+ Sat	Comments
Idle (Low)	1	2	3	4	5	6	15	
Below Normal	1	4	5	6	7	8	15	
Normal	1	6	7	8	9	10	15	
Above Normal	1	8	9	10	11	12	15	
High	1	11	12	13	14	15	15	Only six levels are available (not seven).
Real-time	16	22	23	24	25	26	31	All levels between 16 to 31 can be selected.

The values acceptable to `SetThreadPriority` specify the offset. Five levels correspond to the offsets -2 to +2: THREAD_PRIORITY_LOWEST (-2), THREAD_PRIORITY_BELOW_NORMAL (-1), THREAD_PRIOR-ITY_NORMAL (0), THREAD_PRIORITY_ABOVE_NORMAL (+1), THREAD_PRIORITY_HIGHEST (+2). The remaining two levels, called *Saturation* levels, set the priority to the two extremes supported by that priority class: THREAD_PRIORITY_IDLE (-Sat) and THREAD_PRIORITY_TIME_CRITICAL (+Sat).

The following code example changes the current thread's priority to 11:

```
SetPriorityClass(GetCurrentProcess(), ABOVE_NORMAL_PRIORITY_CLASS);
SetThreadPriority(GetCurrentThread(), THREAD_PRIORITY_ABOVE_NORMAL);
```

 The Real-time priority class does not imply Windows is a real-time OS; Windows does not provide some of the timing guarantees normally provided by true real-time operating systems. Also, since Real-time priorities are very high and compete with many kernel threads doing important work, such a process must be running with administrator privileges; otherwise, attempting to set the priority class to Real-time causes the value to be set to High.

There are other differences between the real-time priorities and the lower priority classes. Consult the *Windows Internals* book for more information.

Table 4-1 shows the problem we will address quite clearly. Only a small set of priorities are available to set directly. We would like to create a driver that would circumvent these limitations and allow setting a thread's priority to any number, regardless of its process priority class.

Driver Initialization

We'll start building the driver in the same way we did in chapter 2. Create a new "WDM Empty Project" named *PriorityBooster* (or another name of your choosing) and delete the INF file created by the wizard. Next, add a new source file to the project, called *PriorityBooster.cpp* (or any other name you prefer). Add the basic #include for the main WDK header and an empty `DriverEntry`:

```
#include <ntddk.h>
```

```
extern "C" NTSTATUS
DriverEntry(_In_ PDRIVER_OBJECT DriverObject, _In_ PUNICODE_STRING RegistryPath) {
    return STATUS_SUCCESS;
}
```

Most software drivers need to do the following in `DriverEntry`:

- Set an Unload routine.
- Set dispatch routines the driver supports.
- Create a device object.
- Create a symbolic link to the device object.

Once all these operations are performed, the driver is ready to take requests.

The first step is to add an Unload routine and point to it from the driver object. Here is the new `DriverEntry` with the Unload routine:

```
// prototypes

void PriorityBoosterUnload(_In_ PDRIVER_OBJECT DriverObject);

// DriverEntry

extern "C" NTSTATUS
DriverEntry(_In_ PDRIVER_OBJECT DriverObject, _In_ PUNICODE_STRING RegistryPath) {
    DriverObject->DriverUnload = PriorityBoosterUnload;

    return STATUS_SUCCESS;
}

void PriorityBoosterUnload(_In_ PDRIVER_OBJECT DriverObject) {
}
```

We'll add code to the Unload routine as needed when we do actual work in `DriverEntry` that needs to be undone.

Next, we need to set up the dispatch routines that we want to support. Practically all drivers must support `IRP_MJ_CREATE` and `IRP_MJ_CLOSE`, otherwise there would be no way to open a handle to any device for this driver. So we add the following to `DriverEntry`:

```
DriverObject->MajorFunction[IRP_MJ_CREATE] = PriorityBoosterCreateClose;
DriverObject->MajorFunction[IRP_MJ_CLOSE] = PriorityBoosterCreateClose;
```

We're pointing the Create and Close major functions to the same routine. This is because, as we'll see shortly, they will actually do the same thing: simply approve the request. In more complex cases, these could be separate functions, where in the Create case the driver can (for instance) check to see who the caller is and only let approved callers succeed with opening a device.

All major functions have the same prototype (they are part of an array of function pointers), so we have to add a prototype for `PriorityBoosterCreateClose`. The prototype for these functions is as follows:

```
NTSTATUS PriorityBoosterCreateClose(_In_ PDEVICE_OBJECT DeviceObject, _In_ PIRP Irp);
```

The function must return `NTSTATUS` and accepts a pointer to a device object and a pointer to an *I/O Request Packet* (IRP). An IRP is the primary object where the request information is stored, for all types of requests. We'll dig deeper into an IRP in chapter 6, but we'll look at the basics later in this chapter, since we require it to complete our driver.

Passing Information to the Driver

The Create and Close operations we set up are required, but certainly not enough. We need a way to tell the driver which thread and to what value to set its priority. From a user mode client's perspective, there are three basic functions it can use: `WriteFile`, `ReadFile` and `DeviceIoControl`.

For our driver's purposes, we can use either `WriteFile` or `DeviceIoControl`. Read doesn't make sense, because we're passing information *to* the driver, rather than from the driver. So which is better, `WriteFile` or `DeviceIoControl`? This is mostly a matter of taste, but the general wisdom here is to use Write if it's really a write operation (logically); for anything else - `DeviceIoControl` is preferred, as it's a generic mechanism for passing data to and from the driver.

Since changing a thread's priority is not a purely Write operation, we'll go with `DeviceIoControl`. This function has the following prototype:

```
BOOL WINAPI DeviceIoControl(
    _In_ HANDLE hDevice,
    _In_ DWORD dwIoControlCode,
    _In_reads_bytes_opt_(nInBufferSize) LPVOID lpInBuffer,
    _In_ DWORD nInBufferSize,
    _Out_writes_bytes_to_opt_(nOutBufferSize,*lpBytesReturned) LPVOID lpOutBuffer,
    _In_ DWORD nOutBufferSize,
    _Out_opt_ LPDWORD lpBytesReturned,
    _Inout_opt_ LPOVERLAPPED lpOverlapped);
```

There are three important pieces to `DeviceIoControl`:

- A control code
- An input buffer
- An output buffer

This means `DeviceIoControl` is a flexible way to communicate with a driver. Several control codes can be supported which would require different semantics passed along with the optional buffers. On the driver side, `DeviceIoControl` corresponds to the `IRP_MJ_DEVICE_CONTROL` major function code. Let's add it to our initialization of dispatch routines:

```
DriverObject->MajorFunction[IRP_MJ_DEVICE_CONTROL] = PriorityBoosterDeviceControl;
```

Client / Driver Communication Protocol

Given that we decided to use `DeviceIoControl` for client/driver communication, we now must define the actual semantics. Clearly, we need a control code and the input buffer. This buffer should contain the two pieces of information required so the driver can do its thing: the thread id and the priority to set for it.

These pieces of information must be usable both by the driver and the client. The client would supply the data, and the driver would act on it. This means these definitions must be in a separate file that must be included by the driver and client code.

For these purpose, we'll add a header file named *PriorityBoosterCommon.h* to the driver project. This file will also be used later by the user mode client.

Within this file, we need to define two things: the data structure the driver expects from clients and the control code for changing a thread's priority. Let's start by declaring a structure that captures the information the driver needs for a client:

```
struct ThreadData {
    ULONG ThreadId;
    int Priority;
};
```

We need the thread's unique ID and the target priority. Thread IDs are 32-bit unsigned integers, so we select `ULONG` as the type (Note that we cannot normally use `DWORD` - a common type defined in user mode headers - because it's not defined in kernel mode headers. `ULONG`, on the other hand, is defined in both). The priority should be a number between 1 and 31, so a simple 32-bit integer will do.

Next we need to define a control code. You may think that any 32-bit number will do, but that is not the case. The control code must be built using the `CTL_CODE` macro, that accepts four arguments that make up the final control code. `CTL_CODE` is defined like so:

```
#define CTL_CODE( DeviceType, Function, Method, Access ) ( \
    ((DeviceType) << 16) | ((Access) << 14) | ((Function) << 2) | (Method))
```

Here is a brief description of the meaning of these macro arguments:

- *DeviceType* - identifies a type of device. This can be one of the FILE_DEVICE_**xxx** constants defined in the WDK headers, but this is mostly for hardware based drivers. For software drivers like ours, the number doesn't matter much. Still, Microsoft's documentation specifies that values for 3rd parties should start with 0x8000.
- *Function* - an ascending number indicating a specific operation. If nothing else, this number must be different between different control codes for the same driver. Again, any number will do, but the official documentation says 3rd party drivers should start with 0x800.
- *Method* - the most important part of the control code. It indicates how the input and output buffers provided by the client pass to the driver. We'll deal with these values in detail in chapter 6. For our driver, we'll use the simplest value METHOD_NEITHER. We'll see its effect later in this chapter.
- *Access* - indicates whether this operation is to the driver (FILE_WRITE_ACCESS), from the driver (FILE_READ_ACCESS), or both ways (FILE_ANY_ACCESS). Typical drivers just use FILE_ANY_-ACCESS and deal with the actual request in the IRP_MJ_DEVICE_CONTROL handler.

Given the above information, we can define our single control code as follows:

```
#define PRIORITY_BOOSTER_DEVICE 0x8000

#define IOCTL_PRIORITY_BOOSTER_SET_PRIORITY CTL_CODE(PRIORITY_BOOSTER_DEVICE, \
    0x800, METHOD_NEITHER, FILE_ANY_ACCESS)
```

Creating the Device Object

We have more initializations to do in DriverEntry. Currently, we don't have any device object and so there is no way to open a handle and reach the driver. A typical software driver needs just one device object, with a symbolic link pointing to it, so that user mode clients can obtain handles.

Creating the device object requires calling the IoCreateDevice API, declared as follows (some SAL annotations omitted/simplified for clarity):

```
NTSTATUS IoCreateDevice(
    _In_         PDRIVER_OBJECT DriverObject,
    _In_         ULONG DeviceExtensionSize,
    _In_opt_     PUNICODE_STRING DeviceName,
    _In_         DEVICE_TYPE DeviceType,
    _In_         ULONG DeviceCharacteristics,
    _In_         BOOLEAN Exclusive,
    _Outptr_     PDEVICE_OBJECT *DeviceObject);
```

The arguments to IoCreateDevice are described below:

- *DriverObject* - the driver object to which this device object belongs to. This should be simply the driver object passed to the DriverEntry function.
- *DeviceExtensionSize* - extra bytes that would be allocated in addition to sizeof(DEVICE_-OBJECT). Useful for associating some data structure with a device. It's less useful for software drivers creating just a single device object, since the state needed for the device can simply be managed by global variables.
- *DeviceName* - the internal device name, typically created under the *Device* Object Manager directory.
- *DeviceType* - relevant to some type of hardware based drivers. For software drivers the value FILE_DEVICE_UNKNOWN should be used.
- *DeviceCharacteristics* - a set of flags, relevant for some specific drivers. Software drivers specify zero or FILE_DEVICE_SECURE_OPEN if they support a true namespace (rarely used by software drivers, beyond the scope of this book).
- *Exclusive* - should more than one file object be allowed to open the same device? Most drivers should specify FALSE, but in some cases TRUE is more appropriate; it forces a single client to the device.
- *DeviceObject* - the returned pointer, passed as pointer to a pointer. If successful, IoCreateDevice allocates the structure from non-paged pool and stores the resulting pointer inside the dereferenced argument.

Before calling IoCreateDevice we must create a UNICODE_STRING to hold the internal device name:

```
UNICODE_STRING devName = RTL_CONSTANT_STRING(L"\\Device\\PriorityBooster");
// RtlInitUnicodeString(&devName, L"\\Device\\ThreadBoost");
```

The device name could be anything but should be in the *Device* object manager directory. There are two ways to initialize a UNICODE_STRING with a constant string. The first is using RtlInitUnicode-String, which works just fine. But RtlInitUnicodeString must count the number of characters in the string to initialize the Length and MaximumLength appropriately. Not a big deal in this case, but there is a quicker way - using the RTL_CONSTANT_STRING macro, which calculates the length of the string statically at compile time, meaning it can only work correctly with constant strings.

Now we can call the IoCreateDevice function:

```
PDEVICE_OBJECT DeviceObject;
NTSTATUS status = IoCreateDevice(
    DriverObject          // our driver object,
    0                     // no need for extra bytes,
    &devName              // the device name,
    FILE_DEVICE_UNKNOWN   // device type,
    0                     // characteristics flags,
    FALSE                 // not exclusive,
    &DeviceObject         // the resulting pointer
    );
if (!NT_SUCCESS(status)) {
    KdPrint(("Failed to create device object (0x%08X)\n", status));
    return status;
}
```

If all goes well, we now have a pointer to our device object. The next step is make this device object accessible to user mode callers by providing a symbolic link. The following lines create a symbolic link and connect it to our device object:

```
UNICODE_STRING symLink = RTL_CONSTANT_STRING(L"\\??\\PriorityBooster");
status = IoCreateSymbolicLink(&symLink, &devName);
if (!NT_SUCCESS(status)) {
    KdPrint(("Failed to create symbolic link (0x%08X)\n", status));
    IoDeleteDevice(DeviceObject);
    return status;
}
```

The `IoCreateSymbolicLink` does the work by accepting the symbolic link and the target of the link. Note that if the creation fails, we must undo everything done so far - in this case just the fact the device object was created - by calling `IoDeleteDevice`. More generally, if `DriverEntry` returns any failure status, the Unload routine is **not** called. If we had more initialization steps to do, we would have to remember to undo everything until that point in case of failure. We'll see a more elegant way of handling this in chapter 5.

Once we have the symbolic link and the device object set up, `DriverEntry` can return success and the driver is now ready to accept requests.

Before we move on we must not forget the Unload routine. Assuming `DriverEntry` completed successfully, the Unload routine must undo whatever was done in `DriverEntry`. In our case, there are two things: device object creation and symbolic link creation. We'll undo them in reverse order:

```
void PriorityBoosterUnload(_In_ PDRIVER_OBJECT DriverObject) {
    UNICODE_STRING symLink = RTL_CONSTANT_STRING(L"\\??\\PriorityBooster");
    // delete symbolic link
    IoDeleteSymbolicLink(&symLink);

    // delete device object
    IoDeleteDevice(DriverObject->DeviceObject);
}
```

Client Code

At this point it's worth writing the user mode client code. Everything we need for the client has already been defined.

Add a new console desktop project to the solution named *Booster* (or some other name of your choosing). The Visual Studio wizard should create a single source file (Visual Studio 2019), and two precompiled header files (*pch.h, pch.cpp*) in Visual Studio 2017. You can safely ignore the precompiled header files for now.

In the *Booster.cpp* file, remove the default "hello, world" code and add the following declaration:

```
#include <windows.h>
#include <stdio.h>
#include "..\PriorityBooster\PriorityBoosterCommon.h"
```

Note that we include the common header file created by the driver and shared with client code.

Change the main function to accept command line arguments. We'll accept a thread ID and a priority using command line arguments and request the driver to change the priority of the thread to the given value.

```
int main(int argc, const char* argv[]) {
    if (argc < 3) {
        printf("Usage: Booster <threadid> <priority>\n");
        return 0;
    }
```

Next we need to open a handle to our device. The "file name" to CreateFile should be the symbolic link prepended with "\\.\". The entire call should look like this:

```
HANDLE hDevice = CreateFile(L"\\\\.\\PriorityBooster", GENERIC_WRITE,
    FILE_SHARE_WRITE, nullptr, OPEN_EXISTING, 0, nullptr);
if (hDevice == INVALID_HANDLE_VALUE)
    return Error("Failed to open device");
```

The *Error* function simply prints some text with the last error occurred:

```
int Error(const char* message) {
    printf("%s (error=%d)\n", message, GetLastError());
    return 1;
}
```

The CreateFile call should reach the driver in its IRP_MJ_CREATE dispatch routine. If the driver is not loaded at this time - meaning there is no device object and no symbolic link - we'll get an error number 2 (file not found). Now that we have a valid handle to our device, it's time to set up the call to DeviceIoControl. First, we need to create a ThreadData structure and fill in the details:

```
ThreadData data;
data.ThreadId = atoi(argv[1]);   // command line first argument
data.Priority = atoi(argv[2]);   // command line second argument
```

Now we're ready to call DeviceIoControl and close the device handle afterwards:

```
DWORD returned;
BOOL success = DeviceIoControl(hDevice,
    IOCTL_PRIORITY_BOOSTER_SET_PRIORITY,    // control code
    &data, sizeof(data),                    // input buffer and length
    nullptr, 0,                             // output buffer and length
    &returned, nullptr);
if (success)
    printf("Priority change succeeded!\n");
else
    Error("Priority change failed!");

CloseHandle(hDevice);
```

DeviceIoControl reaches the driver by invoking the IRP_MJ_DEVICE_CONTROL major function routine.

At this point the client code is done. All that remains is to implement the dispatch routines we declared on the driver side.

The Create and Close Dispatch Routines

Now we're ready to implement the three dispatch routines defined by the driver. The simplest by far are the Create and Close routines. All that's needed is completing the request with a successful status. Here is the complete Create/Close dispatch routine implementation:

```
_Use_decl_annotations_
NTSTATUS PriorityBoosterCreateClose(PDEVICE_OBJECT DeviceObject, PIRP Irp) {
    UNREFERENCED_PARAMETER(DeviceObject);

    Irp->IoStatus.Status = STATUS_SUCCESS;
    Irp->IoStatus.Information = 0;
    IoCompleteRequest(Irp, IO_NO_INCREMENT);
    return STATUS_SUCCESS;
}
```

Every dispatch routine accepts the target device object and an *I/O Request Packet* (IRP). We don't care much about the device object, since we only have one, so it must be the one we created in DriverEntry. The IRP on the other hand, is extremely important. We'll dig deeper into IRPs in chapter 6, but we need to take a quick look at IRPs now.

An IRP is a semi-documented structure that represents a request, typically coming from one of the managers in the Executive: I/O Manager, Plug & Play Manager or Power Manager. With a simple software driver, that would most likely be the I/O Manager. Regardless of the creator of the IRP, the driver's purpose is to handle the IRP, which means looking at the details of the request and doing what needs to be done to complete it.

Every request to the driver always arrives wrapped in an IRP, whether that's a Create, Close, Read or any other IRP. By looking at the IRP's members, we can figure out the type and details of the request (technically, the dispatch routine itself was pointed to based on the request type, so in most cases you already know the request type). It's worth mentioning that an IRP never arrives alone; it's accompanied by one or more structures of type IO_STACK_LOCATION. In simple cases like our driver, there is a single IO_STACK_LOCATION. In more complex cases where there are filter drivers above or below us, multiple IO_STACK_LOCATION instances exist, one for each layer in the device stack. (We'll discuss this more thoroughly in chapter 6). Simply put, some of the information we need is in the base IRP structure and some is in the IO_STACK_LOCATION for our "level" in the device stack.

In the case of Create and Close, we don't need to look into any members. We just need to set the status of the IRP in its IoStatus member (of type IO_STATUS_BLOCK), which has two members:

- *Status* - indicating the status this requests would complete with.
- *Information* - a polymorphic member, meaning different things in different requests. In the case of Create and Close, a zero value is just fine.

To actually complete the IRP, we call `IoCompleteRequest`. This function has a lot to do, but basically it propagates the IRP back to its creator (typically the I/O Manager) and that manager notifies the client that the operation has completed. The second argument is a temporary priority boost value that a driver can provide to its client. In most cases a value of zero is best (`IO_NO_INCREMENT` is defined as zero), because the request completed synchronously, so no reason the caller should get a priority boost. Again, more information on this function is provided in chapter 6.

The last operation to do is return the same status as the one put into the IRP. This may seem like a useless duplication, but it is necessary (the reason will be clearer in a later chapter).

The `DeviceIoControl` Dispatch Routine

This is the crux of the matter. All the driver code so far has lead to this dispatch routine. This is the one doing the actual work of setting a given thread to a requested priority.

The first thing we need to check is the control code. Typical drivers may support many control codes, so we want to fail the request immediately if the control code is not recognized:

```
_Use_decl_annotations_
NTSTATUS PriorityBoosterDeviceControl(PDEVICE_OBJECT, PIRP Irp) {
    // get our IO_STACK_LOCATION
    auto stack = IoGetCurrentIrpStackLocation(Irp); // IO_STACK_LOCATION*
    auto status = STATUS_SUCCESS;

    switch (stack->Parameters.DeviceIoControl.IoControlCode) {
        case IOCTL_PRIORITY_BOOSTER_SET_PRIORITY:
            // do the work
            break;

        default:
            status = STATUS_INVALID_DEVICE_REQUEST;
            break;
    }
```

The key to getting the information for any IRP is to look inside the `IO_STACK_LOCATION` associated with the current device layer. Calling `IoGetCurrentIrpStackLocation` returns a pointer to the correct `IO_STACK_LOCATION`. In our case, there is really just one `IO_STACK_LOCATION`, but in any case calling `IoGetCurrentIrpStackLocation` is the right call to make.

The main ingredient in an `IO_STACK_LOCATION` is a monstrous union member named `Parameters` which holds a set of structures, one for each type of IRP. In the case of `IRP_MJ_DEVICE_CONTROL` the structure to look at is `DeviceIoControl`. In that structure we can find the information conveyed by the client, such as the control code, the buffers and their lengths.

The `switch` statement uses the `IoControlCode` member to determine whether we understand the control code or not. If not, we just set the status to something other than success and break out of the `switch` block.

The last piece of generic code we need is to complete the IRP after the `switch` block, whether it succeeded or not. Otherwise, the client will not get a completion response:

```
Irp->IoStatus.Status = status;
Irp->IoStatus.Information = 0;
IoCompleteRequest(Irp, IO_NO_INCREMENT);
return status;
```

We just complete the IRP with whatever status happens to be. If the control code was not recognized, that would be an failure status. Otherwise, it would depend on the actual work done in the case we do recognize the control code.

The last piece is the most interesting and important one: doing the actual work of changing a thread's priority. The first step is to check whether the buffer we received is large enough to contain a `ThreadData` object. The pointer to the user-provided input buffer is available in the `Type3InputBuffer` member and the input buffer length is at `InputBufferLength`:

```
if (stack->Parameters.DeviceIoControl.InputBufferLength < sizeof(ThreadData)) {
    status = STATUS_BUFFER_TOO_SMALL;
    break;
}
```

> You may be wondering, whether it's actually legal to access the provided buffer. Since this buffer is in user space, we must be in the context of the client's process. And indeed we are, as the caller is the client's thread itself that transitioned to kernel mode as described in chapter 1.

Next, we can assume the buffer is large enough, so let's treat it as a `ThreadData`:

```
auto data = (ThreadData*)stack->Parameters.DeviceIoControl.Type3InputBuffer;
```

If the pointer is `NULL`, then we should abort:

```
if (data == nullptr) {
    status = STATUS_INVALID_PARAMETER;
    break;
}
```

Next, let's see if the priority is in the legal range of 1 to 31, and abort if not:

```
if (data->Priority < 1 || data->Priority > 31) {
    status = STATUS_INVALID_PARAMETER;
    break;
}
```

We're getting closer to our goal. The API we would like to use is KeSetPriorityThread, prototyped as follows:

```
KPRIORITY KeSetPriorityThread(
    _Inout_ PKTHREAD Thread,
    _In_ KPRIORITY Priority);
```

The KPRIORITY type is just an 8-bit integer. The thread itself is identified by a pointer to a KTHREAD object. KTHREAD is one part of the way the kernel manages threads. It's completely undocumented, but the point here is that we have the thread ID from the client and need to somehow get a hold of a pointer to the real thread object in kernel space. The function that can look up a thread by its ID is aptly named PsLookupThreadByThreadId. To get its definition, we need to add another #include:

```
#include <ntifs.h>
```

Note that you must add this #include before *<ntddk.h>*, otherwise you'll get compilation errors.

Now we can turn our thread ID into a pointer:

```
PETHREAD Thread;
status = PsLookupThreadByThreadId(ULongToHandle(data->ThreadId), &Thread);
if (!NT_SUCCESS(status))
    break;
```

There are several important points in this code snippet:

- The lookup function is typed as accepting a HANDLE rather than some kind of ID. So is it a handle or an ID? It's an ID typed as handle. The reason has to do with the way process and thread IDs are generated. These are generated from a global private kernel handle table, so the handle "values" are actual IDs. The ULongToHandle macro provides the necessary casting to make the compiler happy. (Remember that a HANDLE is 64 bit on 64 bit systems, but the thread ID provided by the client is always 32 bit.)

- The resulting pointer is typed as PETHREAD or pointer to ETHREAD. Again, ETHREAD is completely undocumented. Regardless, we seem to have a problem since KeSetPriorityThread accepts a PKTHREAD rather than PETHREAD. It turns out these are the same, because the first member of an ETHREAD is a KTHREAD (the member is named Tcb). We'll prove all this in the next chapter when we use the kernel debugger. The bottom line is we can safely switch PKTHREAD for PETHREAD or vice versa when needed without a hitch.
- PsLookupThreadByThreadId can fail for a variety of reasons such as illegal thread ID or thread that has since terminated. If the call fails, we simply drop out of the switch with whatever status was returned from the function.

Now we are finally ready to change the priority. But wait - what if after the last call succeeds the thread is terminated, just before we set its new priority? Rest assured, this cannot actually happen. Technically, the thread can terminate at that point, but that will not make our pointer a dangling one. This is because the lookup function, if successful, increments the reference count on the kernel thread object, so it cannot die until we explicitly decrement the reference count. Here is the call to make the priority change:

```
KeSetPriorityThread((PKTHREAD)Thread, data->Priority);
```

All that's left to do now is decrement the thread object's reference; otherwise, we have a leak on our hands, which will only be resolved in the next system boot. The function that accomplishes this feat is ObDereferenceObject:

```
ObDereferenceObject(Thread);
```

And we're done! For reference, here is the complete IRP_MJ_DEVICE_CONTROL handler, with some minor cosmetic changes:

```
_Use_decl_annotations_
NTSTATUS PriorityBoosterDeviceControl(PDEVICE_OBJECT, PIRP Irp) {
    // get our IO_STACK_LOCATION
    auto stack = IoGetCurrentIrpStackLocation(Irp); // IO_STACK_LOCATION*
    auto status = STATUS_SUCCESS;

    switch (stack->Parameters.DeviceIoControl.IoControlCode) {
    case IOCTL_PRIORITY_BOOSTER_SET_PRIORITY: {
        // do the work
        auto len = stack->Parameters.DeviceIoControl.InputBufferLength;
        if (len < sizeof(ThreadData)) {
            status = STATUS_BUFFER_TOO_SMALL;
            break;
        }
```

```cpp
        auto data = (ThreadData*)stack->Parameters.DeviceIoControl.Type3InputBuffer;
        if (data == nullptr) {
            status = STATUS_INVALID_PARAMETER;
            break;
        }

        if (data->Priority < 1 || data->Priority > 31) {
            status = STATUS_INVALID_PARAMETER;
            break;
        }

        PETHREAD Thread;
        status = PsLookupThreadByThreadId(ULongToHandle(data->ThreadId), &Thread);
        if (!NT_SUCCESS(status))
            break;

        KeSetPriorityThread((PKTHREAD)Thread, data->Priority);
        ObDereferenceObject(Thread);
        KdPrint(("Thread Priority change for %d to %d succeeded!\n",
            data->ThreadId, data->Priority));
        break;
    }

    default:
        status = STATUS_INVALID_DEVICE_REQUEST;
        break;
    }

    Irp->IoStatus.Status = status;
    Irp->IoStatus.Information = 0;
    IoCompleteRequest(Irp, IO_NO_INCREMENT);
    return status;
}
```

Installing and Testing

At this point we can build the driver and client successfully. Our next step is to install the driver and test its functionality. You can try the following on a virtual machine, or if you're feeling brave enough - on your dev machine.

First, let's install the driver. Open an elevated command window and install using the *sc.exe* tool as we did back in chapter 2:

```
sc create booster type= kernel binPath= c:\Test\PriorityBooster.sys
```

make sure *binPath* includes the full path of the resulting SYS file. The name of the driver (*booster*) in the example is the name of the created registry key, and so must be unique. It doesn't have to be related to the SYS file name.

Now we can load the driver:

```
sc start booster
```

If all is well, the driver would have started successfully. To make sure, we can open *WinObj* and look for our device name and symbolic link. Figure 4-1 shows the symbolic link in *WinObj*.

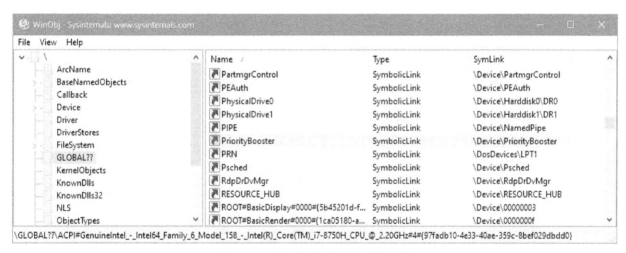

Figure 4-1: Symbolic Link in *WinObj*

Now we can finally run the client executable. Figure 4-2 shows a thread in *Process Explorer* of a *cmd.exe* process selected as an example for which we want set priority to a new value.

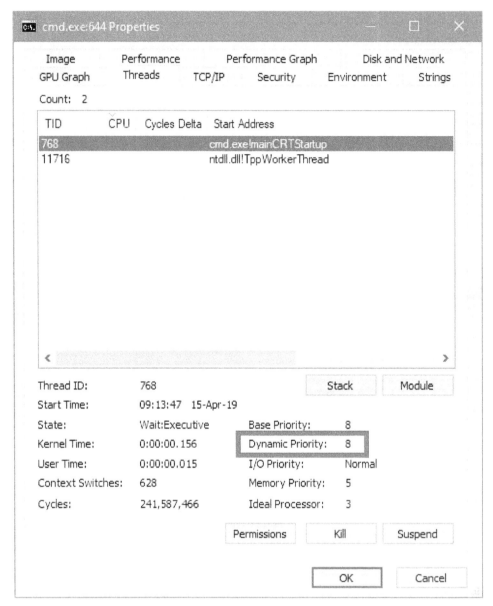

Figure 4-2: Original thread priority

Run the client with the thread ID and the desired priority (replace the thread ID as needed):

```
booster 768 25
```

 If you get an error trying to run the executable, you may need to set the runtime library to a static one instead of a DLL. Go to Project properties, C++ node, **Code Generation**, and select **Multithreaded Debug**.

And voila! See figure 4-3.

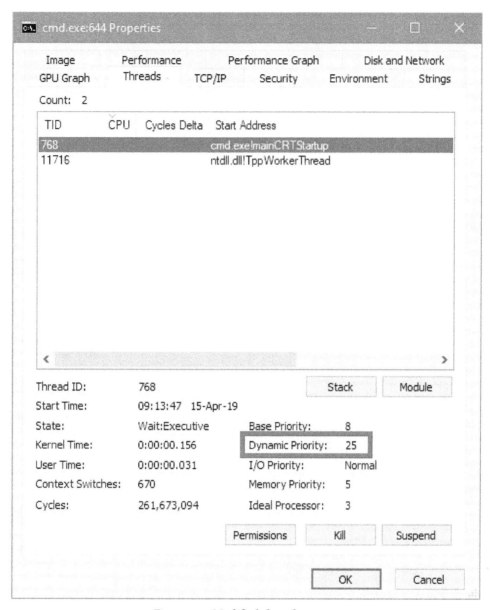

Figure 4-3: Modified thread priority

Summary

We've seen how to build a simple, yet complete, driver, from start to finish. We created a user mode client to communicate with the driver. In the next chapter, we'll tackle debugging, which is something we're bound to do when writing drivers that may not behave as we expect.

Chapter 5: Debugging

Just like with any software, kernel drivers tend to have bugs. Debugging drivers, as opposed to user mode debugging, is more challenging. Driver debugging is essentially debugging an entire machine, not just a specific process or processes. This requires a different mindset. This chapter discussed kernel debugging using the *WinDbg* debugger.

In this chapter:

- **Debugging Tools for Windows**
- **Introduction to WinDbg**
- **Kernel Debugging**
- **Full Kernel Debugging**
- **Kernel Driver Debugging Tutorial**

Debugging Tools for Windows

The *Debugging Tools for Windows* package contains a set of debuggers, tools and documentation focusing on the debuggers within the package. This package can be installed as part of the Windows SDK or the WDK, but there is no real "installation" done. The installation just copies files but does not touch the registry, meaning the package depends only on its own modules and the Windows DLLs. This makes it easy to copy the entire directory to any other directory including to removable media.

The package contains four debuggers: *Cdb.exe*, *Ntsd.Exe*, *Kd.exe* and *WinDbg.exe*. Here is a rundown of the basic functionality of each debugger:

- *Cdb* and *Ntsd* are user mode, console based debuggers. This means they can be attached to processes, just like any other user mode debugger. Both have console UI - type in a command, get a response, and repeat. The only difference between the two is that if launched from a console windows, *Cdb* uses the same console, whereas *Ntsd* opens a new console window. They are otherwise identical.
- *Kd* is a kernel debugger with a console user interface. It can attach to the local kernel (Local Kernel Debugging, described in the next section), or to a another machine.

- *WinDbg* is the only debugger with a graphical user interface. It can be operated in user mode debugging or kernel debugging, depending on the selection performed with its menus or the command line arguments it was launched with.

> A recent alternative to the classic *WinDbg* is *Windbg Preview*, available through the Microsoft store. This is a remake of the classic debugger with much better user interface and experience. It can be installed on Windows 10 version 1607 or later. From a functionality standpoint, it's similar to the classic *WinDbg*. But it is somewhat easier to use because of the modern, convenient UI, and in fact has also solved some bugs in the classic debugger. All the commands we'll see later in this chapter work equally with either debugger.

Although these debuggers may seem different from one another, in fact the user mode debuggers are essentially the same, as are the kernel debuggers. They are all based around a single debugger engine implemented as a DLL (*DbgEng.Dll*). The various debuggers are able to use extension DLLs, that provide most of the power of the debuggers.

> The Debugger Engine is fairly documented in the *Debugging tools for Windows* documentation, and so it is possible to write new debuggers that utilize the same engine.

Other tools that are part of the package include (partial list):

- *Gflags.exe* - the Global Flags tool that allows setting some kernel flags and image flags.
- *ADPlus.exe* - generate a dump file for a process crash or hang.
- *Kill.exe* - a simple tool to terminate process(es) based on process ID, name, or pattern.
- *Dumpchk.exe* - tool to do some general checking of dump files.
- *TList.exe* - lists running processes on the system with various options.
- *Umdh.exe* - analyzes heap allocations in user mode processes.
- *UsbView.exe* - displays a hierarchical view of USB devices and hubs.

Introduction to WinDbg

This section describes the fundamentals of *WinDbg*, but bear in mind everything is essentially the same for the console debuggers, with the exception of the GUI windows.

WinDbg is built around commands. The user enters a command and the debugger responds with text describing the results of the command. With the GUI, some of these results are depicted in dedicated windows, such as locals, stack, threads, etc.

WinDbg supports three types of commands:

- Intrinsic commands - these commands are built-in into the debugger and they operate on the target being debugged.
- Meta commands - these commands start with a period (.) and they operate on the debugging process itself, and not directly on the target being debugged.
- Bang (extension) commands - these commands start with an exclamation point (!), providing much of the power of the debugger. All extension commands are implemented in extension DLLs. By default, the debugger loads a set of predefined extension DLLs, but more can be loaded from the debugger directory or from other sources.

> Writing extension DLLs is possible and is fully documented in the debugger docs. In fact, many such DLLs have been created and can be loaded from their respective source. These DLLs provide new commands that enhance the debugging experience, often targeting specific scenarios.

Tutorial: User mode debugging basics

If you have experience with *WinDbg*, you can safely skip this section.

This tutorial is aimed at getting a basic understanding of *WinDbg* and how to use it for user mode debugging. Kernel debugging is described in the next section.

There are generally two ways to initiate user mode debugging - either launch an executable and attach to it, or attach to an already existing process. We'll use the latter approach in this tutorial, but except for this first step, all other operations are identical.

- Launch *Notepad.*
- Launch *WinDbg* (either the Preview or the classic one. The following screen shots use the Preview).
- Select *File/Attach To Process* and locate the *Notepad* process in the list (see figure 5-1). Then click *Attach*. You should see output similar to figure 5-2.

Figure 5-1: Attaching to a process with WinDbg

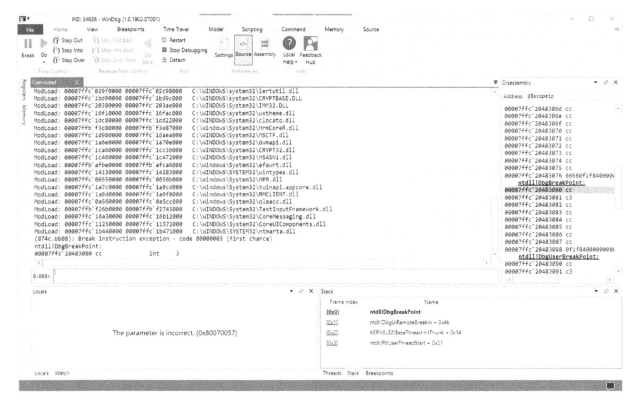

Figure 5-2: First view after process attach

The Command window is the main window of interest - it should always be open. This is the one showing the various responses of commands. Typically, most of the time in a debugging session is spent interacting with this window.

The process now is suspended - we are in a breakpoint induced by the debugger.

- The first command we'll use is ~ which shows information on all threads in the debugged process:

```
0:003> ~
   0  Id: 874c.18068 Suspend: 1 Teb: 00000001`2229d000 Unfrozen
   1  Id: 874c.46ac Suspend: 1 Teb: 00000001`222a5000 Unfrozen
   2  Id: 874c.152cc Suspend: 1 Teb: 00000001`222a7000 Unfrozen
.  3  Id: 874c.bb08 Suspend: 1 Teb: 00000001`222ab000 Unfrozen
```

The exact number of threads you'll see may be different than shown here.

One thing that is very important is the existence of proper symbols. Microsoft provides a public symbol server, which can be used to locate symbols for most modules by Microsoft. This is essential in any low-level debugging.

- To set symbols quickly, enter the **.symfix** command.
- A better approach is to set up symbols once and have them available for all future debugging sessions. To do that, add a system environment variable named **_NT_SYMBOL_PATH** and set it to a string like the following:

```
SRV*c:\Symbols*http://msdl.microsoft.com/download/symbols
```

The middle part (between asterisks) is a local path for caching symbols on your local machine; you can select any path you like. Once this environment variable is set, next invocations of the debugger will find symbols automatically and load them from the Microsoft symbol server as needed.

- To make sure you have proper symbols, enter the **lm** (loaded modules) command:

```
0:003> lm
start               end               module name
00007ff7`53820000 00007ff7`53863000   notepad    (deferred)
00007ffb`afbe0000 00007ffb`afca6000   efswrt     (deferred)

(truncated)

00007ffc`1db00000 00007ffc`1dba8000   shcore     (deferred)
00007ffc`1dbb0000 00007ffc`1dc74000   OLEAUT32   (deferred)
00007ffc`1dc80000 00007ffc`1dd22000   clbcatq    (deferred)
00007ffc`1dd30000 00007ffc`1de57000   COMDLG32   (deferred)
00007ffc`1de60000 00007ffc`1f350000   SHELL32    (deferred)
00007ffc`1f500000 00007ffc`1f622000   RPCRT4     (deferred)
00007ffc`1f630000 00007ffc`1f6e3000   KERNEL32   (pdb symbols)          c:\symbols\k\
ernel32.pdb\3B92DED9912D874A2BD08735BC0199A31\kernel32.pdb
00007ffc`1f700000 00007ffc`1f729000   GDI32      (deferred)
00007ffc`1f790000 00007ffc`1f7e2000   SHLWAPI    (deferred)
00007ffc`1f8d0000 00007ffc`1f96e000   sechost    (deferred)
00007ffc`1f970000 00007ffc`1fc9c000   combase    (deferred)
00007ffc`1fca0000 00007ffc`1fd3e000   msvcrt     (deferred)
00007ffc`1fe50000 00007ffc`1fef3000   ADVAPI32   (deferred)
00007ffc`20380000 00007ffc`203ae000   IMM32      (deferred)
00007ffc`203e0000 00007ffc`205cd000   ntdll      (pdb symbols)          c:\symbols\n\
tdll.pdb\E7EEB80BFAA91532B88FF026DC6B9F341\ntdll.pdb
```

The list of modules shows all modules (DLLs and the EXE) loaded into the debugged process at this time. You can see the start and end virtual addresses into which each module is loaded. Following the module name you can see the symbol status of this module (in parenthesis). Possible values include:

- deferred - the symbols for this module have never been needed in this debugging session and so are not loaded at this time. These will be loaded when needed.
- pdb symbols - this means proper public symbols have been loaded. The local path of the PDB file is displayed.
- export symbols - only exported symbols are available for this DLL. This typically means there are no symbols for this module or they have not been found.
- no symbols - this module symbols were attempted to be located, but nothing was found, not even exported symbols (such modules don't have exported symbols, as is the case of an executable and driver files).

You can force loading of a module's symbols using the command `.reload /f modulename.dll`. This will provide definitive evidence to the availability of symbols for this module.

Symbol paths can also be configured in the debugger's settings dialog.

- Open the *File/Settings* menu and locate *Debugging Settings*. You can then add more paths for symbol searching. This is useful if debugging your own code, so you would like the debugger to search your directories where relevant PDB files may be found (see figure 5-3).

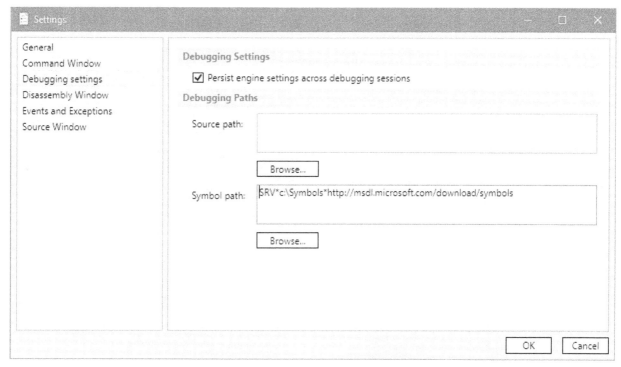

Figure 5-3: Symbols and source paths configuration

- Make sure you have symbols configured correctly before you proceed. To diagnose any issues, you can the !sym noisy command that logs detailed information for symbol load attempts.

Back to the thread list - notice that one of the threads has a dot in front of its data. This is the current thread as far as the debugger is concerned. This means that any command issued that involves a thread where the thread is not specified, will work on that thread. This "current thread" is also shown in the prompt - the number to the right of the colon is the current thread index (3 in this example).

- Enter the **k** command, that shows the stack trace of the current thread:

```
0:003> k
 # Child-SP          RetAddr           Call Site
00 00000001`224ffbd8 00007ffc`204aef5b ntdll!DbgBreakPoint
01 00000001`224ffbe0 00007ffc`1f647974 ntdll!DbgUiRemoteBreakin+0x4b
02 00000001`224ffc10 00007ffc`2044a271 KERNEL32!BaseThreadInitThunk+0x14
03 00000001`224ffc40 00000000`00000000 ntdll!RtlUserThreadStart+0x21
```

You can see the list of calls make on this thread (user mode only of course). The top of stack in the output above is the function DbgBreakPoint located in the module ntdll.dll. The general format of addresses with symbols is modulename!functionname+offset. The offset is optional and could be zero if it's exactly the start of this function. Also notice the module name is without an extension.

In the output above, DbgBreakpoint was called by DbgUiRemoteBreakIn which was called by BaseThreadInitThunk and so on.

> This thread, by the way, was injected by the debugger in order to break into the target forcefully.

- To switch to a different thread, use the following command: ~**ns** where *n* is the thread index. Let's switch to thread 0 and then display its call stack:

```
0:003> ~0s
win32u!NtUserGetMessage+0x14:
00007ffc`1c4b1164 c3              ret
0:000> k
 # Child-SP          RetAddr           Call Site
00 00000001`2247f998 00007ffc`1d802fbd win32u!NtUserGetMessage+0x14
01 00000001`2247f9a0 00007ff7`5382449f USER32!GetMessageW+0x2d
02 00000001`2247fa00 00007ff7`5383ae07 notepad!WinMain+0x267
03 00000001`2247fb00 00007ffc`1f647974 notepad!__mainCRTStartup+0x19f
04 00000001`2247fbc0 00007ffc`2044a271 KERNEL32!BaseThreadInitThunk+0x14
05 00000001`2247fbf0 00000000`00000000 ntdll!RtlUserThreadStart+0x21
```

This is *Notepad*'s main (first) thread. The top of the stack shows the thread waiting for UI messages.

- An alternative way to show the call stack of another thread without switching to it is to use the tilde and thread number before the actual command. The following output is for thread 1's stack:

```
0:000> ~1k
 # Child-SP          RetAddr           Call Site
00 00000001`2267f4c8 00007ffc`204301f4 ntdll!NtWaitForWorkViaWorkerFactory+0x14
01 00000001`2267f4d0 00007ffc`1f647974 ntdll!TppWorkerThread+0x274
02 00000001`2267f7c0 00007ffc`2044a271 KERNEL32!BaseThreadInitThunk+0x14
03 00000001`2267f7f0 00000000`00000000 ntdll!RtlUserThreadStart+0x21
```

- Let's go back to the list of threads:

```
.  0  Id: 874c.18068 Suspend: 1 Teb: 00000001`2229d000 Unfrozen
   1  Id: 874c.46ac Suspend: 1 Teb: 00000001`222a5000 Unfrozen
   2  Id: 874c.152cc Suspend: 1 Teb: 00000001`222a7000 Unfrozen
#  3  Id: 874c.bb08 Suspend: 1 Teb: 00000001`222ab000 Unfrozen
```

Notice the dot has moved to thread 0 (current thread), revealing a hash sign (#) on thread 3. The thread marked with a hash (#) is the one that caused the last breakpoint (which in this case was our initial debugger attach).

The basic information for a thread provided by the ~ command is shown in figure 5-4.

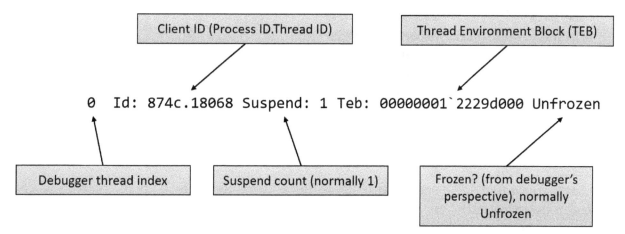

Figure 5-4: Thread information for the ~ command

Most numbers reported by *WinDbg* are hexadecimal by default. To convert a value to decimal, you can use the ? (evaluate expression) command.

- Type the following to get the decimal process ID (you can then compare to the reported PID in Task Manager):

```
0:000> ? 874c
Evaluate expression: 34636 = 00000000`0000874c
```

- You can express decimal numbers with the 0n prefix, so you can get the inverse result as well:

```
0:000> ? 0n34636
Evaluate expression: 34636 = 00000000`0000874c
```

- You can examine the TEB of a thread by using the !teb command. Using !teb without an address shows the TEB of the current thread:

```
0:000> !teb
TEB at 000000012229d000
    ExceptionList:        0000000000000000
    StackBase:            0000000122480000
    StackLimit:           000000012246f000
    SubSystemTib:         0000000000000000
    FiberData:            0000000000001e00
    ArbitraryUserPointer: 0000000000000000
    Self:                 000000012229d000
    EnvironmentPointer:   0000000000000000
    ClientId:             000000000000874c . 0000000000018068
    RpcHandle:            0000000000000000
    Tls Storage:          000001c93676c940
    PEB Address:          000000012229c000
    LastErrorValue:       0
    LastStatusValue:      8000001a
    Count Owned Locks:    0
    HardErrorMode:        0
0:000> !teb 00000001`222a5000
TEB at 00000001222a5000
    ExceptionList:        0000000000000000
    StackBase:            0000000122680000
    StackLimit:           000000012266f000
    SubSystemTib:         0000000000000000
    FiberData:            0000000000001e00
    ArbitraryUserPointer: 0000000000000000
    Self:                 00000001222a5000
    EnvironmentPointer:   0000000000000000
```

```
ClientId:              000000000000874c . 00000000000046ac
RpcHandle:             0000000000000000
Tls Storage:           000001c936764260
PEB Address:           000000012229c000
LastErrorValue:        0
LastStatusValue:       c0000034
Count Owned Locks:     0
HardErrorMode:         0
```

Some data shown by the !teb command is relatively known:

- *StackBase* and *StackLimit* - user mode stack base and limit for the thread.
- *ClientId* - process and thread IDs.
- *LastErrorValue* - last Win32 error code (GetLastError).
- *TlsStorage* - Thread Local Storage (TLS) array for this thread (full explanation of TLS is beyond the scope of this book).
- *PEB Address* - address of the Process Environment Block (PEB), viewable with the !peb command.
- The !teb command (and similar commands) shows parts of the real structure behind the scenes, in this case _TEB. You can always look at the real structure using the dt (display type) command:

```
0:000> dt ntdll!_teb
   +0x000 NtTib              : _NT_TIB
   +0x038 EnvironmentPointer : Ptr64 Void
   +0x040 ClientId           : _CLIENT_ID
   +0x050 ActiveRpcHandle    : Ptr64 Void
   +0x058 ThreadLocalStoragePointer : Ptr64 Void
   +0x060 ProcessEnvironmentBlock : Ptr64 _PEB

   (truncated)

   +0x1808 LockCount         : Uint4B
   +0x180c WowTebOffset      : Int4B
   +0x1810 ResourceRetValue  : Ptr64 Void
   +0x1818 ReservedForWdf    : Ptr64 Void
   +0x1820 ReservedForCrt    : Uint8B
   +0x1828 EffectiveContainerId : _GUID
```

Notice that *WinDbg* is not case sensitive when it comes to symbols. Also, notice the structure name starting with an underscore; this the way all structures are defined in Windows (user mode and kernel mode). Using the typedef name (without the underscore) may or may not work, so always using the underscore is recommended.

 How do you know which module defines a structure you wish to view? If the structure is documented, the module would be listed in the docs for the structure. You can also try specifying the structure without the module name, forcing the debugger to search for it. Generally, you "know" where the structure is defined with experience and sometimes context.

- If you attach an address to the previous command, you can get the actual values of data members:

```
0:000> dt ntdll!_teb 00000001`2229d000
   +0x000 NtTib            : _NT_TIB
   +0x038 EnvironmentPointer : (null)
   +0x040 ClientId         : _CLIENT_ID
   +0x050 ActiveRpcHandle  : (null)
   +0x058 ThreadLocalStoragePointer : 0x000001c9`3676c940 Void
   +0x060 ProcessEnvironmentBlock : 0x00000001`2229c000 _PEB
   +0x068 LastErrorValue   : 0

   (truncated)

   +0x1808 LockCount       : 0
   +0x180c WowTebOffset    : 0n0
   +0x1810 ResourceRetValue : 0x000001c9`3677fd00 Void
   +0x1818 ReservedForWdf  : (null)
   +0x1820 ReservedForCrt  : 0
   +0x1828 EffectiveContainerId : _GUID {00000000-0000-0000-0000-000000000000}
```

Each member is shown with its offset from the beginning of the structure, its name and its value. Simple values are shown directly, while structure values (such as NtTib above) are normally shown with a hyperlink. Clicking this hyperlink provides the details of the structure.

- Click on the NtTib member above to show the details of this data member:

```
0:000> dx -r1 (*((ntdll!_NT_TIB *)0x12229d000))
(*((ntdll!_NT_TIB *)0x12229d000))                    [Type: _NT_TIB]
    [+0x000] ExceptionList    : 0x0 [Type: _EXCEPTION_REGISTRATION_RECORD *]
    [+0x008] StackBase        : 0x122480000 [Type: void *]
    [+0x010] StackLimit       : 0x12246f000 [Type: void *]
    [+0x018] SubSystemTib     : 0x0 [Type: void *]
    [+0x020] FiberData        : 0x1e00 [Type: void *]
    [+0x020] Version          : 0x1e00 [Type: unsigned long]
    [+0x028] ArbitraryUserPointer : 0x0 [Type: void *]
    [+0x030] Self             : 0x12229d000 [Type: _NT_TIB *]
```

The debugger uses the newer dx command to view data.

> If you don't see hyperlinks, you may be using a very old *WinDbg*, where Debugger Markup Language
> (DML) is not on by default. You can turn it on with the .prefer_dml 1 command.

Now let's turn our attention to breakpoints. Let's set a breakpoint when a file is opened by notepad.

- Type the following command to set a breakpoint in the CreateFile API function:

```
0:000> bp kernel32!createfilew
```

Notice the function name is in fact CreateFileW, as there is no function called CreateFile. In code, this is a macro that expands to CreateFileW (wide, Unicode version) or CreateFileA (ASCII or Ansi version) based on a compilation constant named UNICODE. *WinDbg* responds with nothing. This is a good thing.

> The reason there are two sets of functions for most APIs where strings are involved is a historical
> one. In any case, Visual Studio projects define the UNICODE constant by default, so Unicode is the
> norm. This is a good thing - the A functions convert their input to Unicode and call the W functions.

- You can list the existing breakpoints with the bl command:

```
0:000> bl
  0 e Disable Clear  00007ffc`1f652300  0001 (0001)  0:**** KERNEL32!CreateFileW
```

You can see the breakpoint index (0), whether it's enabled or disabled (e=enabled, d=disabled) and you get hyperlinks to disable (bd command) and delete (bc command) the breakpoint.

Now let's let notepad continue execution, until the breakpoint hits:

- Type the g command or press the *Go* button on the toolbar or hit *F5*:

You'll see the debugger showing **_Busy_** in the prompt and the command area shows **Debuggee is running**, meaning you cannot enter commands until the next break.

- Notepad should now be alive. Go to its *File* menu and select *Open....* The debugger should spew details of module loads and then break:

```
Breakpoint 0 hit
KERNEL32!CreateFileW:
00007ffc`1f652300 ff25aa670500    jmp     qword ptr [KERNEL32!_imp_CreateFileW (0000\
7ffc`1f6a8ab0)] ds:00007ffc`1f6a8ab0={KERNELBASE!CreateFileW (00007ffc`1c75e260)}
```

- We have hit the breakpoint! Notice the thread in which it occurred. Let's see what the call stack looks like (it may take a while to show if the debugger needs to download symbols from Microsoft's symbol server):

```
0:002> k
 # Child-SP          RetAddr           Call Site
00 00000001`226fab08 00007ffc`061c8368 KERNEL32!CreateFileW
01 00000001`226fab10 00007ffc`061c5d4d mscoreei!RuntimeDesc::VerifyMainRuntimeModule\
+0x2c
02 00000001`226fab60 00007ffc`061c6068 mscoreei!FindRuntimesInInstallRoot+0x2fb
03 00000001`226fb3e0 00007ffc`061cb748 mscoreei!GetOrCreateSxSProcessInfo+0x94
04 00000001`226fb460 00007ffc`061cb62b mscoreei!CLRMetaHostPolicyImpl::GetRequestedR\
untimeHelper+0xfc
05 00000001`226fb740 00007ffc`061ed4e6 mscoreei!CLRMetaHostPolicyImpl::GetRequestedR\
untime+0x120

(truncated)

21 00000001`226fede0 00007ffc`1df025b2 SHELL32!CFSIconOverlayManager::LoadNonloadedO\
```

```
verlayIdentifiers+0xaa
22 00000001`226ff320 00007ffc`1df022af SHELL32!EnableExternalOverlayIdentifiers+0x46
23 00000001`226ff350 00007ffc`1def434e SHELL32!CFSIconOverlayManager::RefreshOverlay\
Images+0xff
24 00000001`226ff390 00007ffc`1cf250a3 SHELL32!SHELL32_GetIconOverlayManager+0x6e
25 00000001`226ff3c0 00007ffc`1ceb2726 windows_storage!CFSFolder::_GetOverlayInfo+0x\
12b
26 00000001`226ff470 00007ffc`1cf3108b windows_storage!CAutoDestItemsFolder::GetOver\
layIndex+0xb6
27 00000001`226ff4f0 00007ffc`1cf30f87 windows_storage!CRegFolder::_GetOverlayInfo+0\
xbf
28 00000001`226ff5c0 00007ffb`df8fc4d1 windows_storage!CRegFolder::GetOverlayIndex+0\
x47
29 00000001`226ff5f0 00007ffb`df91f095 explorerframe!CNscOverlayTask::_Extract+0x51
2a 00000001`226ff640 00007ffb`df8f70c2 explorerframe!CNscOverlayTask::InternalResume\
RT+0x45
2b 00000001`226ff670 00007ffc`1cf7b58c explorerframe!CRunnableTask::Run+0xb2
2c 00000001`226ff6b0 00007ffc`1cf7b245 windows_storage!CShellTask::TT_Run+0x3c
2d 00000001`226ff6e0 00007ffc`1cf7b125 windows_storage!CShellTaskThread::ThreadProc+\
0xdd
2e 00000001`226ff790 00007ffc`1db32ac6 windows_storage!CShellTaskThread::s_ThreadPro\
c+0x35
2f 00000001`226ff7c0 00007ffc`204521c5 shcore!ExecuteWorkItemThreadProc+0x16
30 00000001`226ff7f0 00007ffc`204305c4 ntdll!RtlpTpWorkCallback+0x165
31 00000001`226ff8d0 00007ffc`1f647974 ntdll!TppWorkerThread+0x644
32 00000001`226ffbc0 00007ffc`2044a271 KERNEL32!BaseThreadInitThunk+0x14
33 00000001`226ffbf0 00000000`00000000 ntdll!RtlUserThreadStart+0x21
```

What can we do at this point? You may wonder what file is being opened. We can get that information based on the calling convention of the CreateFileW function. Since this is a 64-bit process (and the processor is Intel/AMD), the calling convention states that the first integer/pointer arguments are passed in the *RCX*, *RDX*, *R8* and *R9* registers. Since the file name in CreateFileW is the first argument, the relevant register is *RCX*.

> You can get more information on calling conventions in the Debugger documentation (or in several web resources).

- Display the value of the *RCX* register with the r command (you'll get a different value):

```
0:002> r rcx
rcx=00000001226fabf8
```

- We can view the memory pointed by *RCX* with various d (display) commands.

```
0:002> db 00000001226fabf8
00000001`226fabf8  43 00 3a 00 5c 00 57 00-69 00 6e 00 64 00 6f 00  C.:.\.W.i.n.d.o.
00000001`226fac08  77 00 73 00 5c 00 4d 00-69 00 63 00 72 00 6f 00  w.s.\.M.i.c.r.o.
00000001`226fac18  73 00 6f 00 66 00 74 00-2e 00 4e 00 45 00 54 00  s.o.f.t...N.E.T.
00000001`226fac28  5c 00 46 00 72 00 61 00-6d 00 65 00 77 00 6f 00  \.F.r.a.m.e.w.o.
00000001`226fac38  72 00 6b 00 36 00 34 00-5c 00 5c 00 76 00 32 00  r.k.6.4.\.\.v.2.
00000001`226fac48  2e 00 30 00 2e 00 35 00-30 00 37 00 32 00 37 00  ..0...5.0.7.2.7.
00000001`226fac58  5c 00 63 00 6c 00 72 00-2e 00 64 00 6c 00 6c 00  \.c.l.r...d.l.l.
00000001`226fac68  00 00 76 1c fc 7f 00 00-00 00 00 00 00 00 00 00  ..v.............
```

The db command shows the memory in bytes, and ASCII characters on the right. It's pretty clear what the file name is, but because the string is Unicode, it's not super convenient to see.

- Use the du command to view Unicode string more conveniently:

```
0:002> du 00000001226fabf8
00000001`226fabf8  "C:\Windows\Microsoft.NET\Framewo"
00000001`226fac38  "rk64\\v2.0.50727\clr.dll"
```

- You can use a register value directly by prefixing its name with @:

```
0:002> du @rcx
00000001`226fabf8  "C:\Windows\Microsoft.NET\Framewo"
00000001`226fac38  "rk64\\v2.0.50727\clr.dll"
```

Now let's set another breakpoint in the native API that is called by CreateFileW - NtCreateFile:

```
0:002> bp ntdll!ntcreatefile
0:002> bl
   0 e Disable Clear  00007ffc`1f652300  0001 (0001)  0:**** KERNEL32!CreateFileW
   1 e Disable Clear  00007ffc`20480120  0001 (0001)  0:**** ntdll!NtCreateFile
```

Notice the native API never uses W or A - it always works with Unicode strings.

- Continue execution with the g command. The debugger should break:

```
Breakpoint 1 hit
ntdll!NtCreateFile:
00007ffc`20480120 4c8bd1          mov     r10,rcx
```

- Check the call stack again:

```
0:002> k
 # Child-SP          RetAddr           Call Site
00 00000001`226fa938 00007ffc`1c75e5d6 ntdll!NtCreateFile
01 00000001`226fa940 00007ffc`1c75e2c6 KERNELBASE!CreateFileInternal+0x2f6
02 00000001`226faab0 00007ffc`061c8368 KERNELBASE!CreateFileW+0x66
03 00000001`226fab10 00007ffc`061c5d4d mscoreei!RuntimeDesc::VerifyMainRuntimeModule\
+0x2c
04 00000001`226fab60 00007ffc`061c6068 mscoreei!FindRuntimesInInstallRoot+0x2fb
05 00000001`226fb3e0 00007ffc`061cb748 mscoreei!GetOrCreateSxSProcessInfo+0x94
```

(truncated)

- List the next 8 instructions that are about to be executed with the u (unassemble) command:

```
0:002> u
ntdll!NtCreateFile:
00007ffc`20480120 4c8bd1          mov     r10,rcx
00007ffc`20480123 b855000000      mov     eax,55h
00007ffc`20480128 f604250803fe7f01 test    byte ptr [SharedUserData+0x308 (00000000`\
7ffe0308)],1
00007ffc`20480130 7503            jne     ntdll!NtCreateFile+0x15 (00007ffc`20480135)
00007ffc`20480132 0f05            syscall
00007ffc`20480134 c3              ret
00007ffc`20480135 cd2e            int     2Eh
00007ffc`20480137 c3              ret
```

Notice the value 0x55 is copied to the *EAX* register. This is the system service number for NtCreateFile, as described in chapter 1. The syscall instruction shown is the one causing the transition to the kernel and then executing the NtCreateFile system service itself.

- You can step over the next instruction with the p command (step - hit *F10* as alternative). You can step into a function (in case of assembly, this is the call instruction) with the t command (trace - hit *F11* as alternative):

```
0:002> p
Breakpoint 1 hit
ntdll!NtCreateFile:
00007ffc`20480120 4c8bd1              mov      r10,rcx
0:002> p
ntdll!NtCreateFile+0x3:
00007ffc`20480123 b855000000          mov      eax,55h
0:002> p
ntdll!NtCreateFile+0x8:
00007ffc`20480128 f604250803fe7f01 test      byte ptr [SharedUserData+0x308 (00000000`\
7ffe0308)],1 ds:00000000`7ffe0308=00
0:002> p
ntdll!NtCreateFile+0x10:
00007ffc`20480130 7503                jne      ntdll!NtCreateFile+0x15 (00007ffc`20480135\
) [br=0]
0:002> p
ntdll!NtCreateFile+0x12:
00007ffc`20480132 0f05                syscall
```

- Stepping inside a `syscall` is not possible, as we're in user mode. When we step over/into, all is done and we get back a result.

```
0:002> p
ntdll!NtCreateFile+0x14:
00007ffc`20480134 c3                  ret
```

- The return value of functions in x64 calling convention is stored in *EAX* or *RAX*. For system calls, it's an NTSTATUS, so *EAX* contains is the returned status:

```
0:002> r eax
eax=c0000034
```

- We have an error on our hands. We can get the details with the `!error` command:

```
0:002> !error @eax
Error code: (NTSTATUS) 0xc0000034 (3221225524) - Object Name not found.
```

- Disable all breakpoints and let Notepad continue execution normally:

```
0:002> bd *
0:002> g
```

Since we have no breakpoints at this time, we can force break by clicking the *Break* button on the toolbar, or hitting *Ctrl+Break* on the keyboard:

```
874c.16a54): Break instruction exception - code 80000003 (first chance)
ntdll!DbgBreakPoint:
00007ffc`20483080 cc              int     3
```

- Notice the thread number in the prompt. Show all current threads:

```
0:022> ~
   0  Id: 874c.18068 Suspend: 1 Teb: 00000001`2229d000 Unfrozen
   1  Id: 874c.46ac Suspend: 1 Teb: 00000001`222a5000 Unfrozen
   2  Id: 874c.152cc Suspend: 1 Teb: 00000001`222a7000 Unfrozen
   3  Id: 874c.f7ec Suspend: 1 Teb: 00000001`222ad000 Unfrozen
   4  Id: 874c.145b4 Suspend: 1 Teb: 00000001`222af000 Unfrozen

(truncated)

  18  Id: 874c.f0c4 Suspend: 1 Teb: 00000001`222d1000 Unfrozen
  19  Id: 874c.17414 Suspend: 1 Teb: 00000001`222d3000 Unfrozen
  20  Id: 874c.c878 Suspend: 1 Teb: 00000001`222d5000 Unfrozen
  21  Id: 874c.d8c0 Suspend: 1 Teb: 00000001`222d7000 Unfrozen
. 22  Id: 874c.16a54 Suspend: 1 Teb: 00000001`222e1000 Unfrozen
  23  Id: 874c.10838 Suspend: 1 Teb: 00000001`222db000 Unfrozen
  24  Id: 874c.10cf0 Suspend: 1 Teb: 00000001`222dd000 Unfrozen
```

Many threads, right? These were actually created/invoked by the common open dialog, so no direct fault of Notepad.

- Continue exploring the debugger in any way you want!

 Find out the system service numbers for NtWriteFile and NtReadFile.

- If you close Notepad, you'll hit a breakpoint at process termination:

```
ntdll!NtTerminateProcess+0x14:
00007ffc`2047fc14 c3                    ret
0:000> k
 # Child-SP          RetAddr           Call Site
00 00000001`2247f6a8 00007ffc`20446dd8 ntdll!NtTerminateProcess+0x14
01 00000001`2247f6b0 00007ffc`1f64d62a ntdll!RtlExitUserProcess+0xb8
02 00000001`2247f6e0 00007ffc`061cee58 KERNEL32!ExitProcessImplementation+0xa
03 00000001`2247f710 00007ffc`0644719e mscoreei!RuntimeDesc::ShutdownAllActiveRuntim\
es+0x287
04 00000001`2247fa00 00007ffc`1fcda291 mscoree!ShellShim_CorExitProcess+0x11e
05 00000001`2247fa30 00007ffc`1fcda2ad msvcrt!_crtCorExitProcess+0x4d
06 00000001`2247fa60 00007ffc`1fcda925 msvcrt!_crtExitProcess+0xd
07 00000001`2247fa90 00007ff7`5383ae1e msvcrt!doexit+0x171
08 00000001`2247fb00 00007ffc`1f647974 notepad!__mainCRTStartup+0x1b6
09 00000001`2247fbc0 00007ffc`2044a271 KERNEL32!BaseThreadInitThunk+0x14
0a 00000001`2247fbf0 00000000`00000000 ntdll!RtlUserThreadStart+0x21
```

- You can use the q command to quit the debugger. If the process is still alive, it will be terminated. An alternative is to use the .detach command to disconnect from the target without killing it.

Kernel Debugging

User mode debugging involves the debugger attaching to a process, setting breakpoints that cause the process' thread to become suspended, and so on. Kernel mode debugging on the other hand, involves controlling the entire machine with the debugger. This means that if a breakpoint is set and then hit, the entire machine is frozen. Clearly, this cannot be achieved with a single machine. In full kernel debugging, two machines are involved: a host (where the debugger runs) and a target (being debugged). The target can, however, be a virtual machine hosted on the same machine (host) where the debugger executes. Figure 5-5 shows a host and target connected via some connection medium.

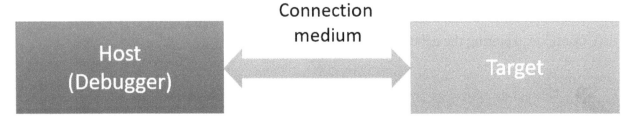

Figure 5-5: Host-target connection

Before we get into full kernel debugging, we'll take a look at its simpler cousin - local kernel debugging.

Local Kernel Debugging

Local kernel debugging (LKD) allows viewing system memory and other system information on the local machine. The primary difference between local and full kernel debugging, is that with LKD there is no way to set up breakpoints, which means you're always looking at the current state of the system. It also means that things change, even while commands are being executed, so some information may not be reliable. With full kernel debugging, commands can only be entered while the target system is in a breakpoint, so system state is unchanged.

To configure LKD, enter the following in an elevated command prompt and then restart the system:

```
bcdedit /debug on
```

After the system is restarted, launch *WinDbg* with elevated privileges. Select the menu *File/Attach To Kernel* (WinDbg preview) or *File/Kernel Debug...* (classic WinDbg). Select the *Local* tab and click *OK*. You should see output similar to the following:

```
Microsoft (R) Windows Debugger Version 10.0.18317.1001 AMD64
Copyright (c) Microsoft Corporation. All rights reserved.


Connected to Windows 10 18362 x64 target at (Sun Apr 21 08:50:59.964 2019 (UTC + 3:0\
0)), ptr64 TRUE


************* Path validation summary **************
Response                      Time (ms)     Location
Deferred                                    SRV*c:\Symbols*http://msdl.microsoft.\
com/download/symbols
Symbol search path is: c:\temp;SRV*c:\Symbols*http://msdl.microsoft.com/download/sym\
bols
Executable search path is:
Windows 10 Kernel Version 18362 MP (12 procs) Free x64
Product: WinNt, suite: TerminalServer SingleUserTS
Built by: 18362.1.amd64fre.19h1_release.190318-1202
Machine Name:
Kernel base = 0xfffff806`466b8000 PsLoadedModuleList = 0xfffff806`46afb2d0
Debug session time: Sun Apr 21 08:51:00.702 2019 (UTC + 3:00)
System Uptime: 0 days 11:33:37.265
```

 Local Kernel Debugging is protected by Secure Boot on Windows 10, Server 2016 and later. To activate LKD you'll have to disable Secure Boot in the machine's BIOS settings. If, for whatever reason, this is not possible, there is an alternative using the Sysinternals *LiveKd* tool. Copy *LiveKd.exe* to the *Debugging Tools for Windows* main directory. Then launch *WinDbg* using LiveKd with the following command: livekd -w.

Note the prompt displays *lkd*. This indicates Local Kernel Debugging is active.

Local kernel Debugging Tutorial

if you're familiar with kernel debugging commands, you can safely skip this section.

- You can display basic information for all processes running on the system with the process
  0 0 command:

```
lkd> !process 0 0
**** NT ACTIVE PROCESS DUMP ****
PROCESS ffff8d0e682a73c0
    SessionId: none  Cid: 0004    Peb: 00000000  ParentCid: 0000
    DirBase: 001ad002  ObjectTable: ffffe20712204b80  HandleCount: 9542.
    Image: System

PROCESS ffff8d0e6832e140
    SessionId: none  Cid: 0058    Peb: 00000000  ParentCid: 0004
    DirBase: 03188002  ObjectTable: ffffe2071220cac0  HandleCount:    0.
    Image: Secure System

PROCESS ffff8d0e683f1080
    SessionId: none  Cid: 0098    Peb: 00000000  ParentCid: 0004
    DirBase: 003e1002  ObjectTable: ffffe20712209480  HandleCount:    0.
    Image: Registry

PROCESS ffff8d0e83099080
    SessionId: none  Cid: 032c    Peb: 5aba7eb000  ParentCid: 0004
    DirBase: 15fa39002  ObjectTable: ffffe20712970080  HandleCount:   53.
    Image: smss.exe

(truncated)
```

For each process, the following information is displayed:

- The address attached to the *PROCESS* text is the EPROCESS address of the process (in kernel space, of course).
- *SessionId* - the session the process is running under.
- *Cid* - (client ID) the unique process ID.
- *Peb* - the address of the *Process Environment Block* (PEB). This address is in user space, naturally.

- *ParentCid* - (parent client ID) the process ID of the parent process. Note that it's possible the parent process no longer exists and this ID can be reused.
- *DirBase* - physical address (sans the lower 12 bits) of the Master Page Directory for this process, used as the basis for virtual to address translation. On x64, this is known as *Page Map Level 4* and on x86 it's *Page Directory Pointer Table* (PDPT).
- *ObjectTable* - pointer to the private handle table for the process.
- *HandleCount* - number of handles in this process.
- *Image* - executable name, or special process name for those not associated with an executable (examples: *Secure System*, *System*, *Mem Compression*).

The !process command accepts at least two arguments. The first indicates the process of interest using its EPROCESS address, where zero means "all or any process". The second argument is the level of details required, where zero means the least amount of detail (a bit mask). A third argument can be added to search for a particular executable.

- List all processes running *csrss.exe*:

```
lkd> !process 0 0 csrss.exe
PROCESS ffff8d0e83c020c0
    SessionId: 0  Cid: 038c    Peb: f599af6000  ParentCid: 0384
    DirBase: 844eaa002  ObjectTable: ffffe20712345480  HandleCount: 992.
    Image: csrss.exe

PROCESS ffff8d0e849df080
    SessionId: 1  Cid: 045c    Peb: e8a8c9c000  ParentCid: 0438
    DirBase: 17afc1002  ObjectTable: ffffe207186d93c0  HandleCount: 1146.
    Image: csrss.exe
```

- List more information for a specific process by specifying its address and a higher level of detail:

```
lkd> !process ffff8d0e849df080 1
PROCESS ffff8d0e849df080
    SessionId: 1  Cid: 045c    Peb: e8a8c9c000  ParentCid: 0438
    DirBase: 17afc1002  ObjectTable: ffffe207186d93c0  HandleCount: 1138.
    Image: csrss.exe
    VadRoot ffff8d0e999a4840 Vads 244 Clone 0 Private 670. Modified 48241. Locked 38\
106.
    DeviceMap ffffe20712213720
    Token                               ffffe207186f38f0
    ElapsedTime                         12:14:47.292
    UserTime                            00:00:00.000
    KernelTime                          00:00:03.468
    QuotaPoolUsage[PagedPool]           423704
    QuotaPoolUsage[NonPagedPool]        37752
    Working Set Sizes (now,min,max)     (1543, 50, 345) (6172KB, 200KB, 1380KB)
    PeakWorkingSetSize                  10222
    VirtualSize                         2101434 Mb
    PeakVirtualSize                     2101467 Mb
    PageFaultCount                      841489
    MemoryPriority                      BACKGROUND
    BasePriority                        13
    CommitCharge                        1012
    Job                                 ffff8d0e83da8080
```

As can be seen from the above output, more information on the process is displayed. Some of this information is hyperlinked, allowing easy further examination. The Job this process is part of (if any) is hyperlinked.

- Click on the Job address hyperlink:

```
lkd> !job ffff8d0e83da8080
Job at ffff8d0e83da8080
  Basic Accounting Information
    TotalUserTime:            0x33db258
    TotalKernelTime:          0x5705d50
    TotalCycleTime:           0x73336f9ae
    ThisPeriodTotalUserTime:  0x33db258
    ThisPeriodTotalKernelTime: 0x5705d50
    TotalPageFaultCount:      0x8617c
    TotalProcesses:           0x3e
    ActiveProcesses:          0xd
    FreezeCount:              0
```

```
    BackgroundCount:            0
    TotalTerminatedProcesses:   0x0
    PeakJobMemoryUsed:          0x38fb5
    PeakProcessMemoryUsed:      0x29366
Job Flags
  [wake notification allocated]
  [wake notification enabled]
  [timers virtualized]
Limit Information (LimitFlags: 0x1800)
Limit Information (EffectiveLimitFlags: 0x1800)
  JOB_OBJECT_LIMIT_BREAKAWAY_OK
  JOB_OBJECT_LIMIT_SILENT_BREAKAWAY_OK
```

> A Job is an object that contains one or more processes, for which it can apply various limitations and monitor various accounting information. A detailed discussion of Jobs is beyond the scope of this book. More information can be found in the *Windows Internals* books.

- As usual, a command such as !job hides some information available in the real data structure. In this case, it's EJOB. Use the command dt nt!_ejob with the job address to see all details.
- The PEB of a process can be viewed as well by clicking its hyperlink. This is similar to the !peb command used in user mode, but the twist here is that the correct process context must be set first, as the address is in user space. Click the *Peb* hyperlink. You should see something like this:

```
lkd> .process /p ffff8d0e849df080; !peb e8a8c9c000
Implicit process is now ffff8d0e`849df080
PEB at 000000e8a8c9c000
    InheritedAddressSpace:    No
    ReadImageFileExecOptions: No
    BeingDebugged:            No
    ImageBaseAddress:         00007ff62fc70000
    NtGlobalFlag:             4400
    NtGlobalFlag2:            0
    Ldr                       00007ffa0ecc53c0
    Ldr.Initialized:          Yes
    Ldr.InInitializationOrderModuleList: 000002021cc04dc0 . 000002021cc15f00
    Ldr.InLoadOrderModuleList:           000002021cc04f30 . 000002021cc15ee0
    Ldr.InMemoryOrderModuleList:         000002021cc04f40 . 000002021cc15ef0
                    Base TimeStamp                       Module
```

```
          7ff62fc70000 78facb67 Apr 27 01:06:31 2034 C:\WINDOWS\system32\csrss.exe
          7ffa0eb60000 a52b7c6a Oct 23 22:22:18 2057 C:\WINDOWS\SYSTEM32\ntdll.dll
          7ffa0ba10000 802fce16 Feb 24 11:29:58 2038 C:\WINDOWS\SYSTEM32\CSRSRV.dll
          7ffa0b9f0000 94c740f0 Feb 04 23:17:36 2049 C:\WINDOWS\system32\basesrv.D\
LL

(truncated)
```

The correct process context is set with the .process meta command and then the PEB is displayed. This is a general technique you need to use to show information that is in user space.

- Repeat the !process command again, but this time with no detail level. More information is shown for the process:

```
kd> !process ffff8d0e849df080
PROCESS ffff8d0e849df080
    SessionId: 1  Cid: 045c    Peb: e8a8c9c000  ParentCid: 0438
    DirBase: 17afc1002  ObjectTable: ffffe207186d93c0  HandleCount: 1133.
    Image: csrss.exe
    VadRoot ffff8d0e999a4840 Vads 243 Clone 0 Private 672. Modified 48279. Locked 34\
442.
    DeviceMap ffffe20712213720
    Token                             ffffe207186f38f0
    ElapsedTime                       12:23:30.102
    UserTime                          00:00:00.000
    KernelTime                        00:00:03.468
    QuotaPoolUsage[PagedPool]         422008
    QuotaPoolUsage[NonPagedPool]      37616
    Working Set Sizes (now,min,max)   (1534, 50, 345) (6136KB, 200KB, 1380KB)
    PeakWorkingSetSize                10222
    VirtualSize                       2101434 Mb
    PeakVirtualSize                   2101467 Mb
    PageFaultCount                    841729
    MemoryPriority                    BACKGROUND
    BasePriority                      13
    CommitCharge                      1014
    Job                               ffff8d0e83da8080

        THREAD ffff8d0e849e0080  Cid 045c.046c  Teb: 000000e8a8ca3000 Win32Thread: f\
fff8d0e865f37c0 WAIT: (WrLpcReceive) UserMode Non-Alertable
            ffff8d0e849e06d8  Semaphore Limit 0x1
        Not impersonating
```

```
        DeviceMap               ffffe20712213720
        Owning Process          ffff8d0e849df080      Image:        csrss.exe
        Attached Process        N/A           Image:        N/A
        Wait Start TickCount     2856062        Ticks: 70 (0:00:00:01.093)
        Context Switch Count     6483          IdealProcessor: 8
        UserTime                00:00:00.421
        KernelTime              00:00:00.437
        Win32 Start Address 0x00007ffa0ba15670
        Stack Init ffff83858295fb90 Current ffff83858295f340
        Base ffff838582960000 Limit ffff838582959000 Call 0000000000000000
        Priority 14 BasePriority 13 PriorityDecrement 0 IoPriority 2 PagePriority 5
GetContextState failed, 0x80004001
Unable to get current machine context, HRESULT 0x80004001
        Child-SP          RetAddr          Call Site
        ffff8385`8295f380 fffff806`466e98c2 nt!KiSwapContext+0x76
        ffff8385`8295f4c0 fffff806`466e8f54 nt!KiSwapThread+0x3f2
        ffff8385`8295f560 fffff806`466e86f5 nt!KiCommitThreadWait+0x144
        ffff8385`8295f600 fffff806`467d8c56 nt!KeWaitForSingleObject+0x255
        ffff8385`8295f6e0 fffff806`46d76c70 nt!AlpcpWaitForSingleObject+0x3e
        ffff8385`8295f720 fffff806`46d162cc nt!AlpcpCompleteDeferSignalRequestAndWai\
t+0x3c
        ffff8385`8295f760 fffff806`46d15321 nt!AlpcpReceiveMessagePort+0x3ac
        ffff8385`8295f7f0 fffff806`46d14e05 nt!AlpcpReceiveMessage+0x361
        ffff8385`8295f8d0 fffff806`46885e95 nt!NtAlpcSendWaitReceivePort+0x105
        ffff8385`8295f990 00007ffa`0ebfd194 nt!KiSystemServiceCopyEnd+0x25 (TrapFram\
e @ ffff8385`8295fa00)
        000000e8`a8e3f798 00007ffa`0ba15778 0x00007ffa`0ebfd194
        000000e8`a8e3f7a0 00000202`1cc85090 0x00007ffa`0ba15778
        000000e8`a8e3f7a8 00000000`00000000 0x00000202`1cc85090

        THREAD ffff8d0e84bbf140  Cid 045c.066c  Teb: 000000e8a8ca9000 Win32Thread: f\
fff8d0e865f4760 WAIT: (WrLpcReply) UserMode Non-Alertable
            ffff8d0e84bbf798  Semaphore Limit 0x1
```

(truncated)

The command lists all threads within the process. Each thread is represented by its ETHREAD address attached to the text "THREAD". The call stack is listed as well - the module prefix "nt" represents the kernel - there is no need to use the "real" kernel module name.

> One of the reasons to use "nt" instead of explicitly stating the kernel's module name is because these are different between 64 and 32 bit systems (*ntoskrnl.exe* on 64 bit, and at least two variants on 32

bit). And it's a lot shorter.

- User mode symbols are not loaded by default, so thread stacks that span to user mode show just numeric addresses. You can load user symbols explicitly with .reload /user:

```
lkd> .reload /user
Loading User Symbols
.................
lkd> !process ffff8d0e849df080
PROCESS ffff8d0e849df080
    SessionId: 1  Cid: 045c    Peb: e8a8c9c000  ParentCid: 0438
    DirBase: 17afc1002  ObjectTable: ffffe207186d93c0  HandleCount: 1149.
    Image: csrss.exe

(truncated)

        THREAD ffff8d0e849e0080  Cid 045c.046c  Teb: 000000e8a8ca3000 Win32Thread: f\
fff8d0e865f37c0 WAIT: (WrLpcReceive) UserMode Non-Alertable
            ffff8d0e849e06d8  Semaphore Limit 0x1
        Not impersonating
        DeviceMap                 ffffe20712213720
        Owning Process            ffff8d0e849df080       Image:         csrss.exe
        Attached Process          N/A            Image:         N/A
        Wait Start TickCount      2895071        Ticks: 135 (0:00:00:02.109)
        Context Switch Count      6684           IdealProcessor: 8
        UserTime                  00:00:00.437
        KernelTime                00:00:00.437
        Win32 Start Address CSRSRV!CsrApiRequestThread (0x00007ffa0ba15670)
        Stack Init ffff83858295fb90 Current ffff83858295f340
        Base ffff838582960000 Limit ffff838582959000 Call 0000000000000000
        Priority 14 BasePriority 13 PriorityDecrement 0 IoPriority 2 PagePriority 5
GetContextState failed, 0x80004001
Unable to get current machine context, HRESULT 0x80004001
        Child-SP          RetAddr           Call Site
        ffff8385`8295f380 fffff806`466e98c2 nt!KiSwapContext+0x76
        ffff8385`8295f4c0 fffff806`466e8f54 nt!KiSwapThread+0x3f2
        ffff8385`8295f560 fffff806`466e86f5 nt!KiCommitThreadWait+0x144
        ffff8385`8295f600 fffff806`467d8c56 nt!KeWaitForSingleObject+0x255
        ffff8385`8295f6e0 fffff806`46d76c70 nt!AlpcpWaitForSingleObject+0x3e
```

```
        ffff8385`8295f720 fffff806`46d162cc nt!AlpcpCompleteDeferSignalRequestAndWai\
t+0x3c
        ffff8385`8295f760 fffff806`46d15321 nt!AlpcpReceiveMessagePort+0x3ac
        ffff8385`8295f7f0 fffff806`46d14e05 nt!AlpcpReceiveMessage+0x361
        ffff8385`8295f8d0 fffff806`46885e95 nt!NtAlpcSendWaitReceivePort+0x105
        ffff8385`8295f990 00007ffa`0ebfd194 nt!KiSystemServiceCopyEnd+0x25 (TrapFram\
e @ ffff8385`8295fa00)
        000000e8`a8e3f798 00007ffa`0ba15778 ntdll!NtAlpcSendWaitReceivePort+0x14
        000000e8`a8e3f7a0 00007ffa`0ebcce7f CSRSRV!CsrApiRequestThread+0x108
        000000e8`a8e3fc30 00000000`00000000 ntdll!RtlUserThreadStart+0x2f
```

```
(truncated)
```

A thread's information can be viewed separately with the !thread command and the address of the thread. Check the debugger documentation for the description of the various pieces of information displayed by this command.

Other generally useful/interesting commands in kernel mode debugging include:

- !pcr - display the Process Control Region (PCR) for a processor specified as an additional index (processor 0 is displayed by default if no index is specified).
- !vm - display memory statistics for the system and processes.
- !running - displays information on threads running on all processors on the system.

We'll look at more specific commands useful for debugging drivers in later chapters.

Full Kernel Debugging

Full kernel debugging requires configuration on the host and target. In this section, we'll see how to configure a virtual machine as a target for kernel debugging. This is the recommended and most convenient setup for kernel driver work (when not developing device drivers for hardware). We'll go through the steps for configuring a Hyper-V virtual machine (VM). If you're using a different virtualization technology (e.g. VMWare or VirtualBox), please consult that vendor's documentation or the web for the correct procedure to get the same results.

The target and host machine must communicate using some connection media. There are several options available. The best option is to use the network. Unfortunately, this requires the host and target to run Windows 8 at the minimum. Since Windows 7 is still a viable target, we'll use another option - the COM (serial) port. Of course most machines don't have serial ports anymore, and in any case we connect to a VM, so no real cables are involved. All virtualization platforms allow redirecting a virtual serial port to a named pipe on the host; this is the configuration we'll use.

Configuring the Target

The target VM must be configured for kernel debugging, similar to local kernel debugging, but with the added connection media set to a virtual serial port on that machine.

One way to do the configuration is using *bcdedit* in an elevated command window:

```
bcdedit /debug on
bcdedit /dbgsettings serial debugport:1 baudrate:115200
```

Change the debug port number according to the actual virtual serial number (typically 1).

The VM must be restarted for these configurations to take effect. Before you do that we can map the serial port to a named pipe. Here is the procedure for Hyper-V virtual machines:

- If the Hyper-V VM is Generation 1 (older), there is a simple UI in the VM's settings to do the configuration. use the *Add Hardware* option to add a serial port if there are none defined. Then configure the serial port to be mapped to a named port of your choosing. Figure 5-6 shows this dialog.

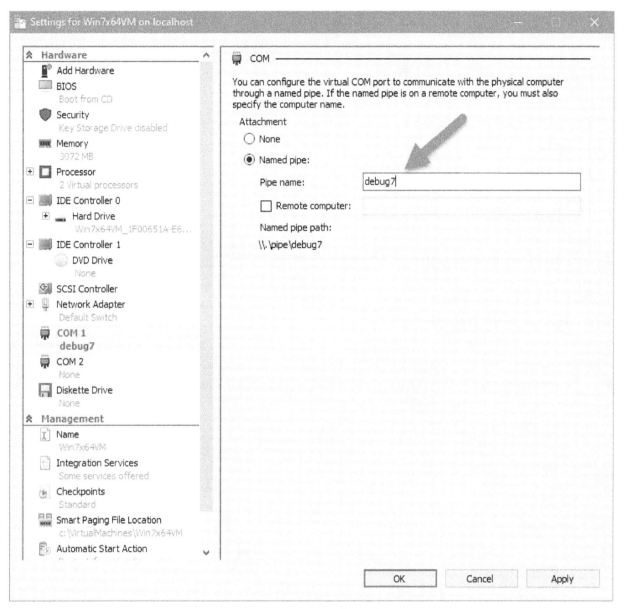

Figure 5-6: Mapping serial port to named pipe for Hyper-V Gen-1 VM

- For Generation 2 VMs, no UI is currently. To configure this, make sure the VM is shut down (although not mandatory in very recent Windows 10 versions) and open an elevated PowerShell window.
- Type the following to set a serial port mapped to a named pipe:

```
Set-VMComPort myvmname -Number 1 -Path \\.\pipe\debug
```

Change the VM name appropriately and the COM port number as set inside the VM earlier with *bcdedit*. Make sure the pipe path is unique.

- You can verify the settings are as expected with Get-VMComPort:

```
Get-VMComPort myvmname

VMName    Name   Path
------    ----   ----
myvmname  COM 1  \\.\pipe\debug
myvmname  COM 2
```

You can boot the VM - the target is now ready.

Configuring the Host

The kernel debugger must be configured to connect with the VM on the same serial port mapped to the same named pipe exposed on the host.

- Launch the kernel debugger and select *File/Attach To Kernel*. Navigate to the *COM* tab. Fill in the correct details as they were set on the target. Figure 5-7 shows what these settings look like.

Figure 5-7: Setting host COM port configuration

- Click OK. The debugger should attach to the target. If it does not, click the *Break* toolbar button. Here is a typical output:

```
Microsoft (R) Windows Debugger Version 10.0.18317.1001 AMD64
Copyright (c) Microsoft Corporation. All rights reserved.


Opened \\.\pipe\debug
Waiting to reconnect...
Connected to Windows 10 18362 x64 target at (Sun Apr 21 11:28:11.300 2019 (UTC + 3:0\
0)), ptr64 TRUE
Kernel Debugger connection established.  (Initial Breakpoint requested)


************* Path validation summary **************
Response                      Time (ms)     Location
Deferred                                    SRV*c:\Symbols*http://msdl.microsoft.\
com/download/symbols
Symbol search path is: SRV*c:\Symbols*http://msdl.microsoft.com/download/symbols
Executable search path is:
Windows 10 Kernel Version 18362 MP (4 procs) Free x64
Product: WinNt, suite: TerminalServer SingleUserTS
Built by: 18362.1.amd64fre.19h1_release.190318-1202
Machine Name:
Kernel base = 0xfffff801`36a09000 PsLoadedModuleList = 0xfffff801`36e4c2d0
Debug session time: Sun Apr 21 11:28:09.669 2019 (UTC + 3:00)
System Uptime: 1 days 0:12:28.864
Break instruction exception - code 80000003 (first chance)
*********************************************************************************
*                                                                               *
*   You are seeing this message because you pressed either                      *
*       CTRL+C (if you run console kernel debugger) or,                          *
*       CTRL+BREAK (if you run GUI kernel debugger),                             *
*   on your debugger machine's keyboard.                                         *
*                                                                               *
*                   THIS IS NOT A BUG OR A SYSTEM CRASH                          *
*                                                                               *
* If you did not intend to break into the debugger, press the "g" key, then      *
* press the "Enter" key now.  This message might immediately reappear.  If it    *
* does, press "g" and "Enter" again.                                            *
*                                                                               *
*********************************************************************************
nt!DbgBreakPointWithStatus:
fffff801`36bcd580 cc              int     3
```

Note the prompt has an index and the word *kd*. The index is the current processor that induced the break. At this point, the target VM is completely frozen. You can now debug normally, bearing in mind anytime you break somewhere, the entire machine is suspended.

Kernel Driver Debugging Tutorial

Once host and target are connected, debugging can begin. We will use the *PriorityBooster* driver we developed in chapter 4 to demonstrate full kernel debugging.

- Install (but don't load) the driver on the target as was done in chapter 4. Make sure you copy the driver's PDB file alongside the driver SYS file itself. This simplifies getting correct symbols for the driver.
- Let's set a breakpoint in DriverEntry. We cannot load the driver because that would cause DriverEntry to execute and we'll miss the chance to set a breakpoint there. Since the driver is not loaded yet, we can use the bu command (unresolved breakpoint) to set a future breakpoint. Break into the target if it's currently running and type the following command:

```
0: kd> bu prioritybooster!driverentry
0: kd> bl
  0 e Disable Clear u        0001 (0001) (prioritybooster!driverentry)
```

The breakpoint is unresolved yet, since our module is not yet loaded.

- Issue the g command to let the target continue, and load the driver with sc start booster (assuming the driver's name is *booster*). If all goes well, the breakpoint should hit, and the source file should load automatically, showing the following output in the command window:

```
0: kd> g
Breakpoint 0 hit
PriorityBooster!DriverEntry:
fffff801`358211d0 4889542410      mov     qword ptr [rsp+10h],rdx
```

Figure 5-8 shows a screenshot of *WinDbg Preview* source window automatically open and the correct line marked. The *Locals* window is also shown as expected.

```
priorityboooster.cpp    ×
    1 #include <ntifs.h>
    2 #include <ntddk.h>
    3 #include "PriorityBoosterCommon.h"
    4
    5 // prototypes
    6
    7 void PriorityBoosterUnload(_In_ PDRIVER_OBJECT DriverObject);
    8 NTSTATUS PriorityBoosterCreateClose(_In_ PDEVICE_OBJECT DeviceObject, _In_ PIRP Irp);
    9 NTSTATUS PriorityBoosterDeviceControl(_In_ PDEVICE_OBJECT DeviceObject, _In_ PIRP Irp);
   10
   11 // DriverEntry
   12
   13 extern "C" NTSTATUS
   14 DriverEntry(_In_ PDRIVER_OBJECT DriverObject, _In_ PUNICODE_STRING RegistryPath) {
   15     UNREFERENCED_PARAMETER(RegistryPath);
   16
   17     DriverObject->DriverUnload = PriorityBoosterUnload;
   18
   19     DriverObject->MajorFunction[IRP_MJ_CREATE] = PriorityBoosterCreateClose;
   20     DriverObject->MajorFunction[IRP_MJ_CLOSE] = PriorityBoosterCreateClose;
   21     DriverObject->MajorFunction[IRP_MJ_DEVICE_CONTROL] = PriorityBoosterDeviceControl;
   22
   23     UNICODE_STRING devName = RTL_CONSTANT_STRING(L"\\Device\\PriorityBooster");
   24     //RtlInitUnicodeString(&devName, L"\\Device\\ThreadBoost");
   25     PDEVICE_OBJECT DeviceObject;
   26     NTSTATUS status = IoCreateDevice(DriverObject, 0, &devName, FILE_DEVICE_UNKNOWN, 0, FALSE, &DeviceObject);
   27     if (!NT_SUCCESS(status)) {
   28         KdPrint(("Failed to create device (0x%08X)\n", status));
   29         return status;
   30     }
   31
   32     UNICODE_STRING symLink = RTL_CONSTANT_STRING(L"\\??\\PriorityBooster");
   33     status = IoCreateSymbolicLink(&symLink, &devName);
   34     if (!NT_SUCCESS(status)) {
   35         KdPrint(("Failed to create symbolic link (0x%08X)\n", status));
   36         IoDeleteDevice(DeviceObject);
   37         return status;
   38     }
```

Locals

Name	Value	Type
⊞ DeviceObject	0xffffdd05fe075e30 : Device for {...}	_DEVICE_OBJECT *
⊞ devName	128	_UNICODE_STRING
status	0	long
⊞ symLink	""	_UNICODE_STRING
DriverObject	0x0	_DRIVER_OBJECT *
⊞ RegistryPath	0xfffff80100000001	_UNICODE_STRING *

Locals | Watch

Figure 5-8: Breakpoint hit in DriverEntry

At this point, you can step over source lines, look at variables in the *Locals* window, and even add expressions to the *Watch* window. You can also change values using the *Locals* window just like would normally do with other debuggers.

The *Command* window is still available as always, but some operations are just easier with the UI. Settings breakpoints, for example, can be done with the normal bp command, but you can simply open a source file (if it's not already open), go to the line where you want to set a breakpoint, and hit *F9* or click the appropriate button on the toolbar. Either way, the bp command will be executed in the *Command* window. The *Breakpoints* window can serve as a quick overview of the currently set breakpoints.

- Issue the k command to see how DriverEntry is being called:

```
2: kd> k
 # Child-SP          RetAddr          Call Site
00 ffffad08`226df898 fffff801`35825020 PriorityBooster!DriverEntry [c:\dev\priorityb\
ooster\prioritybooster\prioritybooster.cpp @ 14]
01 ffffad08`226df8a0 fffff801`37111436 PriorityBooster!GsDriverEntry+0x20 [minkernel\
\tools\gs_support\kmodefastfail\gs_driverentry.c @ 47]
02 ffffad08`226df8d0 fffff801`37110e6e nt!IopLoadDriver+0x4c2
03 ffffad08`226dfab0 fffff801`36ab7835 nt!IopLoadUnloadDriver+0x4e
04 ffffad08`226dfaf0 fffff801`36b39925 nt!ExpWorkerThread+0x105
05 ffffad08`226dfb90 fffff801`36bccd5a nt!PspSystemThreadStartup+0x55
06 ffffad08`226dfbe0 00000000`00000000 nt!KiStartSystemThread+0x2a
```

 If breakpoints seem to fail to setup, it may be a symbols issue. Execute the .reload command and see if the issues are resolved. Setting breakpoints in user space is also possible, but first execute .reload /user to help with that.

It may be the case that a breakpoint should hit only when a specific process is the one executing code. This can be done by adding the /p switch to a breakpoint. In the following example, a breakpoint is set only if the process is *explorer.exe*:

```
2: kd> !process 0 0 explorer.exe
PROCESS ffffdd06042e4080
    SessionId: 2  Cid: 1df8    Peb: 00dee000  ParentCid: 1dd8
    DirBase: 1bf58a002  ObjectTable: ffff960a682133c0  HandleCount: 3504.
    Image: explorer.exe
```

```
2: kd> bp /p ffffdd06042e4080 prioritybooster!priorityboosterdevicecontrol
2: kd> bl
     0 e Disable Clear  fffff801`358211d0  [c:\dev\prioritybooster\prioritybooster\p\
rioritybooster.cpp @ 14]    0001 (0001) PriorityBooster!DriverEntry
     1 e Disable Clear  fffff801`35821040  [c:\dev\prioritybooster\prioritybooster\p\
rioritybooster.cpp @ 63]    0001 (0001) PriorityBooster!PriorityBoosterDeviceContro\
l
    Match process data ffffdd06`042e4080
```

Let's set a normal breakpoint in the switch case for the I/O control code by hitting *F9* on the line in source view, as shown in figure 5-9 (and removing the conditional process breakpoint by hitting *F9* on that line).

```
62 _Use_decl_annotations_
63 NTSTATUS PriorityBoosterDeviceControl(PDEVICE_OBJECT, PIRP Irp) {
64     // get our IO_STACK_LOCATION
65     auto stack = IoGetCurrentIrpStackLocation(Irp);
66     auto status = STATUS_SUCCESS;
67
68     switch (stack->Parameters.DeviceIoControl.IoControlCode) {
69         case IOCTL_PRIORITY_BOOSTER_SET_PRIORITY:
70         {
71             // do the work
72             if (stack->Parameters.DeviceIoControl.InputBufferLength < sizeof(ThreadData))
73                 status = STATUS_BUFFER_TOO_SMALL;
74             break;
75         }
76
```

Figure 5-9: Breakpoint hit in DriverEntry

- Run the test application with some thread ID and priority:

```
booster 2000 30
```

The breakpoint should hit. You can continue debugging normally with a combination of source code and commands.

Summary

In this chapter, we looked at the basics of debugging with *WinDbg*. This is an essential skill to develop, as software of all kinds, including kernel drivers, may have bugs.

In the next chapter we'll delve into some kernel mechanisms we need to get acquainted with as these come up frequently while developing and debugging drivers.

Chapter 6: Kernel Mechanisms

This chapter discussed various mechanisms the Windows kernel provides. Some of these are directly useful for driver writers. Others are mechanisms that a driver developer needs to understand as it helps with debugging and general understanding of activities in the system.

In this chapter:

- Interrupt Request Level
- Deferred Procedure Calls
- Asynchronous Procedure Calls
- Structured Exception Handling
- System Crash
- Thread Synchronization
- High IRQL Synchronization
- Work Items

Interrupt Request Level

In chapter 1, we discussed threads and thread priorities. These priorities are taken into consideration when more threads want to execute than there are available processors. At the same time, hardware devices need to notify the system that something requires attention. A simple example is an I/O operation that is carried out by a disk drive. Once the operation completes, the disk drive notifies completion by requesting an interrupt. This interrupt is connected to an Interrupt Controller hardware that then sends the request to a processor for handling. The next question is, which thread should execute the associated Interrupt Service Routine (ISR)?

Every hardware interrupt is associated with a priority, called *Interrupt Request Level* (IRQL) (not to be confused with an interrupt physical line known as IRQ), determined by the HAL. Each processor's context has its own IRQL, just like any register. IRQLs may or may not be implemented by the CPU hardware, but this is essentially unimportant. IRQL should be treated just like any other CPU register.

The basic rule is that a processor executes the code with the highest IRQL. For example, if a CPU's IRQL is zero at some point, and an interrupt with an associated IRQL of 5 comes in, it will save its state (context) in the current thread's kernel stack, raise its IRQL to 5 and then execute the ISR associated with the interrupt. Once the ISR completes, the IRQL will drop to its previous level, resuming the previous executed code as though the interrupt didn't exist. While the ISR was executing, other interrupts coming in with an IRQL of 5 or less cannot interrupt this processor. If, on the other hand, the IRQL of the new interrupt is above 5, the CPU will save its state again, raise IRQL to the new level, execute the second ISR associated with the second interrupt and when completed, will drop back to IRQL 5, restore its state and continue executing the original ISR. Essentially, raising IRQL blocks code with equal or lower IRQL temporarily. The basic sequence of events when an interrupt occurs is depicted in figure 6-1. Figure 6-2 shows what interrupt nesting looks like.

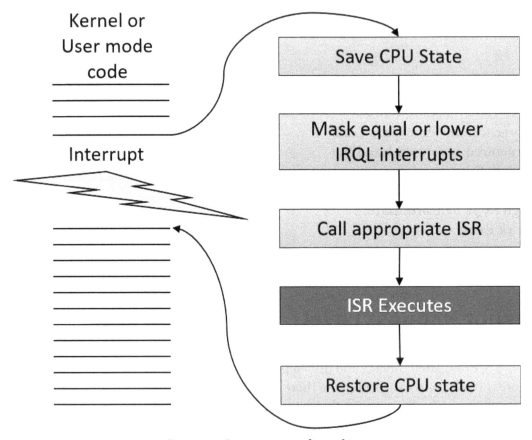

Figure 6-1: Basic interrupt dispatching

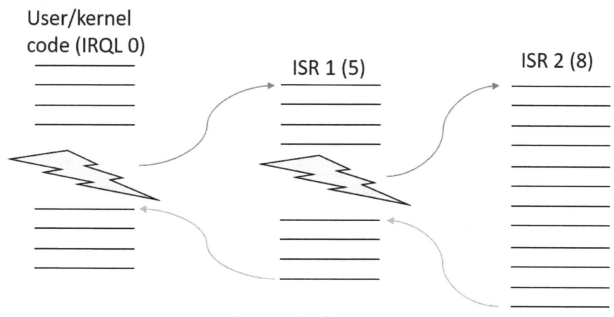

Figure 6-2: Nested interrupts

An important fact for the depicted scenarios in figures 6-1 and 6-2 is that execution of all ISRs is done by the same thread which got interrupted in the first place. Windows does not have a special thread to handle interrupts; they are handled by whatever thread was running at that time on the interrupted processor. As we'll soon discover, context switching is not possible when the IRQL of the processor is 2 or higher, so there is no way another thread can sneak in while these ISRs execute.

> The interrupted thread does not get its quantum reduced because of these "interruptions". It's not its fault, so to speak.

When user mode code is executing, the IRQL is always zero. This is one reason why the term IRQL is not mentioned in any user mode documentation - it's always zero and cannot be changed. Most kernel mode code runs with IRQL zero as well. It's possible, in kernel mode, to raise the IRQL on the current processor.

The important IRQLs are described below:

- PASSIVE_LEVEL in WDK (0) - this is the "normal" IRQL for a CPU. User mode code always runs at this level. Thread scheduling working normally, as described in chapter 1.
- APC_LEVEL (1) - used for special kernel APCs (Asynchronous Procedure Calls will be discussed later in this chapter). Thread scheduling works normally.
- DISPATCH_LEVEL (2) - this is where things change radically. The scheduler cannot wake up on this CPU. Paged memory access is not allowed - such access causes a system crash. Since the scheduler cannot interfere, waiting on kernel objects is not allowed (causes a system crash if used).

- Device IRQL - a range of levels used for hardware interrupts (3 to 11 on x64/ARM/ARM64, 3 to 26 on x86). All rules from IRQL 2 apply here as well.
- Highest level (HIGH_LEVEL) - this is the highest IRQL, masking all interrupts. Used by some APIs dealing with linked list manipulation. The actual values are 15 (x64/ARM/ARM64) and 31 (x86).

When a processor's IRQL is raised to 2 or higher (for whatever reason), certain restrictions apply on the executing code:

- Accessing memory not in physical memory is fatal and causes a system crash. This means accessing data from non-paged pool is always safe, whereas accessing data from paged pool or from user-supplied buffers is not safe and should be avoided.
- Waiting for any dispatcher kernel object (e.g. mutex or event) causes a system crash, unless the wait timeout is zero, which is still allowed. (we'll discuss dispatcher object and waiting later in this chapter in the "Synchronization" section.)

These restrictions are due to the fact that the scheduler "runs" at IRQL 2; so if a processor's IRQL is already 2 or higher, the scheduler cannot wake up on that processor, so context switches (replacing the running thread with another on this CPU) cannot occur. Only higher level interrupts can temporarily divert code into the associated ISR, but it's still the same thread - no context switch can occur; the thread's context is saved, the ISR executes and the thread's state resumes.

> The current IRQL of a processor can be viewed while debugging with the !irql command. An optional CPU number can be specified, which shows the IRQL of that CPU.

> You can view the registered interrupts on a system using the !idt debugger command.

Raising and Lowering IRQL

As previously discussed, in user mode the concept of IRQL is not mentioned and there is no way to change it. In kernel mode, the IRQL can be raised with the KeRaiseIrql function and lowered back with KeLowerIrql. Here is a code snippet that raises the IRQL to DISPATCH_LEVEL (2), and then lowers it back after executing some instructions at this IRQL.

```
// assuming current IRQL <= DISPATCH_LEVEL

KIRQL oldIrql;       // typedefed as UCHAR
KeRaiseIrql(DISPATCH_LEVEL, &oldIrql);

NT_ASSERT(KeGetCurrentIrql() == DISPATCH_LEVEL);

// do work at IRQL DISPATCH_LEVEL

KeLowerIrql(oldIrql);
```

 If you raise IRQL, make sure you lower it in the same function. It's too dangerous to return from a function with a higher IRQL than it was entered. Also, make sure `KeRaiseIrql` actually raises the IRQL and `KeLowerIrql` actually lowers it; otherwise, a system crash will follow.

Thread Priorities vs. IRQLs

IRQL is an attribute of a processor. Priority is an attribute of a thread. Thread priorities only have meaning at IRQL < 2. Once an executing thread raised IRQL to 2 or higher, its priority does not mean anything anymore - it has theoretically an infinite quantum - it will continue execution until it lowers the IRQL to below 2.

Naturally, spending a lot of time at IRQL >= 2 is not a good thing; user-mode code is not running for sure. This is just one reason there are severe restrictions on what executing code can do at these levels.

Task Manager shows the amount of CPU time spent in IRQL 2 or higher using a pseudo-process called *System Interrupts*; *Process Explorer* calls it *Interrupts*. Figure 6-3 shows a screenshot from *Task Manager* and figure 6-4 shows the same information in *Process Explorer*.

Name	PID	Status	User name	Ses...	CPU	Memory (a...	Commit size	Base priority	H...	Th...	Description
System interrupts	-	Running	SYSTEM	0	01	0 K	0 K	N/A	-	-	Deferred procedure calls and interrupt service routines
System Idle Process	0	Running	SYSTEM	0	86	8 K	60 K	N/A	-	12	Percentage of time the processor is idle
System	4	Running	SYSTEM	0	00	20 K	204 K	N/A	9,...	382	NT Kernel & System
Secure System	88	Running	SYSTEM	0	00	80,372 K	184 K	N/A	-	-	NT Kernel & System

(Processes Performance App history Startup Users Details Services)

Figure 6-3: IRQL 2+ CPU time in Task Manager

Process	PID	CPU	Private Bytes	Working Set	Description	User Name
Interrupts	n/a	1.06	0 K	0 K	Hardware Interrupts and DPCs	
System Idle Process	0	83.28	60 K	8 K		NT AUTHORITY\SYSTEM
System	4	0.88	204 K	3,932 K		NT AUTHORITY\SYSTEM
Secure System	88	Suspended	184 K	80,372 K		NT AUTHORITY\SYSTEM

Figure 6-4: IRQL 2+ CPU time in Process Explorer

Deferred Procedure Calls

Figure 6-5 shows a typical sequence of events when a client invokes some I/O operation. In this figure, a user-mode thread opens a handle to a file, and issues a read operation using the ReadFile function. Since the thread can make an asynchronous call, it regains control almost immediately and can do other work. The driver receiving this request, calls the file system driver (e.g. NTFS), which may call other drivers below it, until the request reaches the disk driver, which initiates the operation on the actual disk hardware. At that point, no code needs to execute, since the hardware "does its thing".

When the hardware is done with the read operation, it issues an interrupt. This causes the Interrupt Service Routine associated with the interrupt to execute at Device IRQL (note that the thread handling the request is arbitrary, since the interrupt arrives asynchronously). A typical ISR accesses the device's hardware to get the result of the operation. Its final act should be to complete the initial request.

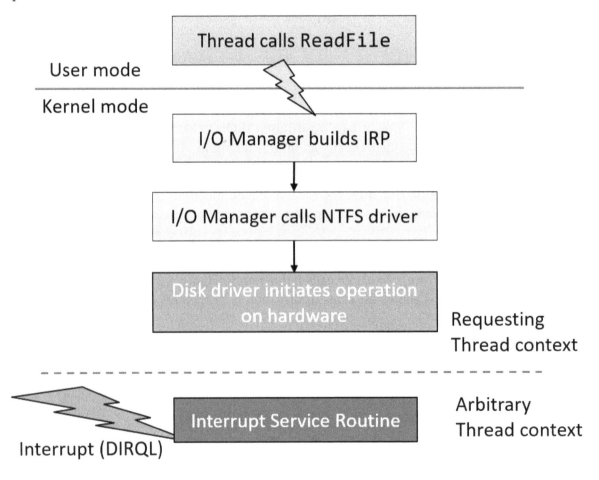

Figure 6-5: Typical I/O request processing (part 1)

As we've seen in chapter 4, completing a request is done by calling IoCompleteRequest. The problem is the documentation states that this function can only be called at IRQL <= DISPATCH_LEVEL (2). This means the ISR cannot call IoCompleteRequest or it will crash the system. So what is the ISR to do?

 You may wonder why is there such a restriction. One of the reasons has to do with the work done by IoCompleteRequest. We'll discuss this in more detail in the next chapter, but the bottom line is that this function is relatively expensive. If the call would have been allowed, that would mean the ISR will take substantially longer to execute, and since it executes in a high IRQL, it will mask off other interrupts for a longer period of time.

The mechanism that allows the ISR to call IoCompleteRequest (and other functions with similar limitations) as soon as possible is using a *Deferred Procedure Call* (DPC). A DPC is an object encapsulating a function that is to be called at IRQL DISPATCH_LEVEL. At this IRQL, calling IoCompleteRequest is permitted.

 You may wonder why does the ISR not simply lower the current IRQL to DISPATCH_LEVEL, call IoCompleteRequest and then raise the IRQL back to its original value. This can cause a deadlock. We'll discuss the reason for that later in this chapter in the section "Spin Locks".

The driver which registered the ISR prepares a DPC in advance, by allocating a KDPC structure from non-paged pool and initializing it with a callback function using KeInitializeDpc. Then, when the ISR is called, just before exiting the function, the ISR requests the DPC to execute as soon as possible by queuing it using KeInsertQueueDpc. When the DPC function executes, it calls IoCompleteRequest. So the DPC serves as a compromise - it's running at IRQL DISPATCH_LEVEL, meaning no scheduling can occur, no paged memory access, etc. but it's not high enough to prevent hardware interrupts from coming in and being served on the same processor.

Every processor on the system has its own queue of DPCs. By default, KeInsertQueueDpc queues the DPC to the current processor's DPC queue. When the ISR returns, before the IRQL can drop back to zero, a check is made to see whetheer DPCs exist in the processor's queue. If there are, the processor drops to IRQL DISPATCH_LEVEL (2) and then processes the DPCs in the queue in a First In First Out (FIFO) manner, calling the respective functions, until the queue is empty. Only then can the processor's IRQL drop to zero, and resume executing the original code that was disturbed at the time the interrupt arrived.

 DPCs can be customized in some ways. Check out the docs for the functions KeSetImportantceDpc and KeSetTargetProcessorDpc.

Figure 6-6 augments figure 6-5 with the DPC routine execution.

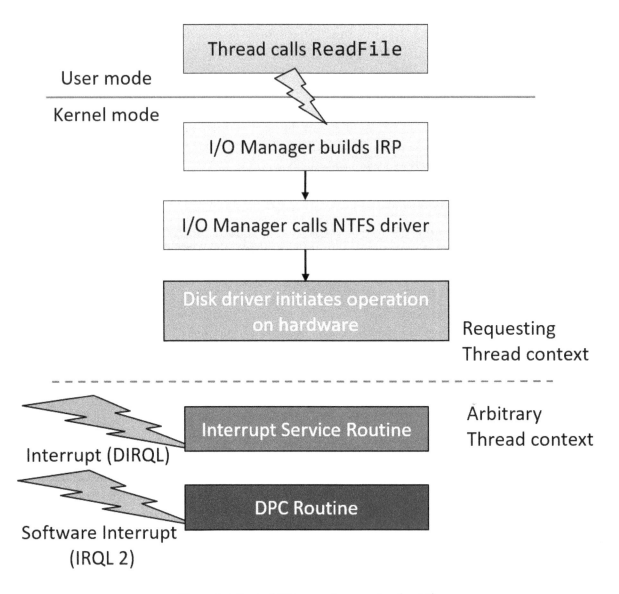

Figure 6-6: Typical I/O request processing (part 2)

Using DPC with a Timer

DPCs were originally created for use by ISRs. However, there are other mechanisms in the kernel that utilize DPCs.

One such use is with a kernel timer. A kernel timer, represented by the KTIMER structure allows setting up a timer to expire some time in the future, based on a relative interval or absolute time. This timer is a dispatcher object and so can be waited upon with KeWaitForSingleObject (discussed later in this chapter in the section "Synchronization"). Although waiting is possible, it's inconvenient for a timer. A simpler approach is to call some callback when the timer expires. This is exactly what the kernel timer provides using a DPC as its callback.

The following code snippet shows how to configure a timer and associate it with a DPC. When the timer expires, the DPC is inserted into a CPU's DPC queue and so executes as soon as possible. Using a DPC is more powerful than a zero IRQL based callback, since it is guaranteed to execute before any user mode code (and most kernel mode code).

```
KTIMER Timer;
KDPC TimerDpc;

void InitializeAndStartTimer(ULONG msec) {
    KeInitializeTimer(&Timer);
    KeInitializeDpc(&TimerDpc,
        OnTimerExpired,     // callback function
        nullptr);           // passed to callback as "context"

    // relative interval is in 100nsec units (and must be negative)
    // convert to msec by multiplying by 10000

    LARGE_INTEGER interval;
    interval.QuadPart = -10000LL * msec;
    KeSetTimer(&Timer, interval, &TimerDpc);
}

void OnTimerExpired(KDPC* Dpc, PVOID context, PVOID, PVOID) {
    UNREFERENCED_PARAMETER(Dpc);
    UNREFERENCED_PARAMETER(context);

    NT_ASSERT(KeGetCurrentIrql() == DISPATCH_LEVEL);

    // handle timer expiration
}
```

Asynchronous Procedure Calls

We've seen in the previous section that DPCs are objects encapsulating a function to be called at IRQL DISPATCH_LEVEL. The calling thread does not matter, as far as DPCs are concerned.

Asynchronous Procedure Calls (APCs) are also data structures that encapsulate a function to be called. But contrary to a DPC, an APC is targeted towards a particular thread, so only that thread can execute the function. This means each thread has an APC queue associated with it.

There are three types of APCs:

- User mode APCs - these execute in user mode at IRQL PASSIVE_LEVEL only when the thread goes into alertable state. This is typically accomplished by calling an API such as SleepEx, WaitForSingleObjectEx, WaitForMultipleObjectsEx and similar APIs. The last argument to these functions can be set to TRUE to put the thread in alertable state. In this state it looks at its APC queue, and if not empty - the APCs now execute until the queue is empty.
- Normal kernel mode APCs - these execute in kernel mode at IRQL PASSIVE_LEVEL and preempt user mode code and user mode APCs.
- Special kernel APCs - these execute in kernel mode at IRQL APC_LEVEL (1) and preempt user mode code, normal kernel APCs, and user mode APCs. These APCs are used by the I/O system to complete I/O operations. The common scenario for this will be discussed in the next chapter.

The APC API is undocumented in kernel mode, so drivers don't usually use APCs directly.

 User mode can use (user mode) APCs by calling certain APIs. For example, calling ReadFileEx or WriteFileEx start an asynchronous I/O operation. When the operation completes, a user mode APC is attached to the calling thread. This APC will execute when the thread enters an alertable state as described earlier. Another useful function in user mode to explicitly generate an APC is QueueUserAPC. Check out the Windows API documentation for more information.

Critical Regions and Guarded Regions

A *Critical Region* prevents user mode and normal kernel APCs from executing (special kernel APCs can still execute). A thread enters a critical region with KeEnterCriticalRegion and leaves it with KeLeaveCriticalRegion. Some functions in the kernel require being inside a critical region, especially when working with executive resources (see the section "Executive Resources" later in this chapter).

A *Guarded Region* prevents all APCs from executing. Call KeEnterGuardedRegion to enter a guarded region and KeLeaveGuardedRegion to leave it. Recursive calls to KeEnterGuardedRegion must be matched with the same number of calls to KeLeaveGuardedRegion.

 Raising the IRQL to APC_LEVEL disables delivery of all APCs.

Structured Exception Handling

An exception is an event that occurs because of a certain instruction that did something that caused the processor to raise an error. Exceptions are in some ways similar to interrupts, the main difference being that an exception is synchronous and technically reproducible under the same conditions, whereas an interrupt is asynchronous and can arrive at any time. Examples of exceptions include division by zero, breakpoint, page fault, stack overflow and invalid instruction.

If an exception occurs, the kernel catches this and allows code to handle the exception, if possible. This mechanism is called *Structured Exception Handling* (SEH) and is available for user mode code as well as kernel mode code.

The kernel exception handlers are called based on the *Interrupt Dispatch Table* (IDT), the same one holding mapping between interrupt vectors and ISRs. Using a kernel debugger, the !idt command shows all these mappings. The low numbered interrupt vectors are in fact exception handlers. Here's a sample output from this command:

```
lkd> !idt

Dumping IDT: fffff8011d941000

00: fffff8011dd6c100 nt!KiDivideErrorFaultShadow
01: fffff8011dd6c180 nt!KiDebugTrapOrFaultShadow      Stack = 0xFFFFF8011D9459D0
02: fffff8011dd6c200 nt!KiNmiInterruptShadow           Stack = 0xFFFFF8011D9457D0
03: fffff8011dd6c280 nt!KiBreakpointTrapShadow
04: fffff8011dd6c300 nt!KiOverflowTrapShadow
05: fffff8011dd6c380 nt!KiBoundFaultShadow
06: fffff8011dd6c400 nt!KiInvalidOpcodeFaultShadow
07: fffff8011dd6c480 nt!KiNpxNotAvailableFaultShadow
08: fffff8011dd6c500 nt!KiDoubleFaultAbortShadow       Stack = 0xFFFFF8011D9453D0
09: fffff8011dd6c580 nt!KiNpxSegmentOverrunAbortShadow
0a: fffff8011dd6c600 nt!KiInvalidTssFaultShadow
0b: fffff8011dd6c680 nt!KiSegmentNotPresentFaultShadow
0c: fffff8011dd6c700 nt!KiStackFaultShadow
0d: fffff8011dd6c780 nt!KiGeneralProtectionFaultShadow
0e: fffff8011dd6c800 nt!KiPageFaultShadow
10: fffff8011dd6c880 nt!KiFloatingErrorFaultShadow
11: fffff8011dd6c900 nt!KiAlignmentFaultShadow

(truncated)
```

Note the function names - most are very descriptive. These entries are connected to Intel/AMD (in this example) faults. Some common examples of exceptions include:

- Division by zero (0)
- Breakpoint (3) - the kernel handles this transparently, passing control to an attached debugger (if any).
- Invalid opcode (6) - this fault is raised by the CPU if it encounters an unknown instruction.

- Page fault (14) - this fault is raised by the CPU if the page table entry used for translating virtual to physical addresses has the Valid bit set to zero, indicating (as far as the CPU is concerned) that the page is not resident in physical memory.

Some other exceptions are raised by the kernel as a result of a previous CPU fault. For example, if a page fault is raised, the Memory Manager's page fault handler will try to locate the page that is not resident in RAM. If the page happens not to exist at all, the Memory Manager will raise an Access Violation exception.

Once an exception is raised, the kernel searches the function where the exception occurred for a handler (except for some exceptions which it handles transparently, such as Breakpoint (3)). If not found, it will search up the call stack, until such handler is found. If the call stack is exhausted, the system will crash.

How can a driver handle these types of exceptions? Microsoft added four keywords to the C language to allow developers to handle such exceptions easily. Table 6-1 shows the added keywords with a brief description.

Table 6-1: Keywords for working with SEH

Keyword	Description
__try	Starts a block of code where exceptions may occur.
__except	Indicates if an exception is handled, and provides the handling code if it is.
__finally	Unrelated to exceptions directly. Provides code that is guaranteed to execute no matter what - whether the __try block is exited normally or because of an exception.
__leave	Provides an optimized mechanism to jump to the __finally block from somewhere within a __try block.

The valid combination of keywords is __try/__except and __try/__finally. However, these can be combined by using nesting to any level.

 These same keywords work in user mode as well, in much the same way.

Using __try/__except

In chapter 4, we implemented a driver that accesses a user mode buffer to get data needed for the driver's operation. We used a direct pointer to the user's buffer. However, this is not guaranteed to be safe. For example, the user mode code (say from another thread) could free the buffer, just before the driver accesses it. In such a case, the driver would cause a system crash, essentially because of a user's error (or malicious intent). Since user data should never be trusted, such access should be wrapped in a __try/__except block to make sure a bad buffer does not crash the driver.

Here is the important part of a revised IRP_MJ_DEVICE_CONTROL handler using an exception handler:

```
case IOCTL_PRIORITY_BOOSTER_SET_PRIORITY:
{
    if (stack->Parameters.DeviceIoControl.InputBufferLength < sizeof(ThreadData)) {
        status = STATUS_BUFFER_TOO_SMALL;
        break;
    }
    auto data = (ThreadData*)stack->Parameters.DeviceIoControl.Type3InputBuffer;
    if (data == nullptr) {
        status = STATUS_INVALID_PARAMETER;
        break;
    }
    __try {
        if (data->Priority < 1 || data->Priority > 31) {
            status = STATUS_INVALID_PARAMETER;
            break;
        }
        PETHREAD Thread;
        status = PsLookupThreadByThreadId(ULongToHandle(data->ThreadId), &Thread);
        if (!NT_SUCCESS(status))
            break;
        KeSetPriorityThread((PKTHREAD)Thread, data->Priority);
        ObDereferenceObject(Thread);
        KdPrint(("Thread Priority change for %d to %d succeeded!\n",
            data->ThreadId, data->Priority));
    }
    __except (EXCEPTION_EXECUTE_HANDLER) {
        // something wrong with the buffer
        status = STATUS_ACCESS_VIOLATION;
    }
    break;
}
```

Placing EXCEPTION_EXECUTE_HANDLER in __except says that any exception is to be handled. We can be more selective by calling GetExceptionCode and looking at the actual exception. If we don't expect this, we can tell the kernel to continue looking for handlers up the call stack:

```
__except (GetExceptionCode() == STATUS_ACCESS_VIOLATION
    ? EXCEPTION_EXECUTE_HANDLER : EXCEPTION_CONTINUE_SEARCH) {
    // handle exception
}
```

Does all this mean that the driver can catch any and all exceptions? If so, the driver will never cause a system crash. Unfortunately (or fortunately, depending on your perspective), this is not the case.

Access violation, for example, is something that can only be caught if the violated address is in user space. If it's in kernel space, it will not be caught and still cause a system crash. This should make sense, because something bad has happened and the kernel will not let the driver get away with it. User mode addresses, on the other hand, are not at the control of the driver, so such exceptions can be caught and handled.

The SEH mechanism can also be used by drivers (and user mode code) to throw custom exceptions. The kernel provides the generic function ExRaiseStatus to raise any exception and some specific functions like ExRaiseAccessViolation.

 You may be wondering how exceptions in high-level languages (C++, Java, .NET, etc.) work. This obviously depends on implementation, but Microsoft's compilers use SEH behind the covers with their own codes for the particular platform. For example, .NET exceptions use the value 0xe0434c52. This value was chosen because the last 3 bytes are the ASCII codes for 'CLR'. 0xe0 is just there to make sure this number does not collide with other exception numbers. The throw C# statement will use the RaiseException API in user mode to raise this exception with some arguments that provide the .NET Common Language Runtime (CLR) the information it needs to recognize the "thrown" object.

Using __try/__finally

Using block of __try and __finally is not directly related to exceptions. This is about making sure some piece of code executes no matter what - whether the code exits cleanly or mid-way because of an exception. This is similar in concept to the finally keyword popular in some high level languages (e.g. Java, C#). Here is a simple example to show the problem:

```
void foo() {
    void* p = ExAllocatePool(PagedPool, 1024);

    // do work with p

    ExFreePool(p);
}
```

The above code seems harmless enough. However, there are several issues with it:

- If an exception is thrown between the allocation and the release, a handler in the caller will be searched but the memory not freed.
- if a return statement used in some conditional between the allocation and release, the buffer will not be freed. This requires the code to be careful to make sure all exit points from the function pass through the code freeing the buffer.

The second bullet can be implemented with careful coding, but is a burden best avoided. The first bullet cannot be handled with standard coding techniques. This is where __try/__finally come in. Using this combination we can make sure the buffer is freed no matter what:

```
void foo() {
    void* p = ExAllocatePool(PagedPool, 1024);
    __try {
        // do work with p
    }
    __finally {
        ExFreePool(p);
    }
}
```

With the above code in place, even if return statements appear within the __try body, the __finally code will be called before actual returning from the function. If some exception occurs, the __finally block runs first before the kernel searches up the call stack for handlers.

__try/__finally is useful not just for memory allocations, but also with other resources, where some acquisition and release need to take place. One common example is when synchronizing threads accessing some shared data. Here is an example acquiring and releasing a fast mutex (fast mutex and other synchronization primitives are described later in this chapter):

```
FAST_MUTEX MyMutex;

void foo() {
    ExAcquireFastMutex(&MyMutex);
    __try {
        // do work while the fast mutex is held
    }
    __finally {
        ExReleaseFastMutex(&MyMutex);
    }
}
```

Using C++ RAII Instead of __try / __finally

Although the preceding examples with __try/__finally work, they are not terribly convenient. Using C++ we can build RAII wrappers that do the right thing without need to use __try/__finally. C++ does not have a finally keyword like C# or Java, but it doesn't need one - it has destructors.

Here is a very simple, bare minimum, example that manages a buffer allocation with a RAII class:

```cpp
template<typename T = void>
struct kunique_ptr {
    kunique_ptr(T* p = nullptr) : _p(p) {}
    ~kunique_ptr() {
        if (_p)
            ExFreePool(_p);
    }

    T* operator->() const {
        return _p;
    }

    T& operator*() const {
        return *_p;
    }

private:
    T* _p;
};
```

The class uses templates to allow working easily with any type of data. An example usage follows:

```cpp
struct MyData {
    ULONG Data1;
    HANDLE Data2;
};

void foo() {
    // take charge of the allocation
    kunique_ptr<MyData> data((MyData*)ExAllocatePool(PagedPool, sizeof(MyData)));
    // use the pointer
    data->Data1 = 10;
    // when the object goes out of scope, the destructor frees the buffer
}
```

> If you don't normally use C++ as your primary programming language, you may find the above code confusing. You can continue working with __try/__finally, but I recommend getting acquainted with this type of code. In any case, even if you struggle with the implementation of kunique_ptr above, you can still use it without needing to understand every little detail.

The `kunique_ptr` type presented is a bare minimum. You should also remove the copy constructor and copy assignment, and possibly allow move copy and assignment (C++ 11 and later, for ownership transfer) and other helpers. Here is a more complete implementation:

```
template<typename T = void>
struct kunique_ptr {
    kunique_ptr(T* p = nullptr) : _p(p) {}

    // remove copy ctor and copy = (single owner)
    kunique_ptr(const kunique_ptr&) = delete;
    kunique_ptr& operator=(const kunique_ptr&) = delete;

    // allow ownership transfer
    kunique_ptr(kunique_ptr&& other) : _p(other._p) {
        other._p = nullptr;
    }

    kunique_ptr& operator=(kunique_ptr&& other) {
        if (&other != this) {
            Release();
            _p = other._p;
            other._p = nullptr;
        }
        return *this;
    }

    ~kunique_ptr() {
        Release();
    }

    operator bool() const {
        return _p != nullptr;
    }

    T* operator->() const {
        return _p;
    }

    T& operator*() const {
        return *_p;
    }

    void Release() {
```

```
    if (_p)
        ExFreePool(_p);
    }

private:
    T* _p;
};
```

We'll build other RAII wrappers for synchronization primitives later in this chapter.

System Crash

As we already know, if an unhandled exception occurs in kernel mode, the system crashes, typically with the "Blue Screen of Death" (BSOD) showing its face (on Windows 8+, that's literally a face - saddy - the inverse of smiley). In this section we'll discuss what happens when the system crashes and how to deal with it.

The system crash has many names, all meaning the same thing - "Blue screen of Death", "System failure", "Bugcheck", "Stop error". The BSOD is not punishment, as may seem at first, but a protection mechanism. If kernel code, which is supposed to be trusted, did something bad, stopping everything is probably the safest approach, as perhaps letting the code continue roaming around may result in an unbootable system if some important files or registry keys get corrupted.

> Recent versions of Windows 10 have some alternate colors for when the system crashes. Green is used for insider builds, and I actually encountered orange as well.

If the crashed system is connected to a kernel debugger, the debugger will break. This allows examining the state of the system before other actions take place.

The system can be configured to perform some operations if the system crashes. This can be done with the *System Properties* UI on the *Advanced* tab. Clicking *Settings…* at the *Startup and Recovery* section brings the *Startup and Recovery* dialog where the *System Failure* section shows the available options. Figure 6-7 shows these two dialogs.

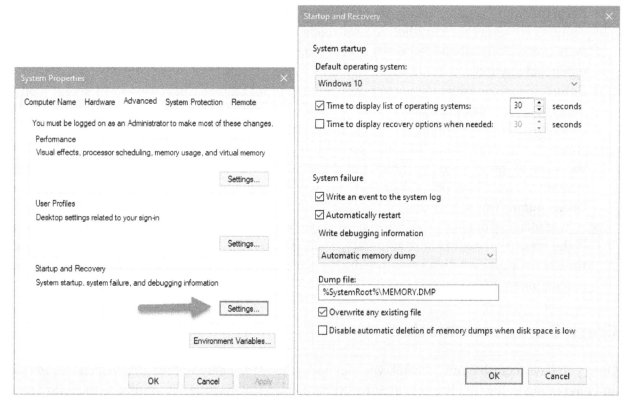

Figure 6-7: Startup and recovery settings

if the system crashes, an event entry can be written to the event log. It's checked by default, and there is no good reason to change it. The system is configured to automatically restart; this has been the default since Windows 2000.

The most important setting is the generation of a dump file. The dump file captures the system state at the time of the crash, so it can later be analyzed by loading the dump file into the debugger. The type of the dump file is important, since it determines what information will be present in the dump. It's important to emphasize that the dump is not written to the target file at crash time, but instead written to the first page file. Only when the system restarts the kernel notices there is dump information in the page file does it copy the data to the target file. The reason has to do with the fact that at system crash time it may be too dangerous to write something to a new file; the system may not be stable enough. The best bet is to write the data to the page file which is already open any way. The downside is that the page file must be large enough to contain the dump, otherwise the dump file will not be written.

The dump type determines what data would be written and hints at the page file size that may be required. Here are the options:

- Small memory dump - a very minimal dump, containing basic system information and information on the thread that caused the crash. Usually this is too little to determine what happened in all but the most trivial cases. The upside is that the file is very small.

- Kernel memory dump - this is the default on Windows 7 and earlier versions. This setting captures all kernel memory but no user mode memory. This is usually good enough, since a system crash can only be caused by kernel code misbehaving. It's extremely unlikely that user mode had anything to do with it.
- Complete memory dump - this provides a dump of all memory, user mode and kernel mode. This is the most complete information available. The downside is the size of the dump, which could be gigantic depending on system RAM and currently used memory.
- Automatic memory dump (Windows 8+) - this is the default on Windows 8 and later. This is the same as kernel memory dump, but the kernel resizes the page file on boot to a size that guarantees with high probability that the page file size would be large enough to contain a kernel dump. This is only done if the page file size is specified as "System managed".
- Active memory dump (Windows 10+) - this is similar to a complete memory dump, except that if the crashed system is hosting guest virtual machines, the memory they were using at the time is not captured. This helps in reducing the dump file size on server systems that may be hosting many VMs.

Crash Dump Information

Once you have a crash dump in hand, you can open it in *WinDbg* by selecting *File/Open Dump File* and navigating to the file. The debugger will spew some basic information similar to the following:

```
Microsoft (R) Windows Debugger Version 10.0.18317.1001 AMD64
Copyright (c) Microsoft Corporation. All rights reserved.


Loading Dump File [C:\Temp\MEMORY.DMP]
Kernel Bitmap Dump File: Kernel address space is available, User address space may n\
ot be available.


************* Path validation summary **************
Response                       Time (ms)     Location
Deferred                                     SRV*c:\Symbols*http://msdl.microsoft.\
com/download/symbols
Symbol search path is: SRV*c:\Symbols*http://msdl.microsoft.com/download/symbols
Executable search path is:
Windows 10 Kernel Version 18362 MP (4 procs) Free x64
Product: WinNt, suite: TerminalServer SingleUserTS
Built by: 18362.1.amd64fre.19h1_release.190318-1202
Machine Name:
Kernel base = 0xfffff803`70abc000 PsLoadedModuleList = 0xfffff803`70eff2d0
Debug session time: Wed Apr 24 15:36:55.613 2019 (UTC + 3:00)
System Uptime: 0 days 0:05:38.923
Loading Kernel Symbols
```

```
.................................Page 2001b5efc too large to be in the dump file.
Page 20001ebfb too large to be in the dump file.
...............................
Loading User Symbols
PEB is paged out (Peb.Ldr = 00000054`34256018).  Type ".hh dbgerr001" for details
Loading unloaded module list
.............
For analysis of this file, run !analyze -v
nt!KeBugCheckEx:
fffff803`70c78810 48894c2408      mov     qword ptr [rsp+8],rcx ss:fffff988`53b0f6b0\
=000000000000000a
```

The debugger suggests running !analyze -v and it's the most common thing to do at the start of dump analysis. Notice the call stack is at KeBugCheckEx, which is the function generating the bugcheck, and is fully documented in the WDK, since drivers may also want to use it if necessary.

The default logic behind !analyze -v performs basic analysis on the thread that caused the crash and shows a few pieces of information related to the crash dump code:

```
2: kd> !analyze -v
*******************************************************************************
*                                                                             *
*                        Bugcheck Analysis                                    *
*                                                                             *
*******************************************************************************

DRIVER_IRQL_NOT_LESS_OR_EQUAL (d1)
An attempt was made to access a pageable (or completely invalid) address at an
interrupt request level (IRQL) that is too high.  This is usually
caused by drivers using improper addresses.
If kernel debugger is available get stack backtrace.
Arguments:
Arg1: ffffd907b0dc7660, memory referenced
Arg2: 0000000000000002, IRQL
Arg3: 0000000000000000, value 0 = read operation, 1 = write operation
Arg4: fffff80375261530, address which referenced memory

Debugging Details:
------------------

(truncated)

DUMP_TYPE:  1
```

```
BUGCHECK_P1: ffffd907b0dc7660

BUGCHECK_P2: 2

BUGCHECK_P3: 0

BUGCHECK_P4: fffff80375261530

READ_ADDRESS: Unable to get offset of nt!_MI_VISIBLE_STATE.SpecialPool
Unable to get value of nt!_MI_VISIBLE_STATE.SessionSpecialPool
 ffffd907b0dc7660 Paged pool


CURRENT_IRQL:  2

FAULTING_IP:
myfault+1530
fffff803`75261530 8b03              mov     eax,dword ptr [rbx]


(truncated)

ANALYSIS_VERSION: 10.0.18317.1001 amd64fre


TRAP_FRAME:  fffff98853b0f7f0 -- (.trap 0xfffff98853b0f7f0)
NOTE: The trap frame does not contain all registers.
Some register values may be zeroed or incorrect.
rax=0000000000000000 rbx=0000000000000000 rcx=ffffd90797400340
rdx=0000000000000880 rsi=0000000000000000 rdi=0000000000000000
rip=fffff80375261530 rsp=fffff98853b0f980 rbp=0000000000000002
 r8=ffffd9079c5cec10  r9=0000000000000000 r10=ffffd907974002c0
r11=ffffd907b0dc1650 r12=0000000000000000 r13=0000000000000000
r14=0000000000000000 r15=0000000000000000
iopl=0          nv up ei ng nz na po nc
myfault+0x1530:
fffff803`75261530 8b03              mov     eax,dword ptr [rbx] ds:00000000`00000000=?\
???????
Resetting default scope


LAST_CONTROL_TRANSFER:  from fffff80370c8a469 to fffff80370c78810


STACK_TEXT:
fffff988`53b0f6a8 fffff803`70c8a469 : 00000000`0000000a ffffd907`b0dc7660 00000000`0\
0000002 00000000`00000000 : nt!KeBugCheckEx
```

```
fffff988`53b0f6b0 fffff803`70c867a5 : ffff8788`e4604080 ffffff4c`c66c7010 00000000`0\
0000003 00000000`00000880 : nt!KiBugCheckDispatch+0x69
fffff988`53b0f7f0 fffff803`75261530 : ffffff4c`c66c7000 00000000`00000000 fffff988`5\
3b0f9e0 00000000`00000000 : nt!KiPageFault+0x465
fffff988`53b0f980 fffff803`75261e2d : fffff988`00000000 00000000`00000000 ffff8788`e\
c7cf520 00000000`00000000 : myfault+0x1530
fffff988`53b0f9b0 fffff803`75261f88 : ffffff4c`c66c7010 00000000`000000f0 00000000`0\
0000001 ffffff30`21ea80aa : myfault+0x1e2d
fffff988`53b0fb00 fffff803`70ae3da9 : ffff8788`e6d8e400 00000000`00000001 00000000`8\
3360018 00000000`00000001 : myfault+0x1f88
fffff988`53b0fb40 fffff803`710d1dd5 : fffff988`53b0fec0 ffff8788`e6d8e400 00000000`0\
0000001 ffff8788`ecdb6690 : nt!IofCallDriver+0x59
fffff988`53b0fb80 fffff803`710d172a : ffff8788`00000000 00000000`83360018 00000000`0\
0000000 fffff988`53b0fec0 : nt!IopSynchronousServiceTail+0x1a5
fffff988`53b0fc20 fffff803`710d1146 : 00000054`344feb28 00000000`00000000 00000000`0\
0000000 00000000`00000000 : nt!IopXxxControlFile+0x5ca
fffff988`53b0fd60 fffff803`70c89e95 : ffff8788`e4604080 fffff988`53b0fec0 00000054`3\
44feb28 fffff988`569fd630 : nt!NtDeviceIoControlFile+0x56
fffff988`53b0fdd0 00007ff8`ba39c147 : 00000000`00000000 00000000`00000000 00000000`0\
0000000 00000000`00000000 : nt!KiSystemServiceCopyEnd+0x25
00000054`344feb48 00000000`00000000 : 00000000`00000000 00000000`00000000 00000000`0\
0000000 00000000`00000000 : 0x00007ff8`ba39c147

(truncated)

FOLLOWUP_IP:
myfault+1530
fffff803`75261530 8b03            mov     eax,dword ptr [rbx]

FAULT_INSTR_CODE:  8d48038b

SYMBOL_STACK_INDEX:  3

SYMBOL_NAME:  myfault+1530

FOLLOWUP_NAME:  MachineOwner

MODULE_NAME: myfault

IMAGE_NAME:  myfault.sys

(truncated)
```

Every crash dump code can have up to 4 numbers that provide more information about the crash. In this case, we can see the code is DRIVER_IRQL_NOT_LESS_OR_EQUAL (0xd1) and the next four numbers named *Arg1* through *Arg4* mean (in order): memory referenced, the IRQL at the time of the call, read vs. write operation and the accessing address.

The command clearly recognizes *myfault.sys* as the faulting module (driver). That's because this is an easy crash - the culprit is on the call stack as can be seen in the *STACK TEXT* section above (you can also simply use the k command to see it again).

> The !analyze -v command is actually extensible and it's possible to add more analysis to that command using an extension DLL. You may be able to find such extensions on the web. Consult the debugger API documentation for more information on how to add your own analysis code to this command.

More complex crash dumps may show calls from the kernel only on the call stack of the offending thread. Before you conclude that you found a bug in the Windows kernel, consider this: Most likely, a driver did something that is not fatal in itself, such as experience a buffer overflow - wrote data beyond its allocated buffer, but unfortunately the memory following that buffer was allocated by some other driver or the kernel and so nothing bad happened at that time. Some time later, the kernel accessed that memory and got bad data and caused a system crash. But the faulting driver is nowhere to be found on any call stack; this is much harder to diagnose.

> One way to help diagnose such issues is using Driver Verifier. We'll look at the basics of Driver Verifier in module 11.

> Once you get the crash dump code, it's helpful to look in the debugger documentation at the topic "Bugcheck Code Reference", where common bugcheck codes are explained more fully with typical causes and ideas on what to investigate next.

Analyzing a Dump File

A dump file is a snapshot of a system. Other than that, it's the same as any kernel debugging sessions. You just can't set breakpoints, and certainly cannot use some go command. All other commands are available as usual. Commands such as !process, !thread, lm, k can be used normally. Here are some other commands and tips:

- The prompt indicates the current processor. Switching processors can be done with the command ~ns where n is the CPU index (it looks like switching threads in user mode).
- The !running command can be used to list the threads that were running on all processors at the time of the crash. Adding -t as an option shows the call stack for each thread. Here is an example with the above crash dump:

```
2: kd> !running -t

System Processors:  (000000000000000f)
  Idle Processors:  (0000000000000002)

      Prcbs             Current          (pri) Next          (pri) Idle
  0     fffff8036ef3f180  ffff8788e91cf080 ( 8)                      fffff8037104840\
0 ..............

 # Child-SP          RetAddr           Call Site
00 00000094`ed6ee8a0 00000000`00000000 0x00007ff8`b74c4b57


  2     ffffb000c1944180  ffff8788e4604080 (12)                     ffffb000c195514\
0 ..............

 # Child-SP          RetAddr           Call Site
00 fffff988`53b0f6a8 fffff803`70c8a469 nt!KeBugCheckEx
01 fffff988`53b0f6b0 fffff803`70c867a5 nt!KiBugCheckDispatch+0x69
02 fffff988`53b0f7f0 fffff803`75261530 nt!KiPageFault+0x465
03 fffff988`53b0f980 fffff803`75261e2d myfault+0x1530
04 fffff988`53b0f9b0 fffff803`75261f88 myfault+0x1e2d
05 fffff988`53b0fb00 fffff803`70ae3da9 myfault+0x1f88
06 fffff988`53b0fb40 fffff803`710d1dd5 nt!IofCallDriver+0x59
07 fffff988`53b0fb80 fffff803`710d172a nt!IopSynchronousServiceTail+0x1a5
08 fffff988`53b0fc20 fffff803`710d1146 nt!IopXxxControlFile+0x5ca
09 fffff988`53b0fd60 fffff803`70c89e95 nt!NtDeviceIoControlFile+0x56
0a fffff988`53b0fdd0 00007ff8`ba39c147 nt!KiSystemServiceCopyEnd+0x25
0b 00000054`344feb48 00000000`00000000 0x00007ff8`ba39c147


  3     ffffb000c1c80180  ffff8788e917e0c0 ( 5)                     ffffb000c1c9114\
0 ..............

 # Child-SP          RetAddr           Call Site
00 fffff988`5683ec38 fffff803`70ae3da9 Ntfs!NtfsFsdClose
01 fffff988`5683ec40 fffff803`702bb5de nt!IofCallDriver+0x59
02 fffff988`5683ec80 fffff803`702b9f16 FLTMGR!FltpLegacyProcessingAfterPreCallbacksC\
ompleted+0x15e
03 fffff988`5683ed00 fffff803`70ae3da9 FLTMGR!FltpDispatch+0xb6
04 fffff988`5683ed60 fffff803`710cfe4d nt!IofCallDriver+0x59
05 fffff988`5683eda0 fffff803`710de470 nt!IopDeleteFile+0x12d
06 fffff988`5683ee20 fffff803`70aea9d4 nt!ObpRemoveObjectRoutine+0x80
07 fffff988`5683ee80 fffff803`723391f5 nt!ObfDereferenceObject+0xa4
08 fffff988`5683eec0 fffff803`72218ca7 Ntfs!NtfsDeleteInternalAttributeStream+0x111
```

```
09 fffff988`5683ef00 fffff803`722ff7cf Ntfs!NtfsDecrementCleanupCounts+0x147
0a fffff988`5683ef40 fffff803`722fe87d Ntfs!NtfsCommonCleanup+0xadf
0b fffff988`5683f390 fffff803`70ae3da9 Ntfs!NtfsFsdCleanup+0x1ad
0c fffff988`5683f6e0 fffff803`702bb5de nt!IofCallDriver+0x59
0d fffff988`5683f720 fffff803`702b9f16 FLTMGR!FltpLegacyProcessingAfterPreCallbacksC\
ompleted+0x15e
0e fffff988`5683f7a0 fffff803`70ae3da9 FLTMGR!FltpDispatch+0xb6
0f fffff988`5683f800 fffff803`710ccc38 nt!IofCallDriver+0x59
10 fffff988`5683f840 fffff803`710d4bf8 nt!IopCloseFile+0x188
11 fffff988`5683f8d0 fffff803`710d9f3e nt!ObCloseHandleTableEntry+0x278
12 fffff988`5683fa10 fffff803`70c89e95 nt!NtClose+0xde
13 fffff988`5683fa80 00007ff8`ba39c247 nt!KiSystemServiceCopyEnd+0x25
14 000000b5`aacf9df8 00000000`00000000 0x00007ff8`ba39c247
```

The command gives a pretty good idea of what was going at the time of the crash.

- The !stacks command lists all thread stacks for all threads by default. A more useful variant
  is a search string that lists only threads where a module or function containing this string
  appears. This allows locating driver's code throughout the system (because it may not have
  been running at the time of the crash, but it's on some thread's call stack). Here's an example
  for the above dump:

```
2: kd> !stacks
Proc.Thread  .Thread  Ticks   ThreadState Blocker
                              [fffff803710459c0 Idle]
   0.000000  fffff80371048400 0000003 RUNNING    nt!KiIdleLoop+0x15e
   0.000000  ffffb000c17b1140 0000ed9 RUNNING    hal!HalProcessorIdle+0xf
   0.000000  ffffb000c1955140 0000b6e RUNNING    nt!KiIdleLoop+0x15e
   0.000000  ffffb000c1c91140 000012b RUNNING    nt!KiIdleLoop+0x15e
                              [ffff8788d6a81300 System]
   4.000018  ffff8788d6b8a080 0005483 Blocked    nt!PopFxEmergencyWorker+0x3e
   4.00001c  ffff8788d6bc5140 0000982 Blocked    nt!ExpWorkQueueManagerThread+0x127
   4.000020  ffff8788d6bc9140 000085a Blocked    nt!KeRemovePriQueue+0x25c

(truncated)


2: kd> !stacks 0 myfault
Proc.Thread  .Thread  Ticks   ThreadState Blocker
                              [fffff803710459c0 Idle]
                              [ffff8788d6a81300 System]

(truncated)
```

```
                    [ffff8788e99070c0 notmyfault64.e]
af4.00160c   ffff8788e4604080 0000006 RUNNING    nt!KeBugCheckEx
```

(truncated)

The address next to each line is the thread's ETHREAD address that can be fed to the !thread command.

System Hang

A system crash is the most common type of dump that is typically investigated. However, there is yet another type of dump that you may need to work with: a hung system. A hung system is a non-responsive or near non-responsive system. Things seem to be halted or deadlocked in some way - the system does not crash, so the first issue to deal with is how to get a dump of the system?

> A dump file contains some system state, it does not have to be related to a crash or any other bad state. There are tools (including the kernel debugger) that can generate a dump file at any time.

If the system is still responsive to some extent, the Sysinternals *NotMyFault* tool can force a system crash and so force a dump file to be generated (this is in fact the way the dump in the previous section was generated). Figure 6-8 shows a screenshot of *NotMyFault*. Selecting the first (default) option and clicking *Crash* immediately crashes the system and will generate a dump file (if configured to do so).

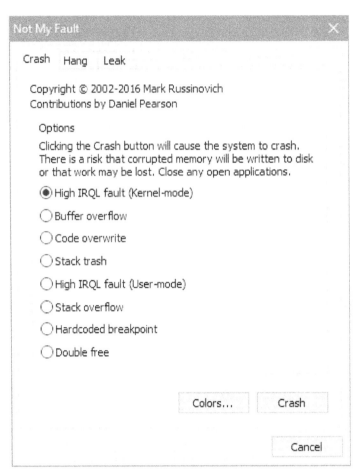

Figure 6-8: NotMyFault

NotMyFault uses a driver, *myfault.sys* that is actually responsible for the crash.

 NotMyFault has 32 and 64 bit versions (the later file name ends with "64"). Remember to use the correct one for the system at hand, otherwise its driver will fail to load.

If the system is completely unresponsive, and you can attach a kernel debugger (the target was configured for debugging), then debug normally or generate a dump file using the .dump command.

If the system is unresponsive but a kernel debugger cannot be attached, it's possible to generate a crash manually if configured in the registry beforehand (this assumes the hang was somehow expected). When a certain key combination is detected, the keyboard driver will generate a crash. Consult this link[1] to get the full details. The crash code in this case is 0xe2 (MANUALLY_INITIATED_-CRASH).

---

[1]https://docs.microsoft.com/en-us/windows-hardware/drivers/debugger/forcing-a-system-crash-from-the-keyboard

Thread Synchronization

Threads sometimes need to coordinate work. A canonical example is a driver using a linked list to gather data items. The driver can be invoked by multiple clients, coming from many threads in one or more processes. This means manipulating the linked list must be done atomically, so it's not corrupted. If multiple threads access the same memory where at least one is a writer (making changes), this is referred to as a *data race*. If a data race occurs, all bets are off and anything can happen. Typically, within a driver, a system crash occurs sooner or later; data corruption is practically guaranteed.

In such a scenario, it's essential that while one thread manipulates the linked list all other threads back off and wait in some way for the first thread to finish its work. Only then another thread (just one) can manipulate the list. This is an example of thread synchronization.

The kernel provides several primitives that help in accomplishing proper synchronization to protect data from concurrent access. The following discussed various primitives and techniques for thread synchronization.

Interlocked Operations

The Interlocked set of functions provide convenient operations that are performed atomically by utilizing the hardware, which means no software objects are involved. IF using these functions gets the job done, then they should be used, as these are as efficient as they possibly can.

A simple example is incrementing an integer by one. Generally, this is not an atomic operations. If two (or more) threads try to perform this at the same time on the same memory location, it's possible (and likely) some of the increments will be lost. Figure 6-9 shows a simple scenario where incrementing a value by 1 done from two threads ends up with result of 1 instead of 2.

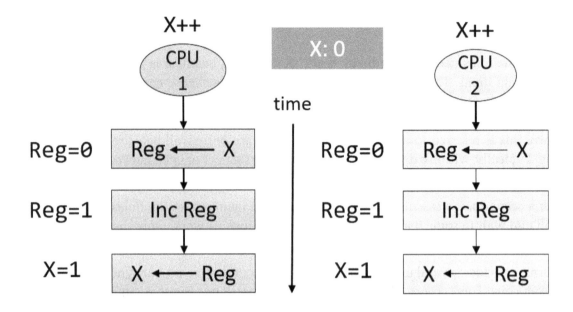

Should be: X=2

Figure 6-9: Concurrent increment

The example in figure 6-9 is extremely simplistic. With real CPUs there are other effects to consider, especially caching, which makes the shown scenario even more likely. CPU caching, store buffers and other aspects of modern CPUs is a non-trivial topic, well beyond the scope of this book.

Table 6-2 lists some of the Interlocked functions available for drivers use.

Table 6-2: Some Interlocked functions

Function	Description
`InterlockedIncrement / InterlockedIncrement16 / InterlockedIncrement64`	Atomically increment a 32/16/64 bit integer by one
`InterlockedDecrement / 16 / 64`	Atomically decrement a 32/16/64 bit integer by one.
`InterlockedAdd / InterlockedAdd64`	Atomically add one 32/64 bit integer to a variable.
`InterlockedExchange / 8 / 16 / 64`	Atomically exchange two 32/8/16/64 bit values.
`InterlockedCompareExchange / 64 / 128`	Atomically compare a variable with a value. If equal exchange with the provided value and return TRUE; otherwise, place the current value in the variable and return FALSE.

The `InterlockedCompareExchange` family of functions are used in *lock-free programming*, a programming technique to perform complex atomic operations without using software objects. This topic is well beyond the scope of this book.

 The functions in table 6-2 are also available in user mode, as these are not really functions, but rather CPU *intrinsics* - special instructions to the CPU.

Dispatcher Objects

The kernel provides a set of primitives known as *Dispatcher Objects*, also called *Waitable Objects*. These objects have a state called **signaled** and **non-signaled**, where the meaning of signaled and non-signaled depends on the type of object. They are called "waitable" because a thread can wait on such objects until they become signaled. While waiting the thread does not consume cpu cycles as it's in a *Waiting* state.

The primary functions used for waiting are `KeWaitForSingleObject` and `KeWaitForMultipleObjects`. Their prototypes (with simplified SAL annotations for clarity) are shown below:

```
NTSTATUS KeWaitForSingleObject (
    _In_ PVOID Object,
    _In_ KWAIT_REASON WaitReason,
    _In_ KPROCESSOR_MODE WaitMode,
    _In_ BOOLEAN Alertable,
    _In_opt_ PLARGE_INTEGER Timeout);

NTSTATUS KeWaitForMultipleObjects (
    _In_ ULONG Count,
    _In_reads_(Count) PVOID Object[],
    _In_ WAIT_TYPE WaitType,
    _In_ KWAIT_REASON WaitReason,
    _In_ KPROCESSOR_MODE WaitMode,
    _In_ BOOLEAN Alertable,
    _In_opt_ PLARGE_INTEGER Timeout,
    _Out_opt_ PKWAIT_BLOCK WaitBlockArray);
```

Here is a rundown of the arguments to these functions:

- *Object* - specifies the object to wait for. Note these functions work with objects, not handles. If you have a handle (maybe provided by user mode), call `ObReferenceObjectByHandle` to get the pointer to the object.

- *WaitReason* - specifies the wait reason. The list of wait reasons is pretty long, but drivers should typically set it to `Executive`, unless it's waiting because of a user request, and if so specify `UserRequest`.
- *WaitMode* - can be `UserMode` or `KernelMode`. Most drivers should specify `KernelMode`.
- *Alertable* - indicates if the thread should be in an alertable state during the wait. Alertable state allows delivering of user mode *Asynchronous Procedure Calls* (APCs). User mode APCs can be delivered if wait mode is `UserMode`. Most drivers should specify `FALSE`.
- *Timeout* - specifies the time to wait. If `NULL` is specified, the wait is indefinite - as long as it takes for the object to become signaled. The units of this argument are in 100nsec chunks, where a negative number is relative wait, while a positive number is absolute wait measured from January 1, 1601 midnight.
- *Count* - the number of objects to wait on.
- *Object[]* - an array of object pointers to wait on.
- *WaitType* - specifies whether to wait for all object to become signaled at once (`WaitAll`) or just one object (`WaitAny`).
- *WaitBlockArray* - an array of structures used internally to manage the wait operation. It's optional if the number of objects is <= `THREAD_WAIT_OBJECTS` (currently 3) - the kernel will use the built-in array present in each thread. If the number of objects is higher, the driver must allocate the correct size of structures from non-paged pool, and deallocate them after the wait is over.

The main return value from `KeWaitForSingleObject` are:

- `STATUS_SUCCESS` - the wait is satisfied because the object state has become signaled.
- `STATUS_TIMEOUT` - the wait is satisfied because the timeout has elapsed.

 Note that all return values from the wait functions pass the `NT_SUCCESS` macro with true.

`KeWaitForMultipleObjects` return values support `STATUS_TIMEOUT` just as `KeWaitForSingleObject`. `STATUS_SUCCESS` is returned if `WaitAll` wait type is specified and all objects became signaled. For `WaitAny` waits, if one of the object became signaled, the return value is its index in the array of objects.

 There are some fine details associated with the wait functions, especially if wait mode is `UserMode` and the wait is alertable. Check the WDK docs for the details.

Table 6-3 lists some of the common dispatcher objects and the meaning of *signaled* and *non-signaled* for these objects.

Table 6-3: Object Types and signaled meaning

Object Type	Signaled meaning	Non-Signaled meaning
Process	process has terminated (for whatever reason)	process has not terminated
Thread	thread has terminated (for whatever reason)	thread has not terminated
Mutex	mutex is free (unowned)	mutex is held
Event	event is set	event is reset
Semaphore	semaphore count is greater than zero	semaphore count is zero
Timer	timer has expired	timer has not yet expired
File	asynchronous I/O operation completed	asynchronous I/O operation is in progress

All the object types from table 6-3 are also exported to user mode. The primary waiting functions in user mode are `WaitForSingleObject` and `WaitForMultipleObjects`.

The following sections will discuss some of common object types useful for synchronization in drivers. Some other objects will discussed as well that are not dispatcher objects, but support waiting for thread synchronization.

Mutex

Mutex is the classic object for the canonical problem of one thread among many that can access a shared resource at any one time.

Mutex is sometimes referred to as *Mutant*. These are the same thing.

A mutex is signaled when it's free. Once a thread calls a wait function and the wait is satisfied, the mutex becomes non-signaled and the thread becomes the owner of the mutex. Ownership is very important for a mutex. It means the following:

- If a thread is the owner of a mutex, it's the only one that can release the mutex.
- A mutex can be acquired more than once by the same thread. The second attempt succeeds automatically since the thread is the current owner of the mutex. This also means the thread needs to release the mutex the same number of times it was acquired; only then the mutex becomes free (signaled) again.

Using a mutex requires allocating a `KMUTEX` structure from non-paged pool. The mutex API contains the following functions working on that `KMUTEX`:

- `KeInitializeMutex` must be called once to initialize the mutex.
- One of the waiting functions, passing the address of the allocated `KMUTEX` structure.

- KeReleaseMutex is called when a thread that is the owner of the mutex wants to release it.

Given the above functions, here is an example using a mutex to access some shared data so that only a single thread does so at a time:

```
KMUTEX MyMutex;
LIST_ENTRY DataHead;

void Init() {
    KeInitializeMutex(&MyMutex, 0);
}

void DoWork() {
    // wait for the mutex to be available

    KeWaitForSingleObject(&MyMutex, Executive, KernelMode, FALSE, nullptr);

    // access DataHead freely

    // once done, release the mutex

    KeReleaseMutex(&MyMutex, FALSE);
}
```

It's important to release the mutex no matter what, so it's better to use __try / __finally to make sure it's done in all circumstances:

```
void DoWork() {
    // wait for the mutex to be available

    KeWaitForSingleObject(&MyMutex, Executive, KernelMode, FALSE, nullptr);
    __try {
        // access DataHead freely

    }
    __finally {
        // once done, release the mutex

        KeReleaseMutex(&MyMutex, FALSE);
    }
}
```

Since using __try/__finally is a little awkward, we can use C++ to create a RAII wrapper for waits. This could also be used for other synchronization primitives.

First, we'll create a mutex wrapper that provides functions named Lock and Unlock:

```cpp
struct Mutex {
    void Init() {
        KeInitializeMutex(&_mutex, 0);
    }

    void Lock() {
        KeWaitForSingleObject(&_mutex, Executive, KernelMode, FALSE, nullptr);
    }

    void Unlock() {
        KeReleaseMutex(&_mutex, FALSE);
    }

private:
    KMUTEX _mutex;
};
```

Then we can create a generic RAII wrapper for waiting for any type that has a Lock and Unlock functions:

```cpp
template<typename TLock>
struct AutoLock {
    AutoLock(TLock& lock) : _lock(lock) {
        lock.Lock();
    }

    ~AutoLock() {
        _lock.Unlock();
    }

private:
    TLock& _lock;
};
```

With these definitions in place, we can replace the code using the mutex with the following:

```
Mutex MyMutex;

void Init() {
    MyMutex.Init();
}

void DoWork() {
    AutoLock<Mutex> locker(MyMutex);

    // access DataHead freely
}
```

 Since locking should be done for as little time as possible, we can use an artificial scope with AutoLock to acquire the mutex as late as possible and release it as soon as possible.

 With C++17, AutoLock can be used without specifying the type like so: AutoLock locker(MyMutex);. Since Visual Studio currently uses C++14 as its default language standard, you'll have to change that in the project properties under the C++ node / Language / C++ Language Standard.

We'll use the same AutoLock type with other synchronization primitives as well.

 What happens if a mutex is not released by a thread and that thread dies? In that case, the kernel releases the mutex explicitly (since no other thread can do so), and the next thread that gets ownership of that mutex receives in its wait function STATUS_ABANDONED - an abandoned mutex. The mutex is acquired normally as far as the other thread is concerned, but this indicates some bug or abnormal condition that caused the first thread to terminate before releasing the mutex.

Fast Mutex

A fast mutex is an alternative to the classic mutex, providing better performance. It's not a dispatcher object, and so has its own API for acquiring and releasing the mutex. It has the following characteristics compared with a regular mutex:

- A fast mutex can't be acquired recursively. Doing so causes a deadlock.
- When a fast mutex is acquired the CPU IRQL is raised to APC_LEVEL (1). This prevents any delivery of APCs to that thread.
- A fast mutex can only be waited on indefinitely - there is no way to specify a timeout.

Because of the first two bullets above, the fast mutex is slightly faster than a regular mutex. In fact, most drivers requiring a mutex use a fast mutex unless there is a compelling reason to use a regular mutex.

A fast mutex is initialized by allocating a FAST_MUTEX structure from non-paged pool and calling ExInitializeFastMutex. Acquiring the mutex is done with ExAcquireFastMutex or ExAcquire-FastMutexUnsafe (if the current IRQL happens to be APC_LEVEL already). Releasing a fast mutex is acomplished with ExReleaseFastMutex or ExReleaseFastMutexUnsafe.

 The fast mutex is not exposed to user mode. User mode code can only use the regular mutex.

From a general usage perspective, the fast mutex is equivalent to a regular mutex. It's just a bit faster.

We can create a C++ wrapper over a fast mutex, so that acquiring and releasing it can be automatically achieved with the AutoLock RAII class defined in the previous section:

```
// fastmutex.h

class FastMutex {
public:
    void Init();

    void Lock();
    void Unlock();

private:
    FAST_MUTEX _mutex;
};

// fastmutex.cpp

#include "FastMutex.h"

void FastMutex::Init() {
    ExInitializeFastMutex(&_mutex);
}

void FastMutex::Lock() {
    ExAcquireFastMutex(&_mutex);
}

void FastMutex::Unlock() {
```

```
    ExReleaseFastMutex(&_mutex);
}
```

Semaphore

The primary goal of a semaphore is to limit something, such as the length of a queue. The semaphore is initialized with its maximum and initial count (typically set to the maximum value) by calling KeInitializeSemaphore. While its internal count is greater than zero, the semaphore is signaled. A thread that calls KeWaitForSingleObject has its wait satisfied and the semaphore count drops by one. This continues until the count reaches zero, at which point the semaphore becomes non-signaled.

As an example, imagine a queue of work items managed by the driver. Some threads want to add items to the queue. Each such thread calls KeWaitForSingleObject to obtain one "count" of the semaphore. As long as the count is greater than zero, the thread continues and adds an item to the queue, increasing its length, and semaphore "loses" a count. Some other threads are tasked with processing work items from the queue. Once a thread removes an item from the queue, it calls KeReleaseSemaphore that increments the count of the semaphore, moving it to the signaled state again, allowing potentially another thread to make progress and add a new item to the queue.

 KeReleaseSemaphore can increment the semaphore's count by more than one, if it so wishes.

 Is a semaphore with a maximum count of one equivalent to a mutex? At first, it seems to be true, but this is not the case. A semaphore lacks ownership, meaning one thread can acquire the semaphore and another can release it. This is a strength, not a weakness, as described in the above example. A Semaphore's purpose is very different from a mutex' one.

Event

An event encapsulates a boolean flag - either true (signaled) or false (non-signaled). The primary purpose of an event is to signal something has happened, to provide *flow synchronization*. For example, if some condition becomes true, an event can be set, and a bunch of threads can be released from waiting and continue working on some data that perhaps is now ready for processing.

The are two types of events, the type being specified at event initialization time:

- Notification event (manual reset) - when this event is set, it releases any number of waiting threads, and the event state remains set (signaled) until explicitly reset.

- Synchronization event (auto reset) - when this event is set, it releases at most one thread (no matter how many are waiting for the event), and once released the event goes back to the reset (non-signaled) state automatically.

An event is created by allocating a KEVENT structure from non-paged pool and then calling KeInitializeEvent to initialize it, specifying the event type (NotificationEvent or SynchronizationEvent) and the initial event state (signaled or non-signaled). Waiting for an event is done normally with the KeWaitXxx functions. Calling KeSetEvent sets the event to the signaled state, while calling KeResetEvent or KeClearEvent resets it (non-signaled state) (the latter function being a bit quicker as it does not return the previous state of the event).

Executive Resource

The classic synchronization problem of accessing a shared resource by multiple threads was dealt with by using a mutex or fast mutex. This works, but mutexes are pessimistic, meaning they allow a single thread to access a shared resource. That may be unfortunate in cases where multiple threads access a shared resource by reading only.

In cases where it's possible to distinguish data changes (writes) vs. just looking at the data (reading) - there is a possible optimization. A thread that requires access to the shared resource can declare its intentions - read or write. If it declares read, other threads declaring read can do so concurrently, improving performance. This is especially useful if the shared data changes slowly, i.e. there are considerably more reads than writes.

> Mutexes by their very nature are concurrency killers, since they enforce a single thread at a time execution. This makes them always work at the expense of possible performance gains with concurrency.

The kernel provides yet another synchronization primitive that is geared towards this scenario, known as *single writer, multiple readers*. This object is the *Executive Resource*, another special object which is not a dispatcher object.

Initializing an executive resource is done by allocating an ERESOURCE structure from non-paged pool and calling ExInitializeResourceLite. Once initialized, threads can acquire either the exclusive lock (for writes) using ExAcquireResourceExclusiveLite or the shared lock by calling ExAcquireResourceSharedLite. Once done the work, a thread releases the executive resource with ExReleaseResourceLite (no matter whether it acquired as exclusive or not). The requirement for using the acquire and release functions is that normal kernel APCs must be disabled. This can be done with KeEnterCtriticalRegion just before the acquire call, and then KeLeaveCriticalRegion just after the release call. The following code snippet demonstrates that:

```
ERESOURCE resource;

void WriteData() {
    KeEnterCriticalRegion();
    ExAcquireResourceExclusiveLite(&resource, TRUE);    // wait until acquired

    // Write to the data

    ExReleaseResourceLite(&resource);
    KeLeaveCriticalRegion();
}
```

Since these calls are so common when working with executive resources, there are functions that perform both operations with a single call:

```
void WriteData() {
    ExEnterCriticalRegionAndAcquireResourceExclusive(&resource);

    // Write to the data

    ExReleaseResourceAndLeaveCriticalRegion(&resource);
}
```

A similar function exists for shared acquisition, ExEnterCriticalRegionAndAcquireResource-Shared. Finally, before freeing the memory the resource occupies, call ExDeleteResourceLite to remove the resource from the kernel's resource list:

```
NTSTATUS ExDeleteResourceLite(
    _Inout_ PERESOURCE Resource);
```

There are other functions for working with executive resources for some specialized cases. Consult the WDK documentation for more information.

 Create appropriate C++ RAII wrappers for executive resources.

High IRQL Synchronization

The sections on synchronization so far have dealt with threads waiting for various types of objects. However, in some scenarios, threads cannot wait - specifically, when the processor's IRQL is DISPATCH_LEVEL (2) or higher. This section discusses these scenarios and how to handle them.

Let's examine an example scenario: A driver has a timer, set up with KeSetTimer and uses a DPC to execute code when the timer expires. At the same time, other functions in the driver, such a IRP_MJ_DEVICE_CONTROL may execute at the same time (runs at IRQL 0). If both these functions need to access a shared resource (e.g. a linked list), they must synchronize access to prevent data corruption.

The problem is that a DPC cannot call KeWaitForSingleObject or any other waiting function - calling any of these is fatal. So how can these functions synchronize access?

The simple case is where the system has a single CPU. In this case, when accessing the shared resource, the low IRQL function just needs to raise IRQL to DISPATCH_LEVEL and then access the resource. During that time a DPC cannot interfere this code since the CPU's IRQL is already 2. Once the code is done with the shared resource, it can lower the IRQL back to zero, allowing the DPC to execute. This prevents execution of these routines at the same time. Figure 6-10 shows this setup.

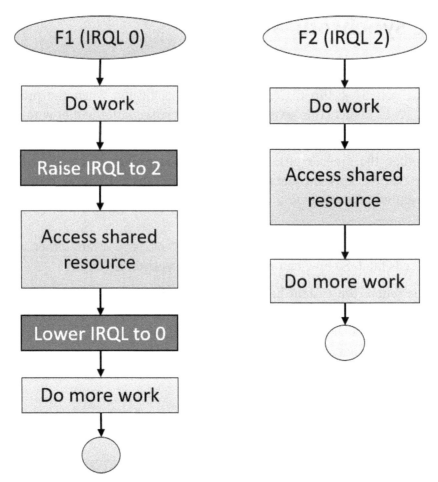

Figure 6-10: High-IRQL synchronization by manipulating IRQL

In standard systems, where there is more than one CPU, this synchronization method is not enough, because the IRQL is a CPU's property, not a system-wide property. If one CPU's IRQL is raised to 2, if a DPC needs to execute, it can interfere another CPU whose IRQL may be zero. In this case, it's possible both functions will execute at the same time, accessing the shared resource, causing a data race.

How can we solve that? We need something like a mutex, but that can synchronize between processors - not threads. That's because when the CPU's IRQL is 2 or higher, the thread itself loses meaning because the scheduler cannot do work on that CPU. This kind of object actually exists - the *Spin Lock*.

The Spin Lock

The Spin Lock is a simple bit in memory that provides atomic test and modify operations via an API. When a CPU tries to acquire a spin lock and it's not currently free, the CPU keeps spinning on the spin lock, busy waiting for it to be released by another CPU (remember, putting the thread into a waiting state cannot be done at IRQL DISPATCH_LEVEL or higher).

In the scenario depicted in the previous section, a spin lock would need to be allocated and initialized. Each function that requires access to the shared data needs to raise IRQL to 2 (if not already there), acquire the spin lock, perform the work on the shared data and finally release the spin lock and lower IRQL back (if applicable; not for a DPC). This chain of events is shown in figure 6-11.

Creating a spin lock requires allocating a KSPIN_LOCK structure from non-paged pool, and calling KeInitializeSpinLock. This puts the spin lock in the unowned state.

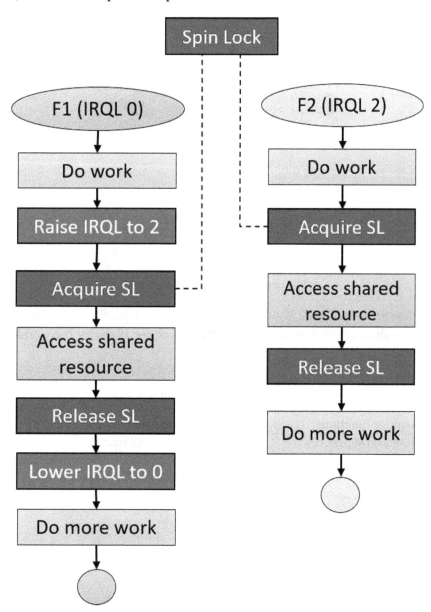

Figure 6-11: High-IRQL synchronization with a Spin Lock

Acquiring a spin lock is always a two-step process: first, raise the IRQL to the proper level, which is the highest level of any function trying to synchronize access to a shared resource. In the previous example, this *associated IRQL* is 2. Second, acquire the spin lock. These two steps are combined by using the appropriate API. This process is depicted in figure 6-12.

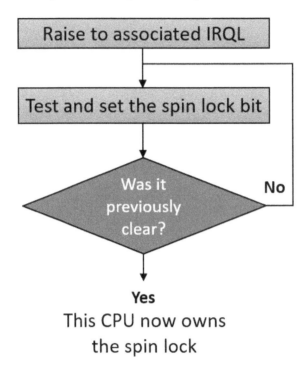

Figure 6-12: Acquiring a Spin Lock

Acquiring and releasing a spin lock is done using an API that performs the two steps outlined in figure 6-12. Table 6-4 shows the relevant APIs and the associated IRQL for the spin locks they operate on.

Table 6-4: APIs for working with spin locks

IRQL	Acquire function	Release function	Remarks
2	KeAcquireSpinLock	KeReleaseSpinLock	
2	KeAcquireSpinLockAtDpcLevel	KeReleaseSpinLockFromDpcLevel	(1)
Device IRQL	KeAcquireInterruptSpinLock	KeReleaseInterruptSpinLock	(2)
HIGH_LEVEL	ExInterlockedXxx	(none)	(3)

Remarks on table 6-4:

1. Can be called at IRQL 2 only. Provides an optimization that just acquires the spin lock without changing IRQLs. Canonical scenario is in a DPC routine.
2. Useful for synchronizing an ISR with any other function. Hardware based drivers with an interrupt source use these routines. The argument is an interrupt object - the spin lock is part of it.
3. 3 functions for manipulating LIST_ENTRY-based linked lists. These functions use the provided spin lock and raise IRQL to HIGH_LEVEL. Because of the high IRQL, these routines can be used in any situation, since raising IRQL is always safe.

If you acquire a spin lock, be sure to release it in the same function. Otherwise, you're risking a deadlock.

 Where do spin locks come from? The scenario described here requires the driver to allocate its own spin lock to protect concurrent access to its own data from high-IRQL functions. Some spin locks exist as part of other objects, such as the KINTERRUPT object used by hardware based drivers that handle interrupts. Another example is a system-wide spin lock known as the *Cancel spin lock*, which is acquired by the kernel before calling a cancellation routine registered by a driver. This is the only case where a driver released a spin lock it has not acquired explicitly.

 If several CPUs try to acquire the same spin lock at the same time, which CPU gets the spin lock first? Normally, there is no order - the CPU with fastest electrons wins :). The kernel does provide an alternative, called *queued spin locks* that serve CPUs on a FIFO basis. These only work with IRQL DISPATCH_LEVEL. The relevant APIs are KeAcquireInStackQueuedSpinLock and KeReleaseInStackQueuedSpinLock. Check the WDK documentation for more details.

 Write a C++ wrapper for a DISPATCH_LEVEL spin lock that works with the AutoLock RAII class defined earlier in this chapter.

Work Items

Sometimes there is a need to run a piece of code on a different thread than the executing one. One way to do that is to create a thread explicitly and task it with running the code. The kernel provides functions that allow a driver to create a separate thread of execution: PsCreateSystemThread and IoCreateSystemThread (available in Windows 8+). These functions are appropriate if the driver needs to run code in the background for a long time. However, for time-bound operations, it's better to use a kernel-provided thread pool that will execute your code on some system worker thread.

 IoCreateSystemThread is preferred because is allows associating a device or driver object with the thread. This makes the I/O system add a reference to the object, which makes sure the driver cannot be unloaded prematurely while the thread is still executing.

 A driver created thread must terminate itself eventually by calling PsTerminateSystemThread. This function never returns if successful.

Work items is the term used to describe functions queued to the system thread pool. A driver can allocate and initialize a work item, pointing to the function the driver wishes to execute, and then the work item can be queued to the pool. This seems very similar to a DPC, the primary difference being work items always execute at IRQL `PASSIVE_LEVEL`, meaning this mechanism can be used to perform operations at IRQL 0 from functions running at IRQL 2. For example, if a DPC routine needs to perform an operation that is not allowed at IRQL 2 (such as opening a file), it can use a work item to perform these operations.

Creating and initializing a work item can be done in one of two ways:

- Allocate and initialize the work item with `IoAllocateWorkItem`. The function return a pointer to the opaque `IO_WORKITEM`. When finished with the work item it must be freed with `IoFreeWorkItem`.
- Allocate an `IO_WORKITEM` structure dynamically with size provided by `IoSizeofWorkItem`. Then call `IoInitializeWorkItem`. When finished with the work item, call `IoUninitialize-WorkItem`.

These functions accept a device object, so make sure the driver is not unloaded while there is a work item queued or executing.

 There is another set of APIs for work items, all start with `Ex`, such as `ExQueueWorkItem`. These functions do not associate the work item with anything in the driver, so theoretically it's possible for the driver to be unloaded while a work item is still in play. Always prefer using the `Io` functions.

To queue the work item, call `IoQueueWorkItem`. Here is its definition:

```
viud IoQueueWorkItem(
    _Inout_ PIO_WORKITEM IoWorkItem,            // the work item
    _In_ PIO_WORKITEM_ROUTINE WorkerRoutine,    // the function to be called
    _In_ WORK_QUEUE_TYPE QueueType,             // queue type
    _In_opt_ PVOID Context);                    // driver-defined value
```

The callback function the driver needs to provide has the following prototype:

```
IO_WORKITEM_ROUTINE WorkItem;

void WorkItem(
  _In_      PDEVICE_OBJECT DeviceObject,
  _In_opt_ PVOID          Context);
```

The system thread pool has several queues, based on the thread priorities that serve these work items. There are several levels defined shown here:

```
typedef enum _WORK_QUEUE_TYPE {
    CriticalWorkQueue,          // priority 13
    DelayedWorkQueue,           // priority 12
    HyperCriticalWorkQueue,     // priority 15
    NormalWorkQueue,            // priority 8
    BackgroundWorkQueue,        // priority 7
    RealTimeWorkQueue,          // priority 18
    SuperCriticalWorkQueue,     // priority 14
    MaximumWorkQueue,
    CustomPriorityWorkQueue = 32
} WORK_QUEUE_TYPE;
```

The documentation indicates `DelayedWorkQueue` must be used, but actually any other supported level can be used.

 There is another function that can be used to queue a work item: `IoQueueWorkItemEx`. This function uses a different callback that has an added parameter which is the work item itself. This is useful if the work item function needs to free the work item before it exits.

Summary

In this chapter we looked at various kernel mechanisms driver developers should be aware of and use. In the next chapter we'll take a closer look at *I/O Request Packets* (IRPs).

Chapter 7: The I/O Request Packet

After a typical driver completes its initialization in `DriverEntry`, its primary job is to handle requests. These requests are packaged as the semi-documented *I/O Request Packet* (IRP) structure. In this chapter, we'll take a deeper look at IRPs and how a driver handles common IRP types.

In This chapter:

- **Introduction to IRPs**
- **Device Nodes**
- **IRP and I/O Stack Location**
- **Dispatch Routines**
- **Accessing User Buffers**
- **Putting it All Together: The Zero Driver**

Introduction to IRPs

An IRP is a structure that is allocated from non-paged pool typically by one of the "managers" in the Executive (I/O Manager, Plug & Play Manager, Power Manager), but can also be allocated by the driver, perhaps for passing a request to another driver. Whichever entity allocating the IRP is also responsible for freeing it.

An IRP is never allocated alone. It's always accompanied by one or more I/O Stack Location structures (`IO_STACK_LOCATION`). In fact, when an IRP is allocated, the caller must specify how many I/O stack locations need to be allocated with the IRP. These I/O stack locations follow the IRP directly in memory. The number of I/O stack locations is the number of device objects in the device stack. We'll discuss device stacks in the next section. When a driver receives an IRP, it gets a pointer to the `IRP` structure itself, knowing it's followed by a set of I/O stack location, one of which is for the driver's use. To get the correct I/O stack location that driver calls `IoGetCurrentIrpStackLocation` (actually a macro). Figure 7-1 shows a conceptual view of an IRP and its associated I/O stack locations.

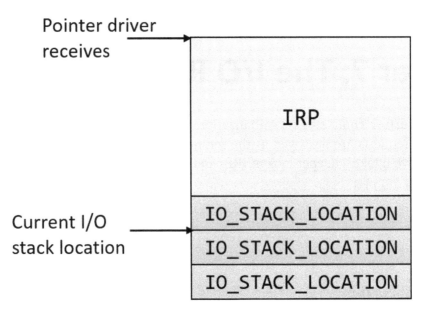

Figure 7-1: IRP and its I/O stack locations

The parameters of the request are somehow "split" between the main IRP structure and the current IO_STACK_LCATION.

Device Nodes

The I/O system in Windows is device-centric, rather than driver-centric. This has several implications:

- Device objects can be named and handles to device objects can be opened. The CreateFile function accepts a symbolic link that lead to a device object name. CreateFile cannot accept a driver's name as argument.
- Windows supports device layering - one device can be layered on top of another. This means that any request destined for the lower device will first reach the uppermost layer. This layering is mostly common for hardware-based device, but it works with any device type.

Figure 7-2 shows an example of several layers of devices, "stacked" one on top of the other. This set of devices is known as a *device stack*, sometimes referred to as *device node*. In the figure there are six layers, or six devices. Each of these devices is actually a DEVICE_OBJECT structure created by calling the standard IoCreateDevice function.

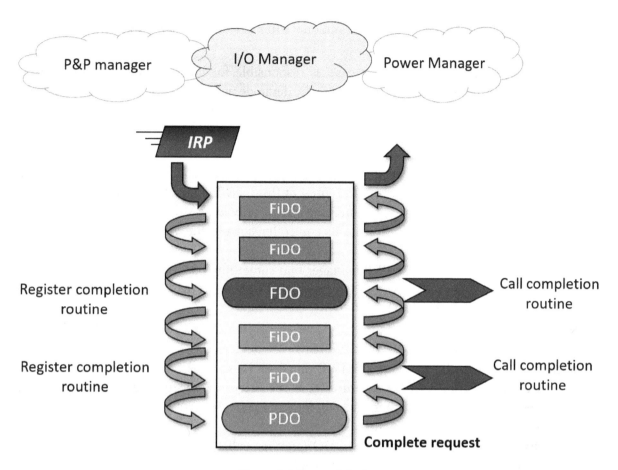

Figure 7-2: Layered devices

The different device objects that comprise the device node (devnode) layers are named according to their role in the devnode. These roles are relevant in a hardware-based device node.

> All the device objects in figure 7-2 are just DEVICE_OBJECT structures, each created by a different driver that is in charge of that layer. More generically, this kind of device node does not have to be related to hardware-based device drivers.

Here is a quick rundown of the meaning of the labels present in figure 7-2:

- *PDO (Physical Device Object)* - Despite the name, there is nothing "physical" about it. This device object is created by a bus driver - the driver that is in charge of the particular bus (e.g. PCI, USB, etc.). This device object represents the fact that there is some device in that slot on that bus.
- *FDO (Functional Device Object)* - This device object is created by the "real" driver; that is, the driver typically provided by the hardware's vendor that understands the details of the device intimately.

- *FiDO* (*Filter Device Object*) - These are optional filter devices created by filter drivers.

The Plug & Play (P&P) Manager in this case, is responsible for loading the appropriate drivers, starting from the bottom. As an example, suppose the devnode in figure 7-2 represents a set of drivers that manage a PCI network card. The sequence of events leading to the creation of this devnode can be summarized as follows:

1. The PCI bus driver (*pci.sys*) recognizes the fact that there is something in that particular slot. It creates a PDO (`IoCreateDevice`) to represent this fact. The bus driver has no idea whether this a network card, video card or something else; it only knows there is something there and can extract the basic information from its controller, such as the Vendor ID and Device ID of the device.
2. The PCI bus driver notifies the P&P manager that something has changed on its bus.
3. The P&P manager requests a list of PDOs managed by the bus driver. It receives back a list of PDOs, in which this new PDO is included.
4. Now the P&P manager's job is to find and load the proper driver for that new PDO. It issues a query to the bus driver to request the full hardware device ID.
5. With this hardware ID in hand, the P&P manager looks in the registry at *HKLM\System\ CurrentControlSet\Enum\PCI\(HardwareID)*. If the driver has been loaded before, it will be registered there, and the P&P manager will load it. Figure 7-3 shows an example hardware ID in the registry (NVIDIA display driver).
6. The driver is loaded, and creates the FDO (another call to `IoCreateDevice`), but adds an additional call to `IoAttachDeviceToDeviceStack`, thus attaching itself over the previous layer (typically the PDO).

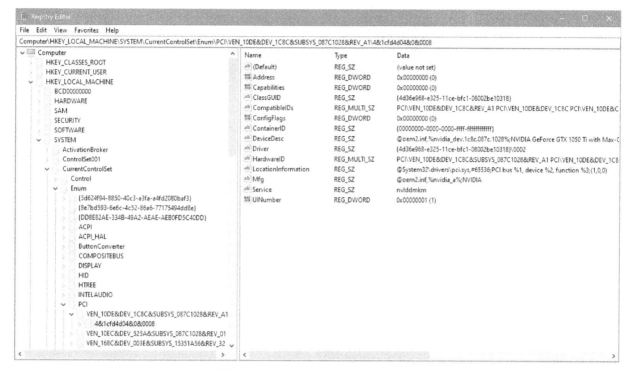

Figure 7-3: Hardware ID information

 The value **Service** in figure 7-3 indirectly points to the actual driver at *HKLMSystemCutr-rentControlSetServices{ServiceName}* where all drivers must be registered.

The filter device objects are loaded as well, if they are registered correctly in the Registry. Lower filters (below the FDO) load in order, from the bottom. Each filter driver loaded creates its own device object and attaches it on top of the previous layer. Upper filters work the same way but are loaded after the FDO. All this means that with operational P&P devnodes, there are at least two layers - PDO and FDO, but there could be more if filters are involved. We'll look at basic filter development for hardware-based drivers in chapter 11.

> Full discussion of Plug & Play and the exact way this kind of devnode is built is beyond the scope of this book. The previous description is incomplete and glances over some details, but it should give you the basic idea. Every devnode is built from the bottom up, regardless of whether this is related to hardware or not.

Lower filters are searched in two locations: the hardware ID key shown in figure 7-3 and in the corresponding class based on the **ClassGuid** value listed under *HKLMSystemCurrentControlSet-ControlClasses*. The value name itself is **LowerFilters** and is a multiple string value holding service names, pointing to the same *Services* key. Upper filters are searched in a similar manner, but the value name is **UpperFilters**. Figure 7-4 shows the registry settings for the *DiskDrive* class where there is a lower filter and an upper filter.

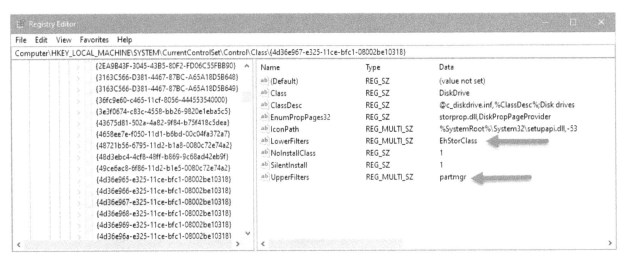

Figure 7-4: The *DiskDrive* class key

IRP Flow

Figure 7-2 shows an example devnode, whether related to hardware or not. An IRP is created by one of the managers in the Executive - for most of our drivers that is the I/O Manager.

The manager creates an IRP with its associated IO_STACK_LOCATIONs - six in the example in figure 7-2. The manager initializes the main IRP structure and the first I/O stack location only. Then it passes the IRP's pointer to the uppermost layer.

A driver receives the IRP in its appropriate dispatch routine. For example, if this is a Read IRP, then the driver will be called in its IRP_MJ_READ index of its MajorFunction array from its driver object. At this point a driver has several options when dealing with IRP:

1. Pass the request down - if the driver's device is not the last device in the devnode, the driver can pass the request along if it's not interesting for the driver. This is typically done by a filter driver that receives a request that it's not interested in, and in order not to hurt the functionality of the device (since the request is actually destined to a lower-layer device), the driver can pass it down. This must be done with two calls:

- Call IoSkipCurrentIrpStackLocation to make sure the next device in line is going to see the same information given to this device - it should see the same I/O stack location.
- Call IoCallDriver passing the lower device object (which the driver received at the time it called IoAttachDeviceToDeviceStack) and the IRP.

Before passing the request down, the driver must prepare the next I/O stack location with proper information. Since the I/O manager only initializes the first I/O stack location, it's the responsibility of each driver to initialize the next one. One way to do that is to call `IoCopyIrpStackLocationToNext` before calling `IoCallDriver`. This works, but is a bit wasteful if the driver just wants the lower layer to see the same information. Calling `IoSkipCurrentIrpStackLocation` is an optimization which does decrements the current I/O stack location pointer inside the IRP, which is later incremented by `IoCallDriver`, so the next layer sees the same `IO_STACK_LOCATION` this driver has seen. This decrement/increment dance is more efficient than making an actual copy.

2. Handle the IRP fully - the driver receiving the IRP can just handle the IRP without propagating it down by eventually calling `IoCompleteRequest`. Any lower devices will never see the request.

3. Do a combination of (1) and (2) - the driver can examine the IRP, do something (such as log the request), and then pass it down. Or it can make some changes to the next I/O stack location, and then pass the request down.

4. Pass the request down and be notified when the request completes by a lower layer device - Any layer (except the lowest one) can set up an I/O completion routine by calling `IoSetCompletion-Routine` before passing the request down. When one of the lower layers completes the request, the driver's completion routine will be called.

5. Start some asynchronous IRP handling - the driver may want to handle the request, but if the request is lengthy (typical of a hardware driver, but also could be the case for a software driver), the driver may mark the IRP as pending by calling `IoMarkIrpPending` and return a `STATUS_PENDING` from its dispatch routine. Eventually, it will have to complete the IRP.

Once some layer calls `IoCompleteRequest`, the IRP turns around and starts "climbing" back towards the originator of the IRP (typically on of the Managers). If completion routines have been registered, they will be invoked in reverse order of registration - i.e. from bottom to top.

In most drivers in this book, layering will not be considered, since the driver is most likely to be part of a single layer devnode. The driver will handle the request then and there.

We'll discuss other aspects of IRP handling in filter drivers in chapter 11.

IRP and I/O Stack Location

Figure 7-5 shows some of the important fields in an IRP.

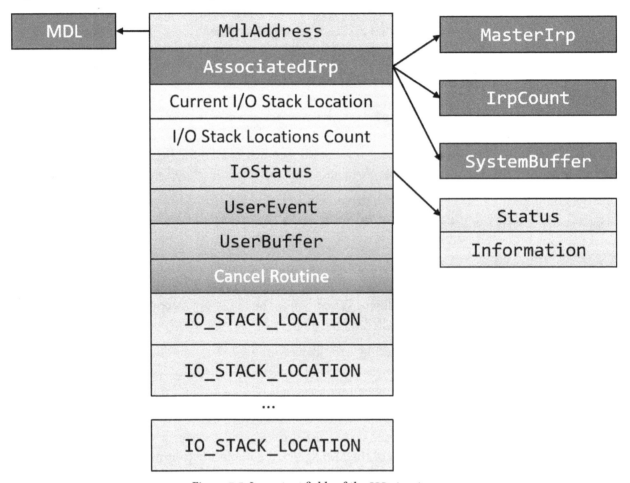

Figure 7-5: Important fields of the IRP structure

Here is a quick rundown of these fields:

- **IoStatus** - contains the Status (NT_STATUS) of the IRP and an Information field. The Information field is a polymorphic one, typed as ULONG_PTR (32 or 64 bit integer), but its meaning depends on the type of IRP. For example, for Read and Write IRPs, its meaning is the number of bytes transferred in the operation.
- **UserBuffer** - contains the raw buffer pointer to the user's buffer for relevant IRPs. Read and Write IRPs, for instance, store the user's buffer pointer in this field. In DeviceIoConttrol IRPs, this points to the output buffer provided in the request.
- **UserEvent** - this is a pointer to an event object (KEVENT) that was provided by a client if the call is asynchronous and such an event was supplied. From user mode, this event can be provided (with a HANDLE) in a OVERLAPPED structure that is mandatory for invoking I/O operations asynchronously.

- **AssociatedIrp** - this union holds three members, only one (at most) of which is valid:
  - **SystemBuffer** - the most often used member. This points to a system-allocated non-paged pool buffer used for Buffered I/O operations. See the section "Buffered I/O" later in this chapter for the details.
  - **MasterIrp** - A pointer to a "master" IRP, if this IRP is an *associated IRP*. This idea is supported by the I/O manager, where one IRP is a "master" that may have several "associated" IRPs. Once all the associated IRPs complete, the master IRP is completed automatically. MasterIrp is valid for an associated IRP - it points to the master IRP.
  - **IrpCount** - for the master IRP itself, this field indicates the number of associated IRPs associated with this master IRP.

> Usage of master and associated IRPs is pretty rare. We will not be using this mechanism in this book.

- **Cancel Routine** - a pointer to a cancel routine that is invoked (if not NULL) if the operation is asked to be canceled, such as with the user mode functions CancelIo and CancelIoEx. Software drivers rarely need cancellation routines, so we will not be using those in this book.
- **MdlAddress** - points to an optional *Memory Descriptor List* (MDL). An MDL is a kernel data structure that knows how to describe a buffer in RAM. MdlAddress is used primarily with Direct I/O (see the section "Direct I/O" later in this chapter).

Every IRP is accompanied by one or more IO_STACK_LOCATIONs. Figure 7-6 shows the important fields in an IO_STACK_LOCATION.

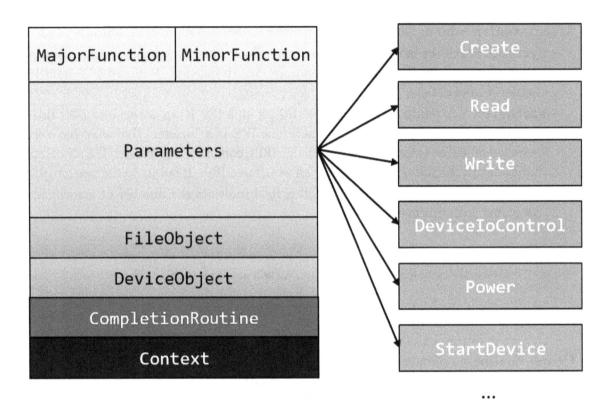

Figure 7-6: Important fields of the IO_STACK_LOCATION structure

Here's a rundown of the fields shown in figure 7-6:

- **MajorFunction** - this is the major function of the IRP (IRP_MJ_CREATE, IRP_MJ_READ, etc.). This field is sometimes useful if the driver points more than one major function code to the same handling routine. In that routine, the driver may want to distinguish the exact function using this field.
- **MinorFunction** - some IRP types have minor functions. These are IRP_MJ_PNP, IRP_MJ_-POWER and IRP_MJ_SYSTEM_CONTROL (WMI). Typical code for these handlers has a switch statement based on the MinorFunction. We will not be using these types of IRPs in this book, except in the case of filter drivers for hardware based devices, which we'll examine in some detail in chapter 11.
- **FileObject** - the FILE_OBJECT associated with this IRP. Not needed in most cases, but is available for dispatch routines that do.
- **DeviceObject** - the device object associated with this IRP. Dispatch routines receive a pointer to this, so typically accessing this field is not needed.
- **CompletionRoutine** - the completion routine that is set for the *previous* (upper) layer (set with IoSetCompletionRoutine).
- **Context** - the argument to pass to the completion routine (if any).
- **Parameters** - this monstrous union contains multiple structures, each valid for a particular operation. For example, in a Read (IRP_MJ_READ) operation, the Parameters.Read structure field should be used to get more information about the Read operation.

The current I/O stack location obtained with IoGetCurrentIrpStackLocation hosts most of the parameters of the request in the Parameters union. It's up to the driver to access the correct structure, as we've already seen in chapter 4 and will see again in this and subsequent chapters.

Viewing IRP Information

While debugging or analyzing kernel dumps, a couple of commands may be useful for searching or examining IRPs.

The !irpfind command can be used to find IRPs - either all IRPs, or IRPs that meet certain criteria. Using !irpfind without any arguments searches the non-paged pool(s) for all IRPs. Check out the debugger documentation on how to specify specific criteria to limit the search. Here's an example of some output when searching for all IRPs:

```
lkd> !irpfind
Unable to get offset of nt!_MI_VISIBLE_STATE.SpecialPool
Unable to get value of nt!_MI_VISIBLE_STATE.SessionSpecialPool

Scanning large pool allocation table for tag 0x3f707249 (Irp?) (ffffbf0a87610000 : f\
fffbf0a87910000)

   Irp            [ Thread ]          irpStack: (Mj,Mn)  DevObj          [Driver]      \
     MDL Process
ffffbf0aa795ca30 [ffffbf0a7fcde080] irpStack: ( c, 2)   ffffbf0a74d20050 [ \FileSyste\
m\Ntfs]
ffffbf0a9a8ef010 [ffffbf0a7fcde080] irpStack: ( c, 2)   ffffbf0a74d20050 [ \FileSyste\
m\Ntfs]
ffffbf0a8e68ea20 [ffffbf0a7fcde080] irpStack: ( c, 2)   ffffbf0a74d20050 [ \FileSyste\
m\Ntfs]
ffffbf0a90deb710 [ffffbf0a808a1080] irpStack: ( c, 2)   ffffbf0a74d20050 [ \FileSyste\
m\Ntfs]
ffffbf0a99d1da90 [0000000000000000] Irp is complete (CurrentLocation 10 > StackCount\
 9)
ffffbf0a74cec940 [0000000000000000] Irp is complete (CurrentLocation 8 > StackCount \
7)
ffffbf0aa0640a20 [ffffbf0a7fcde080] irpStack: ( c, 2)   ffffbf0a74d20050 [ \FileSyste\
m\Ntfs]
ffffbf0a89acf4e0 [ffffbf0a7fcde080] irpStack: ( c, 2)   ffffbf0a74d20050 [ \FileSyste\
m\Ntfs]
ffffbf0a89acfa50 [ffffbf0a7fcde080] irpStack: ( c, 2)   ffffbf0a74d20050 [ \FileSyste\
m\Ntfs]

(truncated)
```

Faced with a specific IRP, the command !irp examines the IRP, providing a nice overview of its data. As always, the dt command can be used with the _IRP type to look at the entire IRP structure. Here's an example of one IRP viewed with !irp:

```
kd> !irp ffffbf0a8bbada20
Irp is active with 13 stacks 12 is current (= 0xffffbf0a8bbade08)
 No Mdl: No System Buffer: Thread ffffbf0a7fcde080:  Irp stack trace.
     cmd  flg cl Device   File     Completion-Context
 [N/A(0), N/A(0)]
     0  0 00000000 00000000 00000000-00000000


    Args: 00000000 00000000 00000000 00000000
 [N/A(0), N/A(0)]
     0  0 00000000 00000000 00000000-00000000

(truncated)

    Args: 00000000 00000000 00000000 00000000
 [N/A(0), N/A(0)]
     0  0 00000000 00000000 00000000-00000000


    Args: 00000000 00000000 00000000 00000000
>[IRP_MJ_DIRECTORY_CONTROL(c), N/A(2)]
     0 e1 ffffbf0a74d20050 ffffbf0a7f52f790 fffff8015c0b50a0-ffffbf0a91d99010 Success\
 Error Cancel pending
        \FileSystem\Ntfs
         Args: 00004000 00000051 00000000 00000000
 [IRP_MJ_DIRECTORY_CONTROL(c), N/A(2)]
     0  0 ffffbf0a60e83dc0 ffffbf0a7f52f790 00000000-00000000
        \FileSystem\FltMgr
     Args: 00004000 00000051 00000000 00000000
```

The !irp commands lists the I/O stack locations and the information stored in them.

Dispatch Routines

We've seen already in chapter 4 that one important aspect of DriverEntry is setting up dispatch routines. These are the functions connected with major function codes. The majorFunction field in DRIVER_OBJECT is the array of function pointers index by the major function code.

All dispatch routines have the same prototype, repeated here for convenience using the DRIVER_-DISPATCH typedef from the WDK (somewhat simplified for clarity):

```
typedef NTSTATUS DRIVER_DISPATCH (
    _In_ PDEVICE_OBJECT DeviceObject,
    _Inout_ PIRP Irp);
```

The relevant dispatch routine (based on the major function code) is the first routine in a driver that sees the request. Normally, it's called by the requesting thread context, i.e. the thread that called the relevant API (e.g. ReadFile) in IRQL PASSIVE_LEVEL (0). However, it's possible that a filter driver sitting on top of this device sent the request down in a different context - it may be some other thread unrelated to the original requestor and even in higher IRQL, such as DISPATCH_LEVEL (2). Robust drivers need to be ready to deal with this kind of situation, even though for software drivers this "inconvenient" context is rare. We'll discuss the way to properly deal with this situation in the section "Accessing User Buffers", later in this chapter.

All dispatch routines follow a certain set of operations:

1. Check for errors - A dispatch routine typically first checks for logical errors, if applicable. For example, read and write operations contain buffers - do these buffers have appropriate sizes? For DeviceIoControl, there is a control code in addition to potentially two buffers. The driver needs to make sure the control code is something it recognizes. If any error is identified, the IRP is completed immediately with appropriate status.
2. Handle the request appropriately.

Here is the list of the most common dispatch routines for a software driver:

- IRP_MJ_CREATE - corresponds to a CreateFile call from user mode or ZwCreateFile in kernel mode. This major function is essentially mandatory, otherwise no client will be able to open a handle to a device controlled by this driver. Most drivers just complete the IRP with a success status.
- IRP_MJ_CLOSE - the opposite of IRP_MJ_CREATE. Called by CloseHandle from user mode or ZwClose from kernel mode when the last handle to the file object is about to be closed. Most drivers just complete the request successfully, but if something meaningful was done in IRP_MJ_CREATE, this is where it should be undone.
- IRP_MJ_READ - corresponds to a read operation, typically invoked from user mode by Read-File or kernel mode with ZwReadFile.
- IRP_MJ_WRITE - corresponds to a write operation, typically invoked from user mode by WriteFile or kernel mode with ZwWriteFile.
- IRP_MJ_DEVICE_CONTROL - corresponds to the DeviceIoControl call from user mode or ZwDeviceIoControlFile from kernel mode (there are other APIs in the kernel that can generate IRP_MJ_DEVICE_CONTROL IRPs).
- IRP_MJ_INTERNAL_DEVICE_CONTROL - similar to IRP_MJ_DEVICE_CONTROL, but only available for kernel callers.

Completing a Request

Once a driver decides to handle an IRP (meaning it's not passing down to another driver), it must eventually complete it. Otherwise, we have a leak on our handles - the requesting thread cannot really terminate and by extension its containing process will linger on as well, resulting in a "zombie process".

Completing a request means calling IoCompleteRequest after filling-in the request status and extra information. If the completion is done in the dispatch routine itself (the common case for software drivers), the routine must return the same status that was placed in the IRP.

The following code snippet shows how to complete a request in a dispatch routine:

```
NTSTATUS MyDispatchRoutine(PDEVICE_OBJECT, PIRP Irp) {
    //...
    Irp->IoStatus.Status = STATUS_XXX;
    Irp->IoStatus.Information = NumberOfBytesTransfered;    // depends on request ty\
pe

    IoCompleteRequest(Irp, IO_NO_INCREMENT);
    return STATUS_XXX;
}
```

 Since the dispatch routine must return the same status as was placed in the IRP, it's tempting to write the last statement like so: return Irp->IoStatus.Status; This, however, will likely result in a system crash. Can you guess why?

After the IRP is completed, touching any of its members is a bad idea. The IRP has probably already been freed and you're touching deallocated memory. It can actually be worse, since another IRP may have been allocated in its place (this is common), and so the code may return the status of some random IRP.

The Information field should be zero in case of an error (a bad status). Its exact meaning for a successful operation depends on the type of IRP.

The IoCompleteRequest accepts two arguments: the IRP itself and an optional value to temporarily increment the original thread's priority (the thread that initiated the request in the first place). In most cases, for software drivers, the thread in question is the executing thread, so a thread boost is inappropriate. The value IO_NO_INCREMENT as defined as zero, so no increment in the above code snippet.

However, the driver may choose to give the thread a boost, regardless whether it's the calling thread or not. In this case, the thread's priority jumps with the given boost, and then it's allowed to execute one quantum with that new priority before the priority decreases by one, it can then get another quantum with the reduced priority, and so on, until its priority returns to its original level. Figure 7-7 illustrates this scenario.

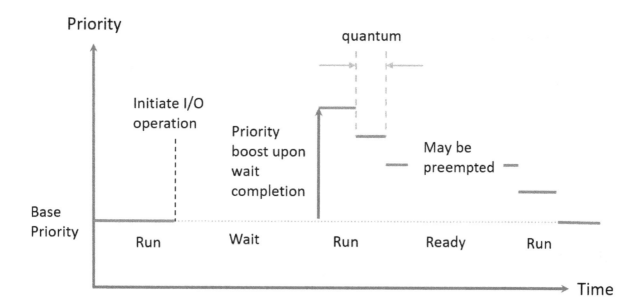

Figure 7-7: Thread priority boost and decay

The thread's priority after the boost can never go above 15. If it's supposed to, it will be 15. If the original thread's priority is above 15, boosting has no effect.

Accessing User Buffers

A given dispatch routine is the first to see the IRP. Some dispatch routines, mainly `IRP_MJ_READ`, `IRP_MJ_WRITE` and `IRP_MJ_DEVICE_CONTROL` accept buffers provided by a client - in most cases from user mode. Typically, a dispatch routine is called in IRQL 0 and in the requesting thread context, which means the buffers pointers provided by user mode are trivially accessible: the IRQL is 0 so page faults are handled normally, and the thread is the requestor, so the pointers are valid in this process context.

However, there could be issues. As we've seen in chapter 6, even in this convenient context (requesting thread and IRQL 0), it's possible for another thread in the client's process to free the passed-in buffer(s), before the driver gets a chance to examine them, and so cause an access violation. The solution we've used in chapter 6 is to use a `__try` / `__except` block to handle any access violation by returning failure to the client.

In some cases, even that is not enough. For example, if we have some code running at IRQL 2 (such as a DPC running as a result of timer expiration), we cannot safely access the user's buffers at this context. There are two issues here:

- IRQL is 2, meaning no page fault handling can occur.

- The thread executing the DPC is an arbitrary one, so the pointer itself has no meaning in whatever process happens to be the current on this processor.

Using exception handling in such a case will not work correctly, because we'll be accessing some memory location that is essentially invalid in this random process context. Even if the access succeeds (because that memory happens to be allocated in this random process and is resident in RAM), we'll be accessing random memory, and certainly not the original buffer provided to the request.

All this means that there must be some way to access the original user's buffer in an inconvenient context. In fact, there are two ways provided by the kernel for this purpose, called *Buffered I/O* and *Direct I/O*. In the next sections we'll see what each of these schemes mean and how to use them.

 Some data structures are always safe to access, since they are allocated from non-paged pool. Common examples are device objects (created with `IoCreateDevice`) and IRPs.

Buffered I/O

Buffered I/O is the simplest of the two ways. To get support for Buffered I/O for Read and Write operations, a flag must be set on the device object like so:

```
DeviceObject->Flags |= DO_BUFFERED_IO;   // DO = Device Object
```

For `IRP_MJ_DEVICE_CONTROL` buffers, see the section "User Buffers for `IRP_MJ_DEVICE_CONTROL`" later in this chapter.

Here are the steps taken by the I/O Manager and the driver when a read or write request arrives:

1. The I/O Manager allocates a buffer from non-paged pool with the same size as the user's buffer. It stores the pointer to this new buffer in the `AssociatedIrp->SystemBuffer` member of the IRP. (The buffer size can be found in the current I/O stack location's `Parameters.Read.Length` or `Parameters.Write.Length`.)
2. For a write request, the I/O Manager copies the user's buffer to the system buffer.
3. Only now the driver's dispatch routine is called. The driver can use the system buffer pointer directly without any checks, because the buffer is in system space (its address is absolute - the same from any process context), and in any IRQL, because the buffer is allocated from non-paged pool, so it cannot be paged out.
4. Once the driver completes the IRP (`IoCompleteRequest`), the I/O manager (for read requests) copies the system buffer back to the user's buffer (the size of the copy is determined by the `IoStatus.Information` field in the IRP set by the driver).
5. Finally, the I/O Manager frees the system buffer.

You may be wondering how does the I/O Manager copy back the system buffer to the original user's buffer from `IoCompleteRequest`. This function can be called from any thread, in IRQL <= 2. The way it's done is by queuing a special kernel APC to the thread requesting the operation in the first place. Once this thread gets a CPU for execution, the first thing it does is run this APC which does the actual copying.

Figures 7-8a to 7-8e illustrate the steps taken with Buffered I/O.

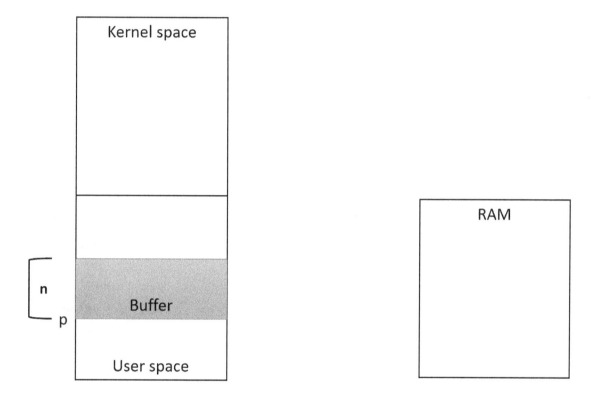

Figure 7-8a: Buffered I/O: initial state

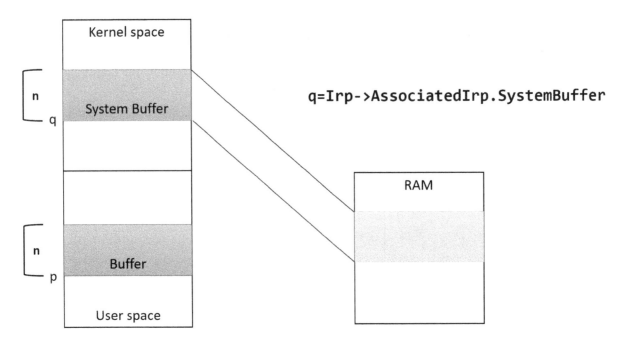

Figure 7-8b: Buffered I/O: system buffer allocated

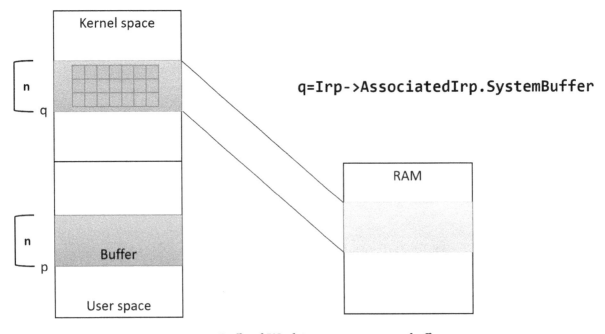

Figure 7-8c: Buffered I/O: driver accesses system buffer

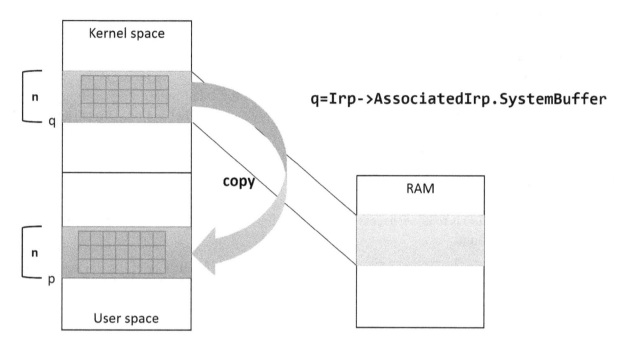

Figure 7-8d: Buffered I/O: on IRP completion, I/O manager copies buffer back (for read)

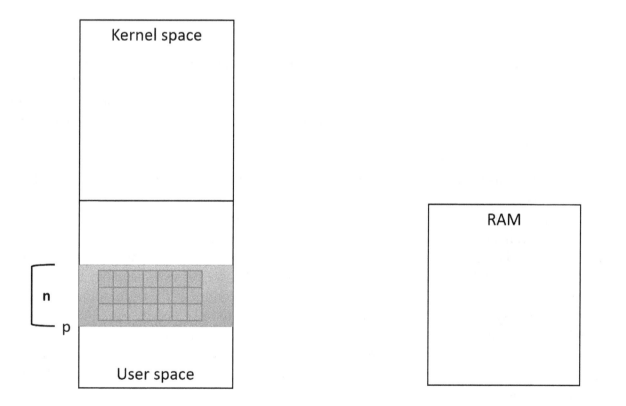

Figure 7-8e: Buffered I/O: final state - I/O manager frees system buffer

Buffered I/O has the following characteristics:

- Easy to use - just specify the flag in the device object and everything else is taken care of by the I/O Manager.
- It always involves a copy - which means it's best used for small buffers (typically up to one page). Large buffers may be expensive to copy. In this case, the other option, Direct I/O, should be used instead.

Direct I/O

The purpose of Direct I/O is to allow access to a user's buffer in any IRQL and any thread but without any copying going around.

For read and write requests, selecting Direct I/O is done with a different flag of the device object:

```
DeviceObject->Flags |= DO_DIRECT_IO;
```

As with Buffered I/O, this selection only affects read and write requests. For `DeviceIoControl` see the next section.

Here are the steps involved in handling Direct I/O:

1. The I/O Manager first makes sure the user's buffer is valid and then faults it into physical memory.
2. It then locks the buffer in memory, so it cannot be paged out until further notice. This solves one of the issues with buffer access - page faults cannot happen, so accessing the buffer in any IRQL is safe.
3. The I/O Manager builds a *Memory Descriptor List* (MDL), a data structure that knows how a buffer is mapped to RAM. The address of this data structure is stored in the `MdlAddress` field of the `IRP`.
4. At this point, the driver gets the call to its dispatch routine. The user's buffer, although locked in RAM, cannot be accessed from an arbitrary thread. When the driver requires access to the buffer, it must call a function that maps the same user buffer to a system address, which by definition is valid in any process context. So essentially, we get two mappings to the same buffer. One is from the original address (valid only in the context of the requestor process) and the other in system space, which is always valid. The API to call is `MmGetSystemAddressFor-MdlSafe`, passing the MDL built by the I/O Manager. The return value is the system address.
5. Once the driver completes the request, the I/O Manager removes the second mapping (to system space), frees the MDL and unlocks the user's buffer, so it can be paged normally just like any other user mode memory.

Figures 7-9a to 7-9f illustrate the steps taken with Direct I/O.

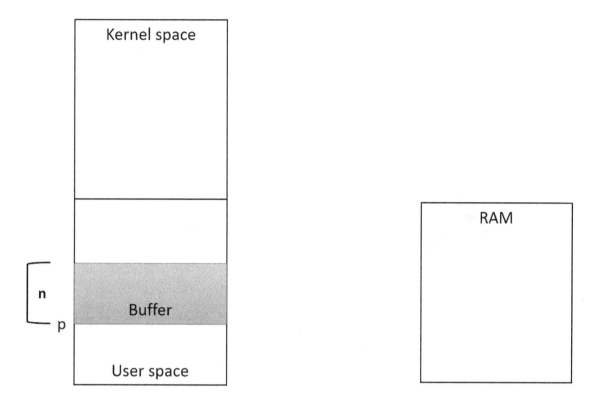

Figure 7-9a: Direct I/O: initial state

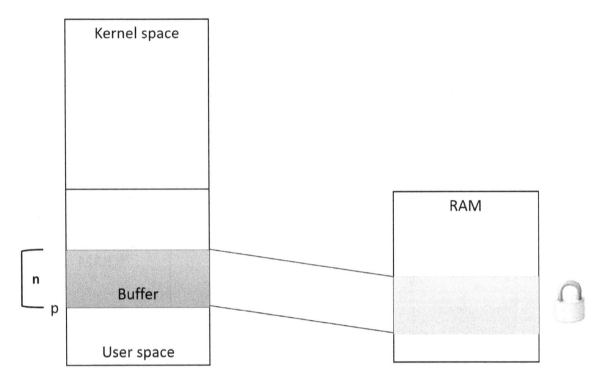

Figure 7-9b: Direct I/O: I/O manager faults buffer's pages to RAM and locks them

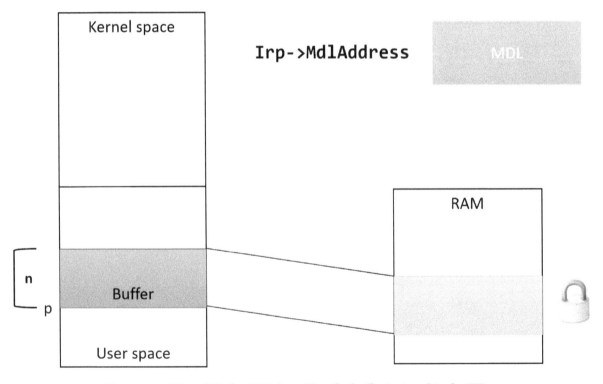

Figure 7-9c: Direct I/O: the MDL describing the buffer is stored in the IRP

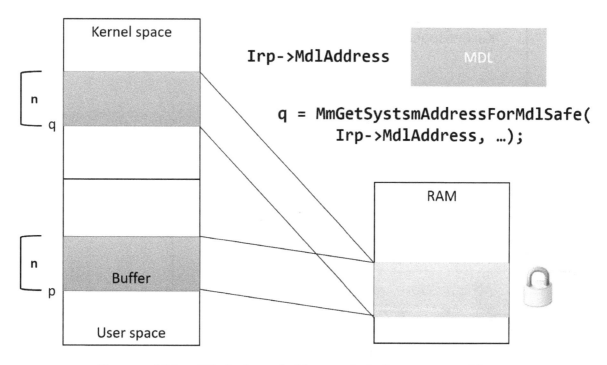

Figure 7-9d: Direct I/O: the driver double-maps the buffer to a system address

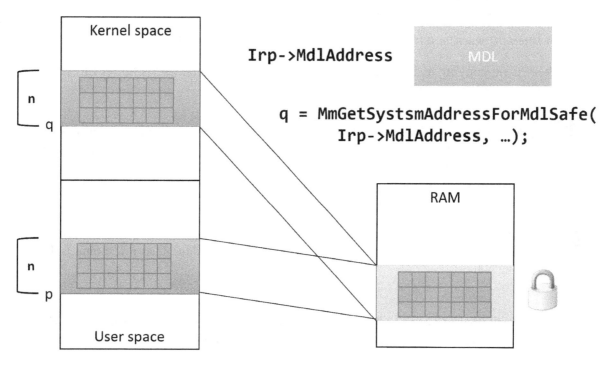

Figure 7-9e: Direct I/O: the driver accesses the buffer using the system address

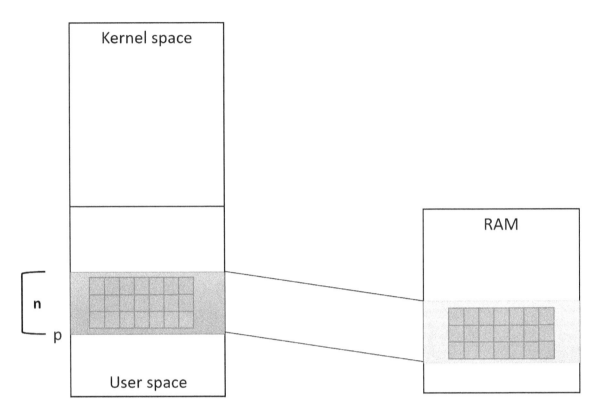

Figure 7-9f: Direct I/O: when the IRP is completed, the I/O manager frees the mapping, the MDL and unlocks the buffer

Notice there is no copying at all. The driver just reads/writes to the user's buffer directly, using a system address.

 Locking the user's buffer is done with the MmProbeAndLockPages API, fully documented in the WDK. Unlocking is done with MmUnlockPages, also documented. This means a driver can use these routines outside the narrow context of Direct I/O.

 Calling MmGetSystemAddressForMdlSafe can be done multiple times. The MDL stores a flag indicating whether the system mapping has already been done. If so, it just returns the existing pointer.

MmGetSystemAddressForMdlSafe accepts the MDL and a page priority (MM_PAGE_PRIORITY enumeration). Most drivers specify NormalPagePriority, but there is also LowPagePriority and HighPagePriority. This priority gives a hint to the system of the importance of the mapping. Check the WDK documentation for more information.

If MmGetSystemAddressForMdlSafe fails, it returns NULL. This means the system is out of system page tables or very low on system page tables (depends on the priority argument above). This should be a rare occurrence, but can happen in very low memory conditions. A driver must check for this;

if NULL is returned, the driver should complete the IRP with the status STATUS_INSUFFICIENT_-RESOURCES.

There is a similar function, called MmGetSystemAddressForMdl, which if it fails, crashes the system. Do not use this function.

Drivers that don't set either of the flags DO_BUFFERED_IO nor DO_DIRECT_IO in the device object flags implicitly use *Neither I/O*, which simply means the driver doesn't get any special help from the I/O manager, and it's up to the driver to deal with the user's buffer.

User Buffers for IRP_MJ_DEVICE_CONTROL

The last two sections discussed Buffered I/O and Direct I/O as they pertain to read and write requests. For IRP_MJ_DEVICE_CONTROL, the buffering access method is supplied on a control code basis. As a reminder, here is the DeviceIoControl user mode function prototype (it's similar with the kernel function ZwDeviceIoControlFile):

```
BOOL DeviceIoControl(
    HANDLE hDevice,               // handle to device or file
    DWORD dwIoControlCode,        // IOCTL code (see <winioctl.h>)
    PVOID lpInBuffer,             // input buffer
    DWORD nInBufferSize,          // size of input buffer
    PVOID lpOutBuffer,            // output buffer
    DWORD nOutBufferSize,         // size of output buffer
    PDWORD lpdwBytesReturned,     // # of bytes actually returned
    LPOVERLAPPED lpOverlapped);   // for async. operation
```

There are three arguments here: the I/O control code, and optional two buffers designated "input" and "output". As it turns out, the way these buffers are accessed depends on the control code, which is very convenient, because different requests may have different requirements related to accessing the user's buffers.

We've already seen in chapter 4 that a control code is made up of four arguments, provided to the CTL_CODE macro, repeated here for convenience:

```
#define CTL_CODE( DeviceType, Function, Method, Access ) ( \
    ((DeviceType) << 16) | ((Access) << 14) | ((Function) << 2) | (Method))
```

The third argument (*Method*) is the key to selecting the buffering method for accessing the input and output buffers provided with DeviceIoControl. Here are the options:

- METHOD_NEITHER - this value means no help is required of the I/O manager, so the driver is left dealing with the buffers on its own. This could be useful, for instance, if the particular code does not require any buffer - the control code itself is all the information needed - it's best to let the I/O manager know that it does not need to do any additional work.
  - In this case, the pointer to the user's input buffer is store in the current I/O stack location's Paramaters.DeviceIoControl.Type3InputBuffer field and the output buffer is stored in the IRP's UserBuffer field.
- METHOD_BUFFERED - this value indicates Buffered I/O for both the input and output buffer. When the request starts, the I/O manager allocates the system buffer from non-paged pool with the size that is the maximum of the lengths of the input and output buffers. It then copies the input buffer to the system buffer. Only now the IRP_MJ_DEVICE_CONTROL dispatch routine is invoked. When the request completes, the I/O manager copies the number of bytes indicated with the IoStatus.Information field in the IRP to the user's output buffer.
  - The system buffer pointer is at the usual location: AssociatedIrp.SystemBuffer inside the IRP structure.
- METHOD_IN_DIRECT and METHOD_OUT_DIRECT - contrary to the intuition, both of these values mean the same thing as far as buffering methods are concerned: the input buffer uses Buffered I/O and the output buffer uses Direct I/O. The only difference between these two values is whether the output buffer can be read (METHOD_IN_DIRECT) or written (METHOD_OUT_DIRECT).

 The last bullet indicates that the output buffer can also be treated as input by using METHOD_-IN_DIRECT.

Table 7-1 summarizes these buffering methods.

Table 7-1: Buffering method based on control code Method argument

Method	Input buffer	Output buffer
METHOD_NEITHER	Neither	Neither
METHOD_BUFFERED	Buffered	Buffered
METHOD_IN_DIRECT	Buffered	Direct
METHOD_OUT_DIRECT	Buffered	Direct

Putting it All Together: The Zero Driver

In this section, we'll use what we've learned in this (and earlier) chapter and build a driver and a client application. The driver is named *Zero* and has the following characteristics:

- For read requests, it zeros out the provided buffer.
- For write requests, it just consumes the provided buffer, similar to a classic *null* device.

The driver will use Direct I/O so as not to incur the overhead of copies, as the buffers provided by the client can potentially be very large.

We'll start the project by creating an "Empty WDM Project" in Visual Studio and and naming it *Zero*. Then we'll delete the created INF file.

Using a Precompiled Header

One technique that we can use that is not specific to driver development, but is generally useful, is using *precompiled headers*. Precompiled headers is a Visual Studio feature that helps with faster compilation times. The precompiled header is a header file that has `#include` statements for headers that rarely change, such as `ntddk.h` for drivers. The precompiled header is compiled once, stored in an internal binary format, and used in subsequent compilations, which become considerably faster.

 Many user mode projects created by Visual Studio already use precompiled headers. Since we're starting with an empty project, we have to set up precompiled headers manually.

Follow these steps to create and use a precompiled header:

- Add a new header file to the project and call it *pch.h*. This file will serve as the precompiled header. Add all rarely-changing `#includes` here:

```
#pragma once

#include <ntddk.h>
```

- Add a source file named *pch.cpp* and put a single `#include` in it: the precompiled header itself:

```
#include "pch.h"
```

- Now comes the tricky part. Letting the compiler know that *pch.h* is the precompiled header and *pch.cpp* is the once creating it. Open project properties, select *All Configurations* and *All Platforms* so you won't need to configure every configuraion/platform separately, navigate to *C/C++ / Precompiled Headers* and set *Precompiled Header* to "Use" and the file name to "pch.h" (see figure 7-10). Click OK and to close the dialog box.

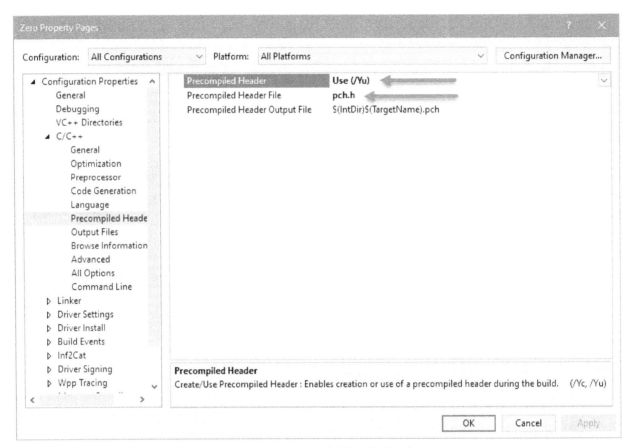

Figure 7-10: Setting precompiled header for the project

- The *pch.cpp* file should be set as the creator of the precompiled header. Right click this file in Solution Explorer, and select *Properties*. Navigate to *C/C++ / Precompiled Headers* and set *Precompiled Header* to "Create" (see figure 7-11). Click OK to accept the setting.

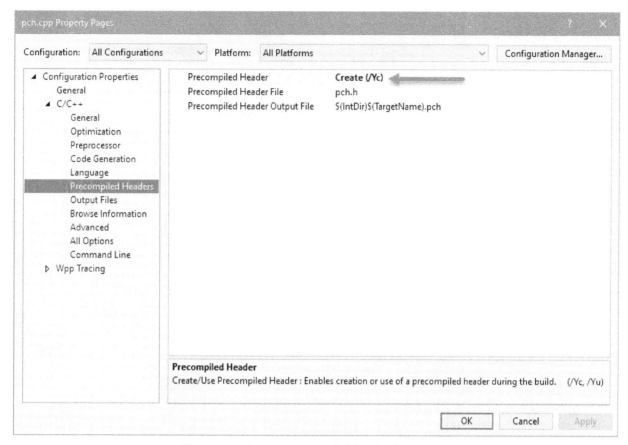

Figure 7-10: Setting precompiled header for pch.cpp

From this point on, every C/CPP file in the project must `#include "pch.h"` as the first thing in the file. Without this include, the project will not compile.

 Make sure there is nothing before this `#include "pch.h"` in a source file. Anything before this line does not get compiled at all!

The `DriverEntry` Routine

The `DriveEntry` routine for the *Zero* driver is very similar to the one we created for the driver in chapter 4. However, in chapter 4's driver the code undo any operation that was already done in case of a later error. We had just two operations that can actually be undone: creation of the device object and creation of the symbolic link. The *Zero* driver is similar, but we'll create a more robust and less error-prone code to handle errors during initialization. Let's start with the basics of setting up an unload routine and the dispatch routines:

```
#define DRIVER_PREFIX "Zero: "

// DriverEntry

extern "C" NTSTATUS
DriverEntry(PDRIVER_OBJECT DriverObject, PUNICODE_STRING RegistryPath) {
    UNREFERENCED_PARAMETER(RegistryPath);

    DriverObject->DriverUnload = ZeroUnload;
    DriverObject->MajorFunction[IRP_MJ_CREATE] = DriverObject->MajorFunction[IRP_MJ_\
CLOSE] = ZeroCreateClose;
    DriverObject->MajorFunction[IRP_MJ_READ] = ZeroRead;
    DriverObject->MajorFunction[IRP_MJ_WRITE] = ZeroWrite;
```

Now we need to create the device object and symbolic link and handle errors in a more general and robust way. The trick we'll use is a do / while(false) block, which is not really a loop, but it allows getting out of the block with a simple break statement in case something goes wrong:

```
    UNICODE_STRING devName = RTL_CONSTANT_STRING(L"\\Device\\Zero");
    UNICODE_STRING symLink = RTL_CONSTANT_STRING(L"\\??\\Zero");
    PDEVICE_OBJECT DeviceObject = nullptr;
    auto status = STATUS_SUCCESS;

    do {
        status = IoCreateDevice(DriverObject, 0, &devName, FILE_DEVICE_UNKNOWN,
            0, FALSE, &DeviceObject);
        if (!NT_SUCCESS(status)) {
            KdPrint((DRIVER_PREFIX "failed to create device (0x%08X)\n",
                status));
            break;
        }
        // set up Direct I/O
        DeviceObject->Flags |= DO_DIRECT_IO;

        status = IoCreateSymbolicLink(&symLink, &devName);
        if (!NT_SUCCESS(status)) {
            KdPrint((DRIVER_PREFIX "failed to create symbolic link (0x%08X)\n",
            status));
            break;
        }
    } while (false);

    if (!NT_SUCCESS(status)) {
```

```
    if (DeviceObject)
        IoDeleteDevice(DeviceObject);
    }
    return status;
```

The pattern is simple: if an error occurs in any call, just break out of the "loop". Outside the loop, check the status, and if it's a failure, undo any operations done so far. With this scheme in hand, it's easy to add more initializations (which we'll need in more complex drivers), while keeping the cleanup code localized and appearing just once.

> It's possible to use goto statements instead of the do / while(false) approach, but as the great Dijkstra wrote "goto considered harmful", so I tend to avoid it if I can.

Notice we're also initializing the device to use Direct I/O for our read and write operations.

The Read Dispatch Routine

Before we get to the actual read dispatch routine, let's create a helper function that simplifies completing an IRP with a given status and information:

```
NTSTATUS CompleteIrp(PIRP Irp, NTSTATUS status = STATUS_SUCCESS, ULONG_PTR info = 0)\
 {
    Irp->IoStatus.Status = status;
    Irp->IoStatus.Information = info;
    IoCompleteRequest(Irp, 0);
    return status;
}
```

Now we can start implementing the read dispatch routine. First we need to check the length of the buffer to make sure it's not zero. If it is, just complete the IRP with a failure status:

```
NTSTATUS ZeroRead(PDEVICE_OBJECT, PIRP Irp) {
    auto stack = IoGetCurrentIrpStackLocation(Irp);
    auto len = stack->Parameters.Read.Length;
    if (len == 0)
        return CompleteIrp(Irp, STATUS_INVALID_BUFFER_SIZE);
```

Note that the length of the user's buffer is provided through the Parameters.Read structure inside the current I/O stack location.

We have configured Direct I/O, so we need to map the locked buffer to system space using MmGet-SystemAddressForMdlSafe:

```
auto buffer = MmGetSystemAddressForMdlSafe(Irp->MdlAddress, NormalPagePriority);
if (!buffer)
    return CompleteIrp(Irp, STATUS_INSUFFICIENT_RESOURCES);
```

The functionality we need to implement is to zero out the given buffer. We can use a simple `memset` call to fill the buffer with zeros and then complete the request:

```
memset(buffer, 0, len);

return CompleteIrp(Irp, STATUS_SUCCESS, len);
}
```

It's important to set the `Information` field to the length of the buffer. This indicates to the client the number of bytes consumed in the operation (in the second to last argument to `ReadFile`). This is all we need for the read operation.

The Write Dispatch Routine

The write dispatch routine is even simpler. All it needs to do is just complete the request with the buffer length provided by the client (essentially swallowing the buffer):

```
NTSTATUS ZeroWrite(PDEVICE_OBJECT, PIRP Irp) {
    auto stack = IoGetCurrentIrpStackLocation(Irp);
    auto len = stack->Parameters.Write.Length;

    return CompleteIrp(Irp, STATUS_SUCCESS, len);
}
```

Note that we don't even bother calling `MmGetSystemAddressForMdlSafe`, as we don't need to access the actual buffer. This is also the reason this call is not made beforehand by the I/O manager: the driver may not even need it, or perhaps need it in certain conditions only; so the I/O manager prepares everything (the MDL) and lets the driver decide when and if to do the actual mapping.

Test Application

We'll add a new console application project to the solution to test the read and write operations. Here is some simple code to test these operations:

```cpp
int Error(const char* msg) {
    printf("%s: error=%d\n", msg, ::GetLastError());
    return 1;
}


int main() {
    HANDLE hDevice = ::CreateFile(L"\\\\.\\Zero", GENERIC_READ | GENERIC_WRITE,
        0, nullptr, OPEN_EXISTING, 0, nullptr);
    if (hDevice == INVALID_HANDLE_VALUE) {
        return Error("failed to open device");
    }

    // test read
    BYTE buffer[64];

    // store some non-zero data
    for (int i = 0; i < sizeof(buffer); ++i)
        buffer[i] = i + 1;

    DWORD bytes;
    BOOL ok = ::ReadFile(hDevice, buffer, sizeof(buffer), &bytes, nullptr);
    if (!ok)
        return Error("failed to read");
    if (bytes != sizeof(buffer))
        printf("Wrong number of bytes\n");

    // check if buffer data sum is zero
    long total = 0;
    for (auto n : buffer)
        total += n;
    if (total != 0)
        printf("Wrong data\n");

    // test write
    BYTE buffer2[1024];     // contains junk
    ok = ::WriteFile(hDevice, buffer2, sizeof(buffer2), &bytes, nullptr);
    if (!ok)
        return Error("failed to write");
    if (bytes != sizeof(buffer2))
        printf("Wrong byte count\n");
    ::CloseHandle(hDevice);
}
```

Add to the driver the following functionality: the driver will count the total number of bytes passed to read and write operations. The driver will expose a control code that allows client code to query the total number of bytes read and written since the driver was loaded.

The solution to the above exercise as well as the complete projects can be found in the book's Github page at https://github.com/zodiacon/windowskernelprogrammingbook.

Summary

In this chapter we learned how to handle IRPs, which drivers deal with all the time. Armed with this knowledge, we can start leveraging more kernel functionality, starting with process and thread callbacks in the next chapter.

Chapter 8: Process and Thread Notifications

One of the powerful mechanisms available for kernel drivers is the ability to be notified when certain important events occur. In this chapter we'll look into some of these events, namely process creation and destruction, thread creation and destruction and image loads.

In this chapter:

- **Process Notifications**
- **Implementing Process Notifications**
- **Providing Data to User Mode**
- **Thread Notifications**
- **Image Load Notifications**
- **Exercises**

Process Notifications

Whenever a process is created or destroyed, interested drivers can be notified by the kernel of that fact. This allows drivers to keep track of processes, possibly associating some data with these processes. At the very minimum, these allows drivers to monitor process creation/destruction in real-time. By "real-time" I mean that the notifications are sent "in-line", as part of process creation; the driver cannot miss any processes that may be created and destroyed quickly.

For process creations, drivers also have the power to stop the process from being created, returning an error to the caller initiating the process creation. This type of power can only be achieved from kernel mode.

> Windows provides other mechanisms for being notified when processes are created or destroyed. For example, using Event Tracing for Windows (ETW), such notifications can be received by a user mode process (running with elevated privileges). However, there is no way in preventing a process from being created. Furthermore, ETW has an inherent notification delay of about 1-3 seconds (performance reasons), so a short-lived process may exit before the notification arrives. At that time

if opening a handle to the created process is attempted, it will fail.

The main API for registering for process notifications is PsSetCreateProcessNotifyRoutineEx, defined like so:

```
NTSTATUS
PsSetCreateProcessNotifyRoutineEx (
    _In_ PCREATE_PROCESS_NOTIFY_ROUTINE_EX NotifyRoutine,
    _In_ BOOLEAN Remove);
```

 There is currently a system-wide limit of 64 registrations, so it's theoretically possible for the registration function to fail.

The first argument is the driver's callback routine, having the following prototype:

```
typedef void
(*PCREATE_PROCESS_NOTIFY_ROUTINE_EX) (
    _Inout_ PEPROCESS Process,
    _In_ HANDLE ProcessId,
    _Inout_opt_ PPS_CREATE_NOTIFY_INFO CreateInfo);
```

The second argument to PsSetCreateProcessNotifyRoutineEx indicates whether the driver is registering or unregistering the callback (FALSE indicates the former). Typically, a driver will call this API with FALSE in its DriverEntry routine and call the same API with TRUE in its unload routine.

The arguments to process notification routine are as follows:

- *Process* - the process object of the newly created process or the process being destroyed.
- *Process Id* - the unique process ID of the process. Although it's declared with type HANDLE, it's in fact an ID.
- *CreateInfo* - a structure that contains detailed information on the process being created. If the process is being destroyed, this argument is NULL.

For process creation, the driver's callback routine is executed by the creating thread. For process exit, the callback is executed by the last thread to exit the process. In both cases, the callback is called inside a critical region (normal kernel APCs disabled).

Starting with Windows 10 version 1607, there is another function for process notifications: PsSetCreateProcessNotifyRoutineEx2. This "extended" function sets up a callback similar to the previous one, but the callback is also invoked on Pico processes. Pico processes are those used to host Linux processes for the Windows Subsystem for Linux (WSL). If a driver is interested in such processes, it must register with the extended function.

A driver using these callbacks must have the IMAGE_DLLCHARACTERISTICS_FORCE_-INTEGRITY flag in its Portable Executable (PE) image header. Without it, the call to the registration function returns STATUS_ACCESS_DENIED (unrelated to driver test signing mode). Currently, Visual Studio does not provide UI for setting this flag. It must be set in the linker command line options with /integritycheck. Figure 8-1 shows the project properties where this setting is specified.

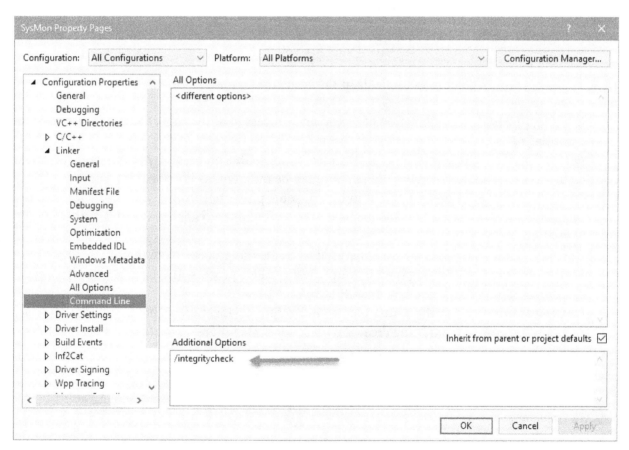

Figure 8-1: /integritycheck linked switch

The data structure provided for process creation is defined like so:

```
typedef struct _PS_CREATE_NOTIFY_INFO {
    _In_ SIZE_T Size;
    union {
        _In_ ULONG Flags;
        struct {
            _In_ ULONG FileOpenNameAvailable : 1;
            _In_ ULONG IsSubsystemProcess : 1;
            _In_ ULONG Reserved : 30;
        };
    };
    _In_ HANDLE ParentProcessId;
    _In_ CLIENT_ID CreatingThreadId;
    _Inout_ struct _FILE_OBJECT *FileObject;
    _In_ PCUNICODE_STRING ImageFileName;
    _In_opt_ PCUNICODE_STRING CommandLine;
    _Inout_ NTSTATUS CreationStatus;
} PS_CREATE_NOTIFY_INFO, *PPS_CREATE_NOTIFY_INFO;
```

Here's a description of the important fields in this structure:

- *CreatingThreadId* - a combination of thread and process Id of the caller to the process creation function.
- *ParentProcessId* - the parent process ID (not a handle). This process may be the same provided by `CreateThreadId.UniqueProcess`, but may be different, as it's possible as part of process creation to pass in a different parent to inherit some properties from.
- *ImageFileName* - the image file name of the executable, available if the flag `FileOpen-NameAvailable` is set.
- *CommandLine* - the full command line used to create the process. Note that it may be `NULL`.
- *IsSubsystemProcess* - this flag is set if this process is a Pico process. This can only be if the driver registered with `PsSetCreateProcessNotifyRoutineEx2`.
- *CreationStatus* - this is the status that would return to the caller. This is where the driver can stop the process from being created by placing some failure status (e.g. `STATUS_ACCESS_-DENIED`).

 Use defensive programming in the process notify callback. This means checking every pointer you're about to access for a non-`NULL` value before the actual access.

Implementing Process Notifications

To demonstrate process notifications, we'll build a driver that gathers information on process creation and destruction and allow this information to be consumed by a user mode client. This is similar to tools such as *Process Monitor* from *Sysinternals*, which uses process (and thread) notifications for reporting process (and thread) activity. During the course of implementing this driver, we'll leverage some of the techniques we learned in previous chapters.

Our driver name is going to be *SysMon* (unrelated to the *SysMon* tool from Sysinternals), and it will store all process creation/destruction information in a linked list (using LIST_ENTRY structures). Since this linked list may be accessed concurrently by multiple threads, we need to protect it with a mutex or a fast mutex; we'll go with fast mutex as it's more efficient.

The data we gather will eventually find its way to user mode, so we should declare common structures that the driver builds and a user mode client receives. We'll add a common header file named *SysMonCommon.h* to the driver project and define a few structures. We'll start with a common header for all information structures defined like so:

```
enum class ItemType : short {
    None,
    ProcessCreate,
    ProcessExit
};


struct ItemHeader {
    ItemType Type;
    USHORT Size;
    LARGE_INTEGER Time;
};
```

 The ItemType enum defined above uses the C++ 11 *scoped enum* feature, where enum values have a scope (ItemType in this case). These enums can also have a non-int size - short in the example. If you're using C, you can just use classic enums, or even #defines.

The ItemHeader structure holds information common to all event types: the type of the event, the time of the event (expressed as a 64-bit integer) and the size of the payload. The size is important, as each event has its own information. If we later wish to pack an array of these events and (say) provide them to a user mode client, the client needs to know where each event ends and the next one begins.

Once we have this common header, we can derive other data structures for particular events. Let's start with simplest - process exit:

```
struct ProcessExitInfo : ItemHeader {
    ULONG ProcessId;
};
```

For process exit event, there is just one interesting piece of information (besides the header) - the exiting process ID.

If you're using C, then inheritance is not available to you. However, you can simulate it by having the first member be of type ItemHeader and then adding the specific members; The memory layout is the same.

```
struct ExitProcessInfo {
    ItemHeader Header;
    ULONG ProcessId;
};
```

The type used for a process ID is ULONG. HANDLE is not a good idea, as user mode may be confused by it. Also, DWORD is not used here, even though user mode headers use the DWORD type a lot (32 bit unsigned integer). In the WDK headers the DWORD type is not defined. Although it's pretty easy to define it explicitly, it's better just to ULONG, which means the same thing and is defined in user mode and kernel mode headers alike.

Since we need to store every such structure as part of a linked list, each data structure must contain a LIST_ENTRY instance that points to the next and previous items. Since these LIST_ENTRY objects should not be exposed to user mode, we will define extended structures containing these entries in a different file, that is not shared with user mode.

In a new file called *SysMon.h* we add a generic structure that holds a LIST_ENTRY together with the actual data structure:

```
template<typename T>
struct FullItem {
    LIST_ENTRY Entry;
    T Data;
};
```

A templated class is used to avoid creating a multitude of types, one for each specific event type. For example, we could create the following structure specifically for a process exit event:

```
struct FullProcessExitInfo {
    LIST_ENTRY Entry;
    ProcessExitInfo Data;
};
```

> We could even inherit from LIST_ENTRY and then just add the ProcessExitInfo structure. But this is not elegant, as our data has nothing to do with LIST_ENTRY, so simply extending it is artificial and should be avoided.

The FullItem<T> type saves the hassle of creating these individual types.

 IF you're using C, then naturally templates are not available, and you must use the above structure approach. I'm not going to mention C again - there is always a workaround that can be used if you have to.

The head of our linked list must be stored somewhere. We'll create a data structure that will hold all the global state of the driver, instead of creating separate global variables. Here is the definition of our structure:

```
struct Globals {
    LIST_ENTRY ItemsHead;
    int ItemCount;
    FastMutex Mutex;
};
```

The FastMutex type used is the same one we developed in chapter 6. Along with the C++ RAII AutoLock wrapper, also from chapter 6.

The DriverEntry Routine

The DriverEntry for the *SysMon* driver is similar to the one in the *Zero* driver from chapter 7. We have to add process notification registration and proper initialization of our Globals object:

```cpp
Globals g_Globals;

extern "C" NTSTATUS
DriverEntry(PDRIVER_OBJECT DriverObject, PUNICODE_STRING) {
    auto status = STATUS_SUCCESS;

    InitializeListHead(&g_Globals.ItemsHead);
    g_Globals.Mutex.Init();

    PDEVICE_OBJECT DeviceObject = nullptr;
    UNICODE_STRING symLink = RTL_CONSTANT_STRING(L"\\??\\sysmon");
    bool symLinkCreated = false;

    do {
        UNICODE_STRING devName = RTL_CONSTANT_STRING(L"\\Device\\sysmon");
        status = IoCreateDevice(DriverObject, 0, &devName,
            FILE_DEVICE_UNKNOWN, 0, TRUE, &DeviceObject);
        if (!NT_SUCCESS(status)) {
            KdPrint((DRIVER_PREFIX "failed to create device (0x%08X)\n",
            status));
            break;
        }
        DeviceObject->Flags |= DO_DIRECT_IO;

        status = IoCreateSymbolicLink(&symLink, &devName);
        if (!NT_SUCCESS(status)) {
            KdPrint((DRIVER_PREFIX "failed to create sym link (0x%08X)\n",
                status));
            break;
        }
        symLinkCreated = true;

        // register for process notifications
        status = PsSetCreateProcessNotifyRoutineEx(OnProcessNotify, FALSE);
        if (!NT_SUCCESS(status)) {
            KdPrint((DRIVER_PREFIX "failed to register process callback (0x%08X)\n",
                status));
            break;
        }
    } while (false);

    if (!NT_SUCCESS(status)) {
        if (symLinkCreated)
```

```
        IoDeleteSymbolicLink(&symLink);
    if (DeviceObject)
        IoDeleteDevice(DeviceObject);
}

DriverObject->DriverUnload = SysMonUnload;
DriverObject->MajorFunction[IRP_MJ_CREATE] =
    DriverObject->MajorFunction[IRP_MJ_CLOSE] = SysMonCreateClose;
DriverObject->MajorFunction[IRP_MJ_READ] = SysMonRead;

return status;
}
```

We'll use the read dispatch routine later to return event information to user mode.

Handling Process Exit Notifications

The process notification function in the code above is OnProcessNotify and has the prototype outlined earlier in this chapter. This callback handles process creations and exits. Let's start with process exit, as it's much simpler than process creation (as we shall soon see). The basic outline of the callback is as follows:

```
void OnProcessNotify(PEPROCESS Process, HANDLE ProcessId,
    PPS_CREATE_NOTIFY_INFO CreateInfo) {
    if (CreateInfo) {
        // process create
    }
    else {
        // process exit
    }
}
```

For process exit we have just the process ID we need to save, along with the header data common to all events. First, we need to allocate storage for the full item representing this event:

```
auto info = (FullItem<ProcessExitInfo>*)ExAllocatePoolWithTag(PagedPool,
    sizeof(FullItem<ProcessExitInfo>), DRIVER_TAG);
if (info == nullptr) {
    KdPrint((DRIVER_PREFIX "failed allocation\n"));
    return;
}
```

If the allocation fails, there is really nothing the driver can do, so it just returns from the callback.

Now it's time to fill the generic information: time, item type and size, all of which are easy to get:

```
auto& item = info->Data;
KeQuerySystemTimePrecise(&item.Time);
item.Type = ItemType::ProcessExit;
item.ProcessId = HandleToULong(ProcessId);
item.Size = sizeof(ProcessExitInfo);

PushItem(&info->Entry);
```

First, we dig into the data item itself (bypassing the LIST_ENTRY) with the info variable. Next, we fill the header information: The item type is well-known, since we are in the branch handling a process exit notification; the time can be obtained with KeQuerySystemTimePrecise that returns the current system time (UTC, not local time) as a 64-bit integer counting from January 1, 1601. Finally, the item size is constant and is the size of the user-facing data structure (not the size of the FullItem<ProcessExitInfo>).

 The KeQuerySystemTimePrecise API is available starting with Windows 8. For earlier versions, the KeQuerySystemTime API should be used instead.

The extra data for a process exit is the process ID. The code uses HandleToULong to make the correct casts to turn a HANDLE object to an unsigned 32-bit integer.

All that's left to do now is add the new item to the end of our linked list. For this purpose, we'll define a function named PushItem:

```
void PushItem(LIST_ENTRY* entry) {
    AutoLock<FastMutex> lock(g_Globals.Mutex);
    if (g_Globals.ItemCount > 1024) {
        // too many items, remove oldest one
        auto head = RemoveHeadList(&g_Globals.ItemsHead);
        g_Globals.ItemCount--;
        auto item = CONTAINING_RECORD(head, FullItem<ItemHeader>, Entry);
        ExFreePool(item);
    }
    InsertTailList(&g_Globals.ItemsHead, entry);
    g_Globals.ItemCount++;
}
```

The code first acquires the fast mutex, as multiple threads may call this function at the same time. Everything after that is done under the protection of the fast mutex.

Next, the driver limits the number of items in the linked list. This is a necessary precaution, as there is no guarantee that a client will consume these events promptly. The driver should never let data be consumed without limit, as this can compromise the system as a whole. The value 1024 chosen here is completely arbitrary. It's better to have this number read from the registry in the driver's service key.

 Implement this limit by reading from the registry in DriverEntry. Hint: you can use APIs such as ZwOpenKey or IoOpenDeviceRegistryKey and then ZwQueryValueKey.

If the item count is above the limit, the code removes the oldest item, essentially treating the linked list as a queue (RemoveHeadList). if the item is removed, its memory must be freed. The pointer to the actual entry is not necessarily the pointer that was originally allocated (in this case it actually is because the LIST_ENTRY object is the first in the FullItem<> structure), so the CONTAINING_RECORD macro is used to get to the beginning of the FullItem<> object. Now ExFreePool can free the item. Figure 8-2 illustrates the layout of FullItem<T> objects.

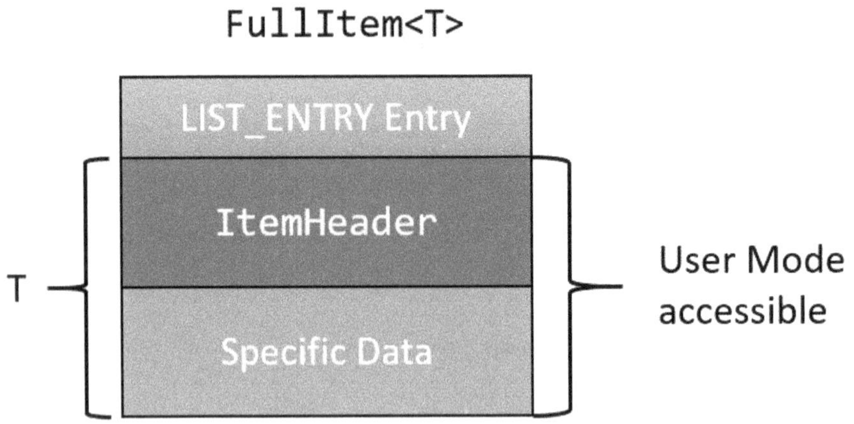

FullItem<T>

Figure 8-2: `FullItem<T>` layout

Finally, the driver calls `InsertTailList` to add the item to the end of the list and the item count is incremented.

> We don't need to use atomic increment/decrement operations in the `PushItem` function because manipulation of the item count is always done under the protection of the fast mutex.

Handling Process Create Notifications

Process create notifications are more complex because the amount of information varies. For example, the command line length is different for different processes. First we need to decide what information to store for process creation. Here is a first try:

```
struct ProcessCreateInfo : ItemHeader {
    ULONG ProcessId;
    ULONG ParentProcessId;
    WCHAR CommandLine[1024];
};
```

We choose to store the process ID, the parent process ID and the command line. Although this structure can work and is fairly easy to deal with because its size is known in advance.

What might be an issue with the above declaration?

The potential issue here is with the command line. Declaring the command line with constant size is simple, but problematic. If the command line is longer than allocated, the driver would have to trim it, possibly hiding important information. If the command line is shorter than the defined limit, the structure is wasting memory.

 Can we use something like this?

```
struct ProcessCreateInfo : ItemHeader {
    ULONG ProcessId;
    ULONG ParentProcessId;
    UNICODE_STRING CommandLine;      // can this work?
};
```

This cannot work. First, UNICODE_STRING is not normally defined in user mode headers. Second (and much worse), the internal pointer to the actual characters normally would point to system space, inaccessible to user mode.

Here is another option, which we'll use in our driver:

```
struct ProcessCreateInfo : ItemHeader {
    ULONG ProcessId;
    ULONG ParentProcessId;
    USHORT CommandLineLength;
    USHORT CommandLineOffset;
};
```

We'll store the command line length and its offset from the beginning of the structure. The actual characters of the command line will follow this structure in memory. In this way, we are not limited by any command line length and are not wasting memory for short command lines.

Given this declaration, we can begin implementation for process creation:

```
USHORT allocSize = sizeof(FullItem<ProcessCreateInfo>);
USHORT commandLineSize = 0;
if (CreateInfo->CommandLine) {
    commandLineSize = CreateInfo->CommandLine->Length;
    allocSize += commandLineSize;
}
auto info = (FullItem<ProcessCreateInfo>*)ExAllocatePoolWithTag(PagedPool,
    allocSize, DRIVER_TAG);
if (info == nullptr) {
    KdPrint((DRIVER_PREFIX "failed allocation\n"));
    return;
}
```

The total size for allocation is based on the command line length (if any). Now it's time to fill in the non-changing information, namely the header and the process and parent IDs:

```
auto& item = info->Data;
KeQuerySystemTimePrecise(&item.Time);
item.Type = ItemType::ProcessCreate;
item.Size = sizeof(ProcessCreateInfo) + commandLineSize;
item.ProcessId = HandleToULong(ProcessId);
item.ParentProcessId = HandleToULong(CreateInfo->ParentProcessId);
```

The item size must be calculated to include the base structure and the command line length.

Next, we need to copy the command line to the address of the end of the base structure and update the length and offset:

```
if (commandLineSize > 0) {
    ::memcpy((UCHAR*)&item + sizeof(item), CreateInfo->CommandLine->Buffer,
        commandLineSize);
    item.CommandLineLength = commandLineSize / sizeof(WCHAR);   // length in WCHARs
    item.CommandLineOffset = sizeof(item);
}
else {
    item.CommandLineLength = 0;
}
PushItem(&info->Entry);
```

Add the image file name to the `ProcessCreateInfo` structure in the same way as the command line. Be careful with the offset calculations.

Providing Data to User Mode

The next thing to consider is how to provide the gathered information to a user mode client. There are several options that could be used, but for this driver we'll let the client poll the driver for information using a read request. The driver will fill the user-provided buffer with as many events as possible, until either the buffer is exhausted or there are no more events in the queue.

We'll start the read request by obtaining the address of the user's buffer with Direct I/O (set up in `DriverEntry`):

```
NTSTATUS SysMonRead(PDEVICE_OBJECT, PIRP Irp) {
    auto stack = IoGetCurrentIrpStackLocation(Irp);
    auto len = stack->Parameters.Read.Length;
    auto status = STATUS_SUCCESS;
    auto count = 0;
    NT_ASSERT(Irp->MdlAddress);   // we're using Direct I/O

    auto buffer = (UCHAR*)MmGetSystemAddressForMdlSafe(Irp->MdlAddress,
        NormalPagePriority);
    if (!buffer) {
        status = STATUS_INSUFFICIENT_RESOURCES;
    }
    else {
```

Now we need to access our linked list and pull items from its head:

```
AutoLock lock(g_Globals.Mutex);      // C++ 17
while (true) {
    if (IsListEmpty(&g_Globals.ItemsHead))   // can also check g_Globals.ItemCount
        break;

    auto entry = RemoveHeadList(&g_Globals.ItemsHead);
    auto info = CONTAINING_RECORD(entry, FullItem<ItemHeader>, Entry);
    auto size = info->Data.Size;
    if (len < size) {
        // user's buffer is full, insert item back
        InsertHeadList(&g_Globals.ItemsHead, entry);
        break;
    }
    g_Globals.ItemCount--;
    ::memcpy(buffer, &info->Data, size);
    len -= size;
    buffer += size;
    count += size;
    // free data after copy
    ExFreePool(info);
}
```

First we obtain the fast mutex, as process notifications can continue to arrive. If the list is empty, there is nothing to do and we break out of the loop. We then pull the head item, and if it's not larger than the remaining user buffer size - copy its contents (sans the LIST_ENTRY field). The loop continues pulling items from the head until either the list is empty or the user's buffer is full.

Finally, we'll complete the request with whatever the status is and set `Information` to the count variable:

```
Irp->IoStatus.Status = status;
Irp->IoStatus.Information = count;
IoCompleteRequest(Irp, 0);
return status;
```

We need to take a look at the unload routine as well. If there are items in the linked list, they must be freed explicitly; otherwise, we have a leak on our hands:

```
void SysMonUnload(PDRIVER_OBJECT DriverObject) {
    // unregister process notifications
    PsSetCreateProcessNotifyRoutineEx(OnProcessNotify, TRUE);

    UNICODE_STRING symLink = RTL_CONSTANT_STRING(L"\\??\\sysmon");
    IoDeleteSymbolicLink(&symLink);
    IoDeleteDevice(DriverObject->DeviceObject);

    // free remaining items
    while (!IsListEmpty(&g_Globals.ItemsHead)) {
        auto entry = RemoveHeadList(&g_Globals.ItemsHead);
        ExFreePool(CONTAINING_RECORD(entry, FullItem<ItemHeader>, Entry));
    }
}
```

The User Mode Client

Once we have all this in place, we can write a user mode client that polls data using `ReadFile` and displays the results.

The `main` function calls `ReadFile` in a loop, sleeping a bit so that the thread is not always consuming CPU. Once some data arrives, it's sent for display purposes:

```
int main() {
    auto hFile = ::CreateFile(L"\\\\.\\SysMon", GENERIC_READ, 0,
        nullptr, OPEN_EXISTING, 0, nullptr);
    if (hFile == INVALID_HANDLE_VALUE)
        return Error("Failed to open file");

    BYTE buffer[1 << 16];    // 64KB buffer

    while (true) {
        DWORD bytes;
        if (!::ReadFile(hFile, buffer, sizeof(buffer), &bytes, nullptr))
            return Error("Failed to read");

        if (bytes != 0)
            DisplayInfo(buffer, bytes);

        ::Sleep(200);
    }
}
```

The DisplayInfo function must make sense of the buffer it's been given. Since all events start with a common header, the function distinguishes the various events based on the ItemType. After the event has been dealt with, the Size field in the header indicates where the next event starts:

```
void DisplayInfo(BYTE* buffer, DWORD size) {
    auto count = size;
    while (count > 0) {
        auto header = (ItemHeader*)buffer;

        switch (header->Type) {
            case ItemType::ProcessExit:
            {
                DisplayTime(header->Time);
                auto info = (ProcessExitInfo*)buffer;
                printf("Process %d Exited\n", info->ProcessId);
                break;
            }

            case ItemType::ProcessCreate:
            {
                DisplayTime(header->Time);
                auto info = (ProcessCreateInfo*)buffer;
                std::wstring commandline((WCHAR*)(buffer + info->CommandLineOffset),
```

```
                        info->CommandLineLength);
                printf("Process %d Created. Command line: %ws\n", info->ProcessId,
                    commandline.c_str());
                break;
            }
            default:
                break;
        }
        buffer += header->Size;
        count -= header->Size;
    }
}
```

To extract the command line properly, the code uses the C++ `wstring` class constructor that can build a string based on a pointer and the string length. The `DisplayTime` helper function formats the time in a human-readable way:

```
void DisplayTime(const LARGE_INTEGER& time) {
    SYSTEMTIME st;
    ::FileTimeToSystemTime((FILETIME*)&time, &st);
    printf("%02d:%02d:%02d.%03d: ",
        st.wHour, st.wMinute, st.wSecond, st.wMilliseconds);
}
```

The driver can be installed and started as done in chapter 4, similar to the following:

```
sc create sysmon type= kernel binPath= C:\Book\SysMon.sys

sc start sysmon
```

Here is some sample output when running *SysMonClient.exe*:

```
C:\Book>SysMonClient.exe
12:06:24.747: Process 13000 Exited
12:06:31.032: Process 7484 Created. Command line: SysMonClient.exe
12:06:42.461: Process 3128 Exited
12:06:42.462: Process 7936 Exited
12:06:42.474: Process 12320 Created. Command line: "C:\$WINDOWS.~BT\Sources\mighost.\
exe" {5152EFE5-97CA-4DE6-BBD2-4F6ECE2ABD7A} /InitDoneEvent:MigHost.{5152EFE5-97CA-4D\
E6-BBD2-4F6ECE2ABD7A}.Event /ParentPID:11908 /LogDir:"C:\$WINDOWS.~BT\Sources\Panthe\
r"
12:06:42.485: Process 12796 Created. Command line: \??\C:\WINDOWS\system32\conhost.e\
```

```
xe 0xffffffff -ForceV1
12:07:09.575: Process 6784 Created. Command line: "C:\WINDOWS\system32\cmd.exe"
12:07:09.590: Process 7248 Created. Command line: \??\C:\WINDOWS\system32\conhost.ex\
e 0xffffffff -ForceV1
12:07:11.387: Process 7832 Exited
12:07:12.034: Process 2112 Created. Command line: C:\WINDOWS\system32\ApplicationFra\
meHost.exe -Embedding
12:07:12.041: Process 5276 Created. Command line: "C:\Windows\SystemApps\Microsoft.M\
icrosoftEdge_8wekyb3d8bbwe\MicrosoftEdge.exe" -ServerName:MicrosoftEdge.AppXdnhjhccw\
3zf0j06tkg3jtqr00qdm0khc.mca
12:07:12.624: Process 2076 Created. Command line: C:\WINDOWS\system32\DllHost.exe /P\
rocessid:{7966B4D8-4FDC-4126-A10B-39A3209AD251}
12:07:12.747: Process 7080 Created. Command line: C:\WINDOWS\system32\browser_broker\
.exe -Embedding
12:07:13.016: Process 8972 Created. Command line: C:\WINDOWS\System32\svchost.exe -k\
 LocalServiceNetworkRestricted
12:07:13.435: Process 12964 Created. Command line: C:\WINDOWS\system32\DllHost.exe /\
Processid:{973D20D7-562D-44B9-B70B-5A0F49CCDF3F}
12:07:13.554: Process 11072 Created. Command line: C:\WINDOWS\system32\Windows.WARP.\
JITService.exe 7f992973-8a6d-421d-b042-6afd93a19631 S-1-15-2-3624051433-2125758914-1\
423191267-1740899205-1073925389-3782572162-737981194 S-1-5-21-4017881901-586210945-2\
666946644-1001 516
12:07:14.454: Process 12516 Created. Command line: C:\Windows\System32\RuntimeBroker\
.exe -Embedding
12:07:14.914: Process 10424 Created. Command line: C:\WINDOWS\system32\MicrosoftEdge\
SH.exe SCODEF:5276 CREDAT:9730 APH:1000000000000017 JITHOST /prefetch:2
12:07:14.980: Process 12536 Created. Command line: "C:\Windows\System32\MicrosoftEdg\
eCP.exe" -ServerName:Windows.Internal.WebRuntime.ContentProcessServer
12:07:17.741: Process 7828 Created. Command line: C:\WINDOWS\system32\SearchIndexer.\
exe /Embedding
12:07:19.171: Process 2076 Exited
12:07:30.286: Process 3036 Created. Command line: "C:\Windows\System32\MicrosoftEdge\
CP.exe" -ServerName:Windows.Internal.WebRuntime.ContentProcessServer
12:07:31.657: Process 9536 Exited
```

Thread Notifications

The kernel provides thread creation and destruction callbacks, similarly to process callbacks. The API to use for registration is PsSetCreateThreadNotifyRoutine and for unregistering there is another API, PsRemoveCreateThreadNotifyRoutine. The arguments provided to the callback routine are the process ID, thread ID and whether the thread is being created or destroyed.

We'll extend the existing *SysMon* driver to receive thread notifications as well as process notifications. First, we'll add enum values for thread events and a structure representing the information, all in the *SysMonCommon.h* header file:

```
enum class ItemType : short {
    None,
    ProcessCreate,
    ProcessExit,
    ThreadCreate,
    ThreadExit
};

struct ThreadCreateExitInfo : ItemHeader {
    ULONG ThreadId;
    ULONG ProcessId;
};
```

Now we can add the proper registration to `DriverEntry`, right after registering for process notifications:

```
status = PsSetCreateThreadNotifyRoutine(OnThreadNotify);
if (!NT_SUCCESS(status)) {
    KdPrint((DRIVER_PREFIX "failed to set thread callbacks (status=%08X)\n", status)\
);
    break;
}
```

The callback routine itself is rather simple, since the event structure has constant size. Here is the thread callback routine in its entirety:

```
void OnThreadNotify(HANDLE ProcessId, HANDLE ThreadId, BOOLEAN Create) {
    auto size = sizeof(FullItem<ThreadCreateExitInfo>);
    auto info = (FullItem<ThreadCreateExitInfo>*)ExAllocatePoolWithTag(PagedPool,
        size, DRIVER_TAG);
    if (info == nullptr) {
        KdPrint((DRIVER_PREFIX "Failed to allocate memory\n"));
        return;
    }
    auto& item = info->Data;
    KeQuerySystemTimePrecise(&item.Time);
    item.Size = sizeof(item);
    item.Type = Create ? ItemType::ThreadCreate : ItemType::ThreadExit;
```

```
    item.ProcessId = HandleToULong(ProcessId);
    item.ThreadId = HandleToULong(ThreadId);

    PushItem(&info->Entry);
}
```

Most of this code should look pretty familiar.

To complete the implementation, we'll add code to the client that knows how to display thread creation and destruction (in `DisplayInfo`):

```
case ItemType::ThreadCreate:
{
    DisplayTime(header->Time);
    auto info = (ThreadCreateExitInfo*)buffer;
    printf("Thread %d Created in process %d\n",
        info->ThreadId, info->ProcessId);
    break;
}

case ItemType::ThreadExit:
{
    DisplayTime(header->Time);
    auto info = (ThreadCreateExitInfo*)buffer;
    printf("Thread %d Exited from process %d\n",
        info->ThreadId, info->ProcessId);
    break;
}
```

Here is some sample output given the updated driver and client:

```
13:06:29.631: Thread 12180 Exited from process 11976
13:06:29.885: Thread 13016 Exited from process 8820
13:06:29.955: Thread 12532 Exited from process 8560
13:06:30.218: Process 12164 Created. Command line: SysMonClient.exe
13:06:30.219: Thread 12004 Created in process 12164
13:06:30.607: Thread 12876 Created in process 10728

...

13:06:33.260: Thread 4524 Exited from process 4484
13:06:33.260: Thread 13072 Exited from process 4484
13:06:33.263: Thread 12388 Exited from process 4484
```

```
13:06:33.264: Process 4484 Exited
13:06:33.264: Thread 4960 Exited from process 5776
13:06:33.264: Thread 12660 Exited from process 5776
13:06:33.265: Process 5776 Exited
13:06:33.272: Process 2584 Created. Command line: "C:\$WINDOWS.~BT\Sources\mighost.e\
xe" {CCD9805D-B15B-4550-94FB-B2AE544639BF} /InitDoneEvent:MigHost.{CCD9805D-B15B-455\
0-94FB-B2AE544639BF}.Event /ParentPID:11908 /LogDir:"C:\$WINDOWS.~BT\Sources\Panther\
"
13:06:33.272: Thread 13272 Created in process 2584
13:06:33.280: Process 12120 Created. Command line: \??\C:\WINDOWS\system32\conhost.e\
xe 0xffffffff -ForceV1
13:06:33.280: Thread 4200 Created in process 12120
13:06:33.283: Thread 4400 Created in process 12120
13:06:33.284: Thread 9632 Created in process 12120
13:06:33.284: Thread 6064 Created in process 12120
13:06:33.289: Thread 2472 Created in process 12120
```

 Add client code that displays the process image name for thread create and exit.

Image Load Notifications

The last callback mechanism we'll look at in this chapter is image load notifications. Whenever an image (EXE, DLL, driver) file loads, the driver can receive a notification.

The PsSetLoadImageNotifyRoutine API registers for these notifications, and PsRemoveImageNo-tifyRoutine is used for unregistering. The callback function has the following prototype:

```
typedef void (*PLOAD_IMAGE_NOTIFY_ROUTINE)(
    _In_opt_ PUNICODE_STRING FullImageName,
    _In_ HANDLE ProcessId,      // pid into which image is being mapped
    _In_ PIMAGE_INFO ImageInfo);
```

> Curiously enough, there is no callback mechanism for image unloads.

The *FullImageName* argument is somewhat tricky. As indicated by the SAL annotation, it's optional and can be NULL. Even if it's not NULL, it doesn't always produce the correct image file name.

The reasons for that are rooted deep in the kernel and are beyond the scope of this book. In most cases, this works fine, and the format of the path is the internal NT format, starting with "\Device\HadrdiskVolumex\..." rather than "c:\...". Translation can be done in a few ways. We'll look at this more closely in chapter 11.

The *ProcessId* argument is the process ID into which the image is loaded. For drivers (kernel images), this value is zero.

The *ImageInfo* argument contains additional information on the image, declared as follows:

```
#define IMAGE_ADDRESSING_MODE_32BIT      3

typedef struct _IMAGE_INFO {
    union {
        ULONG Properties;
        struct {
            ULONG ImageAddressingMode  : 8;   // Code addressing mode
            ULONG SystemModeImage      : 1;   // System mode image
            ULONG ImageMappedToAllPids : 1;   // Image mapped into all processes
            ULONG ExtendedInfoPresent  : 1;   // IMAGE_INFO_EX available
            ULONG MachineTypeMismatch  : 1;   // Architecture type mismatch
            ULONG ImageSignatureLevel  : 4;   // Signature level
            ULONG ImageSignatureType   : 3;   // Signature type
            ULONG ImagePartialMap      : 1;   // Nonzero if entire image is not mapped
            ULONG Reserved             : 12;
        };
    };
    PVOID       ImageBase;
    ULONG       ImageSelector;
    SIZE_T      ImageSize;
    ULONG       ImageSectionNumber;
} IMAGE_INFO, *PIMAGE_INFO;
```

Here is quick rundown of the important fields in this structure:

- *SystemModeImage* - this flag is set for a kernel image, and unset for a user mode image.
- *ImageSignatureLevel* - signing level (Windows 8.1 and later). See SE_SIGNING_LEVEL_ constants in the WDK.
- *ImageSignatureType* - signature type (Windows 8.1 and later). See the SE_IMAGE_SIGNATURE_-TYPE enumeration in the WDK.
- *ImageBase* - the virtual address into which the image is loaded.
- *ImageSize* - the size of the image.
- *ExtendedInfoPresent* - if this flag is set, then IMAGE_INFO is part of a larger structure, IMAGE_-INFO_EX, shown here:

```
typedef struct _IMAGE_INFO_EX {
    SIZE_T              Size;
    IMAGE_INFO          ImageInfo;
    struct _FILE_OBJECT *FileObject;
} IMAGE_INFO_EX, *PIMAGE_INFO_EX;
```

To access this larger structure, a driver uses the CONTAINING_RECORD like so:

```
if (ImageInfo->ExtendedInfoPresent) {
    auto exinfo = CONTAINING_RECORD(ImageInfo, IMAGE_INFO_EX, ImageInfo);
    // access FileObject
}
```

The extended structure adds just one meaningful member - the file object used to manage the image. The driver can add a reference to the object (ObReferenceObject) and use it in other functions as needed.

 Add image load notifications to the *SysMon* driver, collecting user mode image loads only. The client should show the image path, process ID and the image base address.

Exercises

1. Create a driver that monitors process creation and allows a client application to configure executable paths that should not be allowed to execute.
2. Write a driver (or add to the *SysMon* driver) the ability to detect remote thread creations - threads created in processes other than their own. Hint: the first thread in a process is always created "remotely". Notify the user mode client when this occurs. Write a test application that uses CreateRemoteThread to test your detection.

Summary

In this chapter we looked at some of the callback mechanisms provided by the kernel: process, thread and images. In the next chapter, we'll continue with more callback mechanisms - objects and registry.

Chapter 9: Object and Registry Notifications

The kernel provides more ways to intercept certain operations. First, we'll examine object notifications, where obtaining handles to some types of objects can be intercepted. Next, we'll look at registry operation interception.

In this chapter:

- Object Notifications
- The Process Protector Driver
- Registry Notifications
- Implementing Registry Notifications
- Exercises

Object Notifications

The kernel provides a mechanism to notify interested drivers when attempts to open or duplicate a handle to certain object types. The officially supported object types are process, thread, and for Windows 10 - desktop as well.

Desktop Objects

A desktop is a kernel object contained in a Window Station, yet another kernel object, which is in itself part of a Session. A desktop contains windows, menus and hooks. The hooks referred to here are user mode hooks available with the SetWindowsHookEx API.

Normally, when a user logs in, two desktops are created. A desktop named "Winlogon" is created by *Winlogon.exe*. This is the desktop that you see when pressing the *Secure Attention Sequence* key combination(SAS, normally Ctrl+Alt+Del). The second desktop is named "default" and is the normal desktop we know where are normal windows are visible. Switching to another desktop is done with the SwitchDesktop API. For some more details, read this blog post[a].

---
[a]https://scorpiosoftware.net/2019/02/17/windows-10-desktops-vs-sysinternals-desktops/

The registration API to call is `ObRegisterCallbacks`, prototyped like so:

```
NTSTATUS ObRegisterCallbacks (
    _In_ POB_CALLBACK_REGISTRATION CallbackRegistration,
    _Outptr_ PVOID *RegistrationHandle);
```

Prior to registration, an `OB_CALLBACK_REGISTRATION` structure must be initialized, which provides the necessary details about what the driver is registering for. The *RegistrationHandle* is the return value upon a successful registration, which is just an opaque pointer used for unregistration by calling `ObUnRegisterCallbacks`.

> Drivers using `ObRegisterCallbacks` must be linked with the `/integritycheck` switch.

Here is the definition of `OB_CALLBACK_REGISTRATION`:

```
typedef struct _OB_CALLBACK_REGISTRATION {
    _In_ USHORT                      Version;
    _In_ USHORT                      OperationRegistrationCount;
    _In_ UNICODE_STRING              Altitude;
    _In_ PVOID                       RegistrationContext;
    _In_ OB_OPERATION_REGISTRATION   *OperationRegistration;
} OB_CALLBACK_REGISTRATION, *POB_CALLBACK_REGISTRATION;
```

Version is just a constant that must be set to `OB_FLT_REGISTRATION_VERSION` (currently `0x100`). Next, the number of operations that are being registered is specified by *OperationRegistrationCount*. This determines the number of `OB_OPERATION_REGISTRATION` structures that are pointed to by *OperationRegistration*. Each one of these provides information on an object type of interest (process, thread or desktop).

The *Altitude* argument is interesting. It specifies a number (in string form) that affects the order of callbacks invocations for this driver. This is necessary because other drivers may have their own callbacks and the question of which driver is invoked first is answered by the altitude - the higher the altitude, the earlier in the call chain the driver is invoked.

What value should the altitude be? It shouldn't matter in most cases, and is up to the driver. The altitude provided must not collide with altitudes specified by previously registered drivers. The altitude does not have to be an integer number. In fact, it's an infinite precision decimal number, and this is why it's specified as a string. To avoid collision, the altitude should be set to something with random numbers after a decimal point, such as "12345.1762389". The chances of collision in this case are slim. The driver can even truly generate random digits to avoid collisions. If the registration fails with a status of STATUS_FLT_INSTANCE_ALTITUDE_COLLISION, this means altitude collision, so the careful driver can adjust its altitude and try again.

> The concept of Altitude is also used for registry filtering (see "Registry Notifications" later in this chapter) and file system mini-filters (see next chapter).

Finally, *RegistrationContext* is a driver defined value that is passed in as-is to the callback routine(s).

The OB_OPERATION_REGISTRATION structure(s) is where the driver sets up its callbacks, determines which object types and operations are of interest. It's defined like so:

```
typedef struct _OB_OPERATION_REGISTRATION {
    _In_ POBJECT_TYPE                *ObjectType;
    _In_ OB_OPERATION                Operations;
    _In_ POB_PRE_OPERATION_CALLBACK  PreOperation;
    _In_ POB_POST_OPERATION_CALLBACK PostOperation;
} OB_OPERATION_REGISTRATION, *POB_OPERATION_REGISTRATION;
```

ObjectType is a pointer to the object type for this instance registration - process, thread or desktop. These pointers are exported as global kernel variables: PsProcessType, PsThreadType and ExDesktopObjectType, respectively.

The *Operations* field is an bit flags enumeration selecting create/open (OB_OPERATION_HANDLE_CREATE) and/or duplicate (OB_OPERATION_HANDLE_DUPLICATE).

OB_OPERATION_HANDLE_CREATE refers to calls to user mode functions such as CreateProcess, OpenProcess, CreateThread, OpenThread, CreateDesktop, OpenDesktop and similar functions for these object types. OB_OPERATION_HANDLE_DUPLICATE refers to handle duplication for these objects (DuplicateHandle user mode API).

Any time one of these calls is made (from the kernel as well, by the way), one or two callbacks can be registered: a pre-operation callback (*PreOperation* field) and a post-operation callback (*PostOperation*).

Pre-Operation Callback

The pre-operation callback is invoked before the actual create/open/duplicate operation completes, giving a chance to the driver to make changes to the operation's result. The pre-operation callback receives a OB_PRE_OPERATION_INFORMATION structure, defined as shown here:

```
typedef struct _OB_PRE_OPERATION_INFORMATION {
    _In_ OB_OPERATION           Operation;
    union {
        _In_ ULONG Flags;
        struct {
            _In_ ULONG KernelHandle:1;
            _In_ ULONG Reserved:31;
        };
    };
    _In_ PVOID                          Object;
    _In_ POBJECT_TYPE                   ObjectType;
    _Out_ PVOID                         CallContext;
    _In_ POB_PRE_OPERATION_PARAMETERS   Parameters;
} OB_PRE_OPERATION_INFORMATION, *POB_PRE_OPERATION_INFORMATION;
```

Here is a rundown of the structure's members:

- *Operation* - indicates what operation is this (OB_OPERATION_HANDLE_CREATE or OB_OPERA-TION_HANDLE_DUPLICATE).
- *KernelHandle* (inside *Flags*) - indicates this is a kernel handle. Kernel handles can only be created and used by kernel code. This allows the driver to perhaps ignore kernel requests.
- *Object* - the pointer to the actual object for which a handle is being created/opened/duplicated. For processes, this is the EPROCESS address, for thread it's the PETHREAD address.
- *ObjectType* - points to the object type: *PsProcessType, *PsThreadType or *ExDesktopObjectType.
- *CallContext* - a driver-defined value, that is propagated to the post-callback for this instance (if exists).
- *Parameters* - a union specifying additional information based on the *Operation*. This union is defined like so:

```
typedef union _OB_PRE_OPERATION_PARAMETERS {
    _Inout_ OB_PRE_CREATE_HANDLE_INFORMATION      CreateHandleInformation;
    _Inout_ OB_PRE_DUPLICATE_HANDLE_INFORMATION   DuplicateHandleInformation;
} OB_PRE_OPERATION_PARAMETERS, *POB_PRE_OPERATION_PARAMETERS;
```

The driver should inspect the appropriate field based on the operation. For Create operations, the driver receives the following information:

```
typedef struct _OB_PRE_CREATE_HANDLE_INFORMATION {
    _Inout_ ACCESS_MASK            DesiredAccess;
    _In_ ACCESS_MASK               OriginalDesiredAccess;
} OB_PRE_CREATE_HANDLE_INFORMATION, *POB_PRE_CREATE_HANDLE_INFORMATION;
```

The *OriginalDesiredAccess* is the access mask specified by the caller. Consider this user mode code to open a handle to an existing process:

```
HANDLE OpenHandleToProcess(DWORD pid) {
    HANDLE hProcess = OpenProcess(PROCESS_QUERY_INFORMATION | PROCESS_VM_READ,
        FALSE, pid);
    if(!hProcess) {
        // failed to open a handle
    }
    return hProcess;
}
```

In this example, the client tries to obtain a handle to a process with the specified access mask, indicating what are its "intentions" towards that process. The driver's pre-operation callback receives this value in the *OriginalDesiredAccess* field. This value is also copied to *DesiredAccess*. Normally, the kernel will determine, based on the client's security context and the process' security descriptor whether the client can be granted the access it desires.

The driver can, based on its own logic, modify *DesiredAccess* for example by removing some of the access requested by the client:

```
OB_PREOP_CALLBACK_STATUS OnPreOpenProcess(PVOID /* RegistrationContext */,
    POB_PRE_OPERATION_INFORMATION Info) {

    if(/* some logic */) {
        Info->Parameters->CreateHandleInformation.DesiredAccess &= ~PROCESS_VM_READ;
    }
    return OB_PREOP_SUCCESS;
}
```

The above code snippet removes the PROCESS_VM_READ access mask before letting the operation continue normally. If it eventually succeeds, the client will get back a valid handle, but only with PROCESS_QUERY_INFORMATION access mask.

 You can find the complete list of process, thread and desktop access masks in the MSDN documentation.

You cannot add new access mask bits that were not requested by the client.

For duplicate operations, the information provided to the driver is the following:

```
typedef struct _OB_PRE_DUPLICATE_HANDLE_INFORMATION {
    _Inout_ ACCESS_MASK          DesiredAccess;
    _In_ ACCESS_MASK             OriginalDesiredAccess;
    _In_ PVOID                   SourceProcess;
    _In_ PVOID                   TargetProcess;
} OB_PRE_DUPLICATE_HANDLE_INFORMATION, *POB_PRE_DUPLICATE_HANDLE_INFORMATION;
```

The *DesiredAccess* field can be modified as before. The extra information provided are the source process (from which a handle is being duplicated) and the target process (the process the new handle will be duplicated into). This allows the driver to query various properties of these processes before making a decision on how to modify (if at all) the desired access mask.

 How can we get more information on a process given its address? Since the EPROCESS structure is undocumented, and there only a handful of exported and documented functions that deal with such pointers directly - getting detailed information may seem problematic. An alternative is to use ZwQueryInformationProcess to get the information required, but the function requires a handle, which can be obtained by calling ObOpenObjectByPointer. We'll discuss this technique in greater detail in chapter 11.

Post-Operation Callback

Post-operation callbacks are invoked after the operation completes. At this point the driver cannot make any modifications, it can only look at the results. The post-operation callback receives the following structure:

```
typedef struct _OB_POST_OPERATION_INFORMATION {
    _In_ OB_OPERATION  Operation;
    union {
        _In_ ULONG Flags;
        struct {
            _In_ ULONG KernelHandle:1;
            _In_ ULONG Reserved:31;
        };
    };
    _In_ PVOID                        Object;
```

```
    _In_ POBJECT_TYPE                   ObjectType;
    _In_ PVOID                          CallContext;
    _In_ NTSTATUS                       ReturnStatus;
    _In_ POB_POST_OPERATION_PARAMETERS  Parameters;
} OB_POST_OPERATION_INFORMATION, *POB_POST_OPERATION_INFORMATION;
```

This looks similar to the pre-operation callback information, except for the following:

- The final status of the operation is returned in *ReturnStatus*. If successful, it means the client will get back a valid handle (possibly with a reduced access mask).
- The *Parameters* union provided has just one piece of information: the access mask granted to the client (assuming the status is successful).

The Process Protector Driver

The Process Protector driver is an example for using object callbacks. Its purpose is to protect certain processes from termination by denying the PROCESS_TERMINATE access mask from any client that requests it for these "protected" processes.

> The complete driver and client projects are at the usual Github repo[a].
>
> [a]https://github.com/zodiacon/windowskernelprogrammingbook

The driver should keep a list of protected processes. In this driver we'll use a simple limited array to hold the process IDs under the driver's protection. Here is the structure used to hold the driver's global data (defined in *ProcessProtect.h*):

```
#define DRIVER_PREFIX "ProcessProtect: "

#define PROCESS_TERMINATE 1

#include "FastMutex.h"

const int MaxPids = 256;

struct Globals {
    int PidsCount;          // currently protected process count
    ULONG Pids[MaxPids];    // protected PIDs
    FastMutex Lock;
    PVOID RegHandle;        // object registration cookie
```

```
    void Init() {
        Lock.Init();
    }
};
```

 Notice that we must define PROCESS_TERMINATE explicitly, since it's not defined in the WDK headers (only PROCESS_ALL_ACCESS is defined). It's fairly easy to get its definition from user mode headers or documentation.

The main file (*ProcessProtect.cpp*) declares a global variable of type Globals named *g_Data* (and calls Init at the beginning of DriverEntry).

Object Notification Registration

The DriverEntry routine for the *process protector* driver must include registration to object callbacks for processes. First, we prepare the structures for registration:

```
OB_OPERATION_REGISTRATION operations[] = {
    {
        PsProcessType,            // object type
        OB_OPERATION_HANDLE_CREATE | OB_OPERATION_HANDLE_DUPLICATE,
        OnPreOpenProcess, nullptr   // pre, post
    }
};
```

```
OB_CALLBACK_REGISTRATION reg = {
    OB_FLT_REGISTRATION_VERSION,
    1,        // operation count
    RTL_CONSTANT_STRING(L"12345.6171"),       // altitude
    nullptr,        // context
    operations
};
```

The registration is for process objects only, with a pre-callback provided. This callback should remove the PROCESS_TERMINATE from the desired access requested by whatever client.

Now we're ready to do the actual registration:

```
do {
    status = ObRegisterCallbacks(&reg, &g_Data.RegHandle);
    if (!NT_SUCCESS(status)) {
        break;
    }
}
```

Managing Protected Processes

The driver maintains an array of process IDs for processes under its protection. The driver exposes three I/O control codes to allow adding and removing PIDs as well as clearing the entire list. The control codes are defined in *ProcessProtectCommon.h*:

```
#define PROCESS_PROTECT_NAME L"ProcessProtect"

#define IOCTL_PROCESS_PROTECT_BY_PID    \
    CTL_CODE(0x8000, 0x800, METHOD_BUFFERED, FILE_ANY_ACCESS)
#define IOCTL_PROCESS_UNPROTECT_BY_PID  \
    CTL_CODE(0x8000, 0x801, METHOD_BUFFERED, FILE_ANY_ACCESS)
#define IOCTL_PROCESS_PROTECT_CLEAR     \
    CTL_CODE(0x8000, 0x802, METHOD_NEITHER, FILE_ANY_ACCESS)
```

For protecting and unprotecting processes, the handler for IRP_MJ_DEVICE_CONTROL accepts an array of PIDs (not necessarily just one). The handler's skeleton code is the standard switch for known control codes:

```
NTSTATUS ProcessProtectDeviceControl(PDEVICE_OBJECT, PIRP Irp) {
    auto stack = IoGetCurrentIrpStackLocation(Irp);
    auto status = STATUS_SUCCESS;
    auto len = 0;

    switch (stack->Parameters.DeviceIoControl.IoControlCode) {
        case IOCTL_PROCESS_PROTECT_BY_PID:
            //...
            break;

        case IOCTL_PROCESS_UNPROTECT_BY_PID:
            //...
            break;

        case IOCTL_PROCESS_PROTECT_CLEAR:
            //...
```

```
            break;

        default:
            status = STATUS_INVALID_DEVICE_REQUEST;
            break;
    }

    // complete the request
    Irp->IoStatus.Status = status;
    Irp->IoStatus.Information = len;
    IoCompleteRequest(Irp, IO_NO_INCREMENT);
    return status;
}
```

To help with adding and removing PIDs, we'll create two helper functions for this purpose:

```
bool AddProcess(ULONG pid) {
    for(int i = 0; i < MaxPids; i++)
        if (g_Data.Pids[i] == 0) {
            // empty slot
            g_Data.Pids[i] = pid;
            g_Data.PidsCount++;
            return true;
        }
    return false;
}

bool RemoveProcess(ULONG pid) {
    for (int i = 0; i < MaxPids; i++)
        if (g_Data.Pids[i] == pid) {
            g_Data.Pids[i] = 0;
            g_Data.PidsCount--;
            return true;
        }
    return false;
}
```

Notice that the fast mutex is not acquired in these functions, which means the caller must acquire the fast mutex before calling AddProcess or RemoveProcess.

A final help function we'll use searches for a process ID in the array and returns true if found:

```
bool FindProcess(ULONG pid) {
    for (int i = 0; i < MaxPids; i++)
        if (g_Data.Pids[i] == pid)
            return true;
    return false;
}
```

Now we're ready to implement the I/O control codes. For adding a process we need to find an empty "slot" in the process ID array and store the requested PID; of course, we can receive more than one PID.

```
case IOCTL_PROCESS_PROTECT_BY_PID:
{
    auto size = stack->Parameters.DeviceIoControl.InputBufferLength;
    if (size % sizeof(ULONG) != 0) {
        status = STATUS_INVALID_BUFFER_SIZE;
        break;
    }

    auto data = (ULONG*)Irp->AssociatedIrp.SystemBuffer;

    AutoLock locker(g_Data.Lock);

    for (int i = 0; i < size / sizeof(ULONG); i++) {
        auto pid = data[i];
        if (pid == 0) {
            status = STATUS_INVALID_PARAMETER;
            break;
        }
        if (FindProcess(pid))
            continue;

        if (g_Data.PidsCount == MaxPids) {
            status = STATUS_TOO_MANY_CONTEXT_IDS;
            break;
        }

        if (!AddProcess(pid)) {
            status = STATUS_UNSUCCESSFUL;
            break;
        }

        len += sizeof(ULONG);
```

```
    }

    break;
}
```

First, the code checks the buffer size which must be a multiple of four bytes (PIDs) and not zero. Next, the pointer to the system buffer is retrieved (the control code uses METHOD_BUFFERED - see chapter 7 if you need a refresher). Now the fast mutex is acquired and a loop begins.

The loop goes over all PIDs provided in the request and if all the following is true, adds the PID to the array:

- The PID is not zero (always an illegal PID, reserved for the Idle process).
- The PID is not already in the array (FindProcess determines that).
- The number of managed PIDs has not exceeded *MaxPids*.

Removing a PID is similar. We have to find it and then "remove" it by placing a zero in that slot (this is a task for RemoveProcess):

```
case IOCTL_PROCESS_UNPROTECT_BY_PID:
{
    auto size = stack->Parameters.DeviceIoControl.InputBufferLength;
    if (size % sizeof(ULONG) != 0) {
        status = STATUS_INVALID_BUFFER_SIZE;
        break;
    }

    auto data = (ULONG*)Irp->AssociatedIrp.SystemBuffer;

    AutoLock locker(g_Data.Lock);

    for (int i = 0; i < size / sizeof(ULONG); i++) {
        auto pid = data[i];
        if (pid == 0) {
            status = STATUS_INVALID_PARAMETER;
            break;
        }
        if (!RemoveProcess(pid))
            continue;

        len += sizeof(ULONG);

        if (g_Data.PidsCount == 0)
```

```
            break;
    }

    break;
}
```

 Remember that using AutoLock without the templated type requires setting the project's
C++ language standard to C++ 17.

Finally, clearing the list is fairly simple, as long as it's done while holding the lock:

```
case IOCTL_PROCESS_PROTECT_CLEAR:
{
    AutoLock locker(g_Data.Lock);
    ::memset(&g_Data.Pids, 0, sizeof(g_Data.Pids));
    g_Data.PidsCount = 0;
    break;
}
```

The Pre-Callback

The most important piece of the driver is removing the PROCESS_TERMINATE for PIDs that are
currently being protected from termination:

```
OB_PREOP_CALLBACK_STATUS
OnPreOpenProcess(PVOID, POB_PRE_OPERATION_INFORMATION Info) {
    if(Info->KernelHandle)
        return OB_PREOP_SUCCESS;

    auto process = (PEPROCESS)Info->Object;
    auto pid = HandleToULong(PsGetProcessId(process));

    AutoLock locker(g_Data.Lock);
    if (FindProcess(pid)) {
        // found in list, remove terminate access
        Info->Parameters->CreateHandleInformation.DesiredAccess &=
            ~PROCESS_TERMINATE;
    }

    return OB_PREOP_SUCCESS;
}
```

If the handle is a kernel handle, we let the operation continue normally. This makes sense, since we don't want to stop kernel code from working properly.

Now we need the process ID for which a handle is being opened. The data provided in the callback as the object pointer. Fortunately, getting the PID is simple with the `PsGetProcessId` API. It accepts a `PEPROCESS` and returns its ID.

The last part if checking whether we're actually protecting this particular process or not, so we call `FindProcess` under the protection of the lock. If found, we remove the `PROCESS_TERMINATE` access mask.

The Client Application

The client application should be able to add, remove and clear processes by issuing correct `DeviceIo-Control` calls. The command line interface is demonstrated by the following commands (assuming the executable is *Protect.exe*):

Protect.exe add 1200 2820 (protect PIDs 1200 and 2820)

Protect.exe remove 2820 (remove protection from PID 2820)

Protect.exe clear (remove all PIDs from protection)

Here is the `main` function:

```
int wmain(int argc, const wchar_t* argv[]) {
    if(argc < 2)
        return PrintUsage();

    enum class Options {
        Unknown,
        Add, Remove, Clear
    };
    Options option;
    if (::_wcsicmp(argv[1], L"add") == 0)
        option = Options::Add;
    else if (::_wcsicmp(argv[1], L"remove") == 0)
        option = Options::Remove;
    else if (::_wcsicmp(argv[1], L"clear") == 0)
        option = Options::Clear;
    else {
        printf("Unknown option.\n");
        return PrintUsage();
    }

    HANDLE hFile = ::CreateFile(L"\\\\.\\" PROCESS_PROTECT_NAME,
```

```cpp
        GENERIC_WRITE | GENERIC_READ, 0, nullptr, OPEN_EXISTING, 0, nullptr);
    if (hFile == INVALID_HANDLE_VALUE)
        return Error("Failed to open device");

    std::vector<DWORD> pids;
    BOOL success = FALSE;
    DWORD bytes;
    switch (option) {
        case Options::Add:
            pids = ParsePids(argv + 2, argc - 2);
            success = ::DeviceIoControl(hFile, IOCTL_PROCESS_PROTECT_BY_PID,
                pids.data(), static_cast<DWORD>(pids.size()) * sizeof(DWORD),
                nullptr, 0, &bytes, nullptr);
            break;

        case Options::Remove:
            pids = ParsePids(argv + 2, argc - 2);
            success = ::DeviceIoControl(hFile, IOCTL_PROCESS_UNPROTECT_BY_PID,
                pids.data(), static_cast<DWORD>(pids.size()) * sizeof(DWORD),
                nullptr, 0, &bytes, nullptr);
            break;

        case Options::Clear:
            success = ::DeviceIoControl(hFile, IOCTL_PROCESS_PROTECT_CLEAR,
                nullptr, 0, nullptr, 0, &bytes, nullptr);
            break;

    }

    if (!success)
        return Error("Failed in DeviceIoControl");

    printf("Operation succeeded.\n");

    ::CloseHandle(hFile);

    return 0;
}
```

The *ParsePids* helper function parses process IDs and returns them as a std::vector<DWORD> that it's easy to pass as an array by using the data() method on std::vector<T>:

```
std::vector<DWORD> ParsePids(const wchar_t* buffer[], int count) {
    std::vector<DWORD> pids;
    for (int i = 0; i < count; i++)
        pids.push_back(::_wtoi(buffer[i]));
    return pids;
}
```

Finally, the *Error* function is the same we used in previous projects, while *PrintUsage* just displays simple usage information.

The driver is installed normally, and then started:

```
sc create protect type= kernel binPath= c:\book\processprotect.sys
```

```
sc start protect
```

Let's test it by launching process (*Notepad.exe*) as an example, protecting it, and then trying to kill it with *Task Manager*. Figure 9-1 shows the notepad instance running.

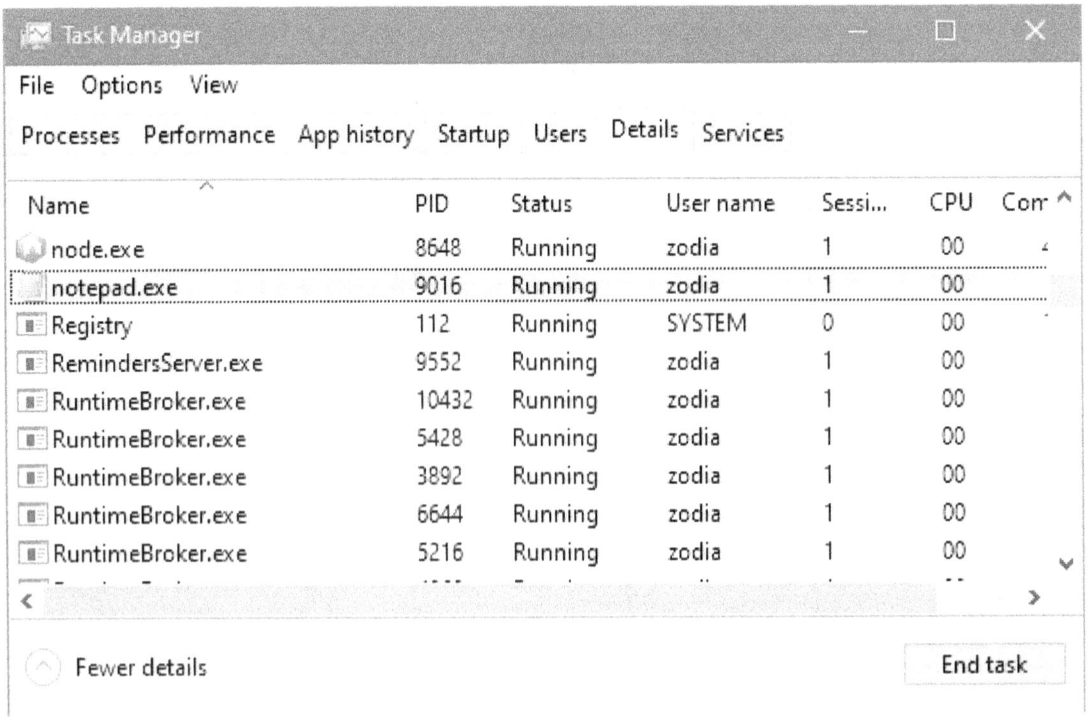

Figure 9-1: Notepad running

Now protect it:

```
protect add 9016
```

Clicking **End task** in Task Manager, pops up an error, shown in figure 9-2.

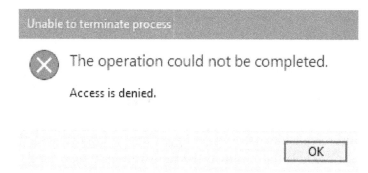

Figure 9-2: Attempting to terminate process

We can remove the protection and try again. This time the process is terminated as expected.

```
protect remove 9016
```

 In the case of notepad, even with protection, clicking the window close button or selecting *File/Exit* from the menu would terminate the process. This is because it's being done internally by calling ExitProcess which does not involve any handles. This means the protection mechanism we devised here is essentially good for processes without user interface.

 Add a control code that allows querying the currently protected processes. You can name the I/O control code IOCTL_PROCESS_QUERY_PIDS.

Registry Notifications

Somewhat similar to object notifications, the Configuration Manager (the part in the Executive that deals with the registry) can be used to register for notifications when registry keys are accesses.

The CmRegisterCallbackEx API is used for registering to such notifications. Its prototype is as follows:

```
NTSTATUS CmRegisterCallbackEx (
    _In_         PEX_CALLBACK_FUNCTION    Function,
    _In_         PCUNICODE_STRING         Altitude,
    _In_         PVOID                    Driver,        // PDRIVER_OBJECT
    _In_opt_     PVOID                    Context,
    _Out_        PLARGE_INTEGER           Cookie,
    _Reserved_   PVOID                    Reserved
```

Function is the callback itself, which we'll look at in a moment. *Altitude* is the driver's callback altitude, which essentially has the same meaning as with object callbacks. The *Driver* argument should be the driver object available in DriverEntry. *Context* is a driver-defined value passed as-is to the callback. Finally, *Cookie* is the result of the registration if successful. This cookie should be passed to CmUnregisterCallback to unregister.

> It's a bit annoying that all the various registration APIs are non consistent with respect to registration/unregistration: CmRegisterCallbackEx returns a LARGE_INTEGER as representing the registration; ObRegisterCallbacks returns a PVOID; process and thread registration functions return nothing (internally use the address of the callback itself to identify the registration). Finally, process and thread unregistration is done with asymmetric APIs. Oh well.

The callback function is fairly generic, shown here:

```
NTSTATUS RegistryCallback (
    _In_ PVOID CallbackContext,
    _In_opt_ PVOID Argument1,
    _In_opt_ PVOID Argument2);
```

CallbackContext is the *Context* argument passed to CmRegisterCallbackEx. The first generic argument is in fact an enumeration, REG_NOTIFY_CLASS, describing the operation for which the callback is invoked, and whether it's pre or post notification. The second argument is a pointer to a specific structure relevant to this type of notification. A driver will typically switch on the notification type like so:

```
NTSTATUS OnRegistryNotify(PVOID, PVOID Argument1, PVOID Argument2) {
    switch ((REG_NOTIFY_CLASS)(ULONG_PTR)Argument1) {
        //...
    }
}
```

Table 9-1 shows some values from the REG_NOTIFY_CLASS enumeration and the corresponding structure passed in as *Argument2*.

Table 9-1: Some registry notifications and associated structures

Notification	Associated structure
RegNtPreDeleteKey	REG_DELETE_KEY_INFORMATION
RegNtPostDeleteKey	REG_POST_OPERATION_INFORMATION
RegNtPreSetValueKey	REG_SET_VALUE_KEY_INFORMATION
RegNtPostSetValueKey	REG_POST_OPERATION_INFORMATION
RegNtPreCreateKey	REG_PRE_CREATE_KEY_INFORMATION
RegNtPostCreateKey	REG_POST_CREATE_KEY_INFORMATION

We can see in table 9-1 that post notifications use the same structure, REG_POST_CREATE_KEY_-INFORMATION.

Handling Pre-Notifications

The callback is called for pre operations before these are carried out by the Configuration Manager. The driver has the following options:

- Returning STATUS_SUCCESS from the callback instructs the Configuration Manager to continue processing the operation normally.
- Return some failure status from the callback. In this case, the Configuration Manager returns to the caller with that status and the post operation will not be invoked.
- Handle the request in some way, and then return STATUS_CALLBACK_BYPASS from the callback. The Configuration Manager returns success to the caller and does not invoke the post operation. The driver must take care to set proper values in the REG_xxx_KEY_INFORMATION provided in the callback.

Handling Post-Operations

After the operation is complete, and assuming the driver did not prevent the post operation from occurring, the callback is invoked after the Configuration Manager performed the operation. The structure provided for post operations is shown here:

```
typedef struct _REG_POST_OPERATION_INFORMATION {
    PVOID     Object;          // input
    NTSTATUS  Status;          // input
    PVOID     PreInformation;  // The pre information
    NTSTATUS  ReturnStatus;    // callback can change the outcome of the operation
    PVOID     CallContext;
    PVOID     ObjectContext;
    PVOID     Reserved;
} REG_POST_OPERATION_INFORMATION,*PREG_POST_OPERATION_INFORMATION;
```

The callback has the following options for a post-operation:

- Look at the operation result and do something benign (log it, for instance).
- Modify the return status by setting a new status value in the `ReturnStatus` field of the post operation structure, and then returning `STATUS_CALLBACK_BYPASS`. The Configuration Manager returns this new status to the caller.
- Modify the output parameters in the `REG_xxx_KEY_INFORMATION` structure and return `STATUS_SUCCESS`. The Configuration Manager returns this new data to the caller.

The `PreInformation` member of the post-operation structure points to the pre-information structure.

Performance Considerations

The registry callback is invoked for every registry operation; there is no a-priori way to filter to certain operations only. This means the callback needs to be as quick as possible since the caller is waiting. Also, there may be more than one driver in the chain of callbacks.

Some registry operations, especially read operations happen in large quantities, so it's better for a driver to avoid processing read operations, if possible. If it must process read operations, it should al least limit its processing to certain keys of interest, such as anything under *HKLM\System\CurrentControlSet* (just an example).

Write and create operations are used much less often, so in these cases the driver can do more if needed.

The bottom line is simple: do as little as possible for as few keys as possible.

Implementing Registry Notifications

We'll extended our *SysMon* driver from chapter 8 to include notifications for some registry operations. As an example, we'll add notifications for writes to somewhere under `HKEY_LOCAL_MACHINE`.

First, we'll define a data structure that would include the reported information (in *SysMonCommon.h*):

```
struct RegistrySetValueInfo : ItemHeader {
    ULONG ProcessId;
    ULONG ThreadId;
    WCHAR KeyName[256];      // full key name
    WCHAR ValueName[64];     // value name
    ULONG DataType;          // REG_xxx
    UCHAR Data[128];         // data
    ULONG DataSize;          // size of data
};
```

For simplicity, we'll use fixed-size arrays for the reported information. In a production-level driver, it's better to make this dynamic to save memory and provide complete information where needed. The *Data* array is the actual written data. Naturally, we have to limit in some way, as it can be almost arbitrarily large.

DataType is one of the REG_xxx type constants, such as REG_SZ, REG_DWORD, REG_BINARY, etc. These values are the same in user mode and kernel mode.

Next we'll add a new event type for this notification:

```
enum class ItemType : short {
    None,
    ProcessCreate,
    ProcessExit,
    ThreadCreate,
    ThreadExit,
    ImageLoad,
    RegistrySetValue    // new value
};
```

In DriverEntry, we need to add registry callback registration as part of the do/while(false) block. The returned cookie representing the registration is stored in our Globals structure:

```
UNICODE_STRING altitude = RTL_CONSTANT_STRING(L"7657.124");
status = CmRegisterCallbackEx(OnRegistryNotify, &altitude, DriverObject,
    nullptr, &g_Globals.RegCookie, nullptr);
if(!NT_SUCCESS(status)) {
    KdPrint((DRIVER_PREFIX "failed to set registry callback (%08X)\n",
        status));
    break;
}
```

Of course we must unregister in the unload routine:

```
CmUnRegisterCallback(g_Globals.RegCookie);
```

Handling Registry Callback

Our callback should only case about writes done to HKEY_LOCAL_MACHINE. First, we switch on the operation of interest:

```
NTSTATUS OnRegistryNotify(PVOID context, PVOID arg1, PVOID arg2) {
    UNREFERENCED_PARAMETER(context);

    switch ((REG_NOTIFY_CLASS)(ULONG_PTR)arg1) {
        case RegNtPostSetValueKey:
        //...
    }
    return STATUS_SUCCESS;
}
```

In this driver we don't care about any other operation, so after the switch we simply return a successful status. Note that we examine the post operation, since only the result is interesting for this driver. Next, inside the case we care about, we cast the second argument to the post operation data and check if the operation succeeded:

```
auto args = (REG_POST_OPERATION_INFORMATION*)arg2;
if (!NT_SUCCESS(args->Status))
    break;
```

If the operation is not successful, we bail out. This is just an arbitrary decision for this driver; indeed, a different driver might actually be interested in these failed attempts, and might want to investigate further.

Next, we need to check if the key in question is under HKLM. If not, we just skip this key. The internal registry paths as viewed by the kernel always start with \REGISTRY\ as the root. After that comes MACHINE\ for the local machine hive - the same as HKEY_LOCAL_MACHINE in user mode code. This means we need to check if the key in question starts with \REGISTRY\MACHINE\.

The key path is not stored in the post-structure and not even stored in the pre-structure directly. Instead, the registry key object itself is provided as part of the post-information structure. We then need to extract the key name with CmCallbackGetKeyObjectIDEx and see if it's starting with \REGISTRY\MACHINE\:

```
static const WCHAR machine[] = L"\\REGISTRY\\MACHINE\\";

PCUNICODE_STRING name;
if (NT_SUCCESS(CmCallbackGetKeyObjectIDEx(&g_Globals.RegCookie, args->Object,
    nullptr, &name, 0))) {
    // filter out none-HKLM writes
    if (::wcsncmp(name->Buffer, machine, ARRAYSIZE(machine) - 1) == 0) {
```

If the condition holds, then we need to capture the information of the operation into our notification structure and push it onto the queue. That information (data type, value name, actual value, etc.) is provided with the pre-information structure that is luckily available as part of the post-information structure we receive directly.

```
auto preInfo = (REG_SET_VALUE_KEY_INFORMATION*)args->PreInformation;
NT_ASSERT(preInfo);

auto size = sizeof(FullItem<RegistrySetValueInfo>);
auto info = (FullItem<RegistrySetValueInfo>*)ExAllocatePoolWithTag(PagedPool,
    size, DRIVER_TAG);
if (info == nullptr)
    break;

// zero out structure to make sure strings are null-terminated when copied
RtlZeroMemory(info, size);

// fill standard data
auto& item = info->Data;
KeQuerySystemTimePrecise(&item.Time);
item.Size = sizeof(item);
item.Type = ItemType::RegistrySetValue;

// get client PID/TID (this is our caller)
item.ProcessId = HandleToULong(PsGetCurrentProcessId());
item.ThreadId = HandleToULong(PsGetCurrentThreadId());

// get specific key/value data
::wcsncpy_s(item.KeyName, name->Buffer, name->Length / sizeof(WCHAR) - 1);
::wcsncpy_s(item.ValueName, preInfo->ValueName->Buffer,
    preInfo->ValueName->Length / sizeof(WCHAR) - 1);
item.DataType = preInfo->Type;
item.DataSize = preInfo->DataSize;
::memcpy(item.Data, preInfo->Data, min(item.DataSize, sizeof(item.Data)));
```

```
PushItem(&info->Entry);
```

The specific pre-information structure (REG_SET_VALUE_KEY_INFORMATION) holds the information we seek. The code is careful not to copy too much so as to overflow the statically-allocated buffers.

Finally, if CmCallbackGetKeyObjectIDEx succeeds, the resulting key name must be explicitly freed:

```
CmCallbackReleaseKeyObjectIDEx(name);
```

Modified Client Code

The client application must be modified to support this new event type. Here is one possible implementation:

```cpp
case ItemType::RegistrySetValue:
{
    DisplayTime(header->Time);
    auto info = (RegistrySetValueInfo*)buffer;
    printf("Registry write PID=%d: %ws\\%ws type: %d size: %d data: ",
        info->ProcessId, info->KeyName, info->ValueName,
        info->DataType, info->DataSize);

    switch (info->DataType) {
        case REG_DWORD:
            printf("0x%08X\n", *(DWORD*)info->Data);
            break;

        case REG_SZ:
        case REG_EXPAND_SZ:
            printf("%ws\n", (WCHAR*)info->Data);
            break;

        case REG_BINARY:
            DisplayBinary(info->Data, min(info->DataSize, sizeof(info->Data)));
            break;

        // add other cases... (REG_QWORD, REG_LINK, etc.)
        default:
            DisplayBinary(info->Data, min(info->DataSize, sizeof(info->Data)));
            break;
```

```
    }
    break;
}
```

`DisplayBinary` is a simple helper function that shows binary data as a series of hex values shown here for completeness:

```
void DisplayBinary(const UCHAR* buffer, DWORD size) {
    for (DWORD i = 0; i < size; i++)
        printf("%02X ", buffer[i]);
    printf("\n");
}
```

Here is some output for this enhanced client and driver:

```
19:22:21.509: Thread 6488 Exited from process 8808
19:22:21.509: Thread 5348 Created in process 8252
19:22:21.510: Thread 5348 Exited from process 8252
19:22:21.531: Registry write PID=7288: \REGISTRY\MACHINE\SOFTWARE\Microsoft\Windows \
Search\FileChangeClientConfigs\{5B8A4E77-3A02-4093-BDDC-B46FAB03AEF5}\FileAttributes\
FilteredOut type: 4 size: 4 data: 0x00000000
19:22:21.531: Registry write PID=7288: \REGISTRY\MACHINE\SOFTWARE\Microsoft\Windows \
Search\FileChangeClientConfigs\{5B8A4E77-3A02-4093-BDDC-B46FAB03AEF5}\UsnSourceFilte\
redOut type: 4 size: 4 data: 0x00000008
19:22:21.531: Registry write PID=7288: \REGISTRY\MACHINE\SOFTWARE\Microsoft\Windows \
Search\FileChangeClientConfigs\{5B8A4E77-3A02-4093-BDDC-B46FAB03AEF5}\UsnReasonFilte\
redOut type: 4 size: 4 data: 0x00000000
19:22:21.531: Registry write PID=7288: \REGISTRY\MACHINE\SOFTWARE\Microsoft\Windows \
Search\FileChangeClientConfigs\{5B8A4E77-3A02-4093-BDDC-B46FAB03AEF5}\ConfigFlags ty\
pe: 4 size: 4 data: 0x00000001
19:22:21.531: Registry write PID=7288: \REGISTRY\MACHINE\SOFTWARE\Microsoft\Windows \
Search\FileChangeClientConfigs\{5B8A4E77-3A02-4093-BDDC-B46FAB03AEF5}\ScopeToMonitor\
 type: 1 size: 270 data: C:\Users\zodia\AppData\Local\Packages\Microsoft.Windows.Con\
tentD19:22:21.531: Registry write PID=7288: \REGISTRY\MACHINE\SOFTWARE\Microsoft\Win\
dows Search\FileChangeClientConfigs\{5B8A4E77-3A02-4093-BDDC-B46FAB03AEF5}\Monitored\
PathRegularExpressionExclusion type: 1 size: 2 data:
19:22:21.531: Registry write PID=7288: \REGISTRY\MACHINE\SOFTWARE\Microsoft\Windows \
Search\FileChangeClientConfigs\{5B8A4E77-3A02-4093-BDDC-B46FAB03AEF5}\ApplicationNam\
e type: 1 size: 36 data: RuntimeBroker.exe
19:22:21.531: Registry write PID=7288: \REGISTRY\MACHINE\SOFTWARE\Microsoft\Windows \
Search\FileChangeClientConfigs\{5B8A4E77-3A02-4093-BDDC-B46FAB03AEF5}\ClientId type:\
 4 size: 4 data: 0x00000001
```

```
19:22:21.531: Registry write PID=7288: \REGISTRY\MACHINE\SOFTWARE\Microsoft\Windows \
Search\FileChangeClientConfigs\{5B8A4E77-3A02-4093-BDDC-B46FAB03AEF5}\VolumeIndex ty\
pe: 4 size: 4 data: 0x00000001
19:22:21.678: Thread 4680 Exited from process 6040
19:22:21.678: Thread 4760 Exited from process 6040
```

 Enhance *SysMon* by adding I/O control codes to enable/disable certain notification types
(processes, threads, image loads, registry).

Exercises

1. Implement a driver that will not allow thread injection into other processes unless the target
   process is being debugged.
2. Implement a driver that protects a registry key from modifications. A client can send the driver
   registry keys to protect or unprotect.
3. Implement a driver that redirects registry write operations coming from selected processes
   (configured by a client application) to their own private key if they access *HKEY_LOCAL_-
   MACHINE*. If the app is writing data, it goes to its private store. If it's reading data, first check the
   private store, and if no value is there go to the real registry key. This is one facet of *application
   sandboxing*.

Summary

In this chapter, we looked at two callback mechanisms supported by the kernel - obtaining handles to
certain objects and registry access. In the next chapter, we'll dive into a new territory of file system
mini-filters.

Chapter 10: Introduction to File System Mini-Filters

File systems are targets for I/O operations to access files. Windows supports several file systems, most notably NTFS, its native file system. File system filtering is the mechanism by which drivers can intercept calls destined to the file system. This is useful for many type of software, such as anti-viruses, backups, encryption and many more.

Windows supported for a long time a filtering model known as *file system filters*, which is now referred to as *file system legacy filters*. A newer model called *file system mini-filters* was developed to replace the legacy filter mechanism. Mini-filters are easier to write in many respects, and are the preferred way to develop file system filtering drivers. In this chapter we'll cover the basics of file system mini-filters.

In this chapter:

- **Introduction**
- **Loading and Unloading**
- **Initialization**
- **Installation**
- **Processing I/O Operations**
- **The Delete Protector Driver**
- **File Names**
- **Contexts**
- **Initiating I/O Requests**
- **The File Backup Driver**
- **User Mode Communication**
- **Debugging**
- **Exercises**

Introduction

Legacy file system filters are notoriously difficult to write. The driver writer has to take care of an assortment of little details, many of them boilerplate, complicating development. Legacy filters cannot be unloaded while the system is running which means the system had to be restarted to load an update version of the driver. With the mini-filter model, drivers can be loaded and unloaded dynamically, thus simplifying the development workflow considerably.

Internally, a legacy filter provided by Windows called the *Filter Manager* is tasked with managing mini-filters. A typical filter layering is shown in figure 10-1.

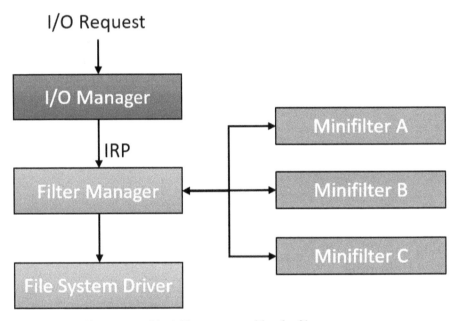

Figure 10-1: Mini-filters managed by the filter manager

Each mini-filter has its own *Altitude*, which determines its relative position in the device stack. The filter manager is the one receiving the IRPs just like any other legacy filter and then calls upon the mini-filters it's managing, in descending order of altitude.

In some unusual cases, there may be another legacy filter in the hierarchy, that may cause a mini-filter "split", where some are higher in altitude than the legacy filter and some lower. In such a case, more than one instance of the filter manager will load, each managing its own mini-filters. Every such filter manager instance is referred to as *Frame*. Figure 10-2 shows such an example with two frames.

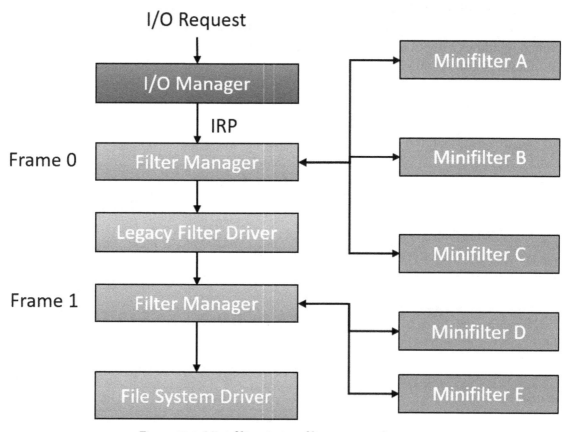

I/O Request

Figure 10-2: Mini-filters in two filter manager frames

Loading and Unloading

Mini-filter drivers must be loaded just like any other driver. The user mode API to use is FilterLoad, passing the driver's name (its key in the registry at *HKLM\System\CurrentControlSet\Services\drivername*). Internally, the kernel FltLoadFilter API is invoked, with the same semantics. Just like any other driver, the SeLoadDriverPrivilege must be present in the caller's token if called from user mode. By default, it's present in admin-level tokens, but not in standard users tokens.

> Loading a mini-filter driver is equivalent to loading a standard software driver. Unloading, however, is not.

Unloading a mini-filter is accomplished with the FilterUnload API in user mode, or FltUnload-Filter in kernel mode. This operation requires the same privilege as for loads, but is not guaranteed to succeed, because the mini-filter's *Filter unload callback* (discussed later) is called, which can fail the request so that driver remains in the system.

Although using APIs to load and unload filters has its uses, during development it's usually easier to
use a built-in tool that can accomplish that (and more) called *fltmc.exe*. Invoking it (from an elevated
command window) without arguments lists the currently loaded mini-filters. Here is the output on
my Windows 10 Pro version 1903 machine:

```
C:\WINDOWS\system32>fltmc

Filter Name                     Num Instances    Altitude    Frame
------------------------------  -------------    --------    -----
bindflt                                     1      409800        0
FsDepends                                   9      407000        0
WdFilter                                   10      328010        0
storqosflt                                  1      244000        0
wcifs                                       3      189900        0
PrjFlt                                      1      189800        0
CldFlt                                      2      180451        0
FileCrypt                                   0      141100        0
luafv                                       1      135000        0
npsvctrig                                   1       46000        0
Wof                                         8       40700        0
FileInfo                                   10       40500        0
```

For each filter, the output shows the driver's name, the number of instances each filter has currently
running (each instance is attached to a volume), its altitude and the filter manager frame it's part of.

You may be wondering why there are drivers with different number of instances. The short answer
is that it's up to the driver to decide whether to attach to a given volume or not (we'll look at this in
more detail later in this chapter).

Loading a driver with *fltmc.exe* is done with the *load* option, like so:

```
fltmc load myfilter
```

Conversely, unloading is done with the *unload* command line option:

```
fltmc unload myfilter
```

fltmc includes other options. Type fltmc -? to get the full list. For example, you can get the details
of all instances for each driver using fltmc instances. Similarly, you can get a list of all volumes
mounted on a system with fltmc volumes. We'll see later in this chapter how this information is
conveyed to the driver.

File system drivers and filters are created in the *FileSystem* directory of the Object Manager
namespace. Figure 10-3 shows this directory in *WinObj*.

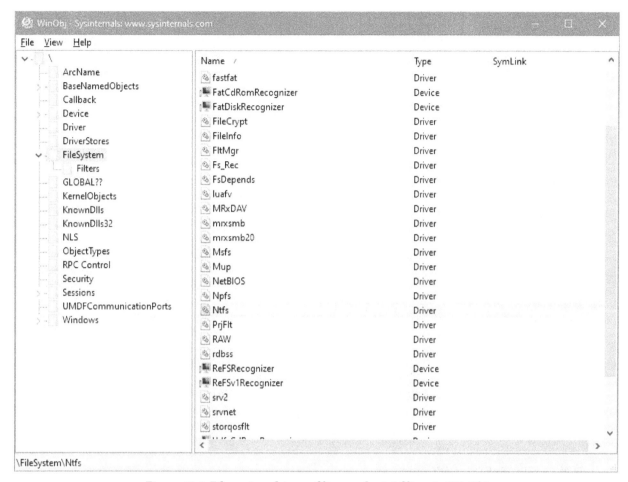

Figure 10-3: File system drivers, filters and mini-filters in WinObj

Initialization

A file system mini-filter driver has a DriverEntry routine, just like any other driver. The driver must register itself as a mini-filter with the filter manager, specifying various settings, such as what operations it wishes to intercept. The driver sets up appropriate structures and then calls FltRegisterFilter to register. If successful, the driver can do further initializations as needed and finally call FltStartFiltering to actually start filtering operations. Note that the driver does **not** need to set up dispatch routines on its own (IRP_MJ_READ, IRP_MJ_WRITE, etc.). This is because the driver is not directly in the I/O path; the filter manager is.

FltRegisterFilter has the following prototype:

```
NTSTATUS FltRegisterFilter (
    _In_ PDRIVER_OBJECT Driver,
    _In_ const FLT_REGISTRATION *Registration,
    _Outptr_ PFLT_FILTER *RetFilte);
```

The required `FLT_REGISTRATION` structure provides all the necessary information for registration. It's defined like so:

```
typedef struct _FLT_REGISTRATION {
    USHORT Size;
    USHORT Version;

    FLT_REGISTRATION_FLAGS Flags;

    const FLT_CONTEXT_REGISTRATION *ContextRegistration;
    const FLT_OPERATION_REGISTRATION *OperationRegistration;

    PFLT_FILTER_UNLOAD_CALLBACK FilterUnloadCallback;
    PFLT_INSTANCE_SETUP_CALLBACK InstanceSetupCallback;
    PFLT_INSTANCE_QUERY_TEARDOWN_CALLBACK InstanceQueryTeardownCallback;
    PFLT_INSTANCE_TEARDOWN_CALLBACK InstanceTeardownStartCallback;
    PFLT_INSTANCE_TEARDOWN_CALLBACK InstanceTeardownCompleteCallback;

    PFLT_GENERATE_FILE_NAME GenerateFileNameCallback;
    PFLT_NORMALIZE_NAME_COMPONENT NormalizeNameComponentCallback;
    PFLT_NORMALIZE_CONTEXT_CLEANUP NormalizeContextCleanupCallback;

    PFLT_TRANSACTION_NOTIFICATION_CALLBACK TransactionNotificationCallback;
    PFLT_NORMALIZE_NAME_COMPONENT_EX NormalizeNameComponentExCallback;

#if FLT_MGR_WIN8
    PFLT_SECTION_CONFLICT_NOTIFICATION_CALLBACK SectionNotificationCallback;
#endif
} FLT_REGISTRATION, *PFLT_REGISTRATION;
```

There is a lot of information encapsulated in this structure. The important fields are described below:

- *Size* must be set to the size of the structure, which may depend on the target Windows version (set in the project's properties). Drivers typically just specify `sizeof(FLT_REGISTRATION)`.
- *Version* is also based on the target Windows version. Drivers use `FLT_REGISTRATION_VER-SION`.
- *Flags* can be zero or a combination of the following values:

- FLTFL_REGISTRATION_DO_NOT_SUPPORT_SERVICE_STOP - the driver does not support a stop request, regardless of other settings.
- FLTFL_REGISTRATION_SUPPORT_NPFS_MSFS - the driver is aware of named pipes and mailslots and wishes to filter requests to these file systems as well (see the sidebar "Pipes and Mailslots" for more information).
- FLTFL_REGISTRATION_SUPPORT_DAX_VOLUME (Windows 10 version 1607 and later) - the driver will support attaching to a Direct Access Volume (DAX), if such a volume is available (see the sidebar "Direct Access Volume").

Pipes and Mailslots

Named pipes is a uni- or bi-directional communication mechanism from a server to one or more clients, implemented as a file system (*npfs.sys*). The Windows API provides specific functions for creating pipe servers and clients. The CreateNamedPipe function can be used to create a named pipe server, to which clients can connect using the normal CreateFile API with a "file name" in this form: \\<server>\pipe\<pipename>.

Mailslots is a uni-directional communication mechanism, implemented as a file system (*msfs.sys*), where a server process opens a mailslot (you can think of it as a mailbox), to which messages can be sent by clients. CreateMailslot is the Windows API to create the mailslot and clients connect with CreateFile with a file name in the form \\<server>\mailslot\<mailslotname>.

Direct Access Volume (DAX or DAS)

Direct access volumes are a relatively new features added to Windows 10 version 1607 ("Anniversary Update") that provides support for a new kind of storage based on direct access to the underlying byte data. This is supported by new type of storage hardware referred to as *Storage Class Memory* - a non-volatile storage medium with RAM-like performance. (more information can be found on the web.)

- *ContextRegistration* - an optional pointer to FLT_CONTEXT_REGISTRATION structure array, where each entry represents a context that driver may use in its work. *Context* refers to some driver-defined data that can be attached to file system entities, such as files and volumes. We'll look at contexts later in this chapter. Some drivers don't need any contexts, and can set this field to NULL.

- *OperationRegistration* - by far the most important field. This is a pointer to an array of
  `FLT_OPERATION_REGISTRATION` structures, each specifying the operation of interest and a pre
  and/or post callback the driver wishes to be called upon. The next section provides the details.
- *FilterUnloadCallback* - specifies a function to be called when the driver is about to be unloaded.
  If `NULL` is specified, the driver cannot be unloaded. If the driver sets a callback and returns a
  successful status, the driver is unloaded; in that case the driver must call `FltUnregisterFil-`
  `ter` to unregister itself before being unloaded. Returning a non-success status does not unload
  the driver.
- *InstanceSetupCallback* - this callback allows the driver to be notified when an instance is about
  to be attached to a new volume. The driver may return `STATUS_SUCCESS` to attach or `STATUS_-`
  `FLT_DO_NOT_ATTACH` if the driver does not wish to attach to this volume.
- *InstanceQueryTeardownCallback* - an optional callback invoked before detaching from a volume. This can happen because of an explicit request to detach using `FltDetachVolume` in
  kernel mode or `FilterDetach` in user mode. If `NULL` is specified by the callback, the detach
  operation is aborted.
- *InstanceTeardownStartCallback* - an optional callback invoked when teardown of an instance
  has started. The driver should complete any pended operations so that instance teardown can
  complete. Specifying `NULL` for this callback does not prevent instance teardown (prevention
  can be achieved with the previous query teardown callback).
- *InstanceTeardownCompleteCallback* - an optional callback invoked after all the pending I/O
  operations complete or canceled.

The rest of the callback fields are all optional and seldom used. These are beyond the scope of this
book.

Operations Callback Registration

A mini-filter driver must indicate which operations it's interested in. This is provided at mini-filter
registration time with an array of `FLT_OPERATION_REGISTRATION` structures defined like so:

```
typedef struct _FLT_OPERATION_REGISTRATION {
    UCHAR MajorFunction;
    FLT_OPERATION_REGISTRATION_FLAGS Flags;
    PFLT_PRE_OPERATION_CALLBACK PreOperation;
    PFLT_POST_OPERATION_CALLBACK PostOperation;

    PVOID Reserved1;    // reserved
} FLT_OPERATION_REGISTRATION, *PFLT_OPERATION_REGISTRATION;
```

The operation itself is identified by a major function code, many of which are the same as the ones
we met in previous chapters: `IRP_MJ_CREATE`, `IRP_MJ_READ`, `IRP_MJ_WRITE` and so on. However,
there are other operations identified with a major function that do not have a real major function

dispatch routine. This abstraction provided by the filter manager helps to isolate the mini-filter from knowing the exact source of the operation - it could be a real IRP or it could be another operation that is abstracted as an IRP. Furthermore, file systems support yet another mechanism for receiving requests, known as *Fast I/O*. Fast I/O is used for synchronous I/O with cached files. Fast I/O requests transfer data between user buffers and the system cache directly, bypassing the file system and storage driver stack, thus avoiding unnecessary overhead. The NTFS file system driver, as a canonical example, supports Fast I/O.

> Fast I/O is initialized by allocating a FAST_IO_DISPATCH structure (containing a long list of callbacks), filling it in, and then setting the FastIoDispatch member of DRIVER_OBJECT to this structure.

This information can be viewed with a kernel debugger by using the !drvobj command as shown here for the NTFS file system driver:

```
lkd> !drvobj \filesystem\ntfs f
Driver object (ffffad8b19a60bb0) is for:
 \FileSystem\Ntfs

Driver Extension List: (id , addr)

Device Object list:
ffffad8c22448050   ffffad8c476e3050   ffffad8c3943f050   ffffad8c208f1050
ffffad8b39e03050   ffffad8b39e87050   ffffad8b39e73050   ffffad8b39d52050
ffffad8b19fc9050   ffffad8b199f3d80

DriverEntry:    fffff8026b609010 Ntfs!GsDriverEntry
DriverStartIo:  00000000
DriverUnload:   00000000
AddDevice:      00000000

Dispatch routines:
[00]  IRP_MJ_CREATE              fffff8026b49bae0   Ntfs!NtfsFsdCreate
[01]  IRP_MJ_CREATE_NAMED_PIPE   fffff80269141d40   nt!IopInvalidDeviceRequest
[02]  IRP_MJ_CLOSE               fffff8026b49d730   Ntfs!NtfsFsdClose
[03]  IRP_MJ_READ                fffff8026b3b3f80   Ntfs!NtfsFsdRead

(truncated)

[19]  IRP_MJ_QUERY_QUOTA         fffff8026b49c700   Ntfs!NtfsFsdDispatchWait
[1a]  IRP_MJ_SET_QUOTA           fffff8026b49c700   Ntfs!NtfsFsdDispatchWait
```

```
[1b] IRP_MJ_PNP                        fffff8026b5143e0   Ntfs!NtfsFsdPnp

Fast I/O routines:
FastIoCheckIfPossible                  fffff8026b5adff0   Ntfs!NtfsFastIoCheckIfPossible
FastIoRead                             fffff8026b49e080   Ntfs!NtfsCopyReadA
FastIoWrite                            fffff8026b46cb00   Ntfs!NtfsCopyWriteA
FastIoQueryBasicInfo                   fffff8026b4d50d0   Ntfs!NtfsFastQueryBasicInfo
FastIoQueryStandardInfo                fffff8026b4d2de0   Ntfs!NtfsFastQueryStdInfo
FastIoLock                             fffff8026b4d6160   Ntfs!NtfsFastLock
FastIoUnlockSingle                     fffff8026b4d6b40   Ntfs!NtfsFastUnlockSingle
FastIoUnlockAll                        fffff8026b5ad2d0   Ntfs!NtfsFastUnlockAll
FastIoUnlockAllByKey                   fffff8026b5ad590   Ntfs!NtfsFastUnlockAllByKey
ReleaseFileForNtCreateSection          fffff8026b3c3670   Ntfs!NtfsReleaseForCreateSection
FastIoQueryNetworkOpenInfo             fffff8026b4d4cb0   Ntfs!NtfsFastQueryNetworkOpenInfo
AcquireForModWrite                     fffff8026b3c4c20   Ntfs!NtfsAcquireFileForModWrite
MdlRead                                fffff8026b46b6a0   Ntfs!NtfsMdlReadA
MdlReadComplete                        fffff8026911aca0   nt!FsRtlMdlReadCompleteDev
PrepareMdlWrite                        fffff8026b46aae0   Ntfs!NtfsPrepareMdlWriteA
MdlWriteComplete                       fffff802696c41e0   nt!FsRtlMdlWriteCompleteDev
FastIoQueryOpen                        fffff8026b4d4940   Ntfs!NtfsNetworkOpenCreate
ReleaseForModWrite                     fffff8026b3c5a40   Ntfs!NtfsReleaseFileForModWrite
AcquireForCcFlush                      fffff8026b3a8690   Ntfs!NtfsAcquireFileForCcFlush
ReleaseForCcFlush                      fffff8026b3c5610   Ntfs!NtfsReleaseFileForCcFlush

Device Object stacks:

!devstack ffffad8c22448050 :
  !DevObj          !DrvObj            !DevExt           ObjectName
  ffffad8c4adcba70 \FileSystem\FltMgr ffffad8c4adcbbc0
> ffffad8c22448050 \FileSystem\Ntfs   ffffad8c224481a0

(truncated)

Processed 10 device objects.
```

The filter manager abstracts I/O operations, regardless of whether they are IRP-based or fast I/O based. Mini-filters can intercept any such request. If the driver is not interested in fast I/O, for example, it can query the actual request type provided by the filter manager with the FLT_IS_FAS-TIO_OPERATION and/or FLT_IS_IRP_OPERATION macros.

Table 10-1 lists some of the common major functions for file system mini-filters with a brief description for each.

Table 10-1: Common major functions

Major function	Dispatch routine?	Description
IRP_MJ_CREATE	Yes	Create or open a file/directory
IRP_MJ_READ	Yes	Read from a file
IRP_MJ_WRITE	Yes	Write to a file
IRP_MJ_QUERY_EA	Yes	Read extended attributes from a file/directory
IRP_MJ_DIRECTORY_CONTROL	Yes	Request sent to a directory
IRP_MJ_FILE_SYSTEM_CONTROL	Yes	File system device I/O control request
IRP_MJ_SET_INFORMATION	Yes	Various information setting for a file (e.g. delete, rename)
IRP_MJ_ACQUIRE_FOR_SECTION_-SYNCHRONIZATION	No	Section (memory mapped file) is being opened
IRP_MJ_OPERATION_END	No	signals the end of array of operations callbacks

The second field in FLT_OPERATION_REGISTRATION is a set of flags which can be zero or a combination of one of the following flags affecting read and write operations:

- FLTFL_OPERATION_REGISTRATION_SKIP_CACHED_IO - do not invoke the callback(s) if it's cached I/O (such as fast I/O operations, which are always cached).
- FLTFL_OPERATION_REGISTRATION_SKIP_PAGING_IO - do not invoke the callback(s) for paging I/O (IRP-based operations only).
- FLTFL_OPERATION_REGISTRATION_SKIP_NON_DASD_IO - do not invoke the callback(s) for DAX volumes.

The next two fields are the pre and post operation callbacks, where at least one must be non-NULL (otherwise, why have that entry in the first place?). Here is an example of initializing an array of FLT_OPERATION_REGISTRATION structures (for an imaginary driver called "Sample"):

```
const FLT_OPERATION_REGISTRATION Callbacks[] = {
    { IRP_MJ_CREATE, 0, nullptr, SamplePostCreateOperation },
    { IRP_MJ_WRITE, FLTFL_OPERATION_REGISTRATION_SKIP_PAGING_IO,
        SamplePreWriteOperation, nullptr },
    { IRP_MJ_CLOSE, 0, nullptr, SamplePostCloseOperation },
    { IRP_MJ_OPERATION_END }
};
```

With this array at hand, registration for a driver that does not require any contexts could be done with the following code:

```
const FLT_REGISTRATION FilterRegistration = {
    sizeof(FLT_REGISTRATION),
    FLT_REGISTRATION_VERSION,
    0,                                  // Flags
    nullptr,                            // Context
    Callbacks,                          // Operation callbacks
    ProtectorUnload,                    // MiniFilterUnload
    SampleInstanceSetup,                // InstanceSetup
    SampleInstanceQueryTeardown,        // InstanceQueryTeardown
    SampleInstanceTeardownStart,        // InstanceTeardownStart
    SampleInstanceTeardownComplete,     // InstanceTeardownComplete
};

PFLT_FILTER FilterHandle;

NTSTATUS
DriverEntry(_In_ PDRIVER_OBJECT DriverObject, _In_ PUNICODE_STRING RegistryPath) {
    NTSTATUS status;
    //... some code
    status = FltRegisterFilter(DriverObject, &FilterRegistration, &FilterHandle);
    if(NT_SUCCESS(status)) {
        // actually start I/O filtering
        status = FltStartFiltering(FilterHandle);
        if(!NT_SUCCESS(status))
            FltUnregisterFilter(FilterHandle);
    }
    return status;
}
```

The Altitude

As we've seen already, file system mini-filters must have an altitude, indicating their relative "position" within the file system filters hierarchy. Contrary to the altitude we've already encountered with object and registry callbacks, a mini-filter's altitude value may be potentially significant.

First, the value of the altitude is not provided as part of mini-filter's registration, but is read from the registry. When the driver is installed, its altitude is written in the proper location in the registry. Figure 10-4 shows the registry entry for the built-in *Fileinfo* mini-filter driver; the Altitude is clearly visible, and is the same value shown earlier with the *fltmc.exe* tool.

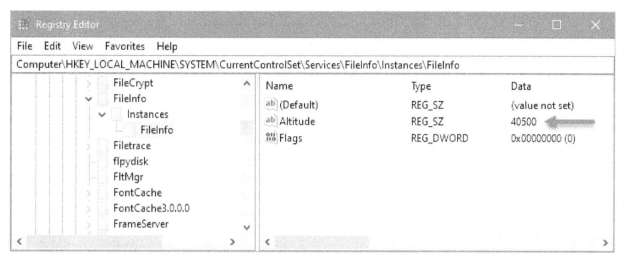

Figure 10-4: Altitude in the registry

Here is an example that should clarify why altitude matters. Suppose there is a mini-filter at altitude 10000 whose job is to encrypt data when written, and decrypt when read. Now suppose another mini-filter whose job is to check data for malicious activity is at altitude 9000. This layout is depicted in figure 10-5.

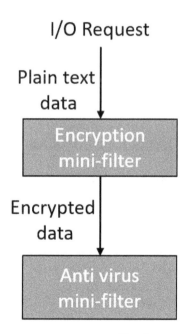

Figure 10-5: Two mini-filter layout

The encryption driver encrypts incoming data to be written, which is then passed on to the anti-virus driver. The anti-virus driver is in a problem, as it sees the encrypted data with no viable way of decrypting it (and even if it could, that would be wasteful). In such a case, the anti-virus driver must have an altitude higher than the encryption driver. How can such a driver guarantee this is in fact the case?

To rectify this (and other similar) situation, Microsoft has defined ranges of altitudes for drivers based on their requirements (and ultimately, their task). In order to obtain a proper altitude, the driver publisher must send an email to Microsoft (fsfcomm@microsoft.com) and ask an altitude be allocated for that driver based on its intended target. Check out this link[2] for the complete list of altitude ranges. In fact, the link shows all drivers that Microsoft has allocated an altitude for, with the file name, the altitude and the publishing company.

  The altitude request email details are located here[3].

  For testing purposes, you can choose any appropriate altitude without going through Microsoft, but you *should* obtain an official altitude for production use.

Table 10-2 shows the list of groups and the altitude range for each group.

Table 10-2: Altitude ranges and load order groups

Altitude range	Group name
420000 - 429999	Filter
400000 - 409999	FSFilter Top
360000 - 389999	FSFilter Activity Monitor
340000 - 349999	FSFilter Undelete
320000 - 329998	FSFilter Anti-Virus
300000 - 309998	FSFilter Replication
280000 - 289998	FSFilter Continuous Backup
260000 - 269998	FSFilter Content Screener
240000 - 249999	FSFilter Quota Management
220000 - 229999	FSFilter System Recovery
200000 - 209999	FSFilter Cluster File System
180000 - 189999	FSFilter HSM
170000 - 174999	FSFilter Imaging (ex: .ZIP)
160000 - 169999	FSFilter Compression
140000 - 149999	FSFilter Encryption
130000 - 139999	FSFilter Virtualization
120000 - 129999	FSFilter Physical Quota management
100000 - 109999	FSFilter Open File
80000 - 89999	FSFilter Security Enhancer
60000 - 69999	FSFilter Copy Protection
40000 - 49999	FSFilter Bottom
20000 - 29999	FSFilter System

[2]https://docs.microsoft.com/en-us/windows-hardware/drivers/ifs/allocated-altitudes
[3]https://docs.microsoft.com/en-us/windows-hardware/drivers/ifs/minifilter-altitude-request

Installation

Figure 10-4 shows that there are additional registry entries that must be set, beyond what is possible with the standard `CreateService` installation API we've been using up until now (indirectly with the *sc.exe* tool). The "proper" way to install a file system mini-filter is to use an INF file.

INF Files

INF files are the classic mechanism used to install hardware based device drivers, but these can be used to install any type of driver. The "File System Mini-Filter" project templates provided by the WDK creates such an INF file, which is almost ready for installation.

> A complete treatment of INF files is beyond the scope of this book. We'll examine the necessary parts for file system mini-filter installation.

INF files use the old INI file syntax, where there are sections in square brackets, and underneath a section there are entries in the form "key=value". These entries are instructions to the installer that parses the file, essentially instructing the installer to do two types of operations: copy files to specific locations and making changes to the registry.

Let's examine a file system mini-filter INF file generated by the WDK project wizard. In Visual Studio, locate the *Device Drivers* node and underneath locate *Devices*. The template to use is *Filter Driver: Filesystem Mini-filter*. Figure 10-6 shows this in Visual Studio 2017.

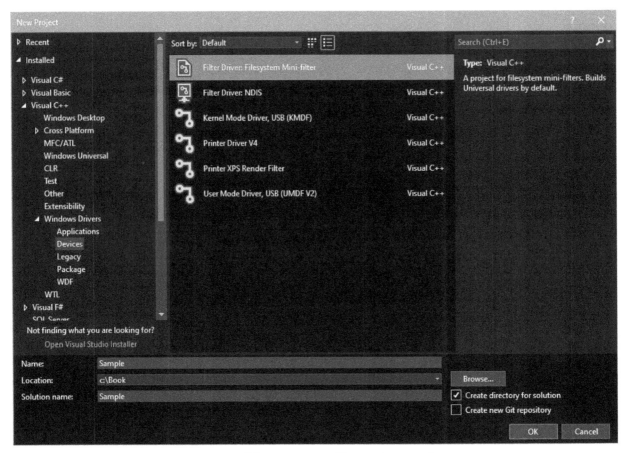

Figure 10-6: File system mini-filter project template

Type a name for the project (*Sample* in figure 10-6) and hit OK. Under the *Driver Files* node in solution explorer, you'll find the INF file named *Sample.inf*.

The Version Section

The *Version* section is mandatory in an INF. The following is generated by the WDK project wizard (slightly modified for readability):

```
[Version]
Signature    = "$Windows NT$"
; TODO - Change the Class and ClassGuid to match the Load Order Group value,
;    see https://msdn.microsoft.com/en-us/windows/hardware/gg462963
; Class        = "ActivityMonitor"
    ;This is determined by the work this filter driver does
; ClassGuid    = {b86dff51-a31e-4bac-b3cf-e8cfe75c9fc2}
    ;This value is determined by the Load Order Group value
Class = "_TODO_Change_Class_appropriately_"
ClassGuid = {_TODO_Change_ClassGuid_appropriately_}
```

```
Provider    = %ManufacturerName%
DriverVer   =
CatalogFile = Sample.cat
```

The *Signature* directive must be set to the magic string "$Windows NT$". The reason for this name is historical, and not important for this discussion.

The *Class* and *ClassGuid* directives are mandatory and specify the class (type or group) to which this driver belongs to. The generated INF contains an example class, *ActivityMonitor* and its associated GUID, both in comments (INF comments are specified after a semicolon until the end of the line). The simplest solution is to uncomment these to lines and remove the dummy *Class* and *ClassGuid* resulting in the following:

```
Class       = "ActivityMonitor"
ClassGuid   = {b86dff51-a31e-4bac-b3cf-e8cfe75c9fc2}
```

 Process Monitor from *Sysinternals* uses an altitude from the *ActivityMonitor* group (385200).

What is this "Class" directive? This is one a set of predefined groups of devices, used mostly by hardware based drivers, but also by mini-filters. For mini-filters, it's roughly based on the groups listed in table 10-2. The complete list of classes is stored in the registry under the key *HKLM\System\CurrentControlSet\Control\Class*. Each class is uniquely identified by a GUID; the string name is just a human-readable helper. Figure 10-7 shows the *ActivityMonitor* class entry in the registry.

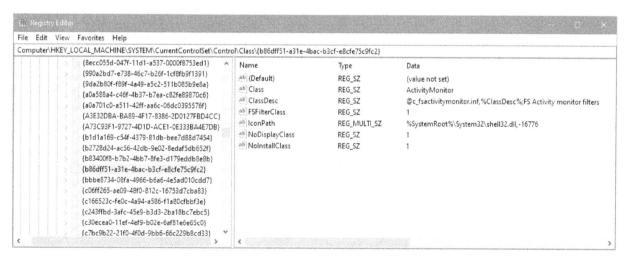

Figure 10-7: The ActivityMonitor class in the registry

Notice the GUID is the key name. The class name itself is provided in the *Class* value. The other values within this key are not important from a practical perspective. The entry that makes this class "eligible" for file system mini-filters is the value *FSFilterClass* having the value of 1.

You can view all the existing classes on a system with the *FSClass.exe* tool, available in my Github *AllTools* repo (https://github.com/zodiacon/AllTools). Here is a sample run:

```
c:\Tools> FSClass.exe
File System Filter Classes version 1.0 (C)2019 Pavel Yosifovich

GUID                                     Name                  Description
------------------------------------------------------------------------------------
{2db15374-706e-4131-a0c7-d7c78eb0289a}  SystemRecovery       FS System recovery filters
{3e3f0674-c83c-4558-bb26-9820e1eba5c5}  ContentScreener      FS Content screener filters
{48d3ebc4-4cf8-48ff-b869-9c68ad42eb9f}  Replication          FS Replication filters
{5d1b9aaa-01e2-46af-849f-272b3f324c46}  FSFilterSystem       FS System filters
{6a0a8e78-bba6-4fc4-a709-1e33cd09d67e}  PhysicalQuotaManagement  FS Physical quota ma\
nagement filters
{71aa14f8-6fad-4622-ad77-92bb9d7e6947}  ContinuousBackup     FS Continuous backup filters
{8503c911-a6c7-4919-8f79-5028f5866b0c}  QuotaManagement      FS Quota management filters
{89786ff1-9c12-402f-9c9e-17753c7f4375}  CopyProtection       FS Copy protection filters
{a0a701c0-a511-42ff-aa6c-06dc0395576f}  Encryption           FS Encryption filters
{b1d1a169-c54f-4379-81db-bee7d88d7454}  AntiVirus            FS Anti-virus filters
{b86dff51-a31e-4bac-b3cf-e8cfe75c9fc2}  ActivityMonitor      FS Activity monitor filters
{cdcf0939-b75b-4630-bf76-80f7ba655884}  CFSMetadataServer    FS CFS metadata server filt\
ers
{d02bc3da-0c8e-4945-9bd5-f1883c226c8c}  SecurityEnhancer     FS Security enhancer filters
{d546500a-2aeb-45f6-9482-f4b1799c3177}  HSM                  FS HSM filters
{e55fa6f9-128c-4d04-abab-630c74b1453a}  Infrastructure       FS Infrastructure filters
{f3586baf-b5aa-49b5-8d6c-0569284c639f}  Compression          FS Compression filters
{f75a86c0-10d8-4c3a-b233-ed60e4cdfaac}  Virtualization       FS Virtualization filters
{f8ecafa6-66d1-41a5-899b-66585d7216b7}  OpenFileBackup       FS Open file backup filters
{fe8f1572-c67a-48c0-bbac-0b5c6d66cafb}  Undelete             FS Undelete filters
```

> Technically, a file system mini-filter can create its own class (with a generated class GUID), putting itself in a category of its own, so to speak. Still the altitude must be selected / requested based on the needs of the driver and the official altitude ranges. (*Process Monitor* creates its own class.)

Back to the *Version* section in the INF - the *Provider* directive is the name of the driver publisher. It doesn't mean much in practical terms, but might appear in some UI, so should be something meaningful. The value set by the WDK template is `%ManufacturerName%`. Anything within percent symbols is sort of a macro - to be replaced by the actual value specified in another section called *Strings*. Here is part of this section:

```
[Strings]
; TODO - Add your manufacturer
ManufacturerName        = "Template"
ServiceDescription      = "Sample Mini-Filter Driver"
ServiceName             = "Sample"
```

Here, *ManufacturerName* is replaced with "Template". The driver writer should replace "Template" with a proper company or product name, whichever makes sense.

The *DriverVer* directive specifies the date/time of the driver and the version. Leaving this empty sets the date to the build date and the version number based on the time of the build. The *CatalogFile* directive points to a catalog file, storing the digital signatures of the driver package (the driver package contains the output files for the driver - typically the SYS, INF and CAT files).

The DefaultInstall Section

The *DefaultInstall* section is the one indicating what operations should execute as part of "running" this INF. By having this section, a driver can be installed using Windows Explorer, by right clicking the INF and selecting **Install**.

> Behind the scenes, a call is made to the `InstallHInfFile` API with the INF file path as the third argument. This same call can also be used by custom applications that want to install the driver programmatically.

 The *DefaultInstall* section should not be used for hardware based device driver installations. *DefaultInstall* is intended for all other kinds of drivers, such as file system mini-filters.

The WDK generated wizard created this:

```
[DefaultInstall]
OptionDesc          = %ServiceDescription%
CopyFiles           = MiniFilter.DriverFiles
```

The *OptionDesc* directive provides a simple description that is used in case the user install the driver using the Plug & Play driver installation wizard (uncommon for file-system mini-filters). The important directive is *CopyFiles* that points to another section (with the given name) that should indicate what files should be copied and to where.

The *CopyFile* directive points to a section named *MiniFilter.DriverFiles* shown here:

```
[MiniFilter.DriverFiles]
%DriverName%.sys
```

%DriverName% points to *Sample.sys*, the driver output file. This file needs to be copied, but to where? The *DestinationDirs* section provides this information:

```
[DestinationDirs]
DefaultDestDir          = 12
MiniFilter.DriverFiles  = 12     ;%windir%\system32\drivers
```

DefaultDestDir is the default directory to copy to if not explicitly specified. The value here is weird (12), but in fact is a magic number pointing to the system's drivers directory, shown in the comment for the second directive. The *System32\Drivers* directory is the canonical location to place drivers in. In previous chapters, we placed our drivers just about anywhere, but drivers should be placed in that *drivers* folder, at least for protection purposes, as this folder is a system one, and so does not allow full access for standard users.

 Some other "magic" numbers referring to special directories are listed below. The complete list is available here[4].

- 10 - Windows directory (*%SystemRoot%*)
- 11 - System directory (*%SystemRoot%\System32*)
- 24 - root directory of system disk (e.g. *C:*)
- 01 - the directory from which the INF file is read from

If these numbers are used as part of a path, they must be enclosed by percent characters. For example: *%10%\Config*.

The second directive we see is in fact the name of the section we just looked at, *MiniFilter.DriverFiles*, essentially specifying the files listed there to be copied to the target directory marked with that magic number again.

> INF file structure and semantics take some getting used to. It's not really a flat file, but actually hierarchical. One value can point to another section, within which another directive value can point to another section and so on. I wish Microsoft would switch to using a file format that is naturally hierarchical (XML or JSON, for example), and ditch this old INI-based format.

The Service Section

The next sections of interest are lated to installation in the services registry key, similarly to what `CreateService` does. This step is mandatory for any driver. First, we see this definition:

---

[4]https://docs.microsoft.com/en-us/windows-hardware/drivers/install/using-dirids

---

```
[DefaultInstall.Services]
AddService = %ServiceName%,,MiniFilter.Service
```

DefaultInstall is appended with ".Services" and such a section is automatically searched. If found, the *AddService* directive points to another section that indicates what information to write to the registry in the service key named *%ServiceName%*. The extra comma is a placeholder for a set of flags, zero in this case (hence the comma). The wizard-generated code follows:

```
[MiniFilter.Service]
DisplayName       = %ServiceName%
Description       = %ServiceDescription%
ServiceBinary     = %12%\%DriverName%.sys        ;%windir%\system32\drivers\
Dependencies      = "FltMgr"
ServiceType       = 2                            ;SERVICE_FILE_SYSTEM_DRIVER
StartType         = 3                            ;SERVICE_DEMAND_START
ErrorControl      = 1                            ;SERVICE_ERROR_NORMAL
; TODO - Change the Load Order Group value
; LoadOrderGroup = "FSFilter Activity Monitor"
LoadOrderGroup = "_TODO_Change_LoadOrderGroup_appropriately_"
AddReg            = MiniFilter.AddRegistry
```

You should recognize most of the directives corresponding to values in the services registry key. *ServiceType* is 2 for a file system related driver (as opposed to 1 for "standard" drivers). *Dependencies* is something we haven't met before - this is a list of services/drivers this service/driver depends on. In the file system mini-filter case, this is the Filter Manager itself.

LoadOrderGroup should be specified based on the mini-filter group names from table 10-2. Finally, the *AddReg* directive points to another section with instructions for adding more registry entries. Here is the fixed *MiniFilter.Service* section:

```
[MiniFilter.Service]
DisplayName       = %ServiceName%
Description       = %ServiceDescription%
ServiceBinary     = %12%\%DriverName%.sys        ;%windir%\system32\drivers\
Dependencies      = "FltMgr"
ServiceType       = 2                            ;SERVICE_FILE_SYSTEM_DRIVER
StartType         = 3                            ;SERVICE_DEMAND_START
ErrorControl      = 1                            ;SERVICE_ERROR_NORMAL
LoadOrderGroup = "FSFilter Activity Monitor"
AddReg            = MiniFilter.AddRegistry
```

AddReg Sections

This section(or sections, there can be any number of these) is used to add custom registry entries for any and all purposes. The wizard generated INF contains the following additions to the registry:

```
[MiniFilter.AddRegistry]
HKR,,"DebugFlags",0x00010001 ,0x0
HKR,,"SupportedFeatures",0x00010001,0x3
HKR,"Instances","DefaultInstance",0x00000000,%DefaultInstance%
HKR,"Instances\"%Instance1.Name%","Altitude",0x00000000,%Instance1.Altitude%
HKR,"Instances\"%Instance1.Name%","Flags",0x00010001,%Instance1.Flags%
```

The syntax for each entry is contains the following in order:

- root key - one of HKLM, HKCU (current user), HKCR (classes root), HKU (users) or HKR (relative to the calling section). In our case, HKR is the service subkey (*HKLMSystemCurrent-ControlSetServicesSample*).
- subkey from the root key (uses the key itself if not specified)
- value name to set
- flags - many are defined, the default is zero which indicates writing of a REG_SZ value. Some other flags:
    - 0x100000 - write REG_MULTI_SZ
    - 0x100001 - write REG_DWORD
    - 0x000001 - write a binary value (REG_BINARY)
    - 0x000002 - no clobber. Do not overwrite an existing value
    - 0x000008 - append a value. The existing value must be REG_MULTI_SZ
- the actual value or values to write/append

The code snippet above sets some defaults for file system mini-filters. The most important value is the altitude, taken from the *%Instance1.Altitude%* in the strings section.

Finalizing the INF

The last piece we need to modify is the altitude itself, in the Strings section. Here is an example for the sample driver:

```
[Strings]
; other entries
;Instances specific information.
DefaultInstance        = "Sample Instance"
Instance1.Name         = "Sample Instance"
Instance1.Altitude     = "360100"
Instance1.Flags        = 0x0               ; Allow all attachments
```

The altitude value was chosen in from the Activity Monitor group altitude range. In a real driver, that number will be returned by Microsoft based on the altitude request discussed earlier.

Lastly, the flags value indicates the driver is fine with attaching to any volume, but in actuality the driver will be queried in its Instance Setup callback, where it can allow or reject attachments.

Installing the Driver

Once the INF file is properly modified, and the driver code compiles, it is ready to be installed. The simplest way to install is to copy the driver package (SYS, INF and CAT files) to the target system, and then right click the INF file in Explorer and select **Install**. This will "run" the INF, executing the required operations.

At this point, the mini-filter is installed, and can be loaded with the *fltmc* command line tool (assuming the driver's name is *sample*):

```
c:\>fltmc load sample
```

Processing I/O Operations

The main function of a file system mini-filter is processing I/O operations by implementing pre and/or post callbacks for the operations of interest. Pre operations allow a mini-filter to reject an operation completely, while post operation allows looking at the result of the operation, and in some cases - making changes to the returned information.

Pre Operation Callbacks

All pre-operation callbacks have the same prototype as follows:

```
FLT_PREOP_CALLBACK_STATUS SomePreOperation (
    _Inout_     PFLT_CALLBACK_DATA Data,
    _In_        PCFLT_RELATED_OBJECTS FltObjects,
    _Outptr_    PVOID *CompletionContext);
```

First, let's look at the possible return values from a pre-operation, typed as the FLT_PREOP_CALL-BACK_STATUS enumeration. Here are the common return values to use:

- FLT_PREOP_COMPLETE indicates the driver is completing the operation. The filter manager does not call the post-operation callback (if registered) and does not forward the request to lower-layer mini-filters.
- FLT_PREOP_SUCCESS_NO_CALLBACK indicates the pre-operation is done with the request and lets it continue flowing to the next filter. The driver does not want its post-operation callback to be called for this operation.
- FLT_PREOP_SUCCESS_WITH_CALLBACK indicates the driver allows the filter manager to propagate the request to lower-layer filters, but it wants its post-callback invoked for this operation.
- FLT_PREOP_PENDING indicates the driver is pending the operation. The filter manager does not continue processing the request until the driver calls FltCompletePendedPreOperation to let the filter manager know it can continue processing this request.
- FLT_PREOP_SYNCHRONIZE is similar to FLT_PREOP_SUCCESS_WITH_CALLBACK, but the driver asks the filter manager to invoke its post-callback on the same thread at IRQL <= APC_LEVEL (normally the post-operation callback can be invoked at IRQL <= DISPATCH_LEVEL by an arbitrary thread).

The *Data* argument provides all the information related to the I/O operation itself, as a FLT_CALL-BACK_DATA structure defined like so:

```
typedef struct _FLT_CALLBACK_DATA {
    FLT_CALLBACK_DATA_FLAGS Flags;
    PETHREAD CONST Thread;
    PFLT_IO_PARAMETER_BLOCK CONST Iopb;
    IO_STATUS_BLOCK IoStatus;

    struct _FLT_TAG_DATA_BUFFER *TagData;

    union {
        struct {
            LIST_ENTRY QueueLinks;
            PVOID QueueContext[2];
        };
        PVOID FilterContext[4];
    };
    KPROCESSOR_MODE RequestorMode;
} FLT_CALLBACK_DATA, *PFLT_CALLBACK_DATA;
```

This structure is also provided in the post-callback. Here is a rundown of the important members of this structure:

- *Flags* may contain zero or a combination of flags, some of which are listed below:
    - FLTFL_CALLBACK_DATA_DIRTY indicates the driver has made changes to the structure and then called FltSetCallbackDataDirty. Every member of the structure can be modified except Thread and RequestorMode.
    - FLTFL_CALLBACK_DATA_FAST_IO_OPERATION indicates this is a fast I/O operation.
    - FLTFL_CALLBACK_DATA_IRP_OPERATION indicates this is an IRP-based operation.
    - FLTFL_CALLBACK_DATA_GENERATED_IO indicates this is an operation generated by another mini-filter.
    - FLTFL_CALLBACK_DATA_POST_OPERATION indicates this is a post-operation, rather than a pre-operation.
- *Thread* is an opaque pointer to the thread requesting this operation.
- *IoStatus* is the status of the request. A pre-operation can set this value and then indicate the operation is complete by returning FLT_PREOP_COMPLETE. A post-operation can look at the final status of the operation.
- *RequestorMode* indicates whether the requestor of the operation is from user mode (UserMode) or kernel mode (KernelMode).
- *Iopb* is in itself a structure holding the detailed parameters of the request, defined like so:

```
    ULONG IrpFlags;
    UCHAR MajorFunction;
    UCHAR MinorFunction;
    UCHAR OperationFlags;
    UCHAR Reserved;
    PFILE_OBJECT TargetFileObject;
    PFLT_INSTANCE TargetInstance;
    FLT_PARAMETERS Parameters;
} FLT_IO_PARAMETER_BLOCK, *PFLT_IO_PARAMETER_BLOCK;
```

The useful member of this structure are the following:

- *TargetFileObject* is the file object that is the target of this operation; it's useful to have when invoking some APIs.
- *Parameters* is a monstrous union providing the actual data for the specific information (similar in concept to the *Paramters* member of an IO_STACK_LOCATION). The driver looks at the proper structure within this union to get to the information it needs. We'll look at some of these structures when we look at specific operation types later in this chapter.

The second argument to the pre-callback is another structure of type FLT_RELATED_OBJECTS. This structure mostly contains opaque handles to the current filter, instance and volume, which are useful in some APIs. Here is the complete definition of this structure:

```
typedef struct _FLT_RELATED_OBJECTS {
    USHORT CONST Size;
    USHORT CONST TransactionContext;
    PFLT_FILTER CONST Filter;
    PFLT_VOLUME CONST Volume;
    PFLT_INSTANCE CONST Instance;
    PFILE_OBJECT CONST FileObject;
    PKTRANSACTION CONST Transaction;
} FLT_RELATED_OBJECTS, *PFLT_RELATED_OBJECTS;
```

The *FileObject* field is the same one accessed through the I/O parameter block's `TargetFileObject` field.

The last argument to the pre-callback is a context value that can be set by the driver. If set, this value is propagated to the post-callback routine for the same request (the default value is `NULL`).

Post Operation Callbacks

All post-operation callbacks have the same prototype as follows:

```
FLT_POSTOP_CALLBACK_STATUS SomePostOperation (
    _Inout_ PFLT_CALLBACK_DATA Data,
    _In_ PCFLT_RELATED_OBJECTS FltObjects,
    _In_opt_ PVOID CompletionContext,
    _In_ FLT_POST_OPERATION_FLAGS Flags);
```

The post-operation function is called at IRQL `<= DISPATCH_LEVEL` in an arbitrary thread context, unless the pre-callback routine returned `FLT_PREOP_SYNCHRONIZE`, in which case the filter manager guarantees the post-callback is invoked at IRQL `< DISPATCH_LEVEL` on the same thread that executed the pre-callback.

In the former case, the driver cannot perform certain types of operations because the IRQL is too high:

- Cannot access paged memory.
- Cannot use kernel APIs that only work at IRQL `< DISPATCH_LEVEL`.
- Cannot acquire synchronization primitives such as mutexes, fast mutexes, executive resources, semaphores, events, etc. (It can acquire spin locks, however.)
- Cannot set, get or delete contexts (see the section "Contexts" later in this chapter), but it can release contexts.

If the driver needs to do any of the above, it somehow must defer its execution to another routine called at IRQL `< DISPATCH_LEVEL`. This can be done in one of two ways:

- The driver calls `FltDoCompletionProcessingWhenSafe` which sets up a callback function that is invoked by a system worker thread at IRQL < DISPATCH_LEVEL (if the post-operation was called at IRQL = DISPATCH_LEVEL).
- The driver posts a work item by calling `FltQueueDeferredIoWorkItem`, which queues a work item that will eventually execute by a system worker thread at IRQL = PASSIVE_LEVEL. In the work item callback, the driver will eventually call `FltCompletePendedPostOperation` to signal the filter manager that the post-operation is complete.

Although using `FltDoCompletionProcessingWhenSafe` is easier, it has some limitations that prevent it from being used in some scenarios:

- Cannot be used for IRP_MJ_READ, IRP_MJ_WRITE or IRP_MJ_FLUSH_BUFFERS because it can cause a deadlock if these operations are completed synchronously by a lower layer.
- Can only be called for IRP-based operations (can check with the FLT_IS_IRP_OPERATION macro).

In any case, using one of these deferring mechanisms is not allowed if the flags argument is set to FLTFL_POST_OPERATION_DRAINING, which means the post-callback is part of volume detaching. In this case, the post callback is called at IRQL < DISPATCH_LEVEL.

Though it seems easy to just return FLT_PREOP_SYNCHRONIZE from the pre-callback to have the pos-callback run in a convenient context, it does carry some overhead with it, which the driver may want to avoid if possible.

The post-create operation (IRP_MJ_CREATE) is guaranteed to be called by the requesting thread at IRQL PASSIVE_LEVEL.

The returned value from the pos-callback is usually FLT_POSTOP_FINISHED_PROCESSING to indicate the driver is finished with this operation. However, if the driver needs to perform work in a work item (because of a high IRQL, for example), the driver can return FLT_POSTOP_MORE_PROCESSING_REQUIRED to tell the filer manager the operation is still pending completion, and in the work item call `FltCompletePendedPostOperation` to let the filter manager know it can continue processing this request.

> There are many little details here, check out the WDK documentation for yet more details. We'll use some of the above mechanisms later in this chapter.

The Delete Protector Driver

Now it's time to put some of the information discussed so far into an actual driver. The driver we'll create will be able to protect certain files from deletion by certain processes. We'll build the driver based on the WDK-provided project template (even though I don't like some of the code generated by that template).

We'll start by creating a new File System Mini-Filter project named *DelProtect* (or another name of your choosing) and let the wizard generate the initial files and code.

Next, we'll take care of the INF file. The class this driver will belong to is "Undelete" (seems reasonable) and we'll select an altitude in that range. Here are the changed sections in the INF:

```
[Version]
Signature    = "$Windows NT$"
Class        = "Undelete"
ClassGuid    = {fe8f1572-c67a-48c0-bbac-0b5c6d66cafb}
Provider     = %ManufacturerName%
DriverVer    =
CatalogFile  = DelProtect.cat


[MiniFilter.Service]
DisplayName    = %ServiceName%
Description    = %ServiceDescription%
ServiceBinary  = %12%\%DriverName%.sys        ;%windir%\system32\drivers\
Dependencies   = "FltMgr"
ServiceType    = 2                            ;SERVICE_FILE_SYSTEM_DRIVER
StartType      = 3                            ;SERVICE_DEMAND_START
ErrorControl   = 1                            ;SERVICE_ERROR_NORMAL
LoadOrderGroup = "FS Undelete filters"
AddReg         = MiniFilter.AddRegistry


[Strings]
ManufacturerName    = "WindowsDriversBook"
ServiceDescription  = "DelProtect Mini-Filter Driver"
ServiceName         = "DelProtect"
DriverName          = "DelProtect"
DiskId1             = "DelProtect Device Installation Disk"


;Instances specific information.
DefaultInstance     = "DelProtect Instance"
Instance1.Name      = "DelProtect Instance"
Instance1.Altitude  = "345101"      ; in the range of the undelete group
Instance1.Flags     = 0x0           ; Allow all attachments
```

Now that we're done with the INF, we can turn our attention to the code. The generated source file is named DelProtect.c and so first we'll rename it to DelProtect.cpp so we can use C++ freely. The DriverEntry provided by the project template already has the mini-filter registration code in place. We need to tweak the callbacks to indicate which are the ones we're actually interested in. So the question is, what major functions are involved in file deletion?

It turns out there are two way to delete a file. One way is to use IRP_MJ_SET_INFORMATION operation. This operation provides a bag of operations, delete just being one of them. The second way to delete a file (and in fact the most common) is to open the file with the FILE_DELETE_ON_CLOSE option flag. The file then is deleted as soon as that last handle to it is closed.

> This flag can be set from user mode in CreateFile with FILE_FLAG_DELETE_ON_CLOSE as one of the flags (second to last argument). The higher level function DeleteFile uses the same flag behind the scenes.

For the driver, we want to support both options for deletion to cover all our bases. The FLT_OPERA-TION_REGISTRATION array must be modified to support these two options like so:

```
CONST FLT_OPERATION_REGISTRATION Callbacks[] = {
    { IRP_MJ_CREATE, 0, DelProtectPreCreate, nullptr },
    { IRP_MJ_SET_INFORMATION, 0, DelProtectPreSetInformation, nullptr },
    { IRP_MJ_OPERATION_END }
};
```

Of course, we need to implement *DelProtectPreCreate* and *DelProtectPreSetInformation* appropriately. Both are pre-callbacks as we want to fail these requests under certain conditions.

Handling Pre-Create

Let's start with the pre-create function (which is somewhat simpler). Its prototype is the same as any pre-callback (just copy it from the generic DelProtectPreOperation provided by the project template):

```
FLT_PREOP_CALLBACK_STATUS DelProtectPreCreate(
    _Inout_ PFLT_CALLBACK_DATA Data,
    _In_ PCFLT_RELATED_OBJECTS FltObjects,
    _Flt_CompletionContext_Outptr_ PVOID *CompletionContext);
```

First we'll check if the operation is originating from kernel mode, and if so, just let it continue uninterrupted:

```
UNREFERENCED_PARAMETER(CompletionContext);
UNREFERENCED_PARAMETER(FltObjects);

if (Data->RequestorMode == KernelMode)
    return FLT_PREOP_SUCCESS_NO_CALLBACK;
```

This is not mandatory, of course, but in most cases we don't want to prevent kernel code from doing work that may be important.

Next we need to check if the flag `FILE_DELETE_ON_CLOSE` exists in the creation request. The structure to look at is the `Create` field under the `Paramaters` inside `Iopb` like so:

```
const auto& params = Data->Iopb->Parameters.Create;
if (params.Options & FILE_DELETE_ON_CLOSE) {
    // delete operation
}
// otherwise, just carry on
return FLT_PREOP_SUCCESS_NO_CALLBACK;
```

The above *params* variable references the `Create` structure defined like so:

```
struct {
    PIO_SECURITY_CONTEXT SecurityContext;
    //
    //  The low 24 bits contains CreateOptions flag values.
    //  The high 8 bits contains the CreateDisposition values.
    //
    ULONG Options;

    USHORT POINTER_ALIGNMENT FileAttributes;
    USHORT ShareAccess;
    ULONG POINTER_ALIGNMENT EaLength;

    PVOID EaBuffer;                  //Not in IO_STACK_LOCATION parameters list
    LARGE_INTEGER AllocationSize;    //Not in IO_STACK_LOCATION parameters list
} Create;
```

Generally, for any I/O operation, the documentation must be consulted to understand what's available and how to use it. In our case, the `Options` field is a combination of flags documented under the `FltCreateFile` function (which we'll use later in this chapter in an unrelated context). The code checks to see if this flag exists, and if so, it means a delete operation is being initiated.

For this driver, we'll block delete operations coming from *cmd.exe* processes. To that end, we need to get the image path of the calling process. Since a create operation is invoked synchronously, we know that the caller is the process attempting to delete something. But how do we get the image path of the current process?

One way would be to use the `NtQueryInformationProcess` native API from the kernel (or its Zw equivalent - `ZwQueryInformationProcess`). It's semi-documented, and its prototype available in the user model header *<wintrnl.h>*. We can just copy its declaration and change to Zw into our source:

```
extern "C" NTSTATUS ZwQueryInformationProcess(
    _In_        HANDLE              ProcessHandle,
    _In_        PROCESSINFOCLASS    ProcessInformationClass,
    _Out_       PVOID               ProcessInformation,
    _In_        ULONG               ProcessInformationLength,
    _Out_opt_   PULONG              ReturnLength);
```

The `PROCESSINFOCLASS` enum is actually mostly available in *<ntddk.h>*. I say "mostly", because it does not provide all supported values. (We'll return to this issue in chapter 11).

For our driver's purposes, we can use the `ProcessImageFileName` value from the `PROCESSINFO-CLASS` enum. With it, we can get the full path of a process' image file. Then we'll be able to compare it to the path of *cmd.exe*.

The documentation for `NtQueryInformationProcess` indicates that for `ProcessImageFileName`, the returned data is a `UNICODE_STRING` structure, that must be allocated by the caller:

```
auto size = 300;        // some arbitrary size enough for cmd.exe image path
auto processName = (UNICODE_STRING*)ExAllocatePool(PagedPool, size);
if (processName == nullptr)
    return FLT_PREOP_SUCCESS_NO_CALLBACK;
RtlZeroMemory(processName, size);   // ensure string will be NULL-terminated
```

Note that we don't allocate just the size of the raw `UNICODE_STRING` structure - where would the API place the actual string? The trick here is to allocate a contiguous buffer and the API itself is going to place the actual characters just after the structure itself in memory and point to it from its internal buffer. Now we can make the API call:

```
auto status = ZwQueryInformationProcess(NtCurrentProcess(), ProcessImageFileName,
    processName, size - sizeof(WCHAR), nullptr);
```

The `NtCurrentProcess` macro returns a pseudo-handle that refers to the current process (practically the same as the `GetCurrentProcess` user mode API).

> *Pseudo-handle* means a handle that need not (and cannot) be closed.

If the call succeeds, we need to compare the process image file name to *cmd.exe*. Here's one simple way to do it:

```
if (NT_SUCCESS(status)) {
    if (wcsstr(processName->Buffer, L"\\System32\\cmd.exe") != nullptr ||
        wcsstr(processName->Buffer, L"\\SysWOW64\\cmd.exe") != nullptr) {
        // do something
    }
}
```

The comparison is not as easy as we would like. The actual path returned from the ZwQueryInformationProcess call is the native path, something like "\Device\HarddiskVolume3\Windows\System32\cmd.exe". For this simple driver, we just look for the substring "System32\cmd.exe" or "SysWOW64\cmd.exe" (the latter is in case the 32-bit *cmd.exe* is invoked). The comparison is cases sensitive, by the way. This is not perfect: what if the case is off? What if someone copies *cmd.exe* to another folder and runs it from there? It's really up to the driver. We could have just as easily compare with "cmd.exe" only. For the purpose of this basic driver, it's good enough.

If this is indeed *cmd.exe*, we need to prevent the operation from succeeding. The standard way of doing this is changing the operation status (Data->IoStatus.Status) to an appropriate failure status and return from the callback FLT_PREOP_COMPLETE to tell the filter manager not to continue with the request.

Here is the entire pre-create callback, slightly modified:

```
_Use_decl_annotations_
FLT_PREOP_CALLBACK_STATUS DelProtectPreCreate(
    PFLT_CALLBACK_DATA Data, PCFLT_RELATED_OBJECTS FltObjects, PVOID*) {
    UNREFERENCED_PARAMETER(FltObjects);

    if (Data->RequestorMode == KernelMode)
        return FLT_PREOP_SUCCESS_NO_CALLBACK;

    auto& params = Data->Iopb->Parameters.Create;
    auto returnStatus = FLT_PREOP_SUCCESS_NO_CALLBACK;

    if (params.Options & FILE_DELETE_ON_CLOSE) {
        // delete operation
        KdPrint(("Delete on close: %wZ\n", &Data->Iopb->TargetFileObject->FileName));
```

```cpp
    auto size = 300;      // some arbitrary size enough for cmd.exe image path
    auto processName = (UNICODE_STRING*)ExAllocatePool(PagedPool, size);
    if (processName == nullptr)
        return FLT_PREOP_SUCCESS_NO_CALLBACK;

    RtlZeroMemory(processName, size);    // ensure string will be NULL-terminated
    auto status = ZwQueryInformationProcess(NtCurrentProcess(),
        ProcessImageFileName, processName, size - sizeof(WCHAR), nullptr);

    if (NT_SUCCESS(status)) {
        KdPrint(("Delete operation from %wZ\n", processName));

        if (wcsstr(processName->Buffer, L"\\System32\\cmd.exe") != nullptr ||
            wcsstr(processName->Buffer, L"\\SysWOW64\\cmd.exe") != nullptr) {
            // fail request
            Data->IoStatus.Status = STATUS_ACCESS_DENIED;
            returnStatus = FLT_PREOP_COMPLETE;
            KdPrint(("Prevent delete from IRP_MJ_CREATE by cmd.exe\n"));
        }
    }
    ExFreePool(processName);
    }
    return returnStatus;
}
```

> The SAL annotation _Use_decl_annotations_ indicates the true SAL annotations are at the function declaration, rather than its declaration **and** implementation. It just makes the implementation a little bit easier to look at.

To build the driver we need to provide something for the IRP_MJ_SET_INFORMATION pre-callback. Here is a simple allow-all implementation:

```
FLT_PREOP_CALLBACK_STATUS DelProtectPreSetInformation(
    _Inout_ PFLT_CALLBACK_DATA Data, _In_ PCFLT_RELATED_OBJECTS FltObjects, PVOID*) {
    UNREFERENCED_PARAMETER(FltObjects);
    UNREFERENCED_PARAMETER(Data);

    return FLT_PREOP_SUCCESS_NO_CALLBACK;
}
```

If we build and deploy the driver, and then test it with something like:

```
del somefile.txt
```

We'll see that although we get to our IRP_MJ_CREATE handler, and we fail the request - the file is still deleted successfully. The reason for this is that *cmd.exe* is somewhat sneaky, and if it fails one way, it tries another. Once using FILE_DLETE_ON_CLOSE fails, it uses IRP_MJ_SET_INFORMATION, and since we allow all operations for IRP_MJ_SET_INFORMATION to go through - the operation succeeds.

Handling Pre-Set Information

We are now ready to implement the pre-set information callback to cover our bases, so to speak, with the second way file deletion is implemented by file systems. We'll start by ignoring kernel callers as with IRP_MJ_CREATE:

```
_Use_decl_annotations_
FLT_PREOP_CALLBACK_STATUS DelProtectPreSetInformation(
    PFLT_CALLBACK_DATA Data, PCFLT_RELATED_OBJECTS FltObjects, PVOID*) {
    UNREFERENCED_PARAMETER(FltObjects);

    if (Data->RequestorMode == KernelMode)
        return FLT_PREOP_SUCCESS_NO_CALLBACK;
```

Since IRP_MJ_SET_INFORMATION is the way to do several types of operations, we need to check if this is in fact a delete operation. The driver must first access the proper structure in the parameters union, declared like so:

```
struct {
    ULONG Length;
    FILE_INFORMATION_CLASS POINTER_ALIGNMENT FileInformationClass;
    PFILE_OBJECT ParentOfTarget;
    union {
        struct {
            BOOLEAN ReplaceIfExists;
            BOOLEAN AdvanceOnly;
        };
        ULONG ClusterCount;
        HANDLE DeleteHandle;
    };
    PVOID InfoBuffer;
} SetFileInformation;
```

`FileInformationClass` indicates which type of operation this instance represents and so we need to check whether this is a delete operation:

```
auto& params = Data->Iopb->Parameters.SetFileInformation;

if (params.FileInformationClass != FileDispositionInformation &&
    params.FileInformationClass != FileDispositionInformationEx) {
    // not a delete operation
    return FLT_PREOP_SUCCESS_NO_CALLBACK;
}
```

The `FileDispositionInformation` enumeration value indicates a delete operation. The `FileDispositionInformationEx` is similar and undocumented, but is used internally by the user mode `DeleteFile` function, so we check for both.

If it is a delete operation, there is yet another check to do, but looking at the information buffer which is of type `FILE_DISPOSITION_INFORMATION` for delete operations and checking the boolean stored there:

```
auto info = (FILE_DISPOSITION_INFORMATION*)params.InfoBuffer;
if (!info->DeleteFile)
    return FLT_PREOP_SUCCESS_NO_CALLBACK;
```

Finally, we are in a delete operation. In the `IRP_MJ_CREATE` case, the callback is called by the requesting thread (and hence the requesting process), so we can just access the current process to find out which image file is used to make the call. In all other major functions, this is not necessary the case and we must look at the `Thread` field in the provided data for the original caller. From this thread, we can get the pointer to the process:

```
// what process did this originate from?
auto process = PsGetThreadProcess(Data->Thread);
NT_ASSERT(process);        // cannot really fail
```

Our goal is to call ZwQueryInformationProcess, but we need a handle for that. This is where the
ObOpenObjectByPointer function comes in. It allows obtaining a handle to an object. It's defined
like so:

```
NTSTATUS ObOpenObjectByPointer(
    _In_ PVOID Object,
    _In_ ULONG HandleAttributes,
    _In_opt_ PACCESS_STATE PassedAccessState,
    _In_ ACCESS_MASK DesiredAccess,
    _In_opt_ POBJECT_TYPE ObjectType,
    _In_ KPROCESSOR_MODE AccessMode,
    _Out_ PHANDLE Handle);
```

The arguments to ObOpenObjectByPointer are described below:

- *Object* is the object for which a handle is needed. It can be any type of kernel object.
- *HandleAttributes* is a set of optional flags. The most useful flag is OBJ_KERNEL_HANDLE (we'll
  discuss other flags in chapter 11). This flag makes the returned handle a kernel handle, which
  is unusable by user mode code and can be used from any process context.
- *PassedAccessState* is an optional pointer to ACCESS_STATE structure, not typically useful for
  drivers - set to NULL.
- *DesiredAccess* is the access mask the handle should be opened with. If the *AccessMode* argument is KernelMode, then this can be zero and the returned handle will be all-powerful.
- *ObjectType* is an optional object type the function can compare the *Object* to, such as *PsProcessType, *PsThreadType and other exported type objects. Specifying NULL does not force
  any check on the passed in object.
- *AccessMode* can be UserMode or KernelMode. Drivers usually specify KernelMode to indicate
  the request is not on behalf of a user mode process. With KernelMode, no access check is made.
- *Handle* is the pointer to the returned handle.

Given the above function, opening a handle to the process follows:

```
HANDLE hProcess;
auto status = ObOpenObjectByPointer(process, OBJ_KERNEL_HANDLE, nullptr, 0,
    nullptr, KernelMode, &hProcess);
if (!NT_SUCCESS(status))
    return FLT_PREOP_SUCCESS_NO_CALLBACK;
```

Once we get a handle to the process, we can query for the process' image file name, and see if it's *cmd.exe*:

```
auto returnStatus = FLT_PREOP_SUCCESS_NO_CALLBACK;
auto size = 300;
auto processName = (UNICODE_STRING*)ExAllocatePool(PagedPool, size);
if (processName) {
    RtlZeroMemory(processName, size);   // ensure string will be NULL-terminated
    status = ZwQueryInformationProcess(hProcess, ProcessImageFileName,
        processName, size - sizeof(WCHAR), nullptr);

    if (NT_SUCCESS(status)) {
        KdPrint(("Delete operation from %wZ\n", processName));

        if (wcsstr(processName->Buffer, L"\\System32\\cmd.exe") != nullptr ||
            wcsstr(processName->Buffer, L"\\SysWOW64\\cmd.exe") != nullptr) {
            Data->IoStatus.Status = STATUS_ACCESS_DENIED;
            returnStatus = FLT_PREOP_COMPLETE;
            KdPrint(("Prevent delete from IRP_MJ_SET_INFORMATION by cmd.exe\n"));
        }
    }
    ExFreePool(processName);
}
ZwClose(hProcess);

return returnStatus;
}
```

Now we can test the complete driver - we'll find that *cmd.exe* is unable to delete files - "access denied" being the returned error.

Some Refactoring

The two pre-callbacks we implemented have a lot of code in common, and so adhering to the DRY principle ("Don't Repeat Yourself"), we can extract the code to open a process handle, get an image file and comparing to *cmd.exe* to a separate function:

```cpp
bool IsDeleteAllowed(const PEPROCESS Process) {
    bool currentProcess = PsGetCurrentProcess() == Process;
    HANDLE hProcess;
    if (currentProcess)
        hProcess = NtCurrentProcess();
    else {
        auto status = ObOpenObjectByPointer(Process, OBJ_KERNEL_HANDLE,
            nullptr, 0, nullptr, KernelMode, &hProcess);
        if (!NT_SUCCESS(status))
            return true;
    }

    auto size = 300;
    bool allowDelete = true;
    auto processName = (UNICODE_STRING*)ExAllocatePool(PagedPool, size);

    if (processName) {
        RtlZeroMemory(processName, size);
        auto status = ZwQueryInformationProcess(hProcess, ProcessImageFileName,
            processName, size - sizeof(WCHAR), nullptr);

        if (NT_SUCCESS(status)) {
            KdPrint(("Delete operation from %wZ\n", processName));

            if (wcsstr(processName->Buffer, L"\\System32\\cmd.exe") != nullptr ||
                wcsstr(processName->Buffer, L"\\SysWOW64\\cmd.exe") != nullptr) {
                allowDelete = false;
            }
        }
        ExFreePool(processName);
    }
    if (!currentProcess)
        ZwClose(hProcess);

    return allowDelete;
}
```

The function accepts an opaque pointer to the process attempting to delete a file. If the process address is the current process (PsGetCurrentProcess) then using a full-fledged open is just a waste of time and the pseudo-handle NtCurrentProcess can be used instead. Otherwise, a full process open is required. We must be careful not to leak resources - freeing the image file buffer and closing the process handle (if it was actually open).

Now we can plug a call to this function to IRP_MJ_CREATE handling. Here is the revised function:

```
_Use_decl_annotations_
FLT_PREOP_CALLBACK_STATUS DelProtectPreCreate(
    PFLT_CALLBACK_DATA Data, PCFLT_RELATED_OBJECTS FltObjects, PVOID*) {
    UNREFERENCED_PARAMETER(FltObjects);

    if (Data->RequestorMode == KernelMode)
        return FLT_PREOP_SUCCESS_NO_CALLBACK;

    auto& params = Data->Iopb->Parameters.Create;
    auto returnStatus = FLT_PREOP_SUCCESS_NO_CALLBACK;

    if (params.Options & FILE_DELETE_ON_CLOSE) {
        // delete operation
        KdPrint(("Delete on close: %wZ\n", &Data->Iopb->TargetFileObject->FileName));

        if (!IsDeleteAllowed(PsGetCurrentProcess())) {
            Data->IoStatus.Status = STATUS_ACCESS_DENIED;
            returnStatus = FLT_PREOP_COMPLETE;
            KdPrint(("Prevent delete from IRP_MJ_CREATE by cmd.exe\n"));
        }
    }
    return returnStatus;
}
```

And the revised IRP_MJ_SET_INFORMATION pre-callback:

```
FLT_PREOP_CALLBACK_STATUS DelProtectPreSetInformation(
    _Inout_ PFLT_CALLBACK_DATA Data, _In_ PCFLT_RELATED_OBJECTS FltObjects, PVOID*) {
    UNREFERENCED_PARAMETER(FltObjects);
    UNREFERENCED_PARAMETER(Data);

    auto& params = Data->Iopb->Parameters.SetFileInformation;

    if (params.FileInformationClass != FileDispositionInformation &&
        params.FileInformationClass != FileDispositionInformationEx) {
        // not a delete operation
        return FLT_PREOP_SUCCESS_NO_CALLBACK;
    }

    auto info = (FILE_DISPOSITION_INFORMATION*)params.InfoBuffer;
    if (!info->DeleteFile)
        return FLT_PREOP_SUCCESS_NO_CALLBACK;
```

```
auto returnStatus = FLT_PREOP_SUCCESS_NO_CALLBACK;

// what process did this originate from?
auto process = PsGetThreadProcess(Data->Thread);
NT_ASSERT(process);

if (!IsDeleteAllowed(process)) {
    Data->IoStatus.Status = STATUS_ACCESS_DENIED;
    returnStatus = FLT_PREOP_COMPLETE;
    KdPrint(("Prevent delete from IRP_MJ_SET_INFORMATION by cmd.exe\n"));
}

return returnStatus;
}
```

Generalizing the Driver

The current driver only checks for delete operations from *cmd.exe*. Let's generalize the driver so that we can register executable names from which delete operations can be prevented.

To that end, we'll create a "classic" device object and symbolic link, just as was done in earlier chapters. This is not a problem, and the driver can serve double-duty: a file system mini-filter and expose a *Control Device Object* (CDO).

We'll manage the executable names in a fixed size array for simplicity, have a fast mutex protecting the array, just as was done in previous chapters. We'll also bring the wrappers we created - FastMutex and AutoLock. Here are the added global variables:

```
const int MaxExecutables = 32;

WCHAR* ExeNames[MaxExecutables];
int ExeNamesCount;
FastMutex ExeNamesLock;
```

The revised DriverEntry has now the additional duty of creating the device object and symbolic link and setting dispatch routines, as well as registering as a mini-filter:

```
PDEVICE_OBJECT DeviceObject = nullptr;
UNICODE_STRING devName = RTL_CONSTANT_STRING(L"\\device\\delprotect");
UNICODE_STRING symLink = RTL_CONSTANT_STRING(L"\\??\\delprotect");
auto symLinkCreated = false;

do {
    status = IoCreateDevice(DriverObject, 0, &devName,
        FILE_DEVICE_UNKNOWN, 0, FALSE, &DeviceObject);
    if (!NT_SUCCESS(status))
        break;

    status = IoCreateSymbolicLink(&symLink, &devName);
    if (!NT_SUCCESS(status))
        break;

    symLinkCreated = true;

    status = FltRegisterFilter(DriverObject, &FilterRegistration, &gFilterHandle);

    FLT_ASSERT(NT_SUCCESS(status));
    if (!NT_SUCCESS(status))
        break;

    DriverObject->DriverUnload = DelProtectUnloadDriver;
    DriverObject->MajorFunction[IRP_MJ_CREATE] =
        DriverObject->MajorFunction[IRP_MJ_CLOSE] = DelProtectCreateClose;
    DriverObject->MajorFunction[IRP_MJ_DEVICE_CONTROL] = DelProtectDeviceControl;
    ExeNamesLock.Init();

    status = FltStartFiltering(gFilterHandle);
} while (false);

if (!NT_SUCCESS(status)) {
    if (gFilterHandle)
        FltUnregisterFilter(gFilterHandle);
    if (symLinkCreated)
        IoDeleteSymbolicLink(&symLink);
    if (DeviceObject)
        IoDeleteDevice(DeviceObject);
}

return status;
```

We'll define a few I/O control codes for adding, removing and clearing the list of executable names (in a new file called *DelProtectCommon.h*):

```
#define IOCTL_DELPROTECT_ADD_EXE    \
    CTL_CODE(0x8000, 0x800, METHOD_BUFFERED, FILE_ANY_ACCESS)
#define IOCTL_DELPROTECT_REMOVE_EXE \
    CTL_CODE(0x8000, 0x801, METHOD_BUFFERED, FILE_ANY_ACCESS)
#define IOCTL_DELPROTECT_CLEAR      \
    CTL_CODE(0x8000, 0x802, METHOD_NEITHER, FILE_ANY_ACCESS)
```

Handling these kinds of control codes is nothing new - here is the complete code for the IRP_MJ_-DEVICE_CONTROL dispatch routine:

```
NTSTATUS DelProtectDeviceControl(PDEVICE_OBJECT, PIRP Irp) {
    auto stack = IoGetCurrentIrpStackLocation(Irp);
    auto status = STATUS_SUCCESS;

    switch (stack->Parameters.DeviceIoControl.IoControlCode) {
        case IOCTL_DELPROTECT_ADD_EXE:
        {
            auto name = (WCHAR*)Irp->AssociatedIrp.SystemBuffer;
            if (!name) {
                status = STATUS_INVALID_PARAMETER;
                break;
            }

            if (FindExecutable(name)) {
                break;
            }

            AutoLock locker(ExeNamesLock);
            if (ExeNamesCount == MaxExecutables) {
                status = STATUS_TOO_MANY_NAMES;
                break;
            }

            for (int i = 0; i < MaxExecutables; i++) {
                if (ExeNames[i] == nullptr) {
                    auto len = (::wcslen(name) + 1) * sizeof(WCHAR);
                    auto buffer = (WCHAR*)ExAllocatePoolWithTag(PagedPool, len,
                        DRIVER_TAG);
                    if (!buffer) {
                        status = STATUS_INSUFFICIENT_RESOURCES;
```

```
                    break;
                }
                ::wcscpy_s(buffer, len / sizeof(WCHAR), name);
                ExeNames[i] = buffer;
                ++ExeNamesCount;
                break;
            }
        }
        break;
    }

    case IOCTL_DELPROTECT_REMOVE_EXE:
    {
        auto name = (WCHAR*)Irp->AssociatedIrp.SystemBuffer;
        if (!name) {
            status = STATUS_INVALID_PARAMETER;
            break;
        }

        AutoLock locker(ExeNamesLock);
        auto found = false;
        for (int i = 0; i < MaxExecutables; i++) {
            if (::_wcsicmp(ExeNames[i], name) == 0) {
                ExFreePool(ExeNames[i]);
                ExeNames[i] = nullptr;
                --ExeNamesCount;
                found = true;
                break;
            }
        }
        if (!found)
            status = STATUS_NOT_FOUND;
        break;
    }

    case IOCTL_DELPROTECT_CLEAR:
        ClearAll();
        break;

    default:
        status = STATUS_INVALID_DEVICE_REQUEST;
        break;
}
```

```
Irp->IoStatus.Status = status;
Irp->IoStatus.Information = 0;
IoCompleteRequest(Irp, IO_NO_INCREMENT);
return status;
}
```

The missing pieces from the above code are the `FindExecutable` and `ClearAll` helper functions defined like so:

```
bool FindExecutable(PCWSTR name) {
    AutoLock locker(ExeNamesLock);
    if (ExeNamesCount == 0)
        return false;

    for (int i = 0; i < MaxExecutables; i++)
        if (ExeNames[i] && ::_wcsicmp(ExeNames[i], name) == 0)
            return true;
    return false;
}

void ClearAll() {
    AutoLock locker(ExeNamesLock);
    for (int i = 0; i < MaxExecutables; i++) {
        if (ExeNames[i]) {
            ExFreePool(ExeNames[i]);
            ExeNames[i] = nullptr;
        }
    }
    ExeNamesCount = 0;
}
```

With the above code in place, we need to make changes to the pre-create callback to search for executable names in the array we're managing. Here is the revised code:

```
_Use_decl_annotations_
FLT_PREOP_CALLBACK_STATUS DelProtectPreCreate(
    PFLT_CALLBACK_DATA Data, PCFLT_RELATED_OBJECTS FltObjects, PVOID*) {
    if (Data->RequestorMode == KernelMode)
        return FLT_PREOP_SUCCESS_NO_CALLBACK;

    auto& params = Data->Iopb->Parameters.Create;
    auto returnStatus = FLT_PREOP_SUCCESS_NO_CALLBACK;

    if (params.Options & FILE_DELETE_ON_CLOSE) {
        // delete operation
        KdPrint(("Delete on close: %wZ\n", &FltObjects->FileObject->FileName));

        auto size = 512;     // some arbitrary size
        auto processName = (UNICODE_STRING*)ExAllocatePool(PagedPool, size);
        if (processName == nullptr)
            return FLT_PREOP_SUCCESS_NO_CALLBACK;

        RtlZeroMemory(processName, size);
        auto status = ZwQueryInformationProcess(NtCurrentProcess(), ProcessImageFile\
Name,
            processName, size - sizeof(WCHAR), nullptr);

        if (NT_SUCCESS(status)) {
            KdPrint(("Delete operation from %wZ\n", processName));

            auto exeName = ::wcsrchr(processName->Buffer, L'\\');
            NT_ASSERT(exeName);

            if (exeName && FindExecutable(exeName + 1)) {   // skip backslash
                Data->IoStatus.Status = STATUS_ACCESS_DENIED;
                KdPrint(("Prevented delete in IRP_MJ_CREATE\n"));
                returnStatus = FLT_PREOP_COMPLETE;
            }
        }
        ExFreePool(processName);
    }
    return returnStatus;
}
```

The main modification in the above code is calling FindExecutable to find out if the current process image executable name is one of the values stored in the array. If it is, we set an "access denied" status and return FLT_PREOP_COMPLETE.

Testing the Modified Driver

Earlier, we tested the driver by deleting files using *cmd.exe*, but that may not be generic enough, so we better create our own test application. There are three ways to delete a file with user mode APIs:

1. Call the DeleteFile function.
2. Call CreateFile with the flag FILE_FLAG_DELETE_ON_CLOSE.
3. Call SetFileInformationByHandle on an open file.

Internally, there are only two ways to delete a file - IRP_MJ_CREATE with the FILE_DELETE_ON_-CLOSE flag and IRP_MJ_SET_INFORMATION with FileDispositionInformation. Clearly, in the above list, item (2) corresponds to the first option and item (3) corresponds to the second option. The only mystery left is DeleteFile - how does it delete a file?

From the driver's perspective it does not matter at all, since it must map to one of the two options the driver handles. From a curiosity point of view, DeleteFile uses IRP_MJ_SET_INFORMATION.

We'll create a console application project named *DelTest*, for which the usage text should be something like this:

```
c:\book>deltest
Usage: deltest.exe <method> <filename>
    Method: 1=DeleteFile, 2=delete on close, 3=SetFileInformation.
```

Let's examine the user mode code for each of these methods (assuming filename is a variable pointing to the file name provided in the command line).

Using DeleteFile is trivial:

```
BOOL success = ::DeleteFile(filename);
```

Opening the file with the delete-on-close flag can be achieved with the following:

```
HANDLE hFile = ::CreateFile(filename, DELETE, 0, nullptr, OPEN_EXISTING,
    FILE_FLAG_DELETE_ON_CLOSE, nullptr);
::CloseHandle(hFile);
```

When the handle is closed, the file should be deleted (if the driver does not prevent it!)

Lastly, using SetFileInformationByHandle:

```
FILE_DISPOSITION_INFO info;
info.DeleteFile = TRUE;
HANDLE hFile = ::CreateFile(filename, DELETE, 0, nullptr, OPEN_EXISTING, 0, nullptr);
BOOL success = ::SetFileInformationByHandle(hFile, FileDispositionInfo,
    &info, sizeof(info));
::CloseHandle(hFile);
```

With this tool in place, we can test our driver. Here are some examples:

```
C:\book>fltmc load delprotect2


C:\book>DelProtectConfig.exe add deltest.exe
Success.


C:\book>DelTest.exe
Usage: deltest.exe <method> <filename>
        Method: 1=DeleteFile, 2=delete on close, 3=SetFileInformation.


C:\book>DelTest.exe 1 hello.txt
Using DeleteFile:
Error: 5


C:\book>DelTest.exe 2 hello.txt
Using CreateFile with FILE_FLAG_DELETE_ON_CLOSE:
Error: 5


C:\book>DelTest.exe 3 hello.txt
Using SetFileInformationByHandle:
Error: 5


C:\book>DelProtectConfig.exe remove deltest.exe
Success.


C:\book>DelTest.exe 1 hello.txt
Using DeleteFile:
Success!
```

File Names

In some mini-filter callbacks, the name of the file being accessed is needed in the majority of cases. At first, this seems like an easy enough detail to find: the FILE_OBJECT structure has a FileName member, which should be exactly that.

Unfortunately, things are not that simple. Files may be opened with a full path or a relative one; rename operations on the same file may be occurring at the same time; some file name information is cached. For these and other internal reasons, the `FileName` field in the file object is not be trusted. In fact, it's only guaranteed to be valid in a `IRP_MJ_CREATE` pre-operation callback, and even there it's not necessarily in the format the driver needs.

To offset this issues, the filter manager provides the `FltGetFileNameInformation` API that can return the correct file name when needed. This function is prototyped as follows:

```
NTSTATUS FltGetFileNameInformation (
    _In_ PFLT_CALLBACK_DATA CallbackData,
    _In_ FLT_FILE_NAME_OPTIONS NameOptions,
    _Outptr_ PFLT_FILE_NAME_INFORMATION *FileNameInformation);
```

The *CallbackData* parameter is the one provided by the filter manager in any callback. The *NameOptions* parameter is a set of flags that specify (among other things) the requested file format. Typical value used by most drivers is `FLT_FILE_NAME_NORMALIZED` (full path name) ORed with `FLT_FILE_NAME_QUERY_DEFAULT` (locate the name in a cache, otherwise query the file system). The result from the call is provided by the last parameter, *FileNameInformation*. The result is an allocated structure that needs to be properly freed by calling `FltReleaseFileNameInformation`.

The `FLT_FILE_NAME_INFORMATION` structure is defined like so:

```
typedef struct _FLT_FILE_NAME_INFORMATION {
    USHORT Size;
    FLT_FILE_NAME_PARSED_FLAGS NamesParsed;
    FLT_FILE_NAME_OPTIONS Format;

    UNICODE_STRING Name;
    UNICODE_STRING Volume;
    UNICODE_STRING Share;
    UNICODE_STRING Extension;
    UNICODE_STRING Stream;
    UNICODE_STRING FinalComponent;
    UNICODE_STRING ParentDir;
} FLT_FILE_NAME_INFORMATION, *PFLT_FILE_NAME_INFORMATION;
```

The main ingredients are the several `UNICODE_STRING` structures that should hold the various components of a file name. Initially, only the `Name` field is initialized to the full file name (depending on the flags used to query the file name information, "full" may be a partial name). If the request specified the flag `FLT_FILE_NAME_NORMALIZED`, then `Name` points to the full path name, in device form. *Device form* means that file such as *c:\mydir\myfile.txt* is stored with the internal device name to which "C:" maps to, such as *\Device\HarddiskVolume3\mydir\myfile.txt*. This makes the driver's job a bit more complicated if it somehow depends on paths provided by user mode (more on that later).

 The driver should never modify this structure, because the filter manager caches it for use with other drivers.

Since only the full name is provided by default (Name field), it's often necessary to split the full path to its constituents. Fortunately, the filter manager provides such a service with the `FltParseFile-NameInformation` API. This one takes the `FLT_FILE_NAME_INFORMATION` object and fills in the other `UNICODE_STRING` fields in the structure.

> Note that `FltParseFileNameInformation` does not allocate anything. It just sets each `UNICODE_-STRING`'s `Buffer` and `Length` to point to the correct part in the full `Name` field. This means there is no "unparse" function and it's not needed.

 In scenarios where a simple C string is available for a full path, the simpler (and weaker) function `FltParseFileName` can be used for getting easy access to the file extension, stream and final component.

File Name Parts

As can be seen from `FLT_FILE_NAME_INFORMATION` declaration, there are several components that make up a full file name. Here is an example for the local file "c:\mydir1\mydir2\myfile.txt":

The volume is the actual device name for which the symbolic link "C:" maps to. Figure 10-8 shows *WinObj* showing the *C:* symbolic link and its target, which is *\Device\HarddiskVolume3* on that machine.

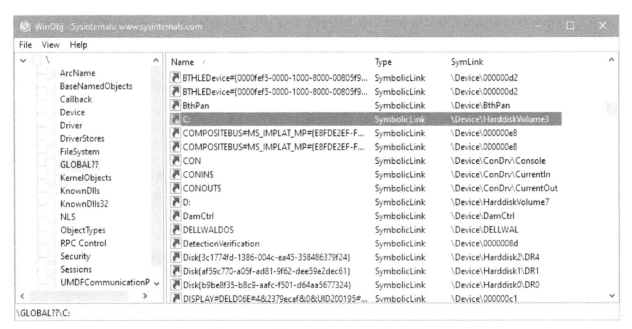

Figure 10-8: Driver Mapping in *WinObj*

The share string is empty for local files (Length is zero). ParentDir is set to the directory only. In our example that would be *\mydir1\mydir2* (not the trailing backslash). The extension is just that, the file extension. In our example this is *txt*. The FinalComponent field stores the file name and stream name (if not using the default stream). For our example, it would be *myfile.txt*.

The Stream component bares some explanation. Some file systems (most notable NTFS) provide the ability to have multiple data "streams" in a single file. Essentially, this means several files can be stored into a single "physical" file. In NTFS, for instance, what we typically think of as a file's data is in fact one of its streams named "$DATA", which is considered the default stream. But it's possible to create/open another stream, that is stored in the same file, so to speak. Tools such as Windows Explorer do not look for these streams, and the sizes of any alternate streams are not shown or returned by standard APIs such as GetFileSize. Stream names are specified with a colon after the file name before the stream name itself. For example, the file name "myfile.txt:mystream" points to an alternate stream named "mystream" within the file "myfile.txt". Alternate streams can be created with the command interpreter as the following example shows:

```
C:\temp>echo hello > hello.txt:mystream


C:\Temp>dir hello.txt
 Volume in drive C is OS
 Volume Serial Number is 1707-9837


 Directory of C:\Temp


22-May-19  11:33                     0 hello.txt
             1 File(s)                0 bytes
```

Notice the zero size of the file. Is the data really in there? Trying to use the type command fails:

```
C:\Temp>type hello.txt:mystream
The filename, directory name, or volume label syntax is incorrect.
```

The type command interpreter does not recognize stream names. We can use the *SysInternals* tool *Streams.exe* to list the names and sizes of alternate streams in files. Here is the command with our *hello.txt* file:

```
C:\Temp>streams -nobanner hello.txt
C:\Temp\hello.txt:
        :mystream:$DATA 8
```

The alternate stream content is not shown. To view (and optionally export to another file) the stream's data, we can use a tool called *NtfsStreams* available on my Github *AllTools* repository. Figure 10-9 shows *NtfsStreams* opening the *hello.txt* file from the previous example. We can clearly see stream's size and data.

> The *$DATA* shown is the stream type, where *$DATA* is that normal data stream (there are other predefined stream types). Custom stream types are specifically used in reparse points (beyond the scope of this book).

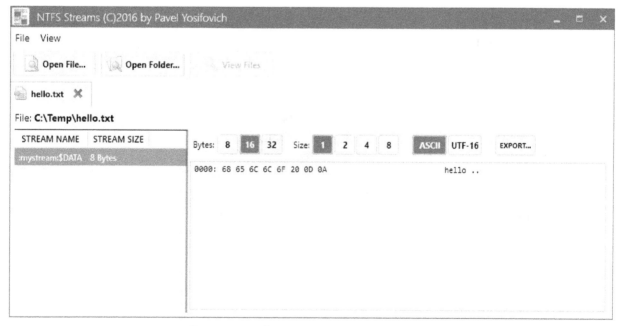

Figure 10-9: Alternate Streams in *NtfsStreams*

Of course alternate streams can be created programmatically by passing the stream name at the end of the filename after a colon, to the CreateFile API. Here is an example (error handling omitted):

```
HANDLE hFile = ::CreateFile(L"c:\\temp\\myfile.txt:stream1",
    GENERIC_WRITE, 0, nullptr, OPEN_ALWAYS, 0, nullptr);

char data[] = "Hello, from a stream";
DWORD bytes;
::WriteFile(hFile, data, sizeof(data), &bytes, nullptr);
::CloseHandle(hFile);
```

> Streams can also be deleted normally with DeleteFile and can be enumerated (this is what *streams.exe* and *ntfsstreams.exe* do) with FindFirstStream and FileNextStream.

RAII FLT_FILE_NAME_INFORMATION wrapper

As discussed in the previous section, calling FltGetFileNameInformation requires calling its opposite function, FltReleaseFileNameInformation. This naturally leads to the possibility of having a RAII wrapper to take care of this, making the surrounding code simpler and less error prone. Here is one possible declaration for such a wrapper:

```
enum class FileNameOptions {
    Normalized = FLT_FILE_NAME_NORMALIZED,
    Opened     = FLT_FILE_NAME_OPENED,
    Short      = FLT_FILE_NAME_SHORT,

    QueryDefault        = FLT_FILE_NAME_QUERY_DEFAULT,
    QueryCacheOnly      = FLT_FILE_NAME_QUERY_CACHE_ONLY,
    QueryFileSystemOnly = FLT_FILE_NAME_QUERY_FILESYSTEM_ONLY,

    RequestFromCurrentProvider = FLT_FILE_NAME_REQUEST_FROM_CURRENT_PROVIDER,
    DoNotCache                 = FLT_FILE_NAME_DO_NOT_CACHE,
    AllowQueryOnReparse        = FLT_FILE_NAME_ALLOW_QUERY_ON_REPARSE
};
DEFINE_ENUM_FLAG_OPERATORS(FileNameOptions);

struct FilterFileNameInformation {
    FilterFileNameInformation(PFLT_CALLBACK_DATA data, FileNameOptions options =
        FileNameOptions::QueryDefault | FileNameOptions::Normalized);
```

```
    ~FilterFileNameInformation();

    operator bool() const {
        return _info != nullptr;
    }

    operator PFLT_FILE_NAME_INFORMATION() const {
        return Get();
    }

    PFLT_FILE_NAME_INFORMATION operator->() {
        return _info;
    }

    NTSTATUS Parse();

private:
    PFLT_FILE_NAME_INFORMATION _info;
};
```

The non-inline functions are defined below:

```
FilterFileNameInformation::FilterFileNameInformation(
    PFLT_CALLBACK_DATA data, FileNameOptions options) {
    auto status = FltGetFileNameInformation(data,
        (FLT_FILE_NAME_OPTIONS)options, &_info);
    if (!NT_SUCCESS(status))
        _info = nullptr;
}

FilterFileNameInformation::~FilterFileNameInformation() {
    if (_info)
        FltReleaseFileNameInformation(_info);
}

NTSTATUS FilterFileNameInformation::Parse() {
    return FltParseFileNameInformation(_info);
}
```

Using this wrapper can be something like the following:

```
FilterFileNameInformation nameInfo(Data);
if(nameInfo) {  // operator bool()
    if(NT_SUCCESS(nameInfo.Parse())) {
        KdPrint(("Final component: %wZ\n", &nameInfo->FinalComponent));
    }
}
```

The Alternate Delete Protector Driver

Let's create an alternative Delete Protector driver, that will be protecting file deletions from certain directories (regardless of the calling process), rather than basing the decision on the caller process or image file.

 Of course, the two approaches could be combined; either in a single driver, or with multiple drivers having different altitudes.

 The driver in this section is named **DelProtect3** in the book samples for chapter 10.

First, we'll need to manage directories to protect (rather than process image file names as in the earlier driver). A complication arises because a user mode client will use directories in the form "c:\somedir"; that is, paths based on symbolic links. As we've seen already a driver gets the real device names rather than the symbolic links. This means we would need to somehow convert DOS-style names (as they're sometimes referred to) to NT-style names (another common referral to internal device names).

To this end, our list of protected directories would have each directory in the two forms, ready to be used where appropriate. Here is the structure definition:

```
struct DirectoryEntry {
    UNICODE_STRING DosName;
    UNICODE_STRING NtName;

    void Free() {
        if (DosName.Buffer) {
            ExFreePool(DosName.Buffer);
            DosName.Buffer = nullptr;
        }
```

```
        if (NtName.Buffer) {
            ExFreePool(NtName.Buffer);
            NtName.Buffer = nullptr;
        }
    }
};
```

Since we will allocate these strings dynamically, we need to free them eventually. The above code adds a Free method that frees the internal string buffers. The choice of using UNICODE_STRING rather than raw C-strings or even a constant size string is somewhat arbitrary, but it should be appropriate for the driver's requirements. In this case I decided to go with UNICODE_STRING objects because the strings themselves can be allocated dynamically and some APIs work with UNICODE_STRING directly.

Now we can store an array of these structures and manage it in a similar way as was done in the previous driver:

```
const int MaxDirectories = 32;

DirectoryEntry DirNames[MaxDirectories];
int DirNamesCount;
FastMutex DirNamesLock;
```

The I/O control codes of the previous driver have changed meaning - they should allow adding and removing directories, which are also strings of course. Here are the updated definitions:

```
#define IOCTL_DELPROTECT_ADD_DIR                 \
    CTL_CODE(0x8000, 0x800, METHOD_BUFFERED, FILE_ANY_ACCESS)
#define IOCTL_DELPROTECT_REMOVE_DIR \
    CTL_CODE(0x8000, 0x801, METHOD_BUFFERED, FILE_ANY_ACCESS)
#define IOCTL_DELPROTECT_CLEAR                   \
    CTL_CODE(0x8000, 0x802, METHOD_NEITHER, FILE_ANY_ACCESS)
```

Next, we need to implement these add/remove/clear operations, starting with add. The first part is making some sanity checks for the input string:

```
case IOCTL_DELPROTECT_ADD_DIR:
{
    auto name = (WCHAR*)Irp->AssociatedIrp.SystemBuffer;
    if (!name) {
        status = STATUS_INVALID_PARAMETER;
        break;
    }

    auto bufferLen = stack->Parameters.DeviceIoControl.InputBufferLength;
    if (bufferLen > 1024) {
        // just too long for a directory
        status = STATUS_INVALID_PARAMETER;
        break;
    }

    // make sure there is a NULL terminator somewhere
    name[bufferLen / sizeof(WCHAR) - 1] = L'\0';

    auto dosNameLen = ::wcslen(name);
    if (dosNameLen < 3) {
        status = STATUS_BUFFER_TOO_SMALL;
        break;
    }
```

Now that we have a proper buffer, we should check if it already exists in our array, and if so, no need to add it again. We'll create a helper function to do this lookup:

```
int FindDirectory(PCUNICODE_STRING name, bool dosName) {
    if (DirNamesCount == 0)
        return -1;

    for (int i = 0; i < MaxDirectories; i++) {
        const auto& dir = dosName ? DirNames[i].DosName : DirNames[i].NtName;
        if (dir.Buffer && RtlEqualUnicodeString(name, &dir, TRUE))
            return i;
    }
    return -1;
}
```

The function goes over the array, looking for a match with the input string. The boolean parameter indicates whether the routine compares the DOS name or the NT name. We use RtlEqualUnicode-String to check for equality, specifying case insensitive test (the last TRUE argument). The function returns the index in which the string was found, or -1 otherwise. Note the function does not acquire any lock, so it's up to the caller to call the function with proper synchronization.

Our add directory handler can now search for the input directory string and just move on if found:

```
AutoLock locker(DirNamesLock);

UNICODE_STRING strName;
RtlInitUnicodeString(&strName, name);
if (FindDirectory(&strName, true) >= 0) {
    // found it, just continue and return success
    break;
}
```

With the fast mutex acquired, we can safely proceed to access the directories array. If the string is not found, we have a new directory to add to the array. First, we should make sure the array is not exhausted:

```
if (DirNamesCount == MaxDirectories) {
    status = STATUS_TOO_MANY_NAMES;
    break;
}
```

At this point we need to traverse the array and look for an empty slot (where the DOS string's buffer pointer is NULL). Once we find it, we'll add the DOS name and do something to convert it to an NT name that we would definitely need later.

```
for (int i = 0; i < MaxDirectories; i++) {
    if (DirNames[i].DosName.Buffer == nullptr) {
        // allow space for trailing backslash and NULL terminator
        auto len = (dosNameLen + 2) * sizeof(WCHAR);
        auto buffer = (WCHAR*)ExAllocatePoolWithTag(PagedPool, len, DRIVER_TAG);
        if (!buffer) {
            status = STATUS_INSUFFICIENT_RESOURCES;
            break;
        }
        ::wcscpy_s(buffer, len / sizeof(WCHAR), name);

        // append a backslash if it's missing
        if (name[dosNameLen - 1] != L'\\')
            ::wcscat_s(buffer, dosNameLen + 2, L"\\");

        status = ConvertDosNameToNtName(buffer, &DirNames[i].NtName);
```

```
            if (!NT_SUCCESS(status)) {
                ExFreePool(buffer);
                break;
            }

            RtlInitUnicodeString(&DirNames[i].DosName, buffer);
            KdPrint(("Add: %wZ <=> %wZ\n", &DirNames[i].DosName, &DirNames[i].NtName));
            ++DirNamesCount;
            break;
        }
    }
}
```

The code is fairly straightforward with the exception of the call to ConvertDosNameToNtName. This is not a built-in function, but something we need to implement ourselves. Here is its declaration:

```
NTSTATUS ConvertDosNameToNtName(_In_ PCWSTR dosName, _Out_ PUNICODE_STRING ntName);
```

How can we convert the DOS name to NT name? Since "C:" and similar are the symbolic links, one approach would be to lookup the symbolic link and find its target, which is the NT name. We'll start with some basic checks:

```
ntName->Buffer = nullptr;      // in case of failure
auto dosNameLen = ::wcslen(dosName);

if (dosNameLen < 3)
    return STATUS_BUFFER_TOO_SMALL;

// make sure we have a driver letter
if (dosName[2] != L'\\' || dosName[1] != L':')
    return STATUS_INVALID_PARAMETER;
```

We expect a directory in the form "X:\...", meaning a drive letter, colon, backslash, and the rest of the path. We don't accept shares in this driver (something like "\myserver\myshare\mydir"). I'll leave this as an exercise to the reader to implement.

Now we need to build the symbolic link, residing under the \??\ Object Manager directory. We can use string manipulation functions to create the full string. In the following code snippet we'll use a type called kstring, which is a string wrapper, similar in concept to the standard C++ std::wstring. Its API is not the same, but fairly readable. We'll detail the implementation of this type in chapter 11.

> You can just change the following code to use various string functions to get the same result. I'll leave it as another exercise for the reader.

We'll start with the base symbolic link directory and add the drive letter provided:

```
kstring symLink(L"\\??\\");
symLink.Append(dosName, 2);   // driver letter and colon
```

Now we need to open the symbolic link using ZwOpenSymbolicLinkObject. For this purpose, we need to prepare an OBJECT_ATTRIBUTES structure common to many open-style APIs where some kind of name is required:

```
UNICODE_STRING symLinkFull;
symLink.GetUnicodeString(&symLinkFull);

OBJECT_ATTRIBUTES symLinkAttr;
InitializeObjectAttributes(&symLinkAttr, &symLinkFull,
    OBJ_KERNEL_HANDLE | OBJ_CASE_INSENSITIVE, nullptr, nullptr);
```

GetUnicodeString is a kstring helper that initializes a UNICODE_STRING based on a kstring. This is necessary because OBJECT_ATTRIBUTES requires a UNICODE_STRING for the name. Initializing OBJECT_ATTRIBUTES is accomplished with the InitializeObjectAttributes macro, requiring the following arguments (in order):

- the pointer to the OBJECT_ATTRIBUTES structure to initialize
- the name of the object
- a set of flags. In this case the handle returned would be a kernel handle and the lookup will be case insensitive
- an optional handle to a root directory in case the name is relative, rather than absolute. NULL in our case
- an optional security descriptor to apply to the object (if created and not opened). NULL in our case

Once the structure is initialized, we are ready to call ZwOpenSymbolicLinkObject:

```
HANDLE hSymLink = nullptr;
auto status = STATUS_SUCCESS;

do {
    // open symbolic link
    status = ZwOpenSymbolicLinkObject(&hSymLink, GENERIC_READ, &symLinkAttr);
    if (!NT_SUCCESS(status))
        break;
```

We'll use the well-known do / while(false) scheme to cleanup the handle if it's valid. ZwOpen-SymbolicLinkObject accepts an output HANDLE, an access mask (GENERIC_READ here means we just want to read information) and the attributes we prepared earlier. This call can certainly fail, if the provided drive letter does not exist, for instance.

If the call succeeds, we need to read the target this symbolic link object points to. The function to get this info is ZwQuerySymbolicLinkObject. We need to prepare a UNICODE_STRING large enough to hold the result (this is also our output parameter from the conversion function):

```
    USHORT maxLen = 1024;          // arbitrary
    ntName->Buffer = (WCHAR*)ExAllocatePool(PagedPool, maxLen);
    if (!ntName->Buffer) {
        status = STATUS_INSUFFICIENT_RESOURCES;
        break;
    }
    ntName->MaximumLength = maxLen;

    // read target of symbolic link
    status = ZwQuerySymbolicLinkObject(hSymLink, ntName, nullptr);
    if (!NT_SUCCESS(status))
        break;
} while (false);
```

Once the do/while block is exited, we need to free the allocated buffer if anything failed. Otherwise, we can append the rest of the input directory to the target NT name we acquired:

```
if (!NT_SUCCESS(status)) {
    if (ntName->Buffer) {
        ExFreePool(ntName->Buffer);
        ntName->Buffer = nullptr;
    }
}
else {
    RtlAppendUnicodeToString(ntName, dosName + 2);      // directory part
}
```

Finally, we just need to close the symbolic link handle if opened successfully:

```
    if (hSymLink)
        ZwClose(hSymLink);

    return status;
}
```

For removing a protected directory, we make similar checks on the provided path and then look it up by its DOS name. If found, we remove it from the array:

```
AutoLock locker(DirNamesLock);
UNICODE_STRING strName;
RtlInitUnicodeString(&strName, name);

int found = FindDirectory(&strName, true);
if (found >= 0) {
    DirNames[found].Free();
    DirNamesCount--;
}
else {
    status = STATUS_NOT_FOUND;
}
break;
```

The clear operation is fairly simple, I'll leave it as an exercise for the reader (the project's source code includes this).

Handling Pre-Create and Pre-Set Information

Now that we have the above infrastructure in place, we can turn our attention to implementing the pre-callbacks, so that any file in one of the protected directories would not be deleted, regardless of the calling process. In both callbacks we need to get the file name to be deleted and locate its directory in our array of directories. We'll create a helper function for this purpose, declared like so:

```
bool IsDeleteAllowed(_In_ PFLT_CALLBACK_DATA Data);
```

Since the file in question is tucked away in the FLT_CALLBACK_DATA structure, this is all that we would need. The first thing to do is get the file name (in this code we will not be using the wrapper introduced earlier to make the API calls more apparent):

```
PFLT_FILE_NAME_INFORMATION nameInfo = nullptr;
auto allow = true;
do {
    auto status = FltGetFileNameInformation(Data,
        FLT_FILE_NAME_QUERY_DEFAULT | FLT_FILE_NAME_NORMALIZED, &nameInfo);
    if (!NT_SUCCESS(status))
        break;

    status = FltParseFileNameInformation(nameInfo);
    if (!NT_SUCCESS(status))
        break;
```

We get the file name information and then parse it, since we need the volume and parent directory only (and the share if we support them). We need to build a UNICODE_STRING that concatenates these three factors:

```
// concatenate volume+share+directory
UNICODE_STRING path;
path.Length = path.MaximumLength =
    nameInfo->Volume.Length + nameInfo->Share.Length + nameInfo->ParentDir.Length;
path.Buffer = nameInfo->Volume.Buffer;
```

Since the full file path is contiguous in memory, the buffer pointer starts at the first component (volume) and the length must be calculated appropriately. All that's left to do now is call FindDirectory to locate (or fail to locate) this directory:

```
    AutoLock locker(DirNamesLock);
    if (FindDirectory(&path, false) >= 0) {
        allow = false;
        KdPrint(("File not allowed to delete: %wZ\n", &nameInfo->Name));
    }
} while (false);
```

Finally, release the file name information and we're done:

```
    if (nameInfo)
        FltReleaseFileNameInformation(nameInfo);
    return allow;
}
```

Back to our pre-callbacks. First, pre-create:

```
_Use_decl_annotations_
FLT_PREOP_CALLBACK_STATUS DelProtectPreCreate(PFLT_CALLBACK_DATA Data,
    PCFLT_RELATED_OBJECTS, PVOID*) {
    if (Data->RequestorMode == KernelMode)
        return FLT_PREOP_SUCCESS_NO_CALLBACK;

    auto& params = Data->Iopb->Parameters.Create;

    if (params.Options & FILE_DELETE_ON_CLOSE) {
        // delete operation
        KdPrint(("Delete on close: %wZ\n", &FltObjects->FileObject->FileName));

        if (!IsDeleteAllowed(Data)) {
            Data->IoStatus.Status = STATUS_ACCESS_DENIED;
            return FLT_PREOP_COMPLETE;
        }
    }
    return FLT_PREOP_SUCCESS_NO_CALLBACK;
}
```

And pre-set information which is very similar:

```
_Use_decl_annotations_
FLT_PREOP_CALLBACK_STATUS DelProtectPreSetInformation(PFLT_CALLBACK_DATA Data,
    PCFLT_RELATED_OBJECTS, PVOID*) {

    if (Data->RequestorMode == KernelMode)
        return FLT_PREOP_SUCCESS_NO_CALLBACK;

    auto& params = Data->Iopb->Parameters.SetFileInformation;

    if (params.FileInformationClass != FileDispositionInformation &&
        params.FileInformationClass != FileDispositionInformationEx) {
        // not a delete operation
        return FLT_PREOP_SUCCESS_NO_CALLBACK;
```

```
    }

    auto info = (FILE_DISPOSITION_INFORMATION*)params.InfoBuffer;
    if (!info->DeleteFile)
        return FLT_PREOP_SUCCESS_NO_CALLBACK;

    if (IsDeleteAllowed(Data))
        return FLT_PREOP_SUCCESS_NO_CALLBACK;

    Data->IoStatus.Status = STATUS_ACCESS_DENIED;
    return FLT_PREOP_COMPLETE;
}
```

Testing the Driver

The configuration client has been updated to send the updated control codes, although the code is very similar to the earlier one since we send strings in add/remove just like before (the project is named **DelProtectConfig3** in the source). Here are some tests:

```
c:\book>fltmc load delprotect3

c:\book>delprotectconfig3 add c:\users\pavel\pictures
Success!

c:\book>del c:\users\pavel\pictures\pic1.jpg
c:\users\pavel\pictures\pic1.jpg
Access is denied.
```

Contexts

In some scenarios it is desirable to attach some data to file system entities such as volumes and files. The filter manager provides this capability through *contexts*. A context is a data structure provided by the mini-filter driver that can be set and retrieved for any file system object. These contexts are connected to the objects they are set on, for as long as these objects are alive.

To use contexts, the driver must declare before hand what contexts it may require and for what type of objects. This is done as part of the registration structure FLT_REGISTRATION. The ContextReg-istration field may point to an array of FLT_CONTEXT_REGISTRATION structures, each of which defines information for a single context. FLT_CONTEXT_REGISTRATION is declared as follows:

```
typedef struct _FLT_CONTEXT_REGISTRATION {
    FLT_CONTEXT_TYPE ContextType;
    FLT_CONTEXT_REGISTRATION_FLAGS Flags;
    PFLT_CONTEXT_CLEANUP_CALLBACK ContextCleanupCallback;
    SIZE_T Size;
    ULONG PoolTag;
    PFLT_CONTEXT_ALLOCATE_CALLBACK ContextAllocateCallback;
    PFLT_CONTEXT_FREE_CALLBACK ContextFreeCallback;
    PVOID Reserved1;
} FLT_CONTEXT_REGISTRATION, *PFLT_CONTEXT_REGISTRATION;
```

Here is a description of the above fields:

- *ContextType* identifies the object type this context would be attached to. The FLT_CONTEXT_-TYPE is typedefed as USHORT and can have one of the following values:

```
    #define FLT_VOLUME_CONTEXT          0x0001
    #define FLT_INSTANCE_CONTEXT        0x0002
    #define FLT_FILE_CONTEXT            0x0004
    #define FLT_STREAM_CONTEXT          0x0008
    #define FLT_STREAMHANDLE_CONTEXT    0x0010
    #define FLT_TRANSACTION_CONTEXT     0x0020
#if FLT_MGR_WIN8
    #define FLT_SECTION_CONTEXT         0x0040
#endif // FLT_MGR_WIN8
    #define FLT_CONTEXT_END             0xffff
```

As can be seen from the above definitions, a context can be attached to a volume, filter instance, file, stream, stream handle, transaction and section (on Windows 8 and later). The last value is a sentinel for indicating this is the end of the list of context definitions. The aside "Context Types" contains more information on the various context types.

Context Types

The filter manager supports several types of contexts:

- Volume contexts are attached to volumes, such as a disk partition (C:, D:, etc.).
- Instance contexts are attached to filter instances. A mini-filter can have several instances running, each attached to a different volume.
- File contexts can be attached to files in general (and not a specific file stream).
- Stream contexts can be attached to file streams, supported by some file systems, such as NTFS. File systems that support a single stream per file (such as FAT) treat stream contexts as file contexts.

- Stream handle contexts can be attached to a stream on a per `FILE_OBJECT`.
- Transaction contexts can be attached to a transaction that is in progress. Specifically, the NTFS file system supports transactions, and such so a context can be attached to a running transaction.
- Section contexts can be attached to section (file mapping) objects created with the function `FltCreateSectionForDataScan` (beyond the scope of this book).

Not all types of contexts are supported on all file systems. The filter manager provides APIs to query this dynamically if desired (for some context types), such as `FltSupportsFileContexts`, `FltSupportsFileContextsEx` and `FltSupportsStreamContexts`.

Context size can be fixed or variable. If fixed size is desired, it's specified in the *Size* field of `FLT_CONTEXT_REGISTRATION`. For a variable sized context, a driver specifies the special value `FLT_VARIABLE_SIZED_CONTEXTS` (-1). Using fixed-size contexts is more efficient, because the filter manager can use lookaside lists for managing allocations and deallocations (see the WDK documentation for more on lookaside lists).

The pool tag is specified with the *PoolTag* field of `FLT_CONTEXT_REGISTRATION`. This is the tag the filter manager will use when actually allocating the context. The next two fields are optional callbacks where the driver provides the allocation and deallocation functions. If these are non-`NULL`, then the *PoolTag* and *Size* fields are meaningless and not used.

Here is an example of building an array of context registration structure:

```
struct FileContext {
    //...
};

const FLT_CONTEXT_REGISTRATION ContextRegistration[] = {
    { FLT_FILE_CONTEXT, 0, nullptr, sizeof(FileContext), 'torP',
        nullptr, nullptr, nullptr },
    { FLT_CONTEXT_END }
};
```

Managing Contexts

To actually use a context, a driver first needs to allocate it by calling `FltAllocateContext`, defined like so:

```
NTSTATUS FltAllocateContext (
    _In_ PFLT_FILTER Filter,
    _In_ FLT_CONTEXT_TYPE ContextType,
    _In_ SIZE_T ContextSize,
    _In_ POOL_TYPE PoolType,
    _Outptr_ PFLT_CONTEXT *ReturnedContext);
```

The *Filter* parameter is the filter's opaque pointer returned by FltRegisterFilter but also available in the FLT_RELATED_OBJECTS structure provided to all callbacks. *ContextType* is one of the supported context macros shown earlier, such as FLT_FILE_CONTEXT. *ContextSize* is the requested context size in bytes (must be greater than zero). *PoolType* can be PagedPool or NonPagedPool, depending on what IRQL the driver is planning to access the context (for volume contexts, NonPaged-Pool must be specified). Finally, the *ReturnedContext* field stores the returned allocated context; PFLT_CONTEXT is typedefed as PVOID.

Once the context has been allocated, the driver can store in that data buffer anything it wishes. Then it must attach the context to an object (this is the reason to create the context in the first place) using one of several functions named FltSetXxxContext where "Xxx" is one of File, Instance, Volume, Stream, StreamHandle, or Transaction. The only exception is a section context which is set with FltCreateSectionForDataScan. Each of the FltSetXxxContext functions has the same generic makeup, shown here for the File case:

```
NTSTATUS FltSetFileContext (
    _In_ PFLT_INSTANCE Instance,
    _In_ PFILE_OBJECT FileObject,
    _In_ FLT_SET_CONTEXT_OPERATION Operation,
    _In_ PFLT_CONTEXT NewContext,
    _Outptr_ PFLT_CONTEXT *OldContext);
```

The function accepts the required parameters for the context at hand. In this file case it's the instance (actually needed in any set context function) and the file object representing the file that should carry this context. The *Operation* parameter can be either FLT_SET_CONTEXT_REPLACE_IF_EXISTS or FLT_SET_CONTEXT_KEEP_IF_EXISTS, which are pretty self explanatory.

NewContext is the context to set, and *OldContext* is an optional parameter that can be used to retrieve the previous context with the operation set to FLT_SET_CONTEXT_REPLACE_IF_EXISTS.

Contexts are reference counted. Allocating a context (FltAllocateContext) and setting a context increment its reference count. The opposite function is FltReleaseContext that must be called a matching number of times to make sure the context is not leaked. Although there is context delete function (FltDeleteContext), it's usually not needed as the filter manager will tear down the context once the file system object holding it is destroyed.

You must pay careful attention to context management, otherwise you may find that the driver cannot be unloaded because a positive reference counted context is still alive, and the file system object it's attached to has not yet been deleted (such as a file or volume). Clearly, this suggests a RAII context handling class could be useful.

The typical scenario would be to allocate a context, fill it, set it on the relevant object and then call FltReleaseContext once, keeping a reference count of one for the context. We will see a practical use of contexts in the "File Backup Driver" section later in this chapter.

Once a context has been set on an object, other callbacks may wish to get a hold of that context. A set of "get" functions provide access to the relevant context, all named in the form FltGetXxxContext, where "Xxx" is one of File, Instance, Volume, Stream, StreamHandle, Transaction or Section. The "get" functions increment the context's reference count and so calling FltReleaseContext is necessary once working with the context is completed.

Initiating I/O Requests

File system mini-filters sometimes need to initiate their own I/O operations. Normally, kernel code would use functions such as ZwCreateFile to open a handle to a file, and then issue I/O operations with functions such as ZwReadFile, ZwWriteFile, ZwDeviceIoControlFile, and some others. Mini-filters don't usually use ZwCreateFile if they need to issue an I/O operation from one of the filter manager's callbacks. The reason has to do with the fact that the I/O operation will travel from the topmost filter down towards the file system itself, meeting the current mini-filter on the way! This is a form of *reentrancy*, which can cause issues if the driver is not careful. It also has a performance penalty because the entire file system stack of filters must be traversed.

Instead, mini-filters use filter manager routines to issue I/O operations that are sent to the next lower filter towards the file system, preventing reentrancy and a possible performance hit. These APIs start with "Flt" and are similar in concept to the "Zw" variants. The main function to use is FltCreateFile (and its extended friends, FltCreateFileEx and FltCreateFileEx2. Here is the prototype of FltCreateFile:

```
NTSTATUS FltCreateFile (
    _In_ PFLT_FILTER Filter,
    _In_opt_ PFLT_INSTANCE Instance,
    _Out_ PHANDLE FileHandle,
    _In_ ACCESS_MASK DesiredAccess,
    _In_ POBJECT_ATTRIBUTES ObjectAttributes,
    _Out_ PIO_STATUS_BLOCK IoStatusBlock,
    _In_opt_ PLARGE_INTEGER AllocationSize,
    _In_ ULONG FileAttributes,
    _In_ ULONG ShareAccess,
```

```
_In_ ULONG CreateDisposition,
_In_ ULONG CreateOptions,
_In_reads_bytes_opt_(EaLength) PVOID EaBuffer,
_In_ ULONG EaLength,
_In_ ULONG Flags);
```

Wow, that's quite a mouthful - this function has many, many options. Fortunately, they are not difficult to understand, but they must be set just right, or the call will fail with some weird status.

As can be seen from the declaration, the first argument is the filter opaque address, used as the base layer for I/O operations through the resulting file handle. The main return value is the *FileHandle* to the open file if successful. We won't go over all the various parameters (refer to the WDK documentation), but we will use this function in the next section.

> The extended function FltCreateFileEx has an additional output parameter which is the FILE_-OBJECT pointer created by the function. FltCreateFileEx2 has an additional input parameter of type IO_DRIVER_CREATE_CONTEXT used to specify additional information to the file system (refer to the WDK documentation for more information).

With the returned handle, the driver can call the standard I/O APIs such as ZwReadFile, ZwWriteFile, etc. The operation will still target lower layers only. Alternatively, the driver can use the returned FILE_OBJECT from FltCreateFileEx or FltCreateFileEx2 with functions such as FltReadFile and FltWriteFile (the latter functions require the file object rather than a handle).

Once the operation is done, FltClose must be called on the returned handle. If a file object was returned as well, its reference count must be decremented with ObDereferenceObject to prevent a leak.

 FltClose actually just calls ZwClose; it's there for consistency.

The File Backup Driver

It's time to put what we learned into practice, specifically using contexts and I/O operations from within a mini-filter driver. The driver we'll build provides automatic backup of a file whenever that file is opened for write access, just before it's being written. In this way, it's possible to revert to the previous file state if desired. In effect - we have a single backup of the file at any point.

The main question is, where will that backup be stored? It's possible to create some "backup" directory within the directory of the file, or perhaps create a root directory for all backups and re-create the backup in the same folder structure starting of the original file, but starting from the backup root directory (the driver can even hide this directory from general access). These options are fine, but for this demo we'll use another option: we'll store the backup of the file *within the file itself*, in an alternate NTFS stream. So essentially, the file would contain its own backup. Then, if needed, we can swap the contexts of the alternate stream with the default stream, effectively restoring the file to its previous state.

We'll start with the File System Mini-filter project template we've used in previous drivers. The driver name is going to be *FileBackup*. Next, we need to fix the INF file as usual. Here are the parts that have been changed:

```
[Version]
Signature   = "$Windows NT$"
Class       = "OpenFileBackup"
ClassGuid   = {f8ecafa6-66d1-41a5-899b-66585d7216b7}
Provider    = %ManufacturerName%
DriverVer   =
CatalogFile = FileBackup.cat


[MiniFilter.Service]
; truncated
LoadOrderGroup = "FS Open file backup filters"


[Strings]
; truncated
Instance1.Altitude   = "100200"
Instance1.Flags      = 0x0
```

We'll rename the *FileBackup.c* file to *FileBackup.cpp* to support C++ code.

Since we'll be using alternate streams, only NTFS can be used, as it's the only "standard" file system in Windows to support alternate file streams. This means the driver should not attach to a volume not using NTFS. The driver needs to modify the default implementation of the "instance setup" callback already set up by the project template. Here is the complete function code with the extra check for NTFS and avoiding file systems that are not NTFS:

```
NTSTATUS FileBackupInstanceSetup(
    _In_ PCFLT_RELATED_OBJECTS FltObjects,
    _In_ FLT_INSTANCE_SETUP_FLAGS Flags,
    _In_ DEVICE_TYPE VolumeDeviceType,
    _In_ FLT_FILESYSTEM_TYPE VolumeFilesystemType) {
    UNREFERENCED_PARAMETER(FltObjects);
    UNREFERENCED_PARAMETER(Flags);
    UNREFERENCED_PARAMETER(VolumeDeviceType);

    if (VolumeFilesystemType != FLT_FSTYPE_NTFS) {
        KdPrint(("Not attaching to non-NTFS volume\n"));
        return STATUS_FLT_DO_NOT_ATTACH;
    }

    return STATUS_SUCCESS;
}
```

Returning STATUS_FLT_DO_NOT_ATTACH denies attachment to the volume in question.

Next, we need to register to the proper requests. The driver needs to intercept write operations, so a pre-operation callback for IRP_MJ_WRITE is needed. Also, we will need to keep track of some state using a file context. The driver may need handling a post-create operation and also a cleanup operation (IRP_MJ_CLEANUP). We'll see later why this is required. For now, given these constraints, we can set up the callback registration structure like so:

```
#define DRIVER_CONTEXT_TAG 'xcbF'
#define DRIVER_TAG 'bF'

const FLT_OPERATION_REGISTRATION Callbacks[] = {
    { IRP_MJ_CREATE, 0, nullptr, FileBackupPostCreate },
    { IRP_MJ_WRITE, FLTFL_OPERATION_REGISTRATION_SKIP_PAGING_IO,
        FileBackupPreWrite, nullptr },
    { IRP_MJ_CLEANUP, 0, nullptr, FileBackupPostCleanup },

    { IRP_MJ_OPERATION_END }
};
```

Next, we'll need some context to keep track of whether a write operation already occurred on a particular open file. Let's define a context structure we'll use:

```
struct FileContext {
    Mutex Lock;
    UNICODE_STRING FileName;
    BOOLEAN Written;
};
```

We'll store the file name itself (will be easier to have it for when backing up the file), a mutex for synchronization purposes and a boolean indicating whether a backup operation already occurred for this file. Again, actual usage of this context will become clearer once we start callback implementation.

Since we have a context, it needs to be registered in an array of contexts like so:

```
const FLT_CONTEXT_REGISTRATION Contexts[] = {
    { FLT_FILE_CONTEXT, 0, nullptr, sizeof(FileContext), DRIVER_CONTEXT_TAG },
    { FLT_CONTEXT_END }
};
```

This array is the pointed to by the full registration structure, shown below:

```
CONST FLT_REGISTRATION FilterRegistration = {
    sizeof(FLT_REGISTRATION),              // Size
    FLT_REGISTRATION_VERSION,              // Version
    0,                                     // Flags

    Contexts,                              // Context
    Callbacks,                             // Operation callbacks

    FileBackupUnload,                      // MiniFilterUnload
    FileBackupInstanceSetup,
    FileBackupInstanceQueryTeardown,
    FileBackupInstanceTeardownStart,
    FileBackupInstanceTeardownComplete,
};
```

Now that we have all the structures set up, we can move on to callback implementation.

The Post Create Callback

Why do we even need a post-create callback? It is actually possible to write the driver without it, but it will help demonstrate some features we haven't seen before. Our goal for post-create is to allocate a file context for files we're interested in. For example, files that are not open for write access are of no interest to the driver.

Why do we use a post callback rather than a pre-callback? If a file open operation fails by some pre-create of another driver, we don't care. Only if the file is opened successfully, then our driver should examine the file further. Implementation starts here:

```
FLT_POSTOP_CALLBACK_STATUS FileBackupPostCreate(
    PFLT_CALLBACK_DATA Data, PCFLT_RELATED_OBJECTS FltObjects,
    PVOID CompletionContext, FLT_POST_OPERATION_FLAGS Flags) {
```

Next, let's extract the parameters of the create operation:

```
const auto& params = Data->Iopb->Parameters.Create;
```

We are only interested in files opened for write access, not from kernel mode, and not new files (since new files do not require backup). Here are the checks to make:

```
if (Data->RequestorMode == KernelMode
    || (params.SecurityContext->DesiredAccess & FILE_WRITE_DATA) == 0
    || Data->IoStatus.Information == FILE_DOES_NOT_EXIST) {
    // kernel caller, not write access or a new file - skip
    return FLT_POSTOP_FINISHED_PROCESSING;
}
```

> Check out the documentation for FLT_PARAMETERS for IRP_MJ_CREATE to get more information on the details shown above.

These kinds of checks are important, as they remove a lot of possible overhead for the driver. The driver should always strive to do as little as possible to reduce its performance impact.

Now that we have a file we care about, we need to prepare a context object to be attached to the file. This context will be needed later when we process the pre-write callback. First, we'll extract the name of the file. The driver needs to call the standard FltGetFileNameInformation. To make it a little easier and less error-prone, we'll use the RAII wrapper presented earlier in this chapter:

```
FilterFileNameInformation fileNameInfo(Data);
if (!fileNameInfo) {
    return FLT_POSTOP_FINISHED_PROCESSING;
}

if (!NT_SUCCESS(fileNameInfo.Parse()))   // FltParseFileNameInformation
    return FLT_POSTOP_FINISHED_PROCESSING;
```

The next step is to decide whether we backup all files or files residing in specific directories. For flexibility, we'll go with the latter approach. Let's create a helper function named `IsBackupDirectory` that should return true for directories we care about. Here is a simple implementation that returns true for any directory which has the name "\pictures\" or "\documents\":

```
bool IsBackupDirectory(_In_ PCUNICODE_STRING directory) {
    // no counted version of wcsstr :(

    ULONG maxSize = 1024;
    if (directory->Length > maxSize)
        return false;

    auto copy = (WCHAR*)ExAllocatePoolWithTag(PagedPool, maxSize + sizeof(WCHAR),
        DRIVER_TAG);
    if (!copy)
        return false;

    RtlZeroMemory(copy, maxSize + sizeof(WCHAR));
    wcsncpy_s(copy, 1 + maxSize / sizeof(WCHAR), directory->Buffer,
        directory->Length / sizeof(WCHAR));
    _wcslwr(copy);

    bool doBackup = wcsstr(copy, L"\\pictures\\") || wcsstr(copy, L"\\documents\\");
    ExFreePool(copy);

    return doBackup;
}
```

The function accepts the directory name only (extracted by `FltParseFileNameInformation`) and needs to look for the above substrings. Unfortunately, This is not as easy as one would like. The natural function to use is `wcsstr` which scans a string for some substring, but it has two issues:

- it's case sensitive, which is inconvenient when files or directories are concerned
- it expects the searched string to be `NULL`-terminated, which is not necessarily the case with `UNICODE_STRING`

Because of the above wrinkles, the code allocates its own string buffer, copies the directory name, and converts the string to lowercase (_wcslwr) before using wcsstr to scan for "\pictures\" and "\documents\".

> Of course, in a production-grade driver, these hard coded strings should come from some configuration utility, the registry or a combination of the above. This is left as an exercise for the reader.

Back at the post-create callback, we call IsBackupDirectory and bail out if it returns false:

```
if (!IsBackupDirectory(&fileNameInfo->ParentDir))
    return FLT_POSTOP_FINISHED_PROCESSING;
```

Next, we have one more check to make. If the file opened is for a non-default stream, then we should not attempt to back up anything. We will only backup the default data stream:

```
if (fileNameInfo->Stream.Length > 0)
    return FLT_POSTOP_FINISHED_PROCESSING;
```

Finally, we are ready to allocate our file context and initialize it:

```
FileContext* context;
auto status = FltAllocateContext(FltObjects->Filter, FLT_FILE_CONTEXT,
    sizeof(FileContext), PagedPool, (PFLT_CONTEXT*)&context);
if (!NT_SUCCESS(status)) {
    KdPrint(("Failed to allocate file context (0x%08X)\n", status));
    return FLT_POSTOP_FINISHED_PROCESSING;
}

context->Written = FALSE;
context->FileName.MaximumLength = fileNameInfo->Name.Length;
context->FileName.Buffer = (WCHAR*)ExAllocatePoolWithTag(PagedPool,
    fileNameInfo->Name.Length, DRIVER_TAG);
if (!context->FileName.Buffer) {
    FltReleaseContext(context);
    return FLT_POSTOP_FINISHED_PROCESSING;
}
RtlCopyUnicodeString(&context->FileName, &fileNameInfo->Name);

// initialize mutex
context->Lock.Init();
```

This code bears some explanation. `FltAllocateContext` allocates a context with the required size and returns a pointer to the allocated memory. `PFLT_CONTEXT` is just a `void*` - we can cast to whatever type we need. The returned context memory is not zeroed, so all members must be initialized properly.

Why do we need this context in the first place? A typical client opens a file for write access and then calls `WriteFile` potentially multiple times. Before the first call to `WriteFile` the driver should back up the existing content of the file. This is why we need the boolean `Written` field - to make sure we make the backup just once before the first write operation. This flag starts as `FALSE` and will turn `TRUE` after the first write operation. This turn of events is depicted in figure 10-10.

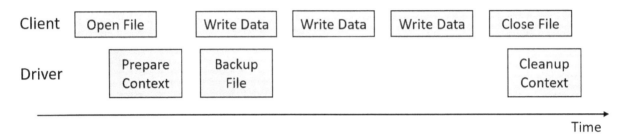

Figure 10-10: Client and driver operations for common write sequence

Next we allocate memory to store the full file name, which we'll need later when actually backing up the file. Technically, we can call `FltGetFileNameInformation` at backup file time, but since this function may fail in some scenarios, it's better to grab the file name now and use it later, making the driver more robust.

The last field in our context is a mutex. We need some synchronization in a non-common, but possible, case, where more than one thread within the client process write to the same file at roughly the same time. In such a case, we need to make sure we make a single backup of the data, otherwise our backup may become corrupted. In all examples thus far where we needed such synchronization, we used a fast mutex, but here we're using a standard mutex. Why? The reason has to do with the operations the driver will call when backing up the file - I/O APIs such as `ZwWriteFile` and `ZwReadFile` can only be called at IRQL `PASSIVE_LEVEL` (0). An acquired fast mutex raises IRQL to `APC_LEVEL` (1), which will cause a deadlock if I/O APIs are used.

The `Mutex` class is the same one shown in chapter 6, which will be used with the RAII `AutoLock` class we've used multiple times in previous chapters.

The context is now initialized, so we need to attach it to the file with `FltSetFileContext`, release the context and finally return from the post-create callback:

```
    status = FltSetFileContext(FltObjects->Instance, FltObjects->FileObject,
        FLT_SET_CONTEXT_KEEP_IF_EXISTS, context, nullptr);
    if (!NT_SUCCESS(status)) {
        KdPrint(("Failed to set file context (0x%08X)\n", status));
        ExFreePool(context->FileName.Buffer);
    }
    FltReleaseContext(context);

    return FLT_POSTOP_FINISHED_PROCESSING;
}
```

The set context APIs allow keeping an existing context (if any) or to replace it (if exists). In this case we choose to keep an existing context in the rare occurrence where two separate callers open the same file for write access and one was quicker to set a context. If a context was already there the returned status is STATUS_FLT_CONTEXT_ALREADY_DEFINED, which is an error status, and if an error status is returned the driver is careful to free the string buffer allocated earlier.

Finally, FltReleaseContext must be called, which if all is well, set the internal reference count of the context to 1 (+1 for allocate, +1 for set, -1 for release). If the context failed to be set, then it will be completely freed.

The Pre-Write Callback

The pre-write callback's job is to make a copy of the file data just before the actual write operation is allowed to go through; this is why a pre-callback is needed here, otherwise in the post-callback the operation would already be completed.

We start with retrieving the file's context. If it does not exist, this means our post-create callback deemed the file uninteresting and we can just move on:

```
FLT_PREOP_CALLBACK_STATUS FileBackupPreWrite(
    PFLT_CALLBACK_DATA Data, PCFLT_RELATED_OBJECTS FltObjects,
        PVOID* CompletionContext) {
    UNREFERENCED_PARAMETER(CompletionContext);
    UNREFERENCED_PARAMETER(Data);

    // get the file context if exists
    FileContext* context;

    auto status = FltGetFileContext(FltObjects->Instance,
        FltObjects->FileObject, (PFLT_CONTEXT*)&context);
    if (!NT_SUCCESS(status) || context == nullptr) {
        // no context, continue normally
```

```
        return FLT_PREOP_SUCCESS_NO_CALLBACK;
    }
```

Once we have a context, we need to make a copy of the file data just once before the first write operation. First, we acquire the mutex and check the written flag from the context. if it's false, then a backup was not created yet and we call a helper function to make the backup:

```
    {
        AutoLock<Mutex> locker(context->Lock);

        if (!context->Written) {
            status = BackupFile(&context->FileName, FltObjects);
            if (!NT_SUCCESS(status)) {
                KdPrint(("Failed to backup file! (0x%X)\n", status));
            }
            context->Written = TRUE;
        }
    }
    FltReleaseContext(context);

    return FLT_PREOP_SUCCESS_NO_CALLBACK;
}
```

The BackupFile helper function is the key to making all this work. One might thing that making a file copy is just an API away; unfortunately, it's not. There is no "CopyFile" function in the kernel. The CopyFile user mode API is a non-trivial function that does quite a bit of work to make copy work. Part of it is reading bytes from the source file and writing to the destination file. But that's not enough in the general case. First, there may be multiple streams to copy (in case of NTFS). Second, there is the question of the security descriptor from the original file which also needs to be copied in certain cases (refer to the documentation for CopyFile to get all details).

The bottom line is that we need to create our own file copy operation. Fortunately, we just need to copy a single file stream - the default stream to another stream inside the same physical file as our backup stream. Here is the start of our BackupFile function:

```
NTSTATUS
BackupFile(_In_ PUNICODE_STRING FileName, _In_ PCFLT_RELATED_OBJECTS FltObjects) {
    HANDLE hTargetFile = nullptr;
    HANDLE hSourceFile = nullptr;
    IO_STATUS_BLOCK ioStatus;
    auto status = STATUS_SUCCESS;
    void* buffer = nullptr;
```

The route we'll take is to open two handles - one (source) handle pointing to the original file (with the default stream to back up) and the other (target) handle to the backup stream. Then, we'll read from the source and write to the target. This is conceptually simple, but as is often the case in kernel programming, the devil is in the details.

We'll start by getting the file size. The file size could be zero, and in that case there is nothing to backup:

```
LARGE_INTEGER fileSize;
status = FsRtlGetFileSize(FltObjects->FileObject, &fileSize);
if (!NT_SUCCESS(status) || fileSize.QuadPart == 0)
    return status;
```

The FsRtlGetFileSize API is recommended whenever the file size is needed given a FILE_OBJECT pointer. The alternative would be using ZwQueryInformationFile to obtain the file size (it has many other types of information it can retrieve), but this requires a file handle and in some cases can cause a deadlock.

Now we're ready to open the source file with FltCreateFile. It's important **not** to use ZwCreate-File, so that the I/O requests are sent to the driver below this driver and not to the top of the file system driver stack. FltCreateFile has many parameters, so the call is not fun to look at:

```
do {
    // open source file
    OBJECT_ATTRIBUTES sourceFileAttr;
    InitializeObjectAttributes(&sourceFileAttr, FileName,
        OBJ_KERNEL_HANDLE | OBJ_CASE_INSENSITIVE, nullptr, nullptr);

    status = FltCreateFile(
        FltObjects->Filter,              // filter object
        FltObjects->Instance,            // filter instance
        &hSourceFile,                    // resulting handle
        FILE_READ_DATA | SYNCHRONIZE,    // access mask
        &sourceFileAttr,                 // object attributes
        &ioStatus,                       // resulting status
        nullptr, FILE_ATTRIBUTE_NORMAL,  // allocation size, file attributes
```

```
        FILE_SHARE_READ | FILE_SHARE_WRITE, // share flags (unimportant here)
        FILE_OPEN,                    // create disposition
        FILE_SYNCHRONOUS_IO_NONALERT, // create options (sync I/O)
        nullptr, 0,                                // extended attributes, EA length
        IO_IGNORE_SHARE_ACCESS_CHECK);        // flags

    if (!NT_SUCCESS(status))
        break;
```

Before calling FltCreateFile, just like other APIs requiring a name, an OBJECT_ATTRIBUTES
structure must be initialized properly with the file name provided to BackupFile. This is the default
file stream that is about to change by a write operation and that's why we're making the backup.
The important arguments in the call are:

- filter and instance objects, which provide the necessary information for the call to go to the
  next lower layer filter (or the file system) rather than go to the top of the file system stack.
- the returned handle, in hSourceFile.
- the access mask set to FILE_READ_DATA and SYNCHRONIZE.
- the create disposition, in this case indicating the file must exist (FILE_OPEN).
- the create options are set to FILE_SYNCHRONOUS_IO_NONALERT indicating synchronous operations through the resulting file handle. The SYNCHRONIZE access mask flag is required for
  synchronous operations to work.
- the flag IO_IGNORE_SHARE_ACCESS_CHECK is important, because the file in question was
  already opened by the client that most likely opened it with no sharing allowed. So we ask
  the file system to ignore share access checks for this call.

> Read the documentation of FltCreateFile to gain a better understanding of all the various options
> this function provides.

Next we need to open or create the backup stream within the same file. We'll name the backup
stream ":backup" and use another call to FltCreateFile to get a handle to the target file:

```
UNICODE_STRING targetFileName;
const WCHAR backupStream[] = L":backup";
targetFileName.MaximumLength = FileName->Length + sizeof(backupStream);
targetFileName.Buffer = (WCHAR*)ExAllocatePoolWithTag(PagedPool,
    targetFileName.MaximumLength, DRIVER_TAG);
if (targetFileName.Buffer == nullptr)
    return STATUS_INSUFFICIENT_RESOURCES;

RtlCopyUnicodeString(&targetFileName, FileName);
RtlAppendUnicodeToString(&targetFileName, backupStream);

OBJECT_ATTRIBUTES targetFileAttr;
InitializeObjectAttributes(&targetFileAttr, &targetFileName,
    OBJ_KERNEL_HANDLE | OBJ_CASE_INSENSITIVE, nullptr, nullptr);

status = FltCreateFile(
    FltObjects->Filter,              // filter object
    FltObjects->Instance,         // filter instance
    &hTargetFile,                    // resulting handle
    GENERIC_WRITE | SYNCHRONIZE, // access mask
    &targetFileAttr,              // object attributes
    &ioStatus,                       // resulting status
    nullptr, FILE_ATTRIBUTE_NORMAL,      // allocation size, file attributes
    0,              // share flags
    FILE_OVERWRITE_IF,               // create disposition
    FILE_SYNCHRONOUS_IO_NONALERT, // create options (sync I/O)
    nullptr, 0, 0);       // extended attributes, EA length, flags

ExFreePool(targetFileName.Buffer);

if (!NT_SUCCESS(status))
    break;
```

The file name is built by concatenating the base file name and the backup stream name. It is opened for write access (GENERIC_WRITE) and overwrites any data that may be present (FILE_OVERWRITE_-IF).

With these two handles, we can start from the source and writing to the target. A simple approach would be to allocate a buffer with the file size, and do the work with a single read and a single write. This could be problematic, however, if the file is very large, possibly causing memory allocation to fail.

There is also the risk of creating a backup for a very large file, possibly consuming lots of disk space. For this kind of driver, backup should probably be avoided when a file is too large (configurable in the registry for instance) or avoid backup if the remaining disk space would be below a certain threshold (again could be configurable). This is left as an exercise for the reader.

The solution would be to allocate a relatively small buffer and just loop around until all the files chunks have been copied. This is the approach we'll use. First, allocate a buffer:

```
ULONG size = 1 << 21;          // 2 MB
buffer = ExAllocatePoolWithTag(PagedPool, size, DRIVER_TAG);
if (!buffer) {
    status = STATUS_INSUFFICIENT_RESOURCES;
    break;
}
```

Now the loop - we'll use offsets, but they can actually be removed because we do synchronous work on the files, each file object keeps track of a file position, incrementing it after every operation.

```
LARGE_INTEGER offset = { 0 };              // read
LARGE_INTEGER writeOffset = { 0 };         // write

ULONG bytes;
auto saveSize = fileSize;
while (fileSize.QuadPart > 0) {
    status = ZwReadFile(
        hSourceFile,
        nullptr,          // optional KEVENT
        nullptr, nullptr,          // no APC
        &ioStatus,
        buffer,
        (ULONG)min((LONGLONG)size, fileSize.QuadPart),          // # of bytes
        &offset,          // offset
        nullptr);          // optional key
    if (!NT_SUCCESS(status))
        break;

    bytes = (ULONG)ioStatus.Information;

    // write to target file
    status = ZwWriteFile(
        hTargetFile,          // target handle
```

```
    nullptr,                // optional KEVENT
    nullptr, nullptr, // APC routine, APC context
    &ioStatus,              // I/O status result
    buffer,                       // data to write
    bytes,          // # bytes to write
    &writeOffset,       // offset
    nullptr);           // optional key

if (!NT_SUCCESS(status))
    break;

// update byte count and offsets
offset.QuadPart += bytes;
writeOffset.QuadPart += bytes;
fileSize.QuadPart -= bytes;
}
```

The loop keeps going as long as there are bytes to transfer. We start with the file size and then decrement it for every chunk transferred. The function that do the actual work are ZwReadFile and ZwWriteFile. The read operation returns the number of actual bytes transferred in the IO_-STATUS_BLOCK's Information field, used to initialize the bytes local variable used for the write operation.

When all is done, there is one last thing to do. Since we may be overwriting a previous backup (that may have been larger than this one), we must set the end of file pointer to the current offset:

```
FILE_END_OF_FILE_INFORMATION info;
info.EndOfFile = saveSize;
NT_VERIFY(NT_SUCCESS(ZwSetInformationFile(hTargetFile, &ioStatus,
    &info, sizeof(info), FileEndOfFileInformation)));
} while (false);
```

The NT_VERIFY macro works like NT_ASSERT in debug builds, but does not throw away its argument in release builds.

Lastly, we need to cleanup everything:

```
    if (buffer)
        ExFreePool(buffer);
    if (hSourceFile)
        FltClose(hSourceFile);
    if (hTargetFile)
        FltClose(hTargetFile);

    return status;
}
```

The Post-Cleanup Callback

Why do we need another callback? Our context is attached to a file, which means it will only be deleted when the file is deleted, which may never happen. We need to free the context when the file is closed by the client.

There are two operations that seem relevant here, IRP_MJ_CLOSE and IRP_MJ_CLEANUP. The close operation seems most intuitive as it's supposed to be called when the last handle to the file is closed. However, due to caching, this does not always happen soon enough. A better approach is to handle IRP_MJ_CLEANUP, which essentially means the file object is no longer needed, even if the last handle is not yet closed. This is a good time to free our context (if exists).

A post-cleanup callback is similar to any other post-callback:

```
FLT_POSTOP_CALLBACK_STATUS FileBackupPostCleanup(
    PFLT_CALLBACK_DATA Data, PCFLT_RELATED_OBJECTS FltObjects,
    PVOID CompletionContext, FLT_POST_OPERATION_FLAGS Flags) {
    UNREFERENCED_PARAMETER(Flags);
    UNREFERENCED_PARAMETER(CompletionContext);
    UNREFERENCED_PARAMETER(Data);
```

We need to grab the file context, and if it exists - free anything dynamically allocated just before deleting it:

```
FileContext* context;

auto status = FltGetFileContext(FltObjects->Instance,
    FltObjects->FileObject, (PFLT_CONTEXT*)&context);
if (!NT_SUCCESS(status) || context == nullptr) {
    // no context, continue normally
    return FLT_POSTOP_FINISHED_PROCESSING;
}

if (context->FileName.Buffer)
    ExFreePool(context->FileName.Buffer);
FltReleaseContext(context);
FltDeleteContext(context);

return FLT_POSTOP_FINISHED_PROCESSING;
}
```

Testing the Driver

We can test the driver by deploying it to a target system as usual, and then working with files in a "documents" or "pictures" directory.

In the following example, I created a *hello.txt* file in the documents folder with the content "Hello, world!", saved the file, and then changed the contents to "Goodbye, world!" and saved again. Figure 10-11 shows *NtfsStreams* open with this file. The following command window shows the file's current contents:

```
c:\users\pavel\documents>type hello.txt
Goodbye, world!
```

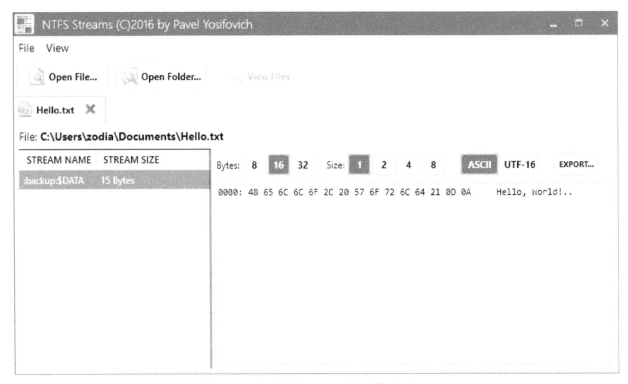

Figure 10-11: NtfsStreams with a file backup

Restoring Backups

How can we restore a backup? We need to copy the ":backup" stream contents over the "normal" file contents. Unfortunately, the CopyFile API cannot do this, as it does not accept alternate streams. Let's write a utility to do the work.

We'll create a new console application project named *FileRestore*. We'll add the following #includes to the *pch.h* file:

```
#include <Windows.h>
#include <stdio.h>
#include <string>
```

The main function should accept the file name as a command line argument:

```
int wmain(int argc, const wchar_t* argv[]) {
    if (argc < 2) {
        printf("Usage: FileRestore <filename>\n");
        return 0;
    }
}
```

Next, we'll open two files, one pointing to the ":backup" stream and the other to the "normal" file. Then, we'll copy in chunks, similarly to the driver `BackupFile` code - but in user mode (all error handling code omitted for brevity):

```cpp
// generate full stream name
std::wstring stream(argv[1]);
stream += L":backup";

HANDLE hSource = ::CreateFile(stream.c_str(), GENERIC_READ, FILE_SHARE_READ,
    nullptr, OPEN_EXISTING, 0, nullptr);

HANDLE hTarget = ::CreateFile(argv[1], GENERIC_WRITE, 0,
    nullptr, OPEN_EXISTING, 0, nullptr);

LARGE_INTEGER size;
::GetFileSizeEx(hSource, &size);

ULONG bufferSize = (ULONG)min((LONGLONG)1 << 21, size.QuadPart);
void* buffer = VirtualAlloc(nullptr, bufferSize,
    MEM_COMMIT | MEM_RESERVE, PAGE_READWRITE);

DWORD bytes;
while (size.QuadPart > 0) {
    ::ReadFile(hSource, buffer,
        (DWORD)(min((LONGLONG)bufferSize, size.QuadPart)),
        &bytes, nullptr);
    ::WriteFile(hTarget, buffer, bytes, &bytes, nullptr);

    size.QuadPart -= bytes;
}

printf("Restore successful!\n");

::CloseHandle(hSource);
::CloseHandle(hTarget);
::VirtualFree(buffer, 0, MEM_DECOMMIT | MEM_RELEASE);

return 0;
}
```

The full source code has proper error handling code for this utility.

 Extend the driver to store an additional stream in the file with the backup time and date.

User Mode Communication

We saw in previous chapters one way of communicating between a driver and a user mode client: using DeviceIoControl. This is certainly a fine way and works well in many scenarios. One of its drawbacks is that the user mode client must initiate the communication. If the driver has something to send to a user mode client (or clients), it cannot do so directly. It must store it and wait for the client to ask for the data.

The filter manager provides an alternative mechanism for bi-directional communication between a file system mini-filter and user mode clients, where any side can send information to the other and even wait for a reply.

The mini-filter creates a *filter communication port* by calling FltCreateCommunicationPort to create such a port and register callbacks for client connection and messages. The user mode client connects to the port by calling FilterConnectCommunicationPort, receiving a handle to the port.

A mini-filter sends a message to its user mode client(s) with FltSendMessage. Conversely, a user mode client calls FilterGetMessage to wait until a message arrives, or calls FilterSendMessage to send a message to the driver. If the driver is expecting a reply, a user mode client calls Filter-ReplyMessage with the reply.

Creating the Communication Port

The FltCreateCommunicationPort function is declared as follows:

```
NTSTATUS FltCreateCommunicationPort (
    _In_ PFLT_FILTER Filter,
    _Outptr_ PFLT_PORT *ServerPort,
    _In_ POBJECT_ATTRIBUTES ObjectAttributes,
    _In_opt_ PVOID ServerPortCookie,
    _In_ PFLT_CONNECT_NOTIFY ConnectNotifyCallback,
    _In_ PFLT_DISCONNECT_NOTIFY DisconnectNotifyCallback,
    _In_opt_ PFLT_MESSAGE_NOTIFY MessageNotifyCallback,
    _In_ LONG MaxConnections);
```

Here is a description of the parameters to FltCreateCommunicationPort:

- *Filter* is the opaque pointer returned from FltRegisterFilter.
- *ServerPort* is an output opaque handle that is used internally to listen to incoming messages from user mode.
- *ObjectAttributes* is the standard attributes structure that must contain the server port name and a security descriptor that would allow user mode clients to connect (more on this later).
- *ServerPortCookie* is an optional driver-defined pointer that can be used to distinguish between multiple open ports in message callbacks.
- *ConnectNotifyCallback* is a callback the driver must provide, called when a new client connects to the port.
- *DisconnectNotifyCallback* is a callback called when a user mode client disconnects from the port.
- *MessageNotifyCallback* is the callback invoked when a message arrives on the port.
- *MaxConnections* indicates the maximum number of clients that can connect to the port. It must be greater than zero.

Successful call to FltCreateCommunicationPort requires the driver to prepare an object attributes and a security descriptor. The simplest security descriptor can be created with FltBuildDefault-SecurityDescriptor like so:

```
PSECURITY_DESCRIPTOR sd;
status = FltBuildDefaultSecurityDescriptor(&sd, FLT_PORT_ALL_ACCESS);
```

The object attributes can then be initialized:

```
UNICODE_STRING portName = RTL_CONSTANT_STRING(L"\\MyPort");
OBJECT_ATTRIBUTES portAttr;
InitializeObjectAttributes(&portAttr, &name,
    OBJ_KERNEL_HANDLE | OBJ_CASE_INSENSITIVE, nullptr, sd);
```

The name of the port is in the object manager namespace, viewable with *WinObj* after port creation. The flags must include OBJ_KERNEL_HANDLE, otherwise the call fails. Notice the last argument being the security descriptor defined earlier. Now the driver is ready to call FltCreateCommunication-Port, typically done after the driver calls FltRegisterFilter (because the returned opaque filter object is needed for the call), but before FltStartFiltering so the port can be ready when actual filtering starts:

```
PFLT_PORT ServerPort;

status = FltCreateCommunicationPort(FilterHandle, &ServerPort, &portAttr, nullptr,
    PortConnectNotify, PortDisconnectNotify, PortMessageNotify, 1);

// free security descriptor
FltFreeSecurityDescriptor(sd);
```

User Mode Connection

User mode clients call FilterConnectCommunicationPort to connect to an open port, declared like so:

```
HRESULT FilterConnectCommunicationPort (
    _In_ LPCWSTR lpPortName,
    _In_ DWORD dwOptions,
    _In_reads_bytes_opt_(wSizeOfContext) LPCVOID lpContext,
    _In_ WORD wSizeOfContext,
    _In_opt_ LPSECURITY_ATTRIBUTES lpSecurityAttributes,
    _Outptr_ HANDLE *hPort);
```

Here is a quick rundown of the parameters:

- *lpPortName* is the port name (such as "\MyPort"). Note that with the default security descriptor created by the driver, only admin level processes are able to connect.
- *dwOptions* is usually zero, but FLT_PORT_FLAG_SYNC_HANDLE in Windows 8.1 and later, indicating the returned handle should work synchronously only. It's not clear why this is needed since the default usage is synchronous anyway.
- *lpContext* and *wSizeOfContext* support a way to send a buffer to the driver at connection time. This could be used as a means of authentication, for example, where some password or token is sent to the driver and the driver will fail requests to connect that don't adhere to some predefined authentication mechanism. In a production driver this is generally a good idea, so that unknown clients could not "hijack" the communication port from legitimate clients.
- *lpSecurityAttributes* is the usual user mode SECURITY_ATTRIBUTES, typically set to NULL.
- *hPort* is the output handle used later by the client to send and receive messages.

This call invokes the driver's client connection notify callback, declared as follows:

```
NTSTATUS PortConnectNotify(
    _In_ PFLT_PORT ClientPort,
    _In_opt_ PVOID ServerPortCookie,
    _In_reads_bytes_opt_(SizeOfContext) PVOID ConnectionContext,
    _In_ ULONG SizeOfContext,
    _Outptr_result_maybenull_ PVOID *ConnectionPortCookie);
```

ClientPort is a unique handle to the client's port which the driver must keep around and use whenever it needs to communicate with that client. *ServerPortCookie* is the same one the driver specified in FltCreateCommunicationPort. The *ConnectionContex* and *SizeOfContex* parameters contain the optional buffer sent by the client. Finally, *ConnectionPortCookie* is an optional value the driver can return as representing this client; it's passed in the client disconnect and message notification routines.

If the driver agrees to accept the client's connection it returns STATUS_SUCCESS. Otherwise, the client will receive a failure HRESULT back at FilterConnectCommunicationPort.

Once the call to FilterConnectCommunicationPort succeeds, the client can start communicating with the driver, and vice-versa.

Sending and Receiving Messages

A mini-filter driver can send a message to clients with FltSendMessage declared like so:

```
NTSTATUS
FLTAPI
FltSendMessage (
    _In_ PFLT_FILTER Filter,
    _In_ PFLT_PORT *ClientPort,
    _In_ PVOID SenderBuffer,
    _In_ ULONG SenderBufferLength,
    _Out_ PVOID ReplyBuffer,
    _Inout_opt_ PULONG ReplyLength,
    _In_opt_ PLARGE_INTEGER Timeout);
```

The first two parameters should be known by now. The driver can send any buffer described by *SenderBuffer* with length *SenderBufferLength*. Typically the driver will define some structure in a common header file the client can include as well so that it can correctly interpret the received buffer. Optionally, the driver may expect a reply, and if so, the *ReplyBuffer* parameter should be non-NULL with the maximum reply length stored in *ReplyLength*. Finally, *Timeout* indicates how long the driver is willing to wait the message to reach the client (and wait for a reply, if one is expected). The timeout has the usual format, described here for convenience:

- if the pointer is NULL, the driver is willing to wait indefinitely.

- if the value is positive, then it's an absolute time in 100nsec units since January 1, 1601 at midnight.
- if the value is negative, it's relative time - the most common case - in the same 100nsec units. For example, to specify one second, specify -100000000. As another example, to specify x milliseconds, multiply x by -10000.

The driver should be careful not to specify NULL from within a callback, because it means that if the client is currently not listening, the thread blocks until it does, which may never happen. It's better to specify some limited value. Even better, if a reply is not needed right away, a work item can be used to send the message and wait for longer if needed (refer to chapter 6 for more information on work items, although the filter manager has its own work item APIs).

From the client's perspective, it can wait for a message from the driver with FilterGetMessage, specifying the port handle received when connecting, a buffer and size for the incoming message and an OVERLAPPED structure than can be used to make the call asynchronous (non-blocking). The received buffer always has a header of type FILTER_MESSAGE_HEADER, followed by the actual data sent by the driver. FILTER_MESSAGE_HEADER is defined like so:

```
typedef struct _FILTER_MESSAGE_HEADER {
    ULONG ReplyLength;
    ULONGLONG MessageId;
} FILTER_MESSAGE_HEADER, *PFILTER_MESSAGE_HEADER;
```

If a reply is expected, *ReplyLength* indicates how many bytes at most are expected. The *MessageId* field allows distinguishing between messages, which the client should use if it calls FilterReply-Message.

A client can initiate its own message with FilterSendMessage which eventually lands in the driver's callback registered in FltCreateCommunicationPort. FilterSendMessage can specify a buffer comprising the message to send and an optional buffer for a reply that may be expected from the mini-filter.

> See the documentation for FilterSendMessage and FilterReplyMessage for the complete details.

Enhanced File Backup Driver

Let's enhance the file backup driver to send notifications to a user mode client when a file has been backed up. First, we'll define some global variable to hold state related to the communication port:

```
PFLT_PORT FilterPort;
PFLT_PORT SendClientPort;
```

FilterPort is the driver's server port and *SendClientPort* is the client port once connected (we will allow a single client only).

We'll have to modify DriverEntry to create the communication port as described in the previous section. Here is the code after FltRegisterFilter succeeds, with error handling omitted:

```
UNICODE_STRING name = RTL_CONSTANT_STRING(L"\\FileBackupPort");
PSECURITY_DESCRIPTOR sd;

status = FltBuildDefaultSecurityDescriptor(&sd, FLT_PORT_ALL_ACCESS);

OBJECT_ATTRIBUTES attr;
InitializeObjectAttributes(&attr, &name,
    OBJ_KERNEL_HANDLE | OBJ_CASE_INSENSITIVE, nullptr, sd);

status = FltCreateCommunicationPort(gFilterHandle, &FilterPort, &attr,
    nullptr, PortConnectNotify, PortDisconnectNotify, PortMessageNotify, 1);

FltFreeSecurityDescriptor(sd);

// Start filtering i/o

status = FltStartFiltering(gFilterHandle);
```

The driver only allows a single client to connect to the port (the last 1 to FltCreateCommunicationPort), which is quite common when a mini-filter works in tandem with a user mode service.

The PortConnectNotify callback is called when a client attempts to connect. Our driver simply stores the client's port and returns success:

```
_Use_decl_annotations_
NTSTATUS PortConnectNotify(
    PFLT_PORT ClientPort, PVOID ServerPortCookie, PVOID ConnectionContext,
    ULONG SizeOfContext, PVOID* ConnectionPortCookie) {
    UNREFERENCED_PARAMETER(ServerPortCookie);
    UNREFERENCED_PARAMETER(ConnectionContext);
    UNREFERENCED_PARAMETER(SizeOfContext);
    UNREFERENCED_PARAMETER(ConnectionPortCookie);

    SendClientPort = ClientPort;
```

```
    return STATUS_SUCCESS;
}
```

When the client disconnects, the PortDisconnectNotify callback is invoked. It's important to close the client port at that time, otherwise the mini-filter will never be unloaded:

```
void PortDisconnectNotify(PVOID ConnectionCookie) {
    UNREFERENCED_PARAMETER(ConnectionCookie);

    FltCloseClientPort(gFilterHandle, &SendClientPort);
    SendClientPort = nullptr;
}
```

In this driver we don't expect any messages from the client - the driver is the only one send messages - so the PostMessageNotify callback has an empty implementation.

Now we need to actually send a message when a file has been backed up successfully. For this purpose, we'll define a message structure common to the driver and the client in its own header file, *FileBackupCommon.h*:

```
struct FileBackupPortMessage {
    USHORT FileNameLength;
    WCHAR FileName[1];
};
```

The message contains the file name length and the file name itself. The message does not have a fixed size and depends on the file name length. In the pre-write callback after a file was backed up successfully we need to allocate and initialize a buffer to send:

```
if (SendClientPort) {
    USHORT nameLen = context->FileName.Length;
    USHORT len = sizeof(FileBackupPortMessage) + nameLen;
    auto msg = (FileBackupPortMessage*)ExAllocatePoolWithTag(PagedPool, len,
        DRIVER_TAG);
    if (msg) {
        msg->FileNameLength = nameLen / sizeof(WCHAR);
        RtlCopyMemory(msg->FileName, context->FileName.Buffer, nameLen);
```

First we check if any client is connected, and if so we allocate a buffer with the proper size to include the file name. Then we copy it to the buffer (RtlCopyMemory, the same as memcpy).

Now we're ready to send the message with a limited timeout:

```
    LARGE_INTEGER timeout;
    timeout.QuadPart = -10000 * 100;        // 100msec
    FltSendMessage(gFilterHandle, &SendClientPort, msg, len,
        nullptr, nullptr, &timeout);
    ExFreePool(msg);
}
```

Finally, in the filter's unload routine we must close the filter communication port (before FltUnreg-isterFilter):

```
FltCloseCommunicationPort(FilterPort);
```

The User Mode Client

Let's build a simple client that opens the port and listens to messages of files being backed up. We'll create a new console application named *FileBackupMon*. In *pch.h* we add the following #includes:

```
#include <Windows.h>
#include <fltUser.h>
#include <stdio.h>
#include <string>
```

fltuser.h is the user mode header where the FilterXxx functions are declared (they are not part of *windows.h*). In the cpp file we must add the import library for where these functions are implemented:

```
#pragma comment(lib, "fltlib")
```

 Alternatively, this library can be added in the project's properties in the Linker node, under Input. Putting this in the source file is easier and more robust, since changes to the project properties will not effect the setting. Without this library, "unresolved external" linker errors will show up.

Our main function needs first to open the communication port:

```
HANDLE hPort;
auto hr = ::FilterConnectCommunicationPort(L"\\FileBackupPort",
    0, nullptr, 0, nullptr, &hPort);
if (FAILED(hr)) {
    printf("Error connecting to port (HR=0x%08X)\n", hr);
    return 1;
}
```

Now we can allocate a buffer for incoming messages and loop around forever waiting for messages. Once a message is received, we'll send it for handling:

```
BYTE buffer[1 << 12];            // 4 KB
auto message = (FILTER_MESSAGE_HEADER*)buffer;

for (;;) {
    hr = ::FilterGetMessage(hPort, message, sizeof(buffer), nullptr);
    if (FAILED(hr)) {
        printf("Error receiving message (0x%08X)\n", hr);
        break;
    }
    HandleMessage(buffer + sizeof(FILTER_MESSAGE_HEADER));
}
```

The buffer here is allocated statically because the message just includes mostly a file name, so a 4KB buffer is more than enough. Once a message is received, we pass the message body to a helper function, HandleMessage, being careful to skip the always-present header.

All that's left now is to do something with the data:

```
void HandleMessage(const BYTE* buffer) {
    auto msg = (FileBackupPortMessage*)buffer;
    std::wstring filename(msg->FileName, msg->FileNameLength);

    printf("file backed up: %ws\n", filename.c_str());
}
```

We build the string based on the pointer and length (fortunately, the C++ standard wstring class has such a convenient constructor). This is important because the string is not NULL-terminated (although we could have zeroed out the buffer before each message receipt, thus making sure zeros are present at the end of the string).

 The client application must be running elevated for the port open to succeed.

Debugging

Debugging file system mini-filter is no different than debugging any other kernel driver. However, the *Debugging Tools for Windows* package has a special extension DLL, *fltkd.dll*, with specific commands to help with mini-filters. This DLL is not one of the default loaded extension DLLs, so the commands must be used with their "full name" that includes the *fltkd* prefix and the command. Alternatively, the DLL can be loaded explicitly with the `.load` command and then the commands can be directly used.

Table 10-3 shows the some of the commands from *fltkd* with a brief description.

Table 10-3: fltkd.dll debugger commands

Command	Description
!help	shows the command list with brief descriptions
!filters	shows information on all loaded mini-filters
!filter	shows information for the specified filter address
!instance	shows information for the specified instance address
!volumes	shows all volume objects
!volume	shows detailed information on the specified volume address
!portlist	shows the server ports for the specified filter
!port	shows information on the specified client port

Here is an example session using some of the above commands:

```
2: kd> .load fltkd
2: kd> !filters


Filter List: ffff8b8f55bf60c0 "Frame 0"
   FLT_FILTER: ffff8b8f579d9010 "bindflt" "409800"
      FLT_INSTANCE: ffff8b8f62ea8010 "bindflt Instance" "409800"
   FLT_FILTER: ffff8b8f5ba06010 "CldFlt" "409500"
      FLT_INSTANCE: ffff8b8f550aaa20 "CldFlt" "180451"
   FLT_FILTER: ffff8b8f55ceca20 "WdFilter" "328010"
      FLT_INSTANCE: ffff8b8f572d6b30 "WdFilter Instance" "328010"
      FLT_INSTANCE: ffff8b8f575d5b30 "WdFilter Instance" "328010"
      FLT_INSTANCE: ffff8b8f585d2050 "WdFilter Instance" "328010"
      FLT_INSTANCE: ffff8b8f58bde010 "WdFilter Instance" "328010"
  FLT_FILTER: ffff8b8f5cdc6320 "storqosflt" "244000"
  FLT_FILTER: ffff8b8f550aca20 "wcifs" "189900"
      FLT_INSTANCE: ffff8b8f551a6720 "wcifs Instance" "189900"
  FLT_FILTER: ffff8b8f576cab30 "FileCrypt" "141100"
  FLT_FILTER: ffff8b8f550b2010 "luafv" "135000"
      FLT_INSTANCE: ffff8b8f550ae010 "luafv" "135000"
```

```
    FLT_FILTER: ffff8b8f633e8c80 "FileBackup" "100200"
        FLT_INSTANCE: ffff8b8f645df290 "FileBackup Instance" "100200"
        FLT_INSTANCE: ffff8b8f5d1a7880 "FileBackup Instance" "100200"
    FLT_FILTER: ffff8b8f58ce2be0 "npsvctrig" "46000"
        FLT_INSTANCE: ffff8b8f55113a60 "npsvctrig" "46000"
    FLT_FILTER: ffff8b8f55ce9010 "Wof" "40700"
        FLT_INSTANCE: ffff8b8f572e2b30 "Wof Instance" "40700"
        FLT_INSTANCE: ffff8b8f5bae7010 "Wof Instance" "40700"
    FLT_FILTER: ffff8b8f55ce8520 "FileInfo" "40500"
        FLT_INSTANCE: ffff8b8f579cea20 "FileInfo" "40500"
        FLT_INSTANCE: ffff8b8f577ee8a0 "FileInfo" "40500"
        FLT_INSTANCE: ffff8b8f58cc6730 "FileInfo" "40500"
        FLT_INSTANCE: ffff8b8f5bae2010 "FileInfo" "40500"
2: kd> !portlist ffff8b8f633e8c80

FLT_FILTER: ffff8b8f633e8c80
    Client Port List          : Mutex (ffff8b8f633e8ed8) List [ffff8b8f5949b7a0-ffff8b\
8f5949b7a0] mCount=1
        FLT_PORT_OBJECT: ffff8b8f5949b7a0
            FilterLink                : [ffff8b8f633e8f10-ffff8b8f633e8f10]
            ServerPort                : ffff8b8f5b195200
            Cookie                    : 0000000000000000
            Lock                      : (ffff8b8f5949b7c8)
            MsgQ                      : (ffff8b8f5949b800)   NumEntries=1 Enabled
            MessageId                 : 0x0000000000000000
            DisconnectEvent           : (ffff8b8f5949b8d8)
            Disconnected              : FALSE


2: kd> !volumes

Volume List: ffff8b8f55bf6140 "Frame 0"
    FLT_VOLUME: ffff8b8f579cb6b0 "\Device\Mup"
        FLT_INSTANCE: ffff8b8f572d6b30 "WdFilter Instance" "328010"
        FLT_INSTANCE: ffff8b8f579cea20 "FileInfo" "40500"
    FLT_VOLUME: ffff8b8f57af8530 "\Device\HarddiskVolume4"
        FLT_INSTANCE: ffff8b8f62ea8010 "bindflt Instance" "409800"
        FLT_INSTANCE: ffff8b8f575d5b30 "WdFilter Instance" "328010"
        FLT_INSTANCE: ffff8b8f551a6720 "wcifs Instance" "189900"
        FLT_INSTANCE: ffff8b8f550aaa20 "CldFlt" "180451"
        FLT_INSTANCE: ffff8b8f550ae010 "luafv" "135000"
        FLT_INSTANCE: ffff8b8f645df290 "FileBackup Instance" "100200"
        FLT_INSTANCE: ffff8b8f572e2b30 "Wof Instance" "40700"
        FLT_INSTANCE: ffff8b8f577ee8a0 "FileInfo" "40500"
```

```
    FLT_VOLUME: ffff8b8f58cc4010 "\Device\NamedPipe"
        FLT_INSTANCE: ffff8b8f55113a60 "npsvctrig" "46000"
    FLT_VOLUME: ffff8b8f58ce8060 "\Device\Mailslot"
    FLT_VOLUME: ffff8b8f58ce1370 "\Device\HarddiskVolume2"
        FLT_INSTANCE: ffff8b8f585d2050 "WdFilter Instance" "328010"
        FLT_INSTANCE: ffff8b8f58cc6730 "FileInfo" "40500"
    FLT_VOLUME: ffff8b8f5b227010 "\Device\HarddiskVolume1"
        FLT_INSTANCE: ffff8b8f58bde010 "WdFilter Instance" "328010"
        FLT_INSTANCE: ffff8b8f5d1a7880 "FileBackup Instance" "100200"
        FLT_INSTANCE: ffff8b8f5bae7010 "Wof Instance" "40700"
        FLT_INSTANCE: ffff8b8f5bae2010 "FileInfo" "40500"

2: kd> !volume ffff8b8f57af8530

FLT_VOLUME: ffff8b8f57af8530 "\Device\HarddiskVolume4"
    FLT_OBJECT: ffff8b8f57af8530  [04000000] Volume
        RundownRef                : 0x00000000000008b2 (1113)
        PointerCount              : 0x00000001
        PrimaryLink               : [ffff8b8f58cc4020-ffff8b8f579cb6c0]
    Frame                     : ffff8b8f55bf6010 "Frame 0"
    Flags                     : [00000164] SetupNotifyCalled EnableNameCaching FilterA\
ttached +100!!
    FileSystemType            : [00000002] FLT_FSTYPE_NTFS
    VolumeLink                : [ffff8b8f58cc4020-ffff8b8f579cb6c0]
    DeviceObject              : ffff8b8f573cab60
    DiskDeviceObject          : ffff8b8f572e7b80
    FrameZeroVolume           : ffff8b8f57af8530
    VolumeInNextFrame         : 0000000000000000
    Guid                      : "\??\Volume{5379a5de-f305-4243-a3ec-311938a2df19}"
    CDODeviceName             : "\Ntfs"
    CDODriverName             : "\FileSystem\Ntfs"
    TargetedOpenCount         : 1104
    Callbacks                 : (ffff8b8f57af8650)
    ContextLock               : (ffff8b8f57af8a38)
    VolumeContexts            : (ffff8b8f57af8a40)  Count=0
    StreamListCtrls           : (ffff8b8f57af8a48)  rCount=29613
    FileListCtrls             : (ffff8b8f57af8ac8)  rCount=22668
    NameCacheCtrl             : (ffff8b8f57af8b48)
    InstanceList              : (ffff8b8f57af85d0)
        FLT_INSTANCE: ffff8b8f62ea8010 "bindflt Instance" "409800"
        FLT_INSTANCE: ffff8b8f575d5b30 "WdFilter Instance" "328010"
        FLT_INSTANCE: ffff8b8f551a6720 "wcifs Instance" "189900"
        FLT_INSTANCE: ffff8b8f550aaa20 "CldFlt" "180451"
```

```
    FLT_INSTANCE: ffff8b8f550ae010 "luafv" "135000"
    FLT_INSTANCE: ffff8b8f645df290 "FileBackup Instance" "100200"
    FLT_INSTANCE: ffff8b8f572e2b30 "Wof Instance" "40700"
    FLT_INSTANCE: ffff8b8f577ee8a0 "FileInfo" "40500"

2: kd> !instance ffff8b8f5d1a7880

FLT_INSTANCE: ffff8b8f5d1a7880 "FileBackup Instance" "100200"
    FLT_OBJECT: ffff8b8f5d1a7880 [01000000] Instance
        RundownRef                 : 0x0000000000000000 (0)
        PointerCount               : 0x00000001
        PrimaryLink                : [ffff8b8f5bae7020-ffff8b8f58bde020]
    OperationRundownRef       : ffff8b8f639c61b0
        Number                    : 3
        PoolToFree                 : ffff8b8f65aad590
        OperationsRefs             : ffff8b8f65aad5c0   (0)
            PerProcessor Ref[0]       : 0x0000000000000000 (0)
            PerProcessor Ref[1]       : 0x0000000000000000 (0)
            PerProcessor Ref[2]       : 0x0000000000000000 (0)
    Flags                     : [00000000]
    Volume                    : ffff8b8f5b227010 "\Device\HarddiskVolume1"
    Filter                    : ffff8b8f633e8c80 "FileBackup"
    TrackCompletionNodes      : ffff8b8f5f3f3cc0
    ContextLock               : (ffff8b8f5d1a7900)
    Context                   : 0000000000000000
    CallbackNodes             : (ffff8b8f5d1a7920)
    VolumeLink                : [ffff8b8f5bae7020-ffff8b8f58bde020]
    FilterLink                : [ffff8b8f633e8d50-ffff8b8f645df300]
```

Exercises

1. Write a file system mini-filter that captures delete operations from *cmd.exe* and instead of deleting them, moves the files to the recycle bin.
2. Extend the file backup driver with the ability to choose the directories where backups will be created.
3. Extend the File Backup driver to include multiple backups, limited by some rule, such as file size, date or maximum number of backup copies.
4. Modify the File Backup driver to back up only the changed data instead of the entire file.
5. Come up with your own ideas for a file system mini-filter driver!

Summary

This chapter was all about file system mini-filters - powerful drivers capable of intercepting any and all file system activity. Mini-filters are a big topic, and this chapter should get you started on this interesting and powerful journey. You can find more information in the WDK documentation, the WDK samples on Github and on some blogs.

In the next (and last) chapter, we'll look at various driver development techniques and other miscellaneous topics that didn't fit well with the chapters so far.

Chapter 11: Miscellaneous Topics

In this last chapter of the book, we'll take a look at various topics that didn't fit well in previous chapters.

In this chapter:

- Driver Signing
- Driver Verifier
- Using the Native API
- Filter Drivers
- Device Monitor
- Driver Hooking
- Kernel Libraries

Driver Signing

Kernel drivers are the only official mechanism to get code into the Windows kernel. As such, kernel drivers can cause a system crash or another form of system instability. The Windows kernel does not have any distinction between "more important" drivers and "less important" drivers. Microsoft naturally would like Windows to be stable, with no system crashes or instabilities. Starting from Windows Vista, on 64 bit systems, Microsoft requires drivers to be signed using a proper certificate acquired from a certificate authority (CA). Without signing, the driver will not load.

Does a signed driver guarantee quality? Does it guarantee the system will not crash? No. It only guarantees the driver files have not changed since leaving the publisher of the driver and that the publisher itself is authentic. It's not a silver bullet against driver bugs, but it does give some sense of confidence in the driver.

For hardware based driver, Microsoft requires these to pass the *Windows Hardware Quality Lab* (WHQL) tests, containing rigorous tests for the stability and driver functionality. If the driver passes these tests, it receives a Microsoft stamp of quality, which the driver publisher can advertise as a sign of quality and trust. Another consequence of passing WHQL is making the driver available through Windows Update, which is important for some publishers,

Starting with Windows 10 version 1607 ("Anniversary update"), for systems that were freshly installed (not upgraded from an earlier version) with secure boot on - Microsoft requires drivers to be signed by Microsoft as well as by the publisher. This is true for all types of drivers, not just related to hardware. Microsoft provides a web portal where drivers can be uploaded (must already be signed by the publisher), tested in some ways by Microsoft and finally signed by Microsoft and returned back to the publisher. It may take some time for Microsoft to return the signed driver the first time the driver is uploaded, but later iterations are fairly fast (several hours).

> The driver that needs to be uploaded includes the binaries only. The source code is not required.

Figure 11-1 shows a driver's image file from Nvidia that is signed by both Nvidia and Microsoft on a Windows 10 19H1 system.

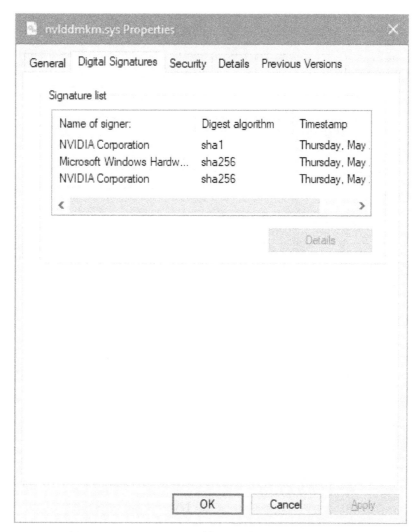

Figure 11-1: Driver signed by vendor and by Microsoft

The first step in driver signing is obtaining a proper certificate from a certificate authority (such as Verisign, Globalsign, Digicert, Symantec, and others) for at least kernel code signing. The CA will validate the identity of the requesting company, and if all is well, will issue a certificate. The downloaded certificate can be installed in the machine's certificate store. Since the certificate must be kept secret and not leak, it is typically installed on a dedicated build machine and the driver signing process is done as part of the build process.

The actual signing operation is done with the *SignTool.exe* tool, part of the Windows SDK. You can use Visual Studio to sign a driver if the certificate is installed in the certificate store on the local machine. Figure 11-2 shows the signing properties in Visual Studio.

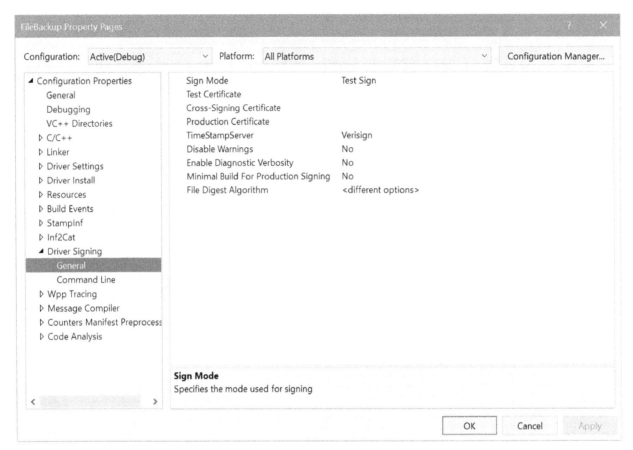

Figure 11-2: Driver signing page in Visual Studio

Visual Studio provides two types of signing: Test sign and production sign. With test signing, a test certificate (a locally-generated certificate that is not trusted globally) is typically used. This allows testing the driver on systems configured with test signing enabled, as we've done throughout this book. Production signing is about using a real certificate to sign the driver for production use.

Test certificates can be generated at will using Visual Studio when selecting a certificate, as shown in figure 11-3.

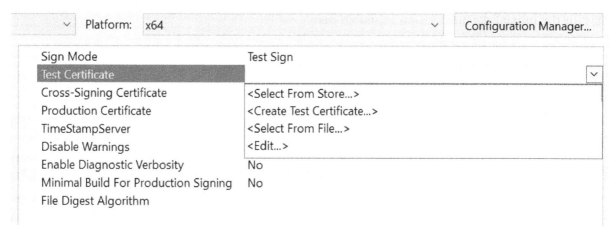

Figure 11-3: Selecting a certificate type in Visual Studio

Figure 11-4 shows an example of production signing a release build of a driver in Visual Studio. Note that the digest algorithm should be *SHA256* rather than the older, less secure, *SHA1*.

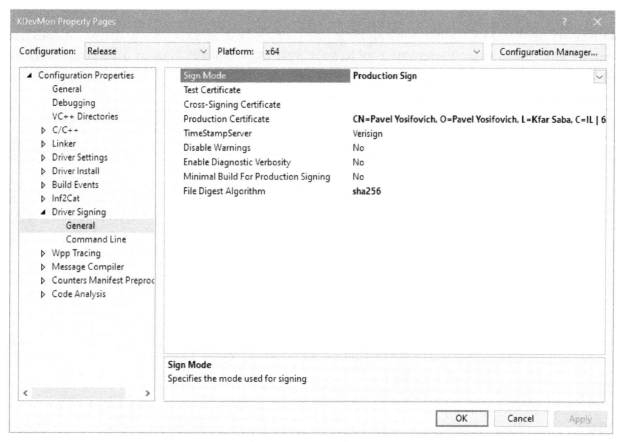

Figure 11-4: Production signing a driver in Visual Studio

Dealing with the various procedures for registering and signing drivers is beyond the scope of this book. Things got more complicated in recent years due to new Microsoft rules and procedures.

Consult the official documentation available here[5].

Driver Verifier

Driver Verifier is a built-in tool that existed in Windows since Windows 2000. Its purpose is to help identify driver bugs and bad coding practices. For example, suppose your driver causes a BSOD in some way, but the driver's code is not on any call stacks in the crash dump file. This typically means that your driver did something which was not fatal at the time, such as writing beyond one of its allocated buffers, where that memory was unfortunately allocated to another driver or the kernel. At that point, there is no crash. However, sometime later that driver or the kernel will use that overflowed data and most likely cause a system crash. There is no easy way to associate the crash with the offending driver. The driver verifier offers an option to allocate memory for the driver in its own "special" pool, where pages at higher and lower addresses are inaccessible, and so will cause an immediate crash upon a buffer overflow or underflow, making it easy to identify the problematic driver.

Driver verifier has a GUI and a command line interface, and can work with any driver - it does not require any source code. The easiest way to start with the verifier is to open it by typing *verifier* in the *Run* dialog or searching for *verifier* when clicking the *Start* button. Either way, the verifier presents its initial user interface shown in figure 11-5.

---

[5]https://docs.microsoft.com/en-us/windows-hardware/drivers/install/kernel-mode-code-signing-policy--windows-vista-and-later-

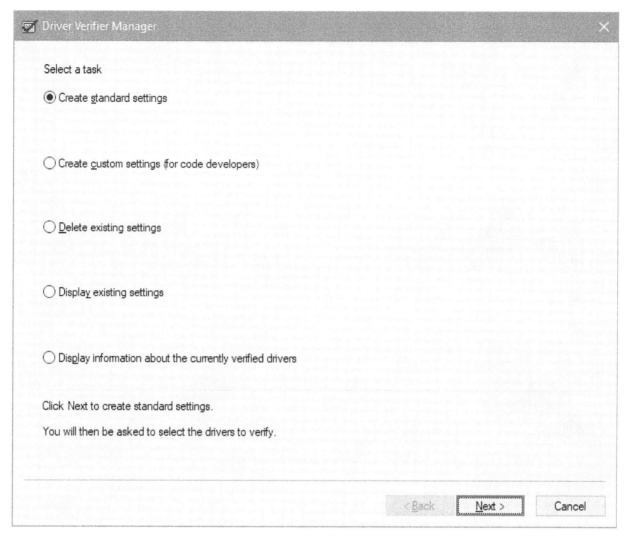

Figure 11-5: Driver Verifier initial window

There are two things that need to be selected: the type of checks to do by the verifier, and the drivers that should be checked. The first page of the wizard is about the checks themselves. The options available on this page are as follows:

- *Create standard settings* selects a predefined set of checks to be performed. We'll see the complete list of available checks in the second page, each with a flag of *Standard* or *Additional*. All those marked *Standard* are selected by this option automatically.
- *Create custom settings* allows fine grained selection of checks by listing all the available checks, shown in figure 11-6.
- *Delete existing settings* deletes all existing verifier settings.
- *Display existing settings* shows the current configured checks and the drivers for which this checks apply.
- *Display information about the currently verified drivers* shows the collected information for the drivers running under the verifier in an earlier session.

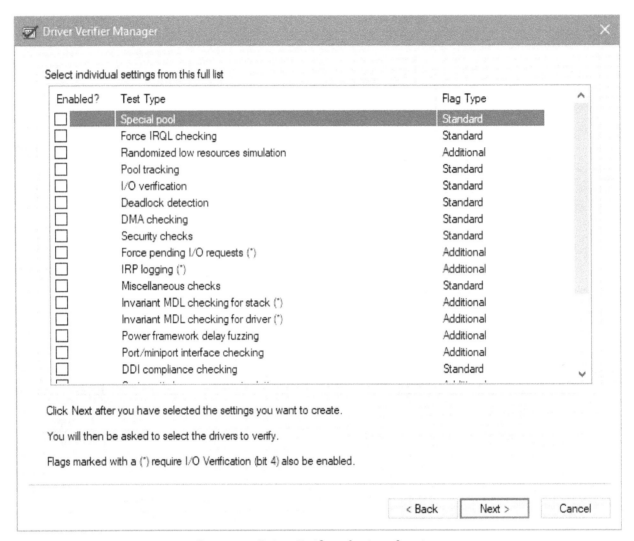

Figure 11-6: Driver Verifier selection of settings

Selecting *Create custom settings* shows the available list of verifier settings, a list that has grown considerably since the early days of Driver Verifier. The flag *Standard* flag indicates this setting is part of the Standard settings that can be selected in the first page of the wizard. Once the settings have been selected, the Verifier shows the next step for selecting the drivers to execute with these settings, shown in figure 11-7.

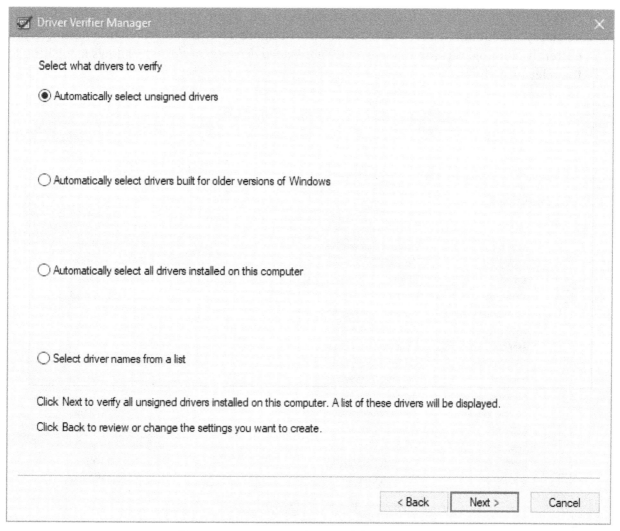

Figure 11-7: Driver Verifier initial driver selection

Here are the possible options:

- *Automatically select unsigned drivers* is mostly relevant for 32 bit systems as 64 bit systems must have signed drivers (unless in test signing mode). Clicking *Next* will list such drivers. Most systems would not have any.
- *Automatically select drivers built for older versions of Windows* is a legacy setting for NT 4 hardware based drivers. Mostly uninteresting for modern systems.
- *Automatically select all drivers installed on the computer* is a catch all option that selects all drivers. This theoretically could be useful if you are presented with a system that crashes but no one has any clue as to offending driver. However, this setting is not recommended, as it slows down the machine (verifier has its costs), because verifier intercepts various operations (based on the previous settings) and typically causes more memory to be used. So it's better in such a scenario to select the first (say) 15 drivers, see if the verifier catches the bad driver, and if not select the next 15 drivers, and so on.

- *Select driver names from a list* is the best option to use, where Verifier presents a list of drivers currently executing on the system, as shown in figure 11-8. If the driver in question is not currently running, clicking *Add currently not loaded driver(s) to the list...* allows navigating to the relevant SYS file(s).

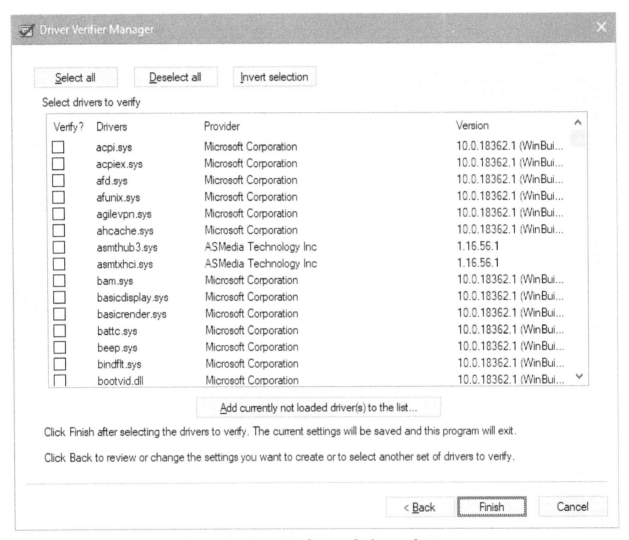

Figure 11-8: Driver Verifier specific driver selection

Finally, clicking *Finish* changes makes the settings permanent until revoked, and the system typically needs to be restarted so that verifier can initialize itself and hook drivers, especially if these are currently executing.

Example Driver Verifier Sessions

Let's start with a simple example involving the *NotMyFault* tool from *Sysinternals*. As discussed in chapter 6, this tool can be used to crash the system in various ways. Figure 11-9 shows *NotMyFault* main UI. Some of the options to crash the system will do so immediately, with the driver *MyFault.sys* appearing on the call stack of the crashing thread. This is an easy crash to diagnose. However, the option *Buffer overflow* may or may not crash the system immediately. If the system crashes somewhat later, than it's unlikely to find *MyFault.sys* on the call stack.

 Make sure you run *NotMyFault64.exe* on a 64-bit system.

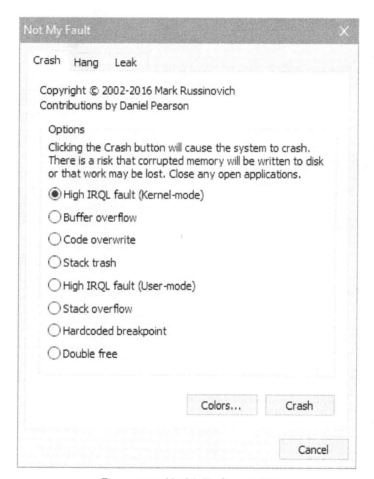

Figure 11-9: NotMyFault main UI

Let's try this (in a virtual machine). It may take several clicks on *Crash* to actually crash the system. Figure 11-10 shows the result on a Windows 7 VM after some clicks on *Crash* and several seconds passing by. Note the BSOD code (BAD_POOL_HEADER). A good guess would be the buffer overflow wrote over some of the metadata of a pool allocation.

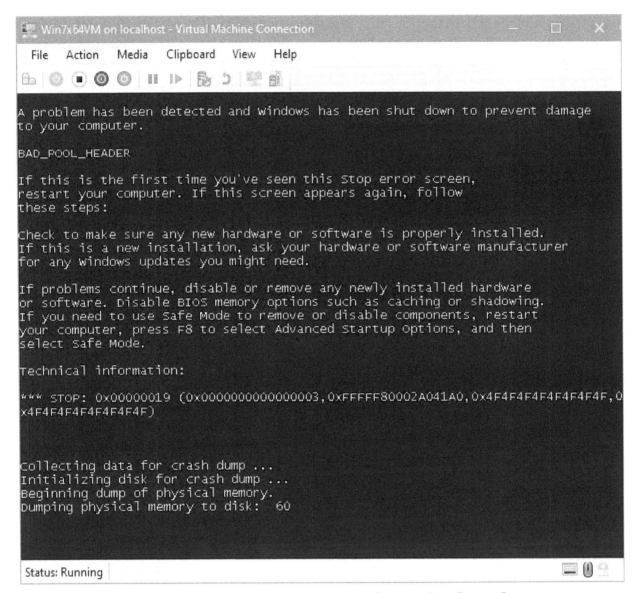

Figure 11-10: NotMyFault causing BSOD on Windows 7 with Buffer overflow

Loading the resulting dump file and looking at the call stack shows this:

```
1: kd> k
 # Child-SP          RetAddr           Call Site
00 fffff880`054be828 fffff800`029e4263 nt!KeBugCheckEx
01 fffff880`054be830 fffff800`02bd969f nt!ExFreePoolWithTag+0x1023
02 fffff880`054be920 fffff800`02b0669b nt!ObpAllocateObject+0x12f
03 fffff880`054be990 fffff800`02c2f012 nt!ObCreateObject+0xdb
04 fffff880`054bea00 fffff800`02b1a7b2 nt!PspAllocateThread+0x1b2
05 fffff880`054bec20 fffff800`02b20d95 nt!PspCreateThread+0x1d2
06 fffff880`054beea0 fffff800`028aaad3 nt!NtCreateThreadEx+0x25d
07 fffff880`054bf5f0 fffff800`028a02b0 nt!KiSystemServiceCopyEnd+0x13
```

```
08  fffff880`054bf7f8  fffff800`02b29a60  nt!KiServiceLinkage
09  fffff880`054bf800  fffff800`0286ac1a  nt!RtlpCreateUserThreadEx+0x138
0a  fffff880`054bf920  fffff800`0285c1c0  nt!ExpWorkerFactoryCreateThread+0x92
0b  fffff880`054bf9e0  fffff800`02857dd0  nt!ExpWorkerFactoryCheckCreate+0x180
0c  fffff880`054bfa60  fffff800`028aaad3  nt!NtReleaseWorkerFactoryWorker+0x1a0
0d  fffff880`054bfae0  00000000`76e1ac3a  nt!KiSystemServiceCopyEnd+0x13
```

Clearly, *MyFault.sys* is nowhere to be found. analyze -v, by the way is no wiser and concludes that the module **nt** is the culprit.

Now let's try the same experiment with Driver Verifier. Choose standard settings and navigate to the *System32\Drivers* to locate *MyFault.sys* (if it's not currently running). Restart the system, run *NotMyFault* again, select *Buffer overflow* and click *Crash*. You will notice that the system crashes immediately, with a BSOD similar to the one shown in figure 11-11.

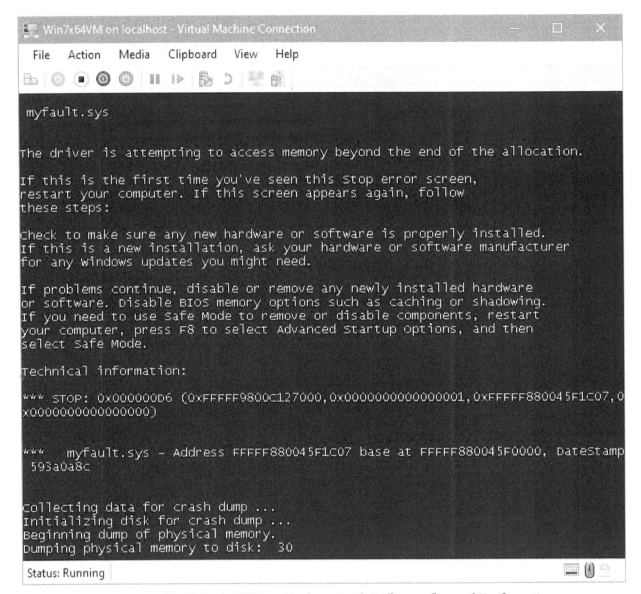

Figure 11-11: NotMyFault BSOD on Windows 7 with Buffer overflow and Verifier active

The BSOD itself is immediately telling. The dump file confirms it with the following call stack:

```
0: kd> k
 # Child-SP          RetAddr           Call Site
00 fffff880`0651c378 fffff800`029ba462 nt!KeBugCheckEx
01 fffff880`0651c380 fffff800`028ecb96 nt!MmAccessFault+0x2322
02 fffff880`0651c4d0 fffff880`045f1c07 nt!KiPageFault+0x356
03 fffff880`0651c660 fffff880`045f1f88 myfault+0x1c07
04 fffff880`0651c7b0 fffff800`02d63d56 myfault+0x1f88
05 fffff880`0651c7f0 fffff800`02b43c7a nt!IovCallDriver+0x566
06 fffff880`0651c850 fffff800`02d06eb1 nt!IopSynchronousServiceTail+0xfa
07 fffff880`0651c8c0 fffff800`02b98296 nt!IopXxxControlFile+0xc51
```

```
08 fffff880`0651ca00 fffff800`028eead3 nt!NtDeviceIoControlFile+0x56
09 fffff880`0651ca70 00000000`777e98fa nt!KiSystemServiceCopyEnd+0x13
```

We have no symbols for *MyFault.sys*, but clearly it's the culprit.

As another example, we apply standard verifier settings to the *DelProtect3* driver from chapter 10. Once the driver is installed, we try to add a folder to protect from deletion like so:

```
delprotectconfig3 add c:\temp
```

We get a system crash initiated by the verifier, with the code BAD_POOL_CALLER (0xc2). Opening the resulting dump file and invoking !analyze -v results in analysis of which the following is a part:

```
BAD_POOL_CALLER (c2)
The current thread is making a bad pool request.  Typically this is at a bad IRQL le\
vel or double freeing the same allocation, etc.
Arguments:
Arg1: 000000000000009b, Attempt to allocate pool with a tag of zero.  This would mak\
e the pool untrackable and worse, corrupt the existing tag tables.
Arg2: 0000000000000001, Pool type
Arg3: 000000000000000c, Size of allocation in bytes
Arg4: fffff8012dcd1297, Caller's address.


FAULTING_SOURCE_CODE:
    113:    return pUnicodeString;
    114: }
    115:
    116: wchar_t* kstring::Allocate(size_t chars, const wchar_t* src) {
>   117:    auto str = static_cast<wchar_t*>(ExAllocatePoolWithTag(m_Pool,
                sizeof(WCHAR) * (chars + 1), m_Tag));
    118:    if (!str) {
    119:        KdPrint(("Failed to allocate kstring of length %d chars\n", chars));
    120:        return nullptr;
    121:    }
    122:    if (src) {
```

Indeed, the kstring object used in the code did not specify a non-zero tag for its allocations. The offending code is part of the ConvertDosNameToNtName function:

```
kstring symLink(L"\\??\\");
```

The fix is easy enough:

```
kstring symLink(L"\\\??\\", PagedPool, DRIVER_TAG);
```

Perhaps the kstring class should be modified to require a tag, without defaulting to zero.

Using the Native API

As we've seen in chapters 1 and 10, the Windows Native API exposed to user mode through *NtDll.Dll*, is the gateway to kernel functionality. The native API indirectly invokes the actual functions in the Executive by placing the system service number in a CPU register (EAX on Intel/AMD), and using a special machine instruction (syscall or sysenter on Intel/AMD platforms), causes a transition from user mode to kernel mode and invocation of the system service dispatcher that uses that register value to call the real system service.

Kernel drivers can enjoy the same API, as already been demonstrated by various Zw-functions. However, a small number of these function are documented, some of which are barely documented - those with "information" in them - NtQuerySystemInformation, NtQueryInformationProcess, NtQueryInformationThread and similar functions. We've already met NtQueryInformationProcess shown here in its Zw version, for easier discussion:

```
NTSTATUS ZwQueryInformationProcess(
    _In_      HANDLE           ProcessHandle,
    _In_      PROCESSINFOCLASS ProcessInformationClass,
    _Out_     PVOID            ProcessInformation,
    _In_      ULONG            ProcessInformationLength,
    _Out_opt_ PULONG           ReturnLength);
```

That PROCESSINFOCLASS enumeration is vast, and contains around 70 values in WDK for build 18362. If you examine the list closely, you'll discover some values are missing. In the official documentation, only 6 values are documented (at the time of this writing), which is a shame. Moreover, the actual supported list is much longer than is provided officially by Microsoft. Again, lots of interesting information that could be used by a driver if needed.

Luckily, an open source project on Github called *Process Hacker* provides much of the missing information, in terms of native API definitions, enumerations and structures expected by these APIs.

 Process Hacker is an open source tool similar to *Process Explorer*. In fact it has some capabilities absent from *Process Explorer* (at the time of writing). The repository URL is https://github.com/processshacker/processhacker.

Process Hacker has all the native API definitions in a separate project, convenient for usage in other projects. The URL is https://github.com/processshacker/phnt. Just as a quick comparison, PROCESS-INFOCLASS in this repository currently has 99 entries, without anything missing, coupled with the data structures expected by the various enumeration values.

The only caveat when using these definitions is that theoretically Microsoft can change almost any of these without warning, as most of these are undocumented. However, this is highly unlikely, as it may break quite a few applications, some of which are from Microsoft. For example, *Process Explorer* uses some of these "undocumented" functions. That said, it's best to test applications and drivers that use these functions for all Windows versions where these applications or drivers are expected to work.

Filter Drivers

The Windows driver model is device-centric as we've seen already in chapter 7. Devices can be layered on top of each other, resulting in the highest layer device getting first crack at an incoming IRP. This same model is used for file system drivers, which we leveraged in chapter 10 with the help of the Filter Manager, which is specialized for file system filters. However, the filtering model is generic and can be utilized for other types of devices. In this section we'll take a closer look at the general model of device filtering, which we'll be able to apply to a broad range of devices, some of which are related to hardware devices while others are not.

The kernel API provides several functions that allow one device to be layered on top of another device. The simplest is probably `IoAttachDevice` which accepts a device object to attach and a target named device object to attach to. Here is its prototype:

```
NTSTATUS IoAttachDevice (
    PDEVICE_OBJECT SourceDevice,
    _In_ PUNICODE_STRING TargetDevice,
    _Out_ PDEVICE_OBJECT *AttachedDevice);
```

The output of the function (besides the status) is another device object to which the *SourceDevice* was actually attached to. This is required since attaching to a named device which is not at the top of its device stack succeeds, but the source device is actually attached on top of the topmost device, which may be another filter. It's important, therefore, to get the real device that the source device attached itself to, as that device should be the target of requests if the driver wishes to propagate them down the device stack. This is illustrated in figure 11-12.

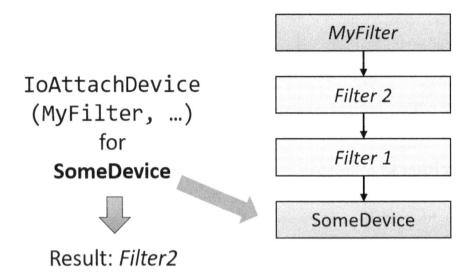

Figure 11-12: Attaching to a named device

Unfortunately, attaching to a device object requires some more work. As discussed in chapter 7, a device can ask the I/O manager to help with accessing a user's buffer with Buffered I/O or Direct I/O (for IRP_MJ_READ and IRP_MJ_WRITE requests) by setting the appropriate flags in the Flags member of the DEVICE_OBJECT. In a layering scenario there are multiple devices, so which device is the one that determines how the I/O manager should help with I/O buffers? It turns out it's always the topmost device. This means that our new filter device should copy the value of DO_BUFFERED_IO and DO_DIRECT_IO flags from the device it actually layered on top of. The default for a device just created with IoCreateDevice has neither of these flags set, so if the new device fails to copy these bits, it most likely will cause the target device to malfunction and even crash, as it would not expect its selected buffering method not being respected.

There are a few other settings that need to be copied from the attached device to make sure the new filter looks the same to the I/O system. We'll see these settings later when we build a complete example of a filter.

What is this device name that IoAttachDevice requires? This is a named device object within the Object Manager's namespace, viewable with the *WinObj* tools we've used before. Most of the named device objects are located in the *\Device* directory, but some are located elsewhere. For example, if we were to attach a filter device object to *Process Explorer*'s device object, the name would be *\Device\ProcExp152* (the name is case insensitive).

Other functions for attaching to another device object include IoAttachDeviceToDeviceStack and IoAttachDeviceToDeviceStackSafe, both accepting another device object to attach to rather than a name of a device. These functions are mostly useful when building filters registered for hardware-based device drivers, where the target device object is provided as part of device node building (partially described in chapter 7 as well). Both return the actual layered device object, just as IoAttachDevice does. The Safe function returns a proper NTSTATUS, while the former returns NULL on failure. Other than that, these functions are identical.

Generally, kernel code can obtain a pointer to a named device object with `IoGetDeviceObject-Pointer` that returns a device object and a file object open for that device based on a device name. Here is the prototype:

```
NTSTATUS IoGetDeviceObjectPointer (
    _In_    PUNICODE_STRING ObjectName,
    _In_    ACCESS_MASK DesiredAccess,
    _Out_   PFILE_OBJECT *FileObject,
    _Out_   PDEVICE_OBJECT *DeviceObject);
```

The desired access is typically `FILE_READ_DATA` or any other that is valid for file objects. The returned file object's reference is incremented, so the driver needs to be careful to decrement that reference eventually (`ObDereferenceObject`) so the file object does not leak. The returned device object can be used as an argument to `IoAttachDeviceToDeviceStack(Safe)`.

Filter Driver Implementation

A filter driver needs to attach a device object over a target device for which filtering is required. We'll discuss later when attachment should occur, but for now let's assume the call to one of the "attach" functions is made at some point. Since the new device object will now become the topmost device in the device stack, any request the driver does not support will bounce back to the client with an "unsupported operation" error. This means that the filter's `DriverEntry` must register for **all** major function codes if it wants to make sure the underlying device object continues to function normally. Here is one way to set this up:

```
for (int i = 0; i < ARRAYSIZE(DriverObject->MajorFunction); i++)
    DriverObject->MajorFunction[i] = HandleFilterFunction;
```

The above code snippet sets all major function codes pointing to the same function. The `Handle-FilterFunction` function must, at the very least, call the lower layered driver using the device object obtained from one of the "attach" functions. Of course, being a filter, the driver will want to do additional work or different work for requests it's interested in, but all the requests it does not care about must be forwarded to the lower layer device, or else that device will not function properly.

This "forward and forget" operation is very common in filters. Let's see how to implement this functionality. The actual call that transfers an IRP to another device is `IoCallDriver`. However, before calling it the current driver must prepare the next I/O stack location for the lower driver's use. Remember that initially, the I/O manager only initializes the first I/O stack location. it's up to every layer to initialize the next I/O stack location before using `IoCallDriver` to pass the IRP down the device stack.

The driver can call `IoGetNextIrpStackLocation` to get a pointer to the next layer's `IO_STACK_-LOCATION` and go ahead and initialize it. In most cases, however, the driver just wants to present to the lower layer the same information it received itself. One function that can help with that is `Io-CopyCurrentIrpStackLocationToNext`, which is pretty self explanatory. This function, however, does **not** just blindly copy the I/O stack location like so:

```
auto current = IoGetCurrentIrpStackLocation(Irp);
auto next = IoCopyCurrentIrpStackLocationToNext(Irp);
*next = *current;
```

Why? The reason is subtle, and has to do with the completion routine. Recall from chapter 7 that a driver can set up a completion routine to be notified once the IRP is completed by a lower layer driver (`IoSetCompletionRoutine/Ex`). The completion pointer (and a driver-defined context argument) are stored in the **next** I/O stack location, and that's why a blind copy would duplicate the higher-level completion routine (if any), which is not what we want. This is exactly what `IoCopyCurrentIrpStackLocationToNext` avoids.

But there is actually a better way if the driver does not need a completion routine and just wants to use "forward and forget", without paying the price of copying the I/O stack location data. This is accomplished by skipping the I/O stack location in such a way so that the next lower layer driver sees the same I/O stack location as this one:

```
IoSkipCurrentIrpStackLocation(Irp);
status = IoCallDriver(LowerDeviceObject, Irp);
```

`IoSkipCurrentIrpStackLocation` simply decrements the internal IRP's I/O stack location's pointer, and `IoCallDriver` increments it, essentially making the lower driver see the same I/O stack location as this layer, without any copying going on; this is the preferred way of propagating the IRP down if the driver does not wish to make changes to the request and it does not require a completion routine.

Attaching Filters

When does a driver call one of the attach functions? The ideal time is when the underlying device (the attach target) is being created; that is, the device node is now being built. This is common in filters for hardware-based device drivers, where filters can be registered in the named values *UpperFilters* and *LowerFilters* we met in chapter 7. For these filters, the proper location for actually creating the new device object and attaching it to an existing device stack is in a callback set with the `AddDevice` member accessible from the driver object like so:

```
DriverObject->DriverExtension->AddDevice = FilterAddDevice;
```

This *AddDevice* callback is invoked when a new hardware device belonging to the driver has been identified by the Plug & Play system. This routine has the following prototype:

```
NTSTATUS AddDeviceRoutine (
    _In_ PDRIVER_OBJECT DriverObject,
    _In_ PDEVICE_OBJECT PhysicalDeviceObject);
```

The I/O system provides the driver with the device object at the bottom of the device stack (*PhysicalDeviceObject* or PDO) to be used in a call to IoAttachDeviceToDeviceStack(Safe). This PDO is one reason why DriverEntry is not a suitable location to make an attach call - at this point the PDO is not yet provided. Furthermore, a second device of the same type may be added into the system (such as a second USB camera), in which case DriverEntry is not going to be called at all; only the *AddDevice* routine will.

Here is an example for implementing an *AddDevice* routine for a filter driver (error handling omitted):

```
struct DeviceExtension {
    PDEVICE_OBJECT LowerDeviceObject;
};

NTSTATUS FilterAddDevice(PDRIVER_OBJECT DriverObject, PDEVICE_OBJECT PDO) {
    PDEVICE_OBJECT DeviceObject;
    auto status = IoCreateDevice(DriverObject, sizeof(DeviceExtension), nullptr,
        FILE_DEVICE_UNKNOWN, 0, FALSE, &DeviceObject);

    auto ext = (DeviceExtension*)DeviceObject->DeviceExtension;
    status = IoAttachDeviceToDeviceStackSafe(
        DeviceObject,               // device to attach
        PDO,                        // target device
        &ext->LowerDeviceObject);   // actual device object

    // copy some info from the attached device

    DeviceObject->DeviceType = ext->LowerDeviceObject->DeviceType;

    DeviceObject->Flags |= ext->LowerDeviceObject->Flags &
        (DO_BUFFERED_IO | DO_DIRECT_IO);

    // important for hardware-based devices

    DeviceObject->Flags &= ~DO_DEVICE_INITIALIZING;
    DeviceObject->Flags |= DO_POWER_PAGABLE;

    return status;
}
```

A few important points for the code above:

- The device object is created without a name. A name is not needed, because the target device is named and is the real target for IRPs, so no need to provide our own name. The filter is going to be invoked regardless.
- In the `IoCreateDevice` call we specify a non-zero size for the second argument, asking the I/O manager to allocate an extra buffer (`DeviceExtension`) along with the actual `DEVICE_OBJECT`. Up until now we used global variables to manage state for a device because we had just one. However, a filter driver may create multiple device objects and attach to multiple device stacks, making it harder to correlate device objects to some state. The device extension mechanism makes it easy to get to a device-specific state given the device object itself. In the above code we capture the lower device object as our state, but this structure can be extended to include more information as needed.
- We copy some information from the lower device object, so that our filter appears to the I/O system as the target device itself. Specifically, we copy the device type and the buffering method flags.
- Finally, we remove the `DO_DEVICE_INITIALIZING` flag (set by the I/O system initially) to indicate to the Plug & Play manager that the device is ready for work. The `DO_POWER_PAGABLE` flag indicates Power IRPs should arrive in IRQL < `DISPATCH_LEVEL`, and is in fact mandatory.

Given the above code, here is a "forward and forget" implementation that uses the lower device as described in the previous section:

```
NTSTATUS FilterGenericDispatch(PDEVICE_OBJECT DeviceObject, PIRP Irp) {
    auto ext = (DeviceExtension*)DeviceObject->DeviceExtension;

    IoSkipCurrentIrpStackLocation(Irp);
    return IoCallDriver(ext->LowerDeviceObject, Irp);
}
```

Attaching Filters at Arbitrary Time

The previous section looked at attaching a filter device in the `AddDevice` callback, called by the plug & Play manager while the device node is being built. For non-hardware based drivers, that don't have registry settings for filters, this `AddDevice` callback is never invoked.

For these more general cases, the filter driver can attach filter devices theoretically at any time, by creating a device object (`IoCreateDevice`) and then using one of the "attach" functions. This means the target device already exists, it's already working, and at some point it gets a filter. The driver must make sure this slight "interruption" does not have any adverse effect on the target device. Most of the operations shown in the previous sections are relevant here as well, such as copying some flags from the lower device. However, some extra care must be taken to make sure the target device's operations are not disrupted.

Using `IoAttachDevice`, the following code creates a device object and attaches it over another named device object (error handling omitted):

```
// use hard-coded name for illustration purposes
UNICODE_STRING targetName = RTL_CONSTANT_STRING(L"\\Device\\SomeDeviceName");

PDEVICE_OBJECT DeviceObject;
auto status = IoCreateDevice(DriverObject, 0, nullptr,
    FILE_DEVICE_UNKNOWN, 0, FALSE, &DeviceObject);

PDEVICE_OBJECT LowerDeviceObject;
status = IoAttachDevice(DeviceObject, &targetName, &LowerDeviceObject);

// copy information

DeviceObject->Flags |= LowerDeviceObject->Flags & (DO_BUFFERED_IO | DO_DIRECT_IO);

DeviceObject->Flags &= ~DO_DEVICE_INITIALIZING;
DeviceObject->Flags |= DO_POWER_PAGABLE;
DeviceObject->DeviceType = LowerDeviceObject->DeviceType;
```

Astute readers may notice that the above code has an inherent race condition. Can you spot it?

This is essentially the same code used in the `AddDevice` callback in the previous section. But in that code there was no race condition. This is because the target device was not yet active - the device node was being built, device by device, from the bottom to the top. The device was not yet in a position to receive requests.

Contrast that with the above code - the target device is working and could be very busy, when suddenly a filter appears. The I/O system makes sure there is no issue while performing the actual attach operation, but once the call to `IoAttachDevice` returns (and in fact even before that), requests continue to come in. Suppose that a read operation comes in just after `IoAttachDevice` returns but before the buffering method flags are set - the I/O manager will see the flags as zero (neither I/O) since it only looks at the topmost device, which is now our filter! So if the target device uses Direct I/O (for example), the I/O manager will not lock the user's buffer, will not create an MDL, etc. This could lead to a system crash if the target driver always assumes that `Irp->MdlAddress` (for example) is non-NULL.

The window of opportunity for failure is very small, but it's better to play it safe.

How can we solve this race condition? We must prepare our new device object fully before actually attaching. We can do that by calling `IoGetDeviceObjectPointer` to get the target device object, copy the required information to our own device (at this time still not attached), and only then call `IoAttachDeviceToDeviceStack(Safe)`. We'll see a complete example later in this chapter.

 Write the appropriate code to use `IoGetDeviceObjectPointer` as described above.

Filter Cleanup

Once a filter is attached, it must be detached at some point. Calling `IoDetachDevice` with the lower device object pointer performs this operation. Notice the lower device object is the argument, **not** the filter's own device object. Finally, `IoDeleteDevice` for the filter's device object should be called, just as we did in all our drivers so far.

The question is when should this cleanup code be called? if the driver is unloaded explicitly, then the normal unload routine should perform these cleanup operations. However, some complication arises in filters for hardware-based drivers. These drivers may need to unload because of a Plug & Play event, such as a user yanking out a device out of the system. A hardware based drivers receives a `IRP_MJ_PNP` request with a minor IRP `IRP_MN_REMOVE_DEVICE` indicating the hardware itself is gone, so the entire device node is not needed and it will be torn down. It's the responsibility of the driver to handle this PnP request properly, detach from the device node and delete the device.

This means that for hardware-based filters, a simple "forward and forget" for `IRP_MJ_PNP` will not suffice. Special treatment is needed for `IRP_MN_REMOVE_DEVICE`. Here is some example code:

```
NTSTATUS FilterDispatchPnp(PDEVICE_OBJECT fido, PIRP Irp) {
    auto ext = (DeviceExtension*)fido->DeviceExtension;
    auto stack = IoGetCurrentIrpStackLocation(Irp);

    UCHAR minor = stack->MinorFunction;
    IoSkipCurrentIrpStackLocation(Irp);
    auto status = IoCallDriver(ext->LowerDeviceObject, Irp);
    if (minor == IRP_MN_REMOVE_DEVICE) {
        IoDetachDevice(LowerDeviceObject);
        IoDeleteDevice(fido);
    }
    return status;
}
```

More on Hardware-Based Filter Drivers

Filters for hardware-based driver have some further complications. The *FilterDispatchPnp* shown in the previous section has a race condition in it. The problem is that while some IRP is being handled, a remove device request might come in (handled on another CPU, for instance). This will cause `IoDeleteDevice` calls in drivers that are part of the device node while a filter is preparing to send the other request down the device stack. A more detailed explanation of this race condition is beyond the scope of this book, but regardless, we need an air-tight solution.

The solution is an object provided by the I/O system called a remove lock, represented by the `IO_REMOVE_LOCK` structure. Essentially, this structure manages a reference count of the number of outstanding IRPs currently being handled and an event that is signaled when the I/O count is zero and a remove operation is in progress. Using an `IO_REMOVE_LOCK` can be summarized as follows:

1. The driver allocates the structure as part of a device extension or a global variable and initializes it once with `IoInitializeRemoveLock`.
2. For every IRP, the driver acquires the remove lock with `IoAcquireRemoveLock` before passing it down to a lower device. if the call fails (`STATUS_DELETE_PENDING`) it means a remove operation is in progress and the driver should return immediately.
3. Once a lower driver is done with the IRP, release the remove lock (`IoReleaseRemoveLock`).
4. When handling `IRP_MN_REMOVE_DEVICE` call `IoReleaseRemoveLockAndWait` before detaching and deleting the device. The call will succeed once all other IRPs are not longer being processed.

With these steps in mind, the generic dispatch passing requests down must be changed as follows (assuming the remove lock was already initialized):

```
struct DeviceExtension {
    IO_REMOVE_LOCK RemoveLock;
    PDEVICE_OBJECT LowerDeviceObject;
};

NTSTATUS FilterGenericDispatch(PDEVICE_OBJECT DeviceObject, PIRP Irp) {
    auto ext = (DeviceExtension*)DeviceObject->DeviceExtension;

    // second argument is unused in release builds
    auto status = IoAcquireRemoveLock(&ext->RemoveLock, Irp);
    if(!NT_SUCCESS(status)) {    // STATUS_DELETE_PENDING
        Irp->IoStatus.Status = status;
        IoCompleteRequest(Irp, IO_NO_INCREMENT);
        return status;
    }
    IoSkipCurrentIrpStackLocation(Irp);
```

```
    status = IoCallDriver(ext->LowerDeviceObject, Irp);

    IoReleaseRemoveLock(&ext->RemoveLock, Irp);
    return status;
}
```

The IRP_MJ_PNP handler must be modified to use the remove lock properly:

```
NTSTATUS FilterDispatchPnp(PDEVICE_OBJECT fido, PIRP Irp) {
    auto ext = (DeviceExtension*)fido->DeviceExtension;
    auto status = IoAcquireRemoveLock(&ext->RemoveLock, Irp);
    if(!NT_SUCCESS(status)) {   // STATUS_DELETE_PENDING
        Irp->IoStatus.Status = status;
        IoCompleteRequest(Irp, IO_NO_INCREMENT);
        return status;
    }

    auto stack = IoGetCurrentIrpStackLocation(Irp);
    UCHAR minor = stack->MinorFunction;

    IoSkipCurrentIrpStackLocation(Irp);
    auto status = IoCallDriver(ext->LowerDeviceObject, Irp);
    if (minor == IRP_MN_REMOVE_DEVICE) {
        // wait if needed
        IoReleaseRemoveLockAndWait(&ext->RemoveLock, Irp);

        IoDetachDevice(ext->LowerDeviceObject);
        IoDeleteDevice(fido);
    }
    else {
        IoReleaseRemoveLock(&ext->RemoveLock, Irp);
    }
    return status;
}
```

Device Monitor

With the information presented thus far it is possible to build a generic driver that can attach to device objects as filters to other devices. This allows for intercepting requests to (almost) any device we're interested in. A companion user mode client will allow adding and removing devices to filter.

We'll create a new *Empty WDM driver* project named *KDevMon* as we've done numerous times. The driver should be able to attach to multiple devices, and on top of that expose its own *Control Device Object* (CDO) to handle a user mode client configuration requests. The CDO will be created in `DriverEntry` as usual, but attachments will be managed separately, controlled by requests from a user mode client.

To manage all the devices currently being filtered, we'll create a helper class named *DevMonManager*. Its primary purpose is to add and remove devices to filter. Each device will be represented by the following structure:

```
struct MonitoredDevice {
    UNICODE_STRING DeviceName;
    PDEVICE_OBJECT DeviceObject;
    PDEVICE_OBJECT LowerDeviceObject;
};
```

For each device, we need to keep the filter device object (the one created by this driver), the lower device object to which it's attached and the device name. The name will be needed for detach purposes. The DevMonManager class holds a fixed array of `MonitoredDevice` structures, a fast mutex to protect the array and some helper functions. Here are the main ingredients in DevMonManager:

```
const int MaxMonitoredDevices = 32;

class DevMonManager {
public:
    void Init(PDRIVER_OBJECT DriverObject);
    NTSTATUS AddDevice(PCWSTR name);
    int FindDevice(PCWSTR name);
    bool RemoveDevice(PCWSTR name);
    void RemoveAllDevices();
    MonitoredDevice& GetDevice(int index);

    PDEVICE_OBJECT CDO;

private:
    bool RemoveDevice(int index);

private:
    MonitoredDevice Devices[MaxMonitoredDevices];
    int MonitoredDeviceCount;
    FastMutex Lock;
    PDRIVER_OBJECT DriverObject;
};
```

Adding a Device to Filter

The most interesting function is DevMonManager::AddDevice which does the attaching. Let's take it step by step.

```
NTSTATUS DevMonManager::AddDevice(PCWSTR name) {
```

First, we have to acquire the mutex in case more than one add/remove/find operation is taking place at the same time. Next, we can make some quick checks to see if all our array slots are taken and that the device in question is not already being filtered:

```
AutoLock locker(Lock);
if (MonitoredDeviceCount == MaxMonitoredDevices)
    return STATUS_TOO_MANY_NAMES;

if (FindDevice(name) >= 0)
    return STATUS_SUCCESS;
```

Now it's time to look for a free array index where we can store information on the new filter being created:

```
for (int i = 0; i < MaxMonitoredDevices; i++) {
    if (Devices[i].DeviceObject == nullptr) {
```

A free slot is indicated by a NULL device object pointer inside the MonitoredDevice structure. Next, we'll try and get a pointer to the device object that we wish to filter with IoGetDeviceObject-Pointer:

```
UNICODE_STRING targetName;
RtlInitUnicodeString(&targetName, name);

PFILE_OBJECT FileObject;
PDEVICE_OBJECT LowerDeviceObject = nullptr;
auto status = IoGetDeviceObjectPointer(&targetName, FILE_READ_DATA,
    &FileObject, &LowerDeviceObject);
if (!NT_SUCCESS(status)) {
    KdPrint(("Failed to get device object pointer (%ws) (0x%8X)\n", name, status));
    return status;
}
```

The result of IoGetDeviceObjectPointer is in fact the topmost device object, which is not necessarily the device object we were targeting. This is fine, since any attach operation will actually attach to the top of the device stack anyway. The function can fail, of course, most likely because a device with that specific name does not exist.

The next step is to create the new filter device object and initialize it, partly based on the device object pointer we just acquired. At the same time, we need to fill the `MonitoredDevice` structure with the proper data. For each created device we want to have a device extension that stores the lower device object, so we can get to it easily at IRP handling time. For this, we define a device extension structure called simply `DeviceExtension` that can hold this pointer (in the *DevMonManager.h* file):

```
struct DeviceExtension {
    PDEVICE_OBJECT LowerDeviceObject;
};
```

Back to `DevMonManager::AddDevice` - let's create the filter device object:

```
PDEVICE_OBJECT DeviceObject = nullptr;
WCHAR* buffer = nullptr;

do {
    status = IoCreateDevice(DriverObject, sizeof(DeviceExtension), nullptr,
        FILE_DEVICE_UNKNOWN, 0, FALSE, &DeviceObject);
    if (!NT_SUCCESS(status))
        break;
```

`IoCreateDevice` is called with the size of the device extension to be allocated in addition to the `DEVICE_OBJECT` structure itself. The device extension is stored in the `DeviceExtension` field in the `DEVICE_OBJECT`, so it's always available when needed. Figure 11-13 shows the effect of calling `IoCreateDevice`.

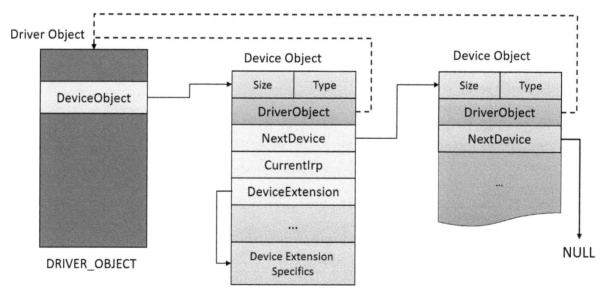

Figure 11-13: The effects of `IoCreateDevice`

Now we can continue with device initialization and the `MonitoredDevice` structure:

```
// allocate buffer to copy device name
buffer = (WCHAR*)ExAllocatePoolWithTag(PagedPool, targetName.Length, DRIVER_TAG);
if (!buffer) {
    status = STATUS_INSUFFICIENT_RESOURCES;
    break;
}

auto ext = (DeviceExtension*)DeviceObject->DeviceExtension;

DeviceObject->Flags |= LowerDeviceObject->Flags & (DO_BUFFERED_IO | DO_DIRECT_IO);
DeviceObject->DeviceType = LowerDeviceObject->DeviceType;

Devices[i].DeviceName.Buffer = buffer;
Devices[i].DeviceName.MaximumLength = targetName.Length;
RtlCopyUnicodeString(&Devices[i].DeviceName, &targetName);
Devices[i].DeviceObject = DeviceObject;
```

> Technically, we could have used `LowerDeviceObject->DeviceType` instead of `FILE_DEVICE_-`
> `UNKNOWN` in the call to `IoCreateDevice` and save the trouble of copying the `DeviceType` field
> explicitly.

At this point the new device object is ready, all that's left is to attach it and finish some more initializations:

```
    status = IoAttachDeviceToDeviceStackSafe(
        DeviceObject,                      // filter device object
        LowerDeviceObject,                 // target device object
        &ext->LowerDeviceObject);          // result
    if (!NT_SUCCESS(status))
        break;

    Devices[i].LowerDeviceObject = ext->LowerDeviceObject;
    // hardware based devices require this
    DeviceObject->Flags &= ~DO_DEVICE_INITIALIZING;
    DeviceObject->Flags |= DO_POWER_PAGABLE;

    MonitoredDeviceCount++;
} while (false);
```

The device is attached, with the resulting pointer saved immediately to the device extension. This is important, as the process of attaching itself generates at least two IRPs - IRP_MJ_CREATE and IRP_MJ_CLEANUP and so the driver must be prepared to handle these. As we shall soon see, this handling requires the lower device object to be available in the device extension.

All that's left now is to clean up:

```cpp
        if (!NT_SUCCESS(status)) {
            if (buffer)
                ExFreePool(buffer);
            if (DeviceObject)
                IoDeleteDevice(DeviceObject);
            Devices[i].DeviceObject = nullptr;
        }
        if (LowerDeviceObject) {
            // dereference - not needed anymore
            ObDereferenceObject(FileObject);
        }
        return status;
    }
}

// should never get here
NT_ASSERT(false);
return STATUS_UNSUCCESSFUL;
}
```

Dereferencing the file object is important; it was obtained by IoGetDeviceObjectPointer. Failure to do so is a kernel leak. Note that we do not need (in fact we must not) dereference the device object returned from IoGetDeviceObjectPointer - it will be dereferenced automatically when the file object's reference drops to zero.

Removing a Filter Device

Removing a device from filtering is fairly straightforward - reversing what AddDevice did:

```
bool DevMonManager::RemoveDevice(PCWSTR name) {
    AutoLock locker(Lock);
    int index = FindDevice(name);
    if (index < 0)
        return false;

    return RemoveDevice(index);
}

bool DevMonManager::RemoveDevice(int index) {
    auto& device = Devices[index];
    if (device.DeviceObject == nullptr)
        return false;

    ExFreePool(device.DeviceName.Buffer);
    IoDetachDevice(device.LowerDeviceObject);
    IoDeleteDevice(device.DeviceObject);
    device.DeviceObject = nullptr;

    MonitoredDeviceCount--;
    return true;
}
```

The important parts are detaching the device and deleting it. FindDevice is a simple helper to locate
a device by name in the array. It returns the index of the device in the array, or -1 if the device is
not found:

```
int DevMonManager::FindDevice(PCWSTR name) {
    UNICODE_STRING uname;
    RtlInitUnicodeString(&uname, name);
    for (int i = 0; i < MaxMonitoredDevices; i++) {
        auto& device = Devices[i];
        if (device.DeviceObject &&
            RtlEqualUnicodeString(&device.DeviceName, &uname, TRUE)) {
            return i;
        }
    }
    return -1;
}
```

The only trick here is to make sure the fast mutex is acquired before calling this function.

Initialization and Unload

The `DriverEntry` routine is fairly standard, creating a CDO that would allow adding and removing filters. The are some differences, however. Most notably, the driver must support all major function codes, as the driver now serves a dual purpose: on the one hand, it provides configuration functionality to add and remove devices when calling the CDO, and on the other hand the major function codes will be called by clients of the filtered devices themselves.

We start `DriverEntry` by creating the CDO and exposing it through a symbolic link as we've seen numerous times:

```
DevMonManager g_Data;

extern "C" NTSTATUS
DriverEntry(PDRIVER_OBJECT DriverObject, PUNICODE_STRING) {
    UNICODE_STRING devName = RTL_CONSTANT_STRING(L"\\Device\\KDevMon");
    PDEVICE_OBJECT DeviceObject;

    auto status = IoCreateDevice(DriverObject, 0, &devName,
        FILE_DEVICE_UNKNOWN, 0, TRUE, &DeviceObject);
    if (!NT_SUCCESS(status))
        return status;

    UNICODE_STRING linkName = RTL_CONSTANT_STRING(L"\\??\\KDevMon");
    status = IoCreateSymbolicLink(&linkName, &devName);
    if (!NT_SUCCESS(status)) {
        IoDeleteDevice(DeviceObject);
        return status;
    }
    DriverObject->DriverUnload = DevMonUnload;
```

Nothing new in this piece of code. Next we must initialize all dispatch routines so that all major functions are supported:

```
    for (auto& func : DriverObject->MajorFunction)
        func = HandleFilterFunction;

    // equivalent to:
    // for (int i = 0; i < ARRAYSIZE(DriverObject->MajorFunction); i++)
    //     DriverObject->MajorFunction[i] = HandleFilterFunction;
```

We've seen similar code earlier in this chapter. The above code uses a C++ reference to change all major functions to point to `HandleFilterFunction`, which we'll meet very soon. Finally, we need to save the returned device object for convenience in the global g_Data (DevMonManager) object and initialize it:

```
g_Data.CDO = DeviceObject;
g_Data.Init(DriverObject);

return status;
}
```

The Init method just initializes the fast mutex and saves the driver object pointer for later use with IoCreateDevice (which we covered in the previous section).

> We will not be using a remove lock in this driver to simplify the code. The reader is encouraged to add support for a remove lock as described earlier in this chapter.

Before we dive into that generic dispatch routine, let's take a closer look at the unload routine. When the driver is unloaded, we need to delete the symbolic link and the CDO as usual, but we also must detach from all currently active filters. Here is the code:

```
void DevMonUnload(PDRIVER_OBJECT DriverObject) {
    UNREFERENCED_PARAMETER(DriverObject);
    UNICODE_STRING linkName = RTL_CONSTANT_STRING(L"\\??\\KDevMon");
    IoDeleteSymbolicLink(&linkName);
    NT_ASSERT(g_Data.CDO);
    IoDeleteDevice(g_Data.CDO);

    g_Data.RemoveAllDevices();
}
```

The key piece here is the call to DevMonManager::RemoveAllDevices. This function is fairly straightforward, leaning on DevMonManager::RemoveDevice for the heavy lifting:

```
void DevMonManager::RemoveAllDevices() {
    AutoLock locker(Lock);
    for (int i = 0; i < MaxMonitoredDevices; i++)
        RemoveDevice(i);
}
```

Handling Requests

The `HandleFilterFunction` dispatch routine is the most important piece of the puzzle. It will be called for all major functions, targeted to one of the filter devices or the CDO. The routine must make that distinction, and this is exactly why we saved the CDO pointer earlier. Our CDO supports create, close and `DeviceIoControl`. Here is the initial code:

```
NTSTATUS HandleFilterFunction(PDEVICE_OBJECT DeviceObject, PIRP Irp) {
    if (DeviceObject == g_Data.CDO) {
        switch (IoGetCurrentIrpStackLocation(Irp)->MajorFunction) {
            case IRP_MJ_CREATE:
            case IRP_MJ_CLOSE:
                return CompleteRequest(Irp);

            case IRP_MJ_DEVICE_CONTROL:
                return DevMonDeviceControl(DeviceObject, Irp);
        }
        return CompleteRequest(Irp, STATUS_INVALID_DEVICE_REQUEST);
    }
```

If the target device is our CDO, we switch on the major function itself. For create and close we simply complete the IRP successfully by calling a helper function we met in chapter 7:

```
NTSTATUS CompleteRequest(PIRP Irp,
    NTSTATUS status = STATUS_SUCCESS,
    ULONG_PTR information = 0);

NTSTATUS CompleteRequest(PIRP Irp, NTSTATUS status, ULONG_PTR information) {
    Irp->IoStatus.Status = status;
    Irp->IoStatus.Information = information;
    IoCompleteRequest(Irp, IO_NO_INCREMENT);
    return status;
}
```

For `IRP_MJ_DEVICE_CONTROL`, we call `DevMonDeviceControl`, which should implement our control codes for adding and removing filters. For all other major functions, we just complete the IRP with an error indicating "unsupported operation".

If the device object is not the CDO, then it must be one of our filters. This is where the driver can do anything with the request: log it, examine it, change it - anything it wants. For our driver we'll just send to the debugger output some pieces of information regarding the request and then send it down to the device underneath the filter.

First, we'll extract our device extension to gain access to the lower device:

```
auto ext = (DeviceExtension*)DeviceObject->DeviceExtension;
```

Next, we'll get the thread that issued the request by digging deep into the IRP and then get the thread and process IDs of the caller:

```
auto thread = Irp->Tail.Overlay.Thread;
HANDLE tid = nullptr, pid = nullptr;
if (thread) {
    tid = PsGetThreadId(thread);
    pid = PsGetThreadProcessId(thread);
}
```

In most cases, the current thread is the same one that made the initial request, but it doesn't have to be - it's possible that a higher-layer filter received the request, did not propagate it immediately for whatever reason, and later propagated it from a different thread.

Now it's time to output the thread and process IDs and the type of operation requested:

```
auto stack = IoGetCurrentIrpStackLocation(Irp);

DbgPrint("Intercepted driver: %wZ: PID: %d, TID: %d, MJ=%d (%s)\n",
    &ext->LowerDeviceObject->DriverObject->DriverName,
    HandleToUlong(pid), HandleToUlong(tid),
    stack->MajorFunction, MajorFunctionToString(stack->MajorFunction));
```

The MajorFunctionToString helper function just returns a string representation of a major function code. For example, for IRP_MJ_READ it returns "IRP_MJ_READ".

At this point the driver can further examine the request. If IRP_MJ_DEVICE_CONTROL was received, it can look at the control code and the input buffer. If it's IRP_MJ_WRITE, it can look at the user's buffer, and so on.

> This driver can be extended to capture these requests and store them in some list (as we did in chapters 8 and 9, for example), and then allow a user mode client to query for this information. This is left as an exercise for the reader.

Finally, since we don't want to hurt the operation of the target device, we'll pass the request along unchanged:

```
        IoSkipCurrentIrpStackLocation(Irp);
        return IoCallDriver(ext->LowerDeviceObject, Irp);
}
```

The DevMonDeviceControl function mentioned earlier is the driver's handler for IRP_MJ_DEVICE_-
CONTROL. This is used to add or remove devices from filtering dynamically. The defined control codes
are as follows (in *KDevMonCommon.h*):

```
#define IOCTL_DEVMON_ADD_DEVICE \
    CTL_CODE(0x8000, 0x800, METHOD_BUFFERED, FILE_ANY_ACCESS)
#define IOCTL_DEVMON_REMOVE_DEVICE \
    CTL_CODE(0x8000, 0x801, METHOD_BUFFERED, FILE_ANY_ACCESS)
#define IOCTL_DEVMON_REMOVE_ALL \
    CTL_CODE(0x8000, 0x802, METHOD_NEITHER, FILE_ANY_ACCESS)
```

The handling code should be fairly easy to understand by now:

```
NTSTATUS DevMonDeviceControl(PDEVICE_OBJECT, PIRP Irp) {
    auto stack = IoGetCurrentIrpStackLocation(Irp);
    auto status = STATUS_INVALID_DEVICE_REQUEST;
    auto code = stack->Parameters.DeviceIoControl.IoControlCode;

    switch (code) {
        case IOCTL_DEVMON_ADD_DEVICE:
        case IOCTL_DEVMON_REMOVE_DEVICE:
        {
            auto buffer = (WCHAR*)Irp->AssociatedIrp.SystemBuffer;
            auto len = stack->Parameters.DeviceIoControl.InputBufferLength;
            if (buffer == nullptr || len < 2 || len > 512) {
                status = STATUS_INVALID_BUFFER_SIZE;
                break;
            }

            buffer[len / sizeof(WCHAR) - 1] = L'\0';
            if (code == IOCTL_DEVMON_ADD_DEVICE)
                status = g_Data.AddDevice(buffer);
            else {
                auto removed = g_Data.RemoveDevice(buffer);
                status = removed ? STATUS_SUCCESS : STATUS_NOT_FOUND;
            }
            break;
        }
```

```
    case IOCTL_DEVMON_REMOVE_ALL:
    {
        g_Data.RemoveAllDevices();
        status = STATUS_SUCCESS;
        break;
    }
    }

    return CompleteRequest(Irp, status);
}
```

Testing the Driver

The user mode console application is again fairly standard, accepting a few commands for adding and removing devices. Here are some examples for issuing commands:

```
devmon add \device\procexp152
devmon remove \device\procexp152
devmon clear
```

Here is the main function of the user mode client (very little error handling):

```
int wmain(int argc, const wchar_t* argv[]) {
    if (argc < 2)
        return Usage();

    auto& cmd = argv[1];

    HANDLE hDevice = ::CreateFile(L"\\\\.\\kdevmon", GENERIC_READ | GENERIC_WRITE,
        FILE_SHARE_READ, nullptr, OPEN_EXISTING, 0, nullptr);
    if (hDevice == INVALID_HANDLE_VALUE)
        return Error("Failed to open device");

    DWORD bytes;
    if (::_wcsicmp(cmd, L"add") == 0) {
        if (!::DeviceIoControl(hDevice, IOCTL_DEVMON_ADD_DEVICE, (PVOID)argv[2],
            static_cast<DWORD>(::wcslen(argv[2]) + 1) * sizeof(WCHAR), nullptr, 0,
            &bytes, nullptr))
            return Error("Failed in add device");
        printf("Add device %ws successful.\n", argv[2]);
```

```
        return 0;
    }
    else if (::_wcsicmp(cmd, L"remove") == 0) {
        if (!::DeviceIoControl(hDevice, IOCTL_DEVMON_REMOVE_DEVICE, (PVOID)argv[2],
            static_cast<DWORD>(::wcslen(argv[2]) + 1) * sizeof(WCHAR), nullptr, 0,
            &bytes, nullptr))
            return Error("Failed in remove device");
        printf("Remove device %ws successful.\n", argv[2]);
        return 0;
    }
    else if (::_wcsicmp(cmd, L"clear") == 0) {
        if (!::DeviceIoControl(hDevice, IOCTL_DEVMON_REMOVE_ALL,
            nullptr, 0, nullptr, 0, &bytes, nullptr))
            return Error("Failed in remove all devices");
        printf("Removed all devices successful.\n");
    }
    else {
        printf("Unknown command.\n");
        return Usage();
    }

    return 0;
}
```

We've seen this kind of code many times before.

The driver can be installed like so:

```
sc create devmon type= kernel binpath= c:\book\kdevmon.sys
```

And started with:

```
sc start devmon
```

As a first example, we'll launch *Process Explorer* (must be running elevated so its driver can be installed if needed), and filter requests coming to it:

```
devmon add \device\procexp152
```

Remember that *WinObj* shows a device named *ProcExp152* in the *Device* directory of the object manager namespace. We can launch *DbgView* from *SysInternals* elevated, and configure it to log kernel output. Here is some example output:

```
1 0.00000000 driver: \Driver\PROCEXP152: PID: 5432, TID: 8820, MJ=14 (IRP_MJ_DEVICE_\
CONTROL)
2 0.00016690 driver: \Driver\PROCEXP152: PID: 5432, TID: 8820, MJ=14 (IRP_MJ_DEVICE_\
CONTROL)
3 0.00041660 driver: \Driver\PROCEXP152: PID: 5432, TID: 8820, MJ=14 (IRP_MJ_DEVICE_\
CONTROL)
4 0.00058020 driver: \Driver\PROCEXP152: PID: 5432, TID: 8820, MJ=14 (IRP_MJ_DEVICE_\
CONTROL)
5 0.00071720 driver: \Driver\PROCEXP152: PID: 5432, TID: 8820, MJ=14 (IRP_MJ_DEVICE_\
CONTROL)
```

It should be no surprise to find out the process ID of *Process Explorer* on that machine is 5432 (and it has a thread with ID 8820). Clearly, *Process Explorer* sends to its driver requests on a timely basis, and it's always `IRP_MJ_DEVICE_CONTROL`.

The devices that we can filter can be viewed with *WinObj*, mostly in the *Device* directory, shown in figure 11-14.

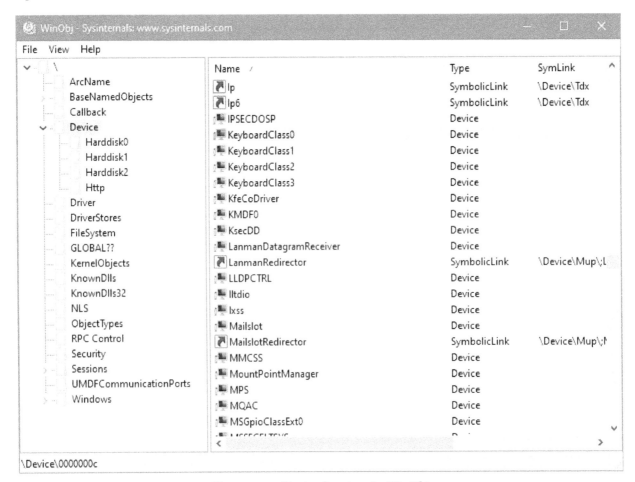

Figure 11-14: Device directory in *WinObj*

Let's filter on *keyboardclass0*, which is managed by the keyboard class driver:

```
devmon add \device\keyboardclass0
```

Now press some keys. You'll see that for every key pressed you get a line of output. Here is some of it:

```
1 11:31:18 driver: \Driver\kbdclass: PID: 612, TID: 740, MJ=3 (IRP_MJ_READ)
2 11:31:18 driver: \Driver\kbdclass: PID: 612, TID: 740, MJ=3 (IRP_MJ_READ)
3 11:31:19 driver: \Driver\kbdclass: PID: 612, TID: 740, MJ=3 (IRP_MJ_READ)
4 11:31:19 driver: \Driver\kbdclass: PID: 612, TID: 740, MJ=3 (IRP_MJ_READ)
5 11:31:20 driver: \Driver\kbdclass: PID: 612, TID: 740, MJ=3 (IRP_MJ_READ)
6 11:31:20 driver: \Driver\kbdclass: PID: 612, TID: 740, MJ=3 (IRP_MJ_READ)
```

What is this process 612? This is an instance of *CSrss.exe* running in the user's session. One of *CSrss'* duties is to get data from input devices. Notice it's a read operation, which means some response buffer is expected from the keyboard class driver. But how can we get it? We'll get to that in the next section.

You can try out other devices. Some may fail to attach (typically those that are open for exclusive access), and some are not suited for this kind of filtering, especially file system drivers.

Here is an example with the *Multiple UNC Provider* device (MUP):

```
devmon add \device\mup
```

Navigate to some network folder and you'll see lots of activity as shown here:

```
001 11:46:19 driver: \FileSystem\FltMgr: PID: 4, TID: 6236, MJ=2 (IRP_MJ_CLOSE)
002 11:46:25 driver: \FileSystem\FltMgr: PID: 7212, TID: 5600, MJ=0 (IRP_MJ_CREATE)
003 11:46:25 driver: \FileSystem\FltMgr: PID: 7212, TID: 5600, MJ=13 (IRP_MJ_FILE_SY\
STEM_CONTROL)
004 11:46:25 driver: \FileSystem\FltMgr: PID: 7212, TID: 5600, MJ=18 (IRP_MJ_CLEANUP\
)
005 11:46:25 driver: \FileSystem\FltMgr: PID: 7212, TID: 5600, MJ=2 (IRP_MJ_CLOSE)
006 11:47:00 driver: \FileSystem\FltMgr: PID: 7212, TID: 4464, MJ=0 (IRP_MJ_CREATE)
007 11:47:00 driver: \FileSystem\FltMgr: PID: 7212, TID: 4464, MJ=13 (IRP_MJ_FILE_SY\
STEM_CONTROL)
...
054 11:47:25 driver: \FileSystem\FltMgr: PID: 7212, TID: 8272, MJ=13 (IRP_MJ_FILE_SY\
STEM_CONTROL)
055 11:47:25 driver: \FileSystem\FltMgr: PID: 7212, TID: 8272, MJ=18 (IRP_MJ_CLEANUP\
)
```

```
056 11:47:25 driver: \FileSystem\FltMgr: PID: 7212, TID: 8272, MJ=2 (IRP_MJ_CLOSE)
057 11:47:25 driver: \FileSystem\FltMgr: PID: 7212, TID: 8272, MJ=5 (IRP_MJ_QUERY_IN\
FORMATION)
...
094 11:47:25 driver: \FileSystem\FltMgr: PID: 6164, TID: 6620, MJ=0 (IRP_MJ_CREATE)
095 11:47:25 driver: \FileSystem\FltMgr: PID: 7212, TID: 7288, MJ=0 (IRP_MJ_CREATE)
096 11:47:25 driver: \FileSystem\FltMgr: PID: 6164, TID: 6620, MJ=5 (IRP_MJ_QUERY_IN\
FORMATION)
097 11:47:25 driver: \FileSystem\FltMgr: PID: 6164, TID: 6620, MJ=18 (IRP_MJ_CLEANUP\
)
098 11:47:25 driver: \FileSystem\FltMgr: PID: 7212, TID: 7288, MJ=5 (IRP_MJ_QUERY_IN\
FORMATION)
099 11:47:25 driver: \FileSystem\FltMgr: PID: 6164, TID: 6620, MJ=2 (IRP_MJ_CLOSE)
100 11:47:25 driver: \FileSystem\FltMgr: PID: 7212, TID: 7288, MJ=12 (IRP_MJ_DIRECTO\
RY_CONTROL)
101 11:47:25 driver: \FileSystem\FltMgr: PID: 6164, TID: 6620, MJ=0 (IRP_MJ_CREATE)
102 11:47:25 driver: \FileSystem\FltMgr: PID: 7212, TID: 7288, MJ=12 (IRP_MJ_DIRECTO\
RY_CONTROL)
103 11:47:25 driver: \FileSystem\FltMgr: PID: 7212, TID: 7288, MJ=18 (IRP_MJ_CLEANUP\
)
104 11:47:25 driver: \FileSystem\FltMgr: PID: 7212, TID: 7288, MJ=2 (IRP_MJ_CLOSE)
105 11:47:25 driver: \FileSystem\FltMgr: PID: 6164, TID: 6620, MJ=5 (IRP_MJ_QUERY_IN\
FORMATION)
106 11:47:25 driver: \FileSystem\FltMgr: PID: 6164, TID: 6620, MJ=12 (IRP_MJ_DIRECTO\
RY_CONTROL)
107 11:47:25 driver: \FileSystem\FltMgr: PID: 6164, TID: 6620, MJ=27 (IRP_MJ_PNP)
```

Notice the layering is on top of the Filter Manager we met in chapter 10. Also notice that multiple processes are involved (both are *Explorer.exe* instances). The MUP device is a volume for the Remote file system. This type of device is best filtered with a file system mini-filter.

 Feel free to experiment!

Results of Requests

The generic dispatch handler we have for the *DevMon* driver only sees requests coming in. These can be examined, but an interesting question remains - how can we get the results of the request? Some driver down the device stack is going to call IoCompleteRequest. If the driver is interested in the results, it must set up an I/O completion routine.

387

As discussed in chapter 7, completion routines are invoked in reverse order of registration when IoCompleteRequest is called. Each layer in the device stack (except the lowest one) can set up a completion routine to be called as part of request completion. At this time, the driver can inspect the IRP's status, examine output buffers, etc.

Setting up a completion routine is done with IoSetCompletionRoutine or (better) IoSetCompletionRoutineEx. Here is the latter's prototype:

```
NTSTATUS IoSetCompletionRoutineEx (
    _In_ PDEVICE_OBJECT DeviceObject,
    _In_ PIRP Irp,
    _In_ PIO_COMPLETION_ROUTINE CompletionRoutine,
    _In_opt_ PVOID Context,      // driver defined
    _In_ BOOLEAN InvokeOnSuccess,
    _In_ BOOLEAN InvokeOnError,
    _In_ BOOLEAN InvokeOnCancel);
```

Most of the parameters are pretty self-explanatory. The last three parameters indicate for which IRP completion status to invoke the completion routine:

- If *InvokeOnSuccess* is TRUE, the completion routine is called if the IRP's status **passes** the NT_-SUCCESS macro.
- If *InvokeOnError* is TRUE, the completion routine is called if the IRP's status **fails** the NT_-SUCCESS macro.
- If *InvokeOnCancel* is TRUE, the completion routine is called if the IRP's status is STATUS_-CANCELLED, which means the request has been canceled.

The completion routine itself must have the following prototype:

```
NTSTATUS CompletionRoutine (
    _In_ PDEVICE_OBJECT DeviceObject,
    _In_ PIRP Irp,
    _In_opt_ PVOID Context);
```

The completion routine is called by an arbitrary thread (the one that called IoCompleteRequest) at IRQL <= DISPATCH_LEVEL (2). This means all the rules from chapter 6 for IRQL 2 must be followed.

What can the completion routine do? It can examine the IRP's status and buffers, and can call IoGetCurrentIrpStackLocation to get more information from the IO_STACK_LOCATION. It must **not** call IoCompleteRequest, because this already happened (this is the reason we are in the completion routine in the first place).

What about the return status? There are actually only two options here: STATUS_MORE_PROCESS-ING_REQUIRED and everything else. Returning that special status tells the I/O manager to stop

(C)2019 Pavel Yosifovich

propagating the IRP up the device stack and cancel the fact the IRP was completed. The driver claims ownership of the IRP and must eventually call `IoCompleteRequest` again (this is not an error). This option is mostly for hardware-based drivers and will not be discussed further in this book.

Any other status returned from the completion routine continues propagation of the IRP up the device stack, possibly calling other completion routines for upper layer drivers. In this case, the driver must mark the IRP as pending if the lower device marked it as one:

```
if (Irp->PendingReturned)
    IoMarkIrpPending(Irp);   // sets SL_PENDING_RETURNED in irpStackLoc->Control
```

This is necessary because the I/O manager does the following after the completion routine returns:

```
Irp->PendingReturned = irpStackLoc->Control & SL_PENDING_RETURNED;
```

 The exact reasons for all these intricacies are beyond the scope of this book. The best source of information on these topics is Walter Oney's excellent book, "Programming the Windows Driver Model", second edition (MS Press, 2003). Although the book is old (covering Windows XP), (and it's about hardware device drivers only), it's still quite relevant and has some great information.

 Implement an I/O completion routine for the *DevMon* driver. I will expand this driver going forward to include completion routines as well.

Driver Hooking

Using filter drivers described in this chapter and in chapter 10 provides a lot of power to a driver developer: the ability to intercept requests to almost any device. In this section I'd like to mention another technique, that although not "official", may be quite useful in certain cases.

This driver hooking technique is based on the idea of replacing dispatch routine pointers of running drivers. This automatically provides "filtering" for all devices managed by that driver. The hooking driver will save the old function pointers and then replace the major function array in the driver object with its own functions. Now any request coming to a device under control of the hooked driver will invoke the hooking driver's dispatch routines. There is no extra device objects or any attaching going on here.

 Some drivers are protected by PatchGuard against these kinds of hooks. A canonical example is the NTFS file system driver - on Windows 8 and later - cannot be hooked in that way. If it is, the system will crash in a few minutes time at most.

PatchGuard (also known as Kernel Patch Protection) is a kernel mechanism that hashes various data structures that are considered important, and if any change is detected - will crash the system. A classic example is the System Service Dispatch Table (SSDT) which points to system services. Starting with Vista (64 bit), this table cannot be hooked.

Drivers have names and thus are part of the Object Manager's namespace, residing in the *Driver* directory, shown with *WinObj* in figure 11-15 (must run elevated).

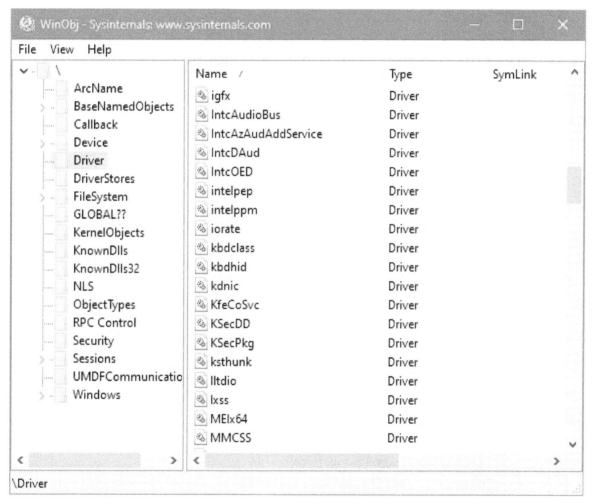

Figure 11-15: The *Driver* directory in *WinObj*

To hook a driver, we need to locate the driver object pointer (DRIVER_OBJECT), and to do that we can use an undocumented, but exported, function that can locate any object given its name:

```
NTSTATUS ObReferenceObjectByName (
    _In_ PUNICODE_STRING ObjectPath,
    _In_ ULONG Attributes,
    _In_opt_ PACCESS_STATE PassedAccessState,
    _In_opt_ ACCESS_MASK DesiredAccess,
    _In_ POBJECT_TYPE ObjectType,
    _In_ KPROCESSOR_MODE AccessMode,
    _Inout_opt_ PVOID ParseContext,
    _Out_ PVOID *Object);
```

Here is an example of calling ObReferenceObjectByName to locate the *kbdclass* driver:

```
UNICODE_STRING name;
RtlInitUnicodeString(&name, L"\\driver\\kbdclass");

PDRIVER_OBJECT driver;
auto status = ObReferenceObjectByName(&name, OBJ_CASE_INSENSITIVE,
    nullptr, 0, *IoDriverObjectType, KernelMode,
    nullptr, (PVOID*)&driver);
if(NT_SUCCESS(status)) {
    // manipulate driver
    ObDereferenceObject(driver);    // eventually
}
```

The hooking driver can now replace the major function pointers, the unload routine, the add device routine, etc. Any such replacement should always save the previous function pointers for unhooking when desired and for forwarding the request to the real driver. Since this replacement must be done atomically, it's best to use InterlockedExchangePointer to make the exchange atomically.

The following code snippet demonstrates this technique:

```
for (int j = 0; j <= IRP_MJ_MAXIMUM_FUNCTION; j++) {
    InterlockedExchangePointer((PVOID*)&driver->MajorFunction[j], MyHookDispatch);
}
InterlockedExchangePointer((PVOID*)&driver->DriverUnload, MyHookUnload);
```

A fairly complete example of this hooking technique can be found in my *DriverMon* project on Github at https://github.com/zodiacon/DriverMon.

Kernel Libraries

In the course of writing drivers, we developed some classes and helper functions that can be used in multiple drivers. It makes sense, though, to package them in a single library that we can then reference instead of copying source files from project to project.

The project templates provided with the WDK don't explicitly provide a static library for drivers, but it's fairly easy to make one. The way to do this is to create a normal driver project (based on *WDM Empty Driver* for example), and then just change the project type to a static library as shown in figure 11-16.

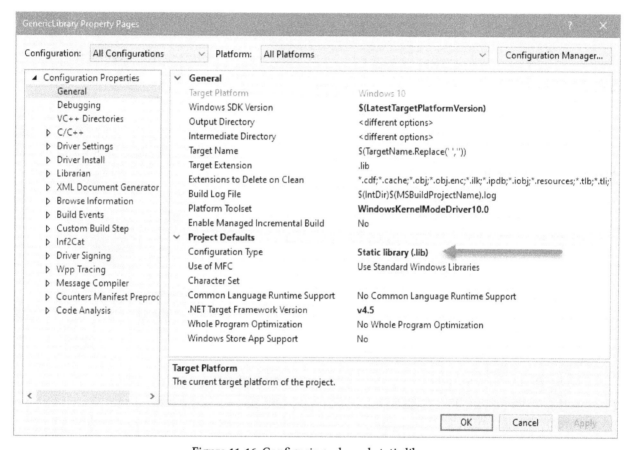

Figure 11-16: Configuring a kernel static library

A driver project that wants to link to this library just needs to add a reference with Visual Studio by right-clicking the *References* node in *Solution Explorer*, choosing *Add Reference...* and checking the library project. Figure 11-17 shows the references node of an example driver after adding the reference.

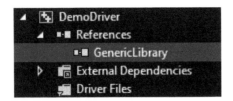

Figure 11-17: Referencing a library

The same can be accomplished in the "old style" by adding the LIB file as an input to the Linker using the project's properties, or using `#pragma comment(lib, "genericlibrary.lib")` in some source file.

Summary

We covered a lot of ground in this book, as the kernel driver space is very large. Even so, you should consider this book an introduction to the world of kernel device drivers. Some topics we have not covered in this book include:

- Hardware-based device drivers
- Network drivers and filters
- Windows Filtering Platform (WFP)
- More file system mini-filters topics
- Other general development techniques: lookaside lists, bitmaps, AVL trees
- Specific technology-related types of drivers: Human Interface Device (HID), display, audio, imaging, bluetooth, storage, ...

Some of these topics are good candidates for a future "advanced" book.

Microsoft has documented all the above driver types, and there are the official samples on Github, which are updated regularly. This should be your first place to look for more information.

We have come to the end of this book. I wish you happy kernel programming!